Mega-city growth and the future

Note to the reader from the UNU

The Mega-city Project of the United Nations University (UNU) was initiated in 1990 as part of the UNU's Programme on Alternative Rural-Urban Configurations. The objective of the project was to examine the growth of large metropolitan agglomerations, especially in the developing world, in regard to the patterns and projections of their growth, the demographic and economic causes, and the social, economic, and environmental consequences. Following a global examination of the mega-city phenomenon, reported in this volume, a series of studies were undertaken in Asia, Latin America, and Africa. The project is intended to provide new data, analyses, and insights that will enhance our understanding of mega-cities and contribute to their improved management.

Mega-city growth and the future

Edited by Roland J. Fuchs, Ellen Brennan, Joseph Chamie, Fu-chen Lo, and Juha I. Uitto

United Nations University Press

TOKYO • NEW YORK • PARIS

Second impression 1999

United Nations University Press
The United Nations University, 53-70, Jingumae 5-chome,
Shibuya-ku, Tokyo, 150-8925, Japan
Tel: +81-3-3499-2811 Fax: +81-3-3406-7345
E-mail: sales@hq.unu.edu
http://www.unu.edu

United Nations University Office in North America
2 United Nations Plaza, Room DC2-1462-70, New York, NY
10017 USA
Tel: +1-212-963-6387 Fax: +1-212-371-9454
E-mail: unuona@igc.apc.org

United Nations University Press is the publishing division of the United Nations University.

Cover design by Apex Production, Hong Kong

Printed in Hong Kong

UNUP-820
ISBN 92-808-820-6

Contents

Introduction

Roland J. Fuchs

Vice-Rector, United Nations University, Tokyo

Mankind's future will unfold largely in urban settings. As the world moves into the twenty-first century, it will also mark a demographic divide, passing from an age when most of its population resided in rural areas to one in which most will be urban residents. This is essentially due to the rapid urban growth occurring in developing countries, which, over the next 20 years, must absorb nearly one billion *additional* urban residents, as many as they had *in total* in 1990. A major challenge for mankind is, therefore, an informed response to such unprecedented urban growth and the intelligent management of urban settlements, which, in the future, will serve as the abiding place of the majority of mankind.

A particular problem is posed by the emergence of a number of urban agglomerations of a scale unprecedented in human history. This century began with perhaps a dozen cities claiming 1 million residents or more. By the year 2000, there will be several hundred cities of that size. Among them, it is estimated there will be 28 cities with populations exceeding an arbitrary threshold of 8 million population, thereby qualifying as mega-cities. The world's largest metropolitan area, that of Tokyo, will encompass nearly 30 million people. However, the vast majority of the mega-cities, and the most rapidly growing, are to be found in the developing countries. There they serve simultaneously as national and regional engines of economic growth, centres of technological and cultural creativity, homes for the poor and deprived, and the sites and sources of environmental pollution.

Only recently have cities of this size been conceptualized as a distinct phenomenon deserving special consideration because of the unique characteristics posed by their size, the impacts of mega-cities on their inhabitants, and the enormous problems they present of management. As a result, the world still has little systematic, as opposed to anecdotal, knowledge and experience to draw upon. Particularly in the case of mega-cities in the developing world, as noted by Janice Perlman, "no precedent exists for feeding, sheltering, or transporting so many people . . . , nor for removing their waste products, or providing clean water." It is not simply a case of scaling up solutions devised for smaller urban centres, or transferring technology from the relatively few mega-cities in the developed world (some of which also find themselves in a growing web of difficulties), but to devise new and creative solutions applicable at such large scales that will lead to economically and socially viable, as well as environmentally sustainable, cities.

This book is the initial product of a UNU Programme on Mega-city Growth and Management intended to address various aspects of the global mega-city phenomenon. It is based on an October 1990 conference jointly organized by the UNU and the Population Division of the United Nations with the support of the Tokyo Metropolitan Government. That conference brought together leading scholars and planners concerned with mega-city issues from both the developed and developing countries, as well as officials from the World Bank and major development assistance agencies. In the conference, participants explored a great range of issues relating to mega-cities: the demographic and economic causes of mega-city growth and its morphology; the economic and social consequences of this growth; and numerous management issues and approaches.

The conference revealed many areas of broad agreement, e.g., on the need to conceptualize and define the mega-city along a greater range of dimensions than size alone, and to revamp data-gathering relating to mega-cities. Similarly, there were broad areas of agreement as to promising policy approaches that could be successfully implemented, given an adequate political will. However, there were also apparent differences of opinion in such matters as the role of economic versus spatial planning approaches; the role of the private versus public sectors, etc. There was no attempt to achieve an artificial consensus, since differences in interpretations or policy recommendations reflect the current state of knowledge and the needs for both basic and policy-relevant research as suggested in many papers.

An overview of the papers, which gives an indication of the main themes of the presentations, and which can serve as a guide to the reader, follows.

Overview

The initial chapter, prepared by Nancy Yu-ping Chen and Larry Heligman of the Population Division of the United Nations, describes the trends of population growth in those urban agglomerations projected to reach 8 million people by the year 2000. While in 1950 there were only two such mega-cities – New York and London – both in the developed world, in the year 2000 it is expected there will be 28, all but 6 in the developing countries. These 28 agglomerations grew at an average rate of 2.5 per cent during the decade 1980–1990; but, while the rates of growth for megalopolises in the developed regions were low, below 0.7 per cent per year, they were typically over 3.0 per cent in the developing countries. The growth rates of this latter group were highly correlated with national population growth rates, even though such mega-cities generally comprise only a small proportion of national populations.

The limitations of our current conceptual and data base for a realistic demographic assessment of mega-cities, their role in the larger development process, and for policy formulation and evaluation are examined in chapter 2 by Sidney Goldstein. The definitions of what constitute urban places and urban populations differ internationally and change over time, as do political boundaries, making historical and comparative research difficult. There is, moreover, a fundamental need to give far more attention to the basic concept of "mega-city." Rather than size alone, Goldstein argues that a more comprehensive set of criteria based on such variables as size, financial resources, industrial/commercial structure, political role, educational facilities and scientific personnel, service functions, and the position in the world system should be considered for classifying selected cities as "mega-cities."

The provision of data for small areal units within the large metropolis is of major importance, given their polycentric evolution and the fact that many mega-cities occupy several political jurisdictions. Because of the role played by mega-cities in national development and their rapid internal change, it can be argued that census, vital statistics, and even survey data sets should, in the future, all be ordered by subunits of the city.

That the pattern of mega-city development may take different forms in different regions of the world and that the "urban transition" and the transition of the space economy are not uniform global processes is argued by T.G. McGee in chapter 3, which treats the extended metropolitan regions of Asia. While noting several types of urban regions in Asia, McGee concentrates on those urban regions characterized by urban cores, and the corridors linking the major urban foci, and large numbers of smaller and medium-sized urban centres.

Such interlocked urban regions are typified by the Taipei-Kaohsiung corridor, the four major coastal zones of China, and the Bangkok metropolitan region. Such regions were previously characterized by dense populations engaged in wetland agriculture. Now they reflect the increasing growth of non-agricultural activity, off-farm employment, intensive labour flows and commuting, and extreme mixtures of land uses with agriculture, cottage industry, industrial estates, suburban developments, and others found side by side. No clear urban-rural distinction is possible as provided for in conventional planning models. They present a challenge to planners, who must take advantage of their dynamic growth features while solving the adverse side-effects brought about by environmental deterioration, transportation, and infrastructural problems.

The effect of macroeconomic forces, including current global adjustments and shifting techno-economic paradigms on the world city system, is the subject of chapter 4 by Fu-chen Lo. The growth of large cities has been differentially affected, he argues, by various global economic forces, such as the rise of third world debt, the decline in commodity prices, globalization of the world economy, technological innovation, the international relocation of industry, and comparative national economic performance in a global context. Latin American and African cities are plagued by regional and national problems of high debt, inflation, and dependence on primary commodities, which result in massive rural-urban migrations, rapid demographic, but sluggish, economic growth, and an inability to finance the necessary urban infrastructure. Cities in the medium growth category range from US and European cities, characterized by deindustrialization and employment shifts to the service sector, to the more traditional, domestically oriented cities of the Middle East and South Asia that are less affected by current global adjustments. In contrast, the cities of East Asia and South-East Asia are experiencing the most rapid economic growth and are increasingly brought together by international trade and inter-industrial linkages.

Lo concludes with an analysis of shifting techno-economic paradigms, i.e., the evolution of technology and product life cycles, and their effects on mega-cities. He distinguishes traditional mega-cities in developing countries from those in centrally planned societies, which are less affected by the cyclical turns of the world economy and advances in science and technology; network world cities, found in both developing and developed countries, which are greatly affected by the shifts in the techno-economic paradigms; and finally the dominant world cities still found largely in developed countries, which are the predominant centres of technological innovation and diffusion, management and finance, and serve as focal points of a network of other world cities.

The relations between technology and the city, and the potentials offered by technologies for reshaping the mega-city, are explored by George Bugliarello in chapter 5. The concentration of population that is the essence of a city, he points out, has been made possible by various technological advances – in agriculture, water and energy supply, waste removal, construction, communication, etc. Such advances have influenced the size, location, and morphology of cities. Emerging and future technologies similarly will have a major impact and open new possibilities, including unprecedented sensing, communication, information, and feedback capabilities for managing urban systems, integrating supplies and services, and also for linking entire systems of cities. However, the possibilities and constraints of technology barely figure in the consciousness of urban administrators and citizens. The author argues that mega-cities – which are larger than many countries – should create strong technology and development offices to develop and coordinate technology aspects of the city and serve as a catalyst of socio-technological innovation.

The impacts of mega-cities upon the remainder of the national space through redistributive mechanisms are treated in chapter 6 by Laurent Davezies and Rémy Prud'homme. Until recently such large cities have been viewed by many politicians and academicians as exploiting the remainder of the country and hence as being "too large." Increasingly, however, they are viewed as the locomotives of growth for their countries, driving the private sector by providing "agglomeration economies."

The authors examine another facet of their impact, that on the public economy, which is between 25 and 50 per cent of GNP in most of the countries, and their redistributive role. In examining budget-induced transfers in selected case-studies, it appears that primate cities "heavily subsidize the rest of the country," i.e., they provide much more public funds than they consume. The impact of public price-induced transfers (e.g., electricity, communications) is less clear, but overall there may also be a net transfer out of the mega-city since public entities often ignore the economies of scale of large cities in setting utility prices. There have been few studies of pricing-policy-induced transfers (e.g., agriculture, import substitution), but recent trends towards deregulation suggest that there is also now a net transfer to rural areas. Overall, in contrast to the perceived wisdom, mega-cities thus serve to redistribute wealth to the remainder of the national space economy.

In examining the economic impacts of third world mega-cities, one must ask, "Is size itself a significant explanation of the many difficulties third world mega-cities pose for their inhabitants and governance?" Andrew M. Hamer, in chapter 7, makes a strong case that "size *per se* is *not* the issue." Instead, it is "mismanagement at both the regional and local levels, and wrong-headed national urbanization policies." The growth of mega-cities is a natural outcome of urbanization economies of agglomeration; with time and development the concentration within the metropolitan region will yield to decentralization, to trunk routes, and secondary cities. Examining case-studies across mega-cities reveals a great variety of outcomes, suggesting the importance of country-specific factors and local governance, as opposed to size.

Hamer hypothesizes that the income base exists in mega-cities to finance near universal access to "adequate" housing and public services, but this is blocked by inadequate policy and regulatory frameworks. International experience demonstrates the futility of attempts to regulate the size of mega-cities through direct controls on growth or movement of people. The proper policy levers, in any case, are not directly size-related. To encourage appropriate deconcentration, decentralization, and restructuring, governments should scale back subsidies and make sure the mega-city pays its own way. Infrastructure should be tailored to the income and effective demands of each mega-city's population. Pollution and congestion can be addressed by proper regulatory frameworks rather than size controls. Urban poverty cannot be attacked in a positive manner until the rural-urban transition has been largely completed, although, again, proper policies will mitigate the problem. Hamer completes his article by addressing the requirements for an effective local management framework that could address the various "symptoms of disorganization" common to many third world mega-cities and turn them into more manageable entities.

The social and welfare impacts of mega-city development are described in chapter 8, a contribution of Aprodicio Laquian. While it is true that mega-city development is rooted in its specific country or regional context, Laquian claims mega-cities have more in common with each other than with their own hinterlands. The author then goes on to examine a number of global trends. To begin with, spurred by the information revolution, and despite a decline in metropolitan growth rates, there is a continuing urbanization as a social process, involving secularization of society, the loss of primary group relationships, the erosion of kinship and other ties, differentiation of the roles between production and consumption, etc. A second major trend is a growing gap between the very rich and the very poor, and an "urbanization of poverty." Urban infrastructure, housing, and social services have fallen far behind needs and the mega-city poor, women especially, have been affected severely. A third trend has been the weakening of metropolitan-wide governments, a concept popular in past decades but recently weakened by the growth of conservative ideology, economic recession, and the growing assertiveness of local units of governments. Yet another trend is the growing pathology of many mega-cities, evident in crimes, often drug-related. Finally, there are the problems associated with changes in demographic structure, which differ in developing and developed countries. The former must cope with ever younger populations resulting from continuing inflow of migrants and high fertility. An especially acute problem is that of street children, for whom the street is the habitual abode. In developed countries, on the other hand, the problem is an aging population, often left with inadequate pensions and family support, and a growing army of the homeless. The author goes on to examine possible avenues of solution, as well as priority research needs.

The impacts of mega-city growth on families and households is the subject of chapter 9 by Eleonora Barbieri Masini. Megapolization, she points out, is much more than a purely demographic phenomenon; it has many enduring repercussions on society and lifestyles in such matters as family size, the function of the family as a social institution and group, the social status of its members, family habits, etc. The size of family units is definitely diminishing. The lack of space and co-residence is a cause of increasingly difficult relations between generations and creates particular problems for the aged. However, despite the lack of co-residence, a form of extended family may survive for several generations, but it is now spread over the urban area and weakened by physical separation.

Family authority structures also change with a tendency for a greater equality between husband and wife, and between parents and those with less authority, i.e., between parents and children. There also arises an accentuation of age differences and a marginalization of some family members, e.g., the old, while the young attach themselves to peer groups, further weakening family influence and authority. New support groups arise, such as neighbourhood alliances, adjusted to the needs of life in the mega-city.

Some of these general observations are derived from case-studies conducted under a UNU project, but there is the need for much more empirical research, especially to determine the impact of the greater distances involved in life in mega-cities and the resulting family dispersion, family vulnerability and responses, and desirable support mechanisms.

Mega-city management policies are the subject of the third and final section of the book. Ellen Brennan presents an overview of this issue based on studies of 13 mega-cities, conducted by the Population Division of the United Nations. Her report surveys several topics: current spatial strategies; urban land policy; urban services (housing, water supply, transport, environmental protection); and institutional development.

Despite some successes, there have been numerous failures as well in promoting spatial strategies, such as polycentric development, and failures in devising effective land development policies and land use controls. The reasons include inaccurate predictions of population growth, excessive reliance on engineering and architectural approaches, and failures to implement programmes because of conflicts with vested interests, including land speculators.

A test of the effectiveness of management in developing country mega-cities is the ability to deliver basic urban services to a rapidly growing metropolitan population. Although some developing country mega-cities have made significant progress in meeting the needs of their populations, most mega-cities suffer from severe service deficits – often more than 50 per cent of the population lacks many basic services. There are already many examples of successful approaches to such problems, which could be emulated and implemented. The explanations for widespread management failure are discussed by the author. Policies are designed for the interests of the élites rather than for redistribution; pride and prestige lead to reluctance to lower public service standards to realistic levels; planners trained in developed countries cannot adapt their skills to developing country situations; and so on. But there are grounds for optimism that innovative policy interventions, relying on appropriate cost recovery schemes and market signals, and implemented by metropolitan level authorities, could successfully address many mega-city management problems.

The critical problems of financing infrastructure in developing country mega-cities is discussed in authoritative detail by Johannes F. Linn and Deborah L. Wetzel. The infrastructure needs of the mega-cities in developing countries are severe and apparently beyond the scope of traditional solutions. One of the most important constraints has been the lack of adequate financial means to support the needed investments, as well as the operation and maintenance of the required facilities. The paper explores a large range of alternative measures that would permit redressing the obvious problems of infrastructure and financing in the mega-cities of developing countries. It focuses on several broad areas of possible reform of existing practices.

Decentralizing expenditure responsibility and revenue authority to urban governments in the mega-cities is likely to result in more efficient infrastructure service provision, greater self-reliance by cities on their own resources, and the strengthening of a country's pluralistic political structure.

Greater reliance on their own resources means that urban governments in mega-cities need to look principally towards a reform of the property tax, automotive taxation, sales taxes and user charges for efficient, equitable, stable, and growing sources of public revenues. Infrastructure in mega-cities offers scope for increased involvement by the private sector in the provision and financing of social and physical infrastructure services.

None of the above approaches will work in isolation. They represent a mutually reinforcing package of measures that need to be pursued across the board. Only then can serious progress be made in dealing with the mega-problems of mega-cities without endangering the macroeconomic stability of the country as a whole, and without imposing an undue burden on the economies of the cities themselves, or on the economy of the rest of the country.

Critical issues of land and shelter in mega-cities are the subject of chapter 12 by Alan Gilbert. His emphasis is on the housing of the poorer half, and in Africa and parts of Asia, two-thirds of the population. Mega-cities in developing countries have in common with other cities problems of poor housing, low incomes, inequality, lack of well-paying jobs, shortages of services, and inadequate public transportation. They face additional problems with respect to land availability, since in some cases there is no land available for expansion close to the city.

The problems of land and shelter are seen as so severe in many cities "that it is futile to pretend they can be solved. They can only be reduced," and the paper suggests a number of concrete ways to go about this, although it is recognized that in the last analysis, the problem, as in other areas, is one of materializing the necessary political will.

A major theme of the paper is that there is evidence that self-help housing is becoming less accessible for the poor than previously, and that, therefore, more attention must be paid to increasing the support of rental housing. Rental housing and shared housing, for various reasons, have been neglected by both governments and the research community. There is a danger that continued neglect of rental housing solutions will result in a serious deterioration of living and housing conditions in third world mega-cities.

How transportation can be used as a tool to improve the viability, development, and welfare of mega-cities is addressed by Ralph Gakenheimer in chapter 13. Transportation management policies are seen in the context of the basic objectives of urban policy and economic development as formulated by the World Bank – increasing urban productivity, alleviating urban poverty, and improving the urban environment. In addition, they are viewed from the standpoint of the general strategic objectives for all sectors of urban policy and planning: guiding physical development, enhancing productive relationships among economic activities, improving the programming and pricing of infrastructure, and restructuring governance. Six interrelated strategic decisions for transportation are then considered: how to price and finance transportation, how to choose transport modes, how to improve the mobility of the poor, how to control automobile usage, how to protect the environment, and how to create sustainable institutions. Finally, the author makes the case that mega-cities, because they have a concentration of professional capabilities and are clearing-houses for international intelligence about urban problems and solutions, must serve as models providing prototype solutions for smaller cities afflicted with similar problems.

The dual challenge of poverty and mega-cities is the topic of chapter 14 by Om Prakash Mathur. He begins by noting that despite the growing concern with global poverty, issues relating to poverty in mega-cities, which account for a significant proportion of the urban poor, have not been separately examined, and policy responses have also failed to distinguish poverty problems of mega-cities from other urban places. He contends that the incidence of poverty in mega-cities is the greatest challenge on the urban agenda of the 1990s and a challenge that cannot be addressed by conventional poverty alleviation strategies and service delivery systems. Also, while community-based approaches have been effective in other urban settings, it is far from clear that they can be multiplied and scaled up to the levels necessary to replace existing interventions. An organized research effort, he stresses, is needed to better understand the syndrome of mega-city poverty, and to seek appropriate policy responses.

His paper has three parts. In the first part, he presents evidence of poverty levels and service deprivation in mega-cities, showing that they are unprecedented in human history. The second part deals with the nature of existing policy responses to mega-city poverty problems and argues that such responses have not been designed specifically for mega-cities and have had, in most cases, only marginal impacts on living conditions of the poor. The final part of the paper points out that the world will witness in the 1990s the emergence of many more mega-cities, wielding enormous economic power within and across developing countries. The future economic growth in many countries will heavily depend on the productivity of these mega-cities; maintaining the productivity of the cities in turn will mean overcoming vast deficiencies in infrastructure and services.

Deteriorating environmental conditions in cities of the developing world are a threat to both the role of these cities as the engines of economic growth and the health of their inhabitants, particularly the urban poor, who are disproportionately at risk from lack of adequate infrastructures for delivery of safe water supplies, sanitation service, and waste removal. Underlying many of the inappropriate and ineffective actions undertaken in response by governments and international agencies is a set of misperceptions by public officials, the subject of chapter 15, "Myths of Environmental Management and the Urban Poor," contributed by Yok-shiu F. Lee. The first myth is that global environmental concern is a first world problem, not a third world issue, i.e., the failure to recognize the environmental conditions facing the urban poor as a global environmental problem. Some 600 million urban poor of the third world are now housed in health- and life-threatening environmental situations. A second myth is that "environmental management can be ignored in the early stages of development." A third is that "environmental damage is too expensive," perpetuated by the adoption of inappropriate standards and technologies. A fourth is that poverty "causes" environmental deterioration and that the urban poor generate wastes that degrade their habitat, when in reality it is the governments that have failed to provide basic services and infrastructure. A fifth is that the urban poor should be more self-reliant in managing their living environment, when in reality their efforts at self-reliance are handicapped by government actions and inactions. The final "myth" is that the only choices in managing the urban environment are the market and the state, when there is already much evidence of the constructive role that can be played by initiatives of community organizations and NGOs.

A fitting conclusion to this volume is the final chapter by G. Shabbir Cheema, in which he examines priority urban management issues in developing countries, and derives a research agenda for the 1990s. Because policies and programmes to control rural to urban migrations and the diffusion of urban population have not been successful, there is an increasing recognition that the growth of cities is inevitable and that the solutions to the problems of cities depend heavily on their effective management. Urban management is a holistic concept. It is aimed at strengthening the capacity of government and non-governmental organizations to identify policy and programme alternatives and to implement them with optimal results. The challenge of urban management is, therefore, to effectively respond to the problems and issues of individual cities to enable them to perform their functions. The most common issues faced by these cities are improving financial structure and management; providing shelter, basic urban services and infrastructure; improving urban information systems; strengthening the role of the urban informal sector; and strengthening urban institutional capacities, including the role of municipal governments. For each issue, the author outlines priority issues that should be addressed in policy-relevant research.

Conclusion

This volume, which presents an overview by leading scholars and planners concerned with issues of mega-cities, is but the first product of a longer range UNU programme concerned with the challenge of the growth of mega-cities. In preparation are volumes examining mega-city problems in greater detail at the regional level: in Asia, Latin America, and Africa. Also under way are studies of Tokyo and aspects of the Japanese experience in the management of the mega-city. The United Nations Population Division also has an ongoing research programme on mega-cities. To date 13 monographs have been published in the mega-city series. The series is being expanded to include additional cities in Latin America, Africa, and Asia. It is anticipated that these studies collectively will help lead to a greater understanding of the mega-city phenomenon in its various manifestations and suggest the policy measures required to meet the challenge posed by mega-cities, their management, and transformation into sustainable human settlements.

Part 1
The growth of mega-cities

1

Growth of the world's megalopolises

Nancy Yu-ping Chen and Larry Heligman

The authors are respectively Population Affairs Officer and Chief, Population Division, United Nations, New York

Introduction

In 1950, New York was the largest agglomeration in the world, containing 12.3 million persons: 50 per cent more than London (at 8.7 million persons) and nearly twice the population of Tokyo (6.7 million). In 1950, Mexico City and São Paulo were relatively "small" cities, having populations of 3.1 million and 2.4 million persons, respectively. Presently, a city with New York's 1950 population size would be only the world's sixth largest city. Twenty cities have now reached the 8 million milestone, topped by Mexico City (at 20.2 million).

This document describes the trend of population growth in the 28 urban agglomerations projected by the United Nations to reach 8 million persons by the year 2000. The estimated and projected city sizes presented are taken from the recent 1990 Revision of the United Nations Population Division's estimates and projections of urban and rural populations and urban agglomerations [4, 5]. An urban agglomeration is considered in United Nations Population Division studies to be an area with a population concentration that usually includes a central city and surrounding urbanized localities and is demarcated without respect to administrative boundaries [3]. This paper uses the term "city" interchangeably with "urban agglomeration," although technically city refers to an administrative (usually smaller) area. The term "megalopolis" is used here to refer to an agglomeration that has reached 8 million in population.

In the following we note the changes in the number and in the regional distribution of cities of 8 million or more, and their past and projected trends of population growth from 1950 to 1990. The population growth of these cities is considered in the context of urban and total national population growth.

The world's largest urban agglomerations

Growth in the number of megalopolises and their regional distribution

In 1950, New York and London were the world's only megalopolises. By 1970, eight new megalopolises had arisen. Three were in the more developed regions (Tokyo, Los Angeles, and Paris), but five were found in the less developed regions. Of these five, three were in Latin America – Mexico City (Mexico), São Paulo (Brazil), and Buenos Aires (Argentina) and two were in China (Shanghai and Beijing) (tables 1 and 2).

By 1990, another two megalopolises were added to those in the more developed regions – Moscow (USSR) and Osaka (Japan) – while London fell from the list as its estimated population size declined to 7.7 million in 1980. The number of megalopolises from the less developed regions reached 14 in 1990 (compared to 6 from the more developed regions). Of the 14 present-day megalopolises in the less developed regions, 4 are in Latin America (Mexico City, São Paulo, Buenos Aires, and Rio de Janeiro), 9 are in Asia (Shanghai, Calcutta, Bombay, Beijing, Jakarta, Delhi, Tianjin, Seoul, and Manila), and 1 (Cairo) is in Africa.

Eight more megalopolises are projected for the year 2000, at which time there will be 28. All 8 are expected to be from the less developed regions: 6 of the 8 will be located in Asia (Dacca, Karachi, Bangkok, Istanbul, Teheran, and Bangalore), 1 in Africa (Lagos, Nigeria), and 1 in Latin America (Lima, Peru).

Table 1 **Population size of urban agglomerations with 8 million or more in 2000**

Agglomeration	Country	1950	1960	1970 (in millions)	1980	1990	2000
Bangalore	India	0.8	1.2	1.6	2.8	5.0	8.2
Bangkok	Thailand	1.4	2.2	3.1	4.7	7.2	10.3
Beijing	China	3.9	6.3	8.1	9.0	10.8	14.0
Bombay	India	2.9	4.1	5.8	8.1	11.2	15.4
Buenos Aires	Argentina	5.0	6.8	8.4	9.9	11.5	12.9
Cairo	Egypt	2.4	3.7	5.3	6.9	9.0	11.8
Calcutta	India	4.4	5.5	6.9	9.0	11.8	15.7
Dacca	Bangladesh	0.4	0.6	1.5	3.3	6.6	12.2
Delhi	India	1.4	2.3	3.5	5.6	8.8	13.2
Istanbul	Turkey	1.1	1.7	2.8	4.4	6.7	9.5
Jakarta	Indonesia	2.0	2.8	3.9	6.0	9.3	13.7
Karachi	Pakistan	1.0	1.8	3.1	4.9	7.7	11.7
Lagos	Nigeria	0.3	0.8	2.0	4.4	7.7	12.9
Lima	Peru	1.0	1.7	2.9	4.4	6.2	8.2
Los Angeles	USA	4.0	6.5	8.4	9.5	11.9	13.9
Manila	Philippines	1.5	2.3	3.5	6.0	8.5	11.8
Mexico City	Mexico	3.1	5.4	9.4	14.5	20.2	25.6
Moscow	Russia	4.8	6.3	7.1	8.2	8.8	9.0
New York	USA	12.3	14.2	16.2	15.6	16.2	16.8
Osaka	Japan	3.8	5.7	7.6	8.3	8.5	8.6
Paris	France	5.4	7.2	8.3	8.5	8.5	8.6
Rio de Janeiro	Brazil	2.9	4.9	7.0	8.8	10.7	12.5
São Paulo	Brazil	2.4	4.7	8.1	12.1	17.4	22.1
Seoul	Korea, Republic of	1.0	2.4	5.3	8.3	11.0	12.7
Shanghai	China	5.3	8.8	11.2	11.7	13.4	17.0
Teheran	Iran (Islamic Rep. of)	1.0	1.9	3.3	5.1	6.8	8.5
Tianjin	China	2.4	3.6	5.2	7.3	9.4	12.7
Tokyo	Japan	6.7	10.7	14.9	16.9	18.1	19.0

Source: Ref. 5.
Notes:
Bangkok refers to Bangkok-Thonburi.
Cairo refers to Cairo-Giza-Imbâba.
Lima refers to Lima-Callao.
Los Angeles refers to Los Angeles–Long Beach.
Manila refers to Metro Manila.
New York refers to New York–North-eastern New Jersey.
Osaka refers to Osaka-Kobe.
Tokyo refers to Tokyo-Yokohama.

The population of Greater London exceeded 8 million in 1950 (8.7 million) and 1960 (9.1 million), but has been under 8 million since 1980.

Table 2 **List of urban agglomerations of 8 million or more persons by develpment region: 1950, 1970, 1990, and 2000**

More developed regions			
1950	1970	1990	2000
New York	New York	New York	New York
London	London	Tokyo	Tokyo
	Tokyo	Los Angeles	Los Angeles
	Los Angeles	Paris	Paris
	Paris	Moscow	Moscow
		Osaka	Osaka

Less developed regions			
1950	1970	1990	2000
None	Mexico City	Mexico City	Mexico City
	São Paulo	São Paulo	São paulo
	Shanghai	Shanghai	Shanghai
	Beijing	Beijing	Beijing
	Buenos Aires	Buenos Aires	Buenos Aires
		Calcutta	Calcutta
		Bombay	Bombay
		Jakarta	Jakarta
		Delhi	Delhi
		Tianjin	Tianjin
		Seoul	Seoul
		Rio de Janeiro	Rio de Janeiro
		Cairo	Cairo
		Manila	Manila
			Lagos
			Dacca
			Karachi
			Bangkok
			Istanbul
			Teheran
			Bangalore
			Lima

Source: Ref. 5.

Rank of the megalopolises

Between 1985 and 1990, Mexico City surpassed Tokyo-Yokohama in population and became the largest megalopolis in the world. The United Nations estimates that Mexico City had 20.2 million inhabitants in 1990, exceeding the populations of Tokyo (18.1 million), São Paulo (17.4 million), and New York (16.2 million).

Table 3 **World's 10 largest urban agglomerations, ranked by population (in millions), 1950–2000**

1950		1960	
Rank, agglomeration	Population	Rank, agglomeration	Population
1. New York	12.3	1. New York	14.2
2. London	8.7	2. Tokyo	10.7
3. Tokyo	6.7	3. London	9.1
4. Paris	5.4	4. Shanghai	8.8
5. Shanghai	5.3	5. Paris	7.2
6. Buenos Aires	5.0	6. Buenos Aires	6.8
7. Chicago	4.9	7. Los Angeles	6.5
8. Moscow	4.8	8. Moscow	6.3
9. Calcutta	4.4	9. Beijing	6.3
10. Los Angeles	4.0	10. Chicago	6.0
1970		1980	
1. New York	16.2	1. Tokyo	16.9
2. Tokyo	14.9	2. New York	15.6
3. Shanghai	11.2	3. Mexico City	14.5
4. Mexico City	9.4	4. São Paulo	12.1
5. London	8.6	5. Shanghai	11.7
6. Buenos Aires	8.4	6. Buenos Aires	9.9
7. Los Angeles	8.4	7. Los Angeles	9.5
8. Paris	8.3	8. Calcutta	9.0
9. Beijing	8.1	9. Beijing	9.0
10. São Paulo	8.1	10. Rio de Janeiro	8.8
1990		2000	
1. Mexico City	20.2	1. Mexico City	25.6
2. Tokyo	18.1	2. São Paulo	22.1
3. São Paulo	17.4	3. Tokyo	19.0
4. New York	16.2	4. Shanghai	17.0
5. Shanghai	13.4	5. New York	16.8
6. Los Angeles	11.9	6. Calcutta	15.7
7. Calcutta	11.8	7. Bombay	15.4
8. Buenos Aires	11.5	8. Beijing	14.0
9. Bombay	11.2	9. Los Angeles	13.9
10. Seoul	11.0	10. Jakarta	13.7

Source: Ref. 5.

As indicated in table 3, the list comprising the 10 largest cities has changed considerably during the last 20 years and is projected to alter significantly again during the next decade. From 1970 to 1990, London, Paris, and Beijing fell from the list (from ranks 5, 8, 9 to 23, 19, and 11) and were replaced by Calcutta, Bombay, and Seoul. In general, the populations of cities in the more developed regions increased at a slower pace, so those cities moved from the top. Tokyo remained the second largest city (although it was the largest city for a short time between 1970 and 1990); New York dropped from being the first to the fourth most populous city, and, as indicated, Paris and London are now off the list altogether. Los Angeles provides the exception, moving from rank 7 in 1970 to number 6 in 1990. Correspondingly, among agglomerations in the less developed regions, Mexico City rose from fourth largest to largest, and São Paulo from tenth to third. Calcutta, Bombay, and Seoul joined the list between 1970 and 1990. Exceptions were Shanghai, which fell from third to fifth, Buenos Aires, which moved from sixth to eighth, and Beijing, which dropped to eleventh and thus off the list.

Mexico City is projected to retain its first ranking in 2000, reaching a population size of 25.6 million persons, and São Paulo is projected to be the second largest city, reaching 22.1 million persons. The United Nations projects that Buenos Aires and Seoul will fall from the list of the 10 largest cities, ranking twelfth and fifteenth in 2000. They are expected to be replaced by Beijing and Jakarta. Hence, the United Nations projects that, by the year 2000, 6 of the 10 largest cities of the world will be in Asia (Tokyo, Shanghai, Beijing, Calcutta, Bombay, and Jakarta), 2 in Latin America (Mexico City and São Paulo), and 2 in North America (New York and Los Angeles).

Concentration of urban population in megalopolises

The megalopolises of many countries contain a very large percentage of the country's total urban population (see table 4). Of the 28 cities considered in this document (i.e., those that will reach a population of 8 million in 2000), 11 represent 20 per cent or more of the country's total urban population. Another 5 contain between 15 and 20 per cent of the nation's urban population. Such primacy of the megalopolis within the urban hierarchy is common in the less developed regions but is not as characteristic of the largest agglomerations in the more developed regions.

Within Asia, over one-half of Thailand's urban population resides

Table 4 **Percentage of urban population living in urban agglomerations, 1950–2000**

Agglomeration	Country	1950	1960	1970	1980	1990	2000
Africa							
Cairo	Egypt	37.1	37.8	38.2	38.7	37.0	34.1
Lagos	Nigeria	8.6	12.5	17.9	20.6	20.2	19.9
Latin America							
Buenos Aires	Argentina	45.0	44.6	44.8	42.4	41.3	40.1
Lima	Peru	35.9	36.7	38.7	39.7	41.3	41.3
Mexico City	Mexico	26.3	28.0	30.1	31.0	31.4	30.8
Rio de Janeiro	Brazil	14.9	15.1	13.2	10.9	9.5	8.6
São Paulo	Brazil	12.6	14.4	15.1	15.1	15.4	15.3
Asia							
Bangalore	India	1.2	1.5	1.5	1.8	2.2	2.4
Bangkok	Thailand	64.9	65.1	65.5	58.7	56.8	54.7
Beijing	China	6.4	5.0	5.6	4.6	2.8	2.3
Bombay	India	4.7	5.1	5.3	5.1	4.9	4.6
Calcutta	India	7.2	6.9	6.3	5.7	5.1	4.7
Dacca	Bangladesh	23.7	24.5	29.6	33.0	35.0	35.2
Delhi	India	2.3	2.9	3.2	3.5	3.8	3.9
Istanbul	Turkey	24.3	21.3	20.5	22.6	19.4	19.3
Jakarta	Indonesia	19.9	19.8	19.1	17.9	16.4	15.9
Karachi	Pakistan	14.9	16.7	19.1	20.7	19.6	19.0
Manila	Philippines	27.1	27.2	28.6	33.0	31.9	31.2
Seoul	Korea, Republic of	23.5	34.1	40.9	38.2	35.7	33.6
Shanghai	China	8.8	7.1	7.7	6.0	3.5	2.8
Teheran	Iran (Islamic Rep. of)	22.2	25.8	28.2	26.4	21.9	19.6
Tianjin	China	3.9	2.9	3.6	3.7	2.5	2.1
More developed regions							
Los Angeles	USA	4.1	5.2	5.6	5.7	6.4	6.8
Moscow	Russia	6.8	6.0	5.2	4.9	4.7	4.3
New York	USA	12.6	11.2	10.7	9.3	8.7	8.2
Osaka	Japan	9.1	9.8	10.2	9.4	9.0	8.7
Paris	France	23.2	25.4	23.1	21.6	20.4	19.4
Tokyo	Japan	16.0	18.2	20.0	19.0	19.1	19.0

Source: Ref. 5.

in Bangkok, and approximately one-third of the urban populations of the Republic of Korea, Bangladesh, and the Philippines resides in Seoul, Dacca, and Manila, respectively. Jakarta, Karachi, Istanbul, and Teheran hold between 15 and 20 per cent of each nation's urban population.

Thailand, the Republic of Korea, Bangladesh, the Philippines, Indonesia, Pakistan, Turkey, and Iran each contain only one megalopolis, and each megalopolis is generally between three and four times the size of the next largest urban agglomeration in the country: In 1990, the population of Jakarta was 3.7 times that of Bandung; Seoul was 2.8 times that of Pusan; Dacca, 2.9 times that of Chittagong; Istanbul, 2.6 times that of Ankara; Karachi, 1.9 times that of Lahore; and Teheran, 3.6 times that of Mashhad. Similar figures are not available in the United Nations database for second largest agglomerations in the Philippines and Thailand, but 1980 census data for these two countries [2] indicate that Metropolitan Manila is nearly 10 times larger than Davao (Mindanao) and Bangkok Metropolis is 55 times larger than Chiang Mai.

The situation is very different, however, for China and India. These countries are large in size and population. The urban population of China is spread among three megalopolises, 35 other agglomerations of at least 1 million residents, plus smaller urban areas. India's urban population resides in three megalopolises, an additional agglomeration (Bangalore) projected to reach megalopolis status by 2000, 20 other agglomerations of at least 1 million inhabitants, and numerous other urban areas. The three megalopolises of Shanghai, Beijing, and Tianjin together accounted for only nine per cent of China's urban population in 1990; Shanghai (the largest) accounts for just 3.5 per cent. In fact, the share of the urban population residing in these three cities declined rapidly from 19 per cent in 1950 and 17 per cent in 1970 to 9 per cent in 1990; the rapid urbanization of the 1980s in China was partially characterized by large growth of other urban agglomerations and smaller towns. Calcutta, Bombay, and Delhi, plus Bangalore, together accounted for 16 per cent of the urban population of India in 1990. Calcutta and Bombay each accounted for 5 per cent, Delhi for just under 4 per cent, and Bangalore for 2 per cent.

Among the Latin American megalopolises, 31 per cent of the urban population of Mexico and 41 per cent of the urban population of both Peru and Argentina currently reside in Mexico City, Lima, and Buenos Aires, respectively. In 1990, the population of Mexico City was 6.4 times that of the next largest Mexican city, Guadalajara, and the population of Buenos Aires was 10 times that of Córdoba. Brazil is the only Latin American country with two megalopolises. The populations of São Paulo and Rio de Janeiro combined make up 25 per cent of Brazil's urban population; 15 per cent reside in São Paulo and 10 per cent in Rio de Janeiro.

About 37 per cent of Egypt's urban population resides in Cairo, a figure that has been more or less constant since at least 1950. Cairo and Alexandria (Egypt's next largest city with 3.7 million residents in 1990) comprise slightly over half of the urban population of Egypt. The Nigerian city of Lagos consisted of 7.7 million residents in 1990 and will certainly attain the 8 million mark within the next few years. Lagos has been a fast growing city in a less urbanized country; it absorbed one-fifth of Nigeria's total urban growth between 1950 and 1990, and the percentage of the urban population residing in Lagos rose from 9 per cent in 1950 to 20 per cent in 1990. Lagos's population is about six times that of Ibadan, the next largest agglomeration.

The more developed regions present six agglomerations that reached a population of 8 million persons before 1990. Currently, the populations of New York and Los Angeles, and the population of Moscow, form only a small share of the urban population of the United States and of the USSR. New York comprises 9 per cent of the US urban population, and Los Angeles comprises 6 per cent. Moscow comprises 5 per cent of the urban population of the USSR. The urban populations of Japan and France are much more concentrated. In 1990, 19 per cent of the urban population of Japan lived in Tokyo and another 9 per cent in Osaka. Paris in 1990 had 8.5 million persons, which is 20 per cent of the total urban population of France and 7.3 times the population of Lyons (1.2 million persons) and 7.8 times the population of Marseilles (1.1 million persons).

Growth rates among the megalopolises

Levels and trends

In this section, we describe the levels and trends of the growth rates of the 28 cities projected to reach megalopolis status by the year 2000. As indicated in table 5, on average, these 28 agglomerations grew at an average rate of 2.5 per cent per year during the 1980–1990 decade. This rate is nearly the same as that for the previous decade (1970–1980) but significantly lower than that observed during previous periods. From 1950 to 1960 and from 1960 to 1970 these agglomerations grew at a rate of 3.9 per cent per year and 3.3 per cent per year, respectively.

These aggregate averages mask a wide disparity of growth rates among the various cities. During the 1980–1990 period, individual city growth rates varied from under 1 per cent per year in Moscow

Table 5 **Average annual rate of change of urban agglomerations with 8 million or more in 2000**

Agglomeration	Country	1950–1960	1960–1970	1970–1980	1980–1990	1990–2000
Africa		*5.1*	*5.0*	*4.3*	*3.9*	*3.9*
Cairo	Egypt	4.3	3.6	2.6	2.7	2.7
Lagos	Nigeria	9.7	9.8	7.7	5.6	5.1
Latin America		*4.9*	*4.2*	*3.3*	*2.8*	*2.1*
Buenos Aires	Argentina	3.0	2.2	1.6	1.5	1.1
Lima	Peru	5.5	5.5	4.1	3.4	2.7
Mexico City	Mexico	5.4	5.5	4.3	3.3	2.4
Rio de Janeiro	Brazil	5.4	3.6	2.2	2.0	1.5
São Paulo	Brazil	6.6	5.4	4.1	3.6	2.4
Asia		*4.4*	*3.7*	*3.3*	*3.3*	*3.3*
Bangalore	India	4.3	3.2	5.5	5.7	5.0
Bangkok	Thailand	4.6	3.7	4.2	4.1	3.6
Beijing	China	4.7	2.5	1.1	1.8	2.6
Bombay	India	3.4	3.6	3.3	3.3	3.2
Calcutta	India	2.1	2.3	2.7	2.7	2.8
Dacca	Bangladesh	4.3	8.4	7.8	7.0	6.0
Delhi	India	5.0	4.4	4.5	4.6	4.1
Istanbul	Turkey	4.8	4.7	4.6	4.1	3.6
Jakarta	Indonesia	3.4	3.4	4.2	4.4	4.0
Karachi	Pakistan	5.9	5.2	4.6	4.4	4.1
Manila	Philippines	3.9	4.4	5.2	3.5	3.3
Seoul	Korea, Republic of	8.4	8.1	4.4	2.8	1.5
Shanghai	China	5.1	2.3	0.5	1.3	2.4
Teheran	Iran (Islamic Rep. of)	5.9	5.6	4.4	2.9	2.3
Tianjin	China	4.2	3.7	3.3	2.5	3.1
More developed regions		*3.1*	*2.1*	*0.7*	*0.7*	*0.5*
Los Angeles	USA	4.8	2.5	1.3	2.2	1.6
Moscow	Russia	2.6	1.2	1.4	0.8	0.2
New York	USA	1.4	1.3	−0.4	0.4	0.3
Osaka	Japan	4.1	2.8	0.9	0.2	0.1
Paris	France	2.8	1.4	0.2	−0.03	0.1
Tokyo	Japan	4.6	3.3	1.3	0.7	0.5
All agglomerations		*3.9*	*3.3*	*2.5*	*2.5*	*2.4*

Source: Ref. 5.

(0.8 per cent), Tokyo (0.7 per cent), New York (0.4 per cent), Osaka (0.2 per cent), and Paris (−0.03 per cent) to over 4 per cent per year in Dacca (7.0 per cent), Bangalore (5.7 per cent), Lagos (5.6 per cent), Delhi (4.6 per cent), Karachi (4.4 per cent), Jakarta (4.4 per cent), Istanbul (4.1 per cent), and Bangkok (4.1 per cent).

From the above list, it is evident that megalopolises experiencing low growth rates are found in the more developed regions and those with high growth rates are located in the less developed regions. Aggregation of megalopolis growth rates by major area shows that during the 1980–1990 period, megalopolises in more developed regions grew 0.7 per cent per year, whereas megalopolises in Asia, Latin America, and Africa grew annually at 3.3 per cent, 2.8 per cent, and 3.9 per cent, respectively.

All megalopolises in the more developed regions, except Los Angeles, grew at a rate under 1 per cent per year during 1980–1990. In fact, Paris exhibited a small population loss during 1980–1990, as had New York during the previous decade. According to United Nations estimates, all but Los Angeles experienced lower growth rates during 1980–1990 than during the previous decade and all but Paris are projected to exhibit lower growth rates during 1990–2000 than during the preceding decade.

On average, growth rates of megalopolises in the more developed regions have declined continuously, from over 3 per cent per year during 1950–1960 to 2.1 per cent annually for 1960–1970 and 0.7 per cent thereafter. During the 1950–1960 decade, three cities (Los Angeles, Tokyo, and Osaka) increased by more than 4 per cent per year. During the 1960–1970 decade, only one city, Tokyo, increased above 3 per cent per year, and from 1970 onwards, growth rates were below 2 per cent per year for all cities but Los Angeles.

Population growth rates among the 15 megalopolises of Asia averaged 3.3 per cent per year during the 1980–1990 period. Megalopolis growth rates exceeded 5 per cent per year in Bangalore and Dacca. With the exception of Beijing and Shanghai, all megalopolises grew faster than 2.5 per cent per year. Population growth rates have been declining in five Asian megalopolises: Seoul (from 8.4 per cent per year during 1950–1960 to 2.8 per cent per year for 1980–1990); Beijing (from 4.7 per cent to 1.8 per cent); Teheran (5.9 per cent to 2.9 per cent); Shanghai (5.1 per cent to 1.3 per cent); and Tianjin (4.2 per cent to 2.5 per cent). In the other megalopolises, population growth rates have remained high.

Currently, four urban agglomerations in Latin America are megalopolises: Buenos Aires, Mexico City, Rio de Janeiro, and São Paulo. By the end of the twentieth century, Lima's population is expected to reach 8.2 million. São Paulo, Lima, and Mexico City exhibited rapid growth rates above 3 per cent per year during 1980–1990, whereas Buenos Aires and Rio de Janeiro exhibited growth rates under 2 per cent per year. The growth rates of all Latin American megalopolises have been declining. In fact, all but Buenos Aires exhibited growth rates above 5 per cent per year during the 1950s. The decline of the population growth rate of Rio de Janeiro has been particularly sharp – from 5.4 per cent per year during the 1950s to 3.6 per cent in the 1960s, 2.2 per cent in the 1970s, and 2.0 per cent for the 1980–1990 decade.

In 1990, the African continent had only one megalopolis – Cairo, but Lagos is projected to exceed 8 million population before 2000. Cairo is estimated to be currently growing at 2.6 per cent per year. This rate is about the same as that during 1970–1980 but is well below the growth rates experienced during the 1950s (4.3 per cent per year) and 1960s (3.6 per cent). The population growth of Lagos during the past 40 years has indeed been rapid. The United Nations estimates that its population grew at a rate of nearly 10 per cent per year between 1950 and 1970, 7.7 per cent during 1970–1980, and 5.6 per cent per year during 1980–1990.

Relationship with national growth rates

The speed at which a city grows is partially explained by the rate of natural increase at the national level and the forces that lead to rural-to-urban migration in general [1]. Here, this relationship is explored on a statistical basis using the United Nations 1990 revisions of estimated world population size and city size. This is done in two ways. This section investigates whether megalopolises exhibiting rapid growth are located in countries whose total populations are also increasing rapidly. The analysis here is undertaken for the 1970–1980 decade only. This period has been chosen because of its relative recency and because the United Nations estimates of city and total populations are generally well grounded on recorded census and survey figures.

Figure 1 presents the cross-sectional relationship between the total growth rate and city growth rate for the 1970–1980 period. The figure shows a strong statistical relationship that appears nearly linear,

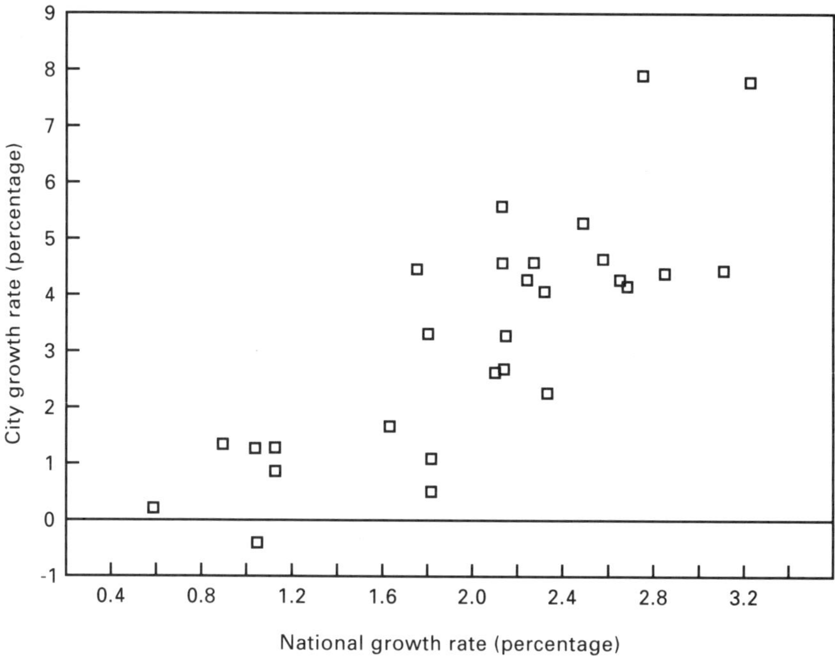

Fig. 1 **Cross-sectional relationship between national population growth rates and mega-city population growth rates, 1970–1980 (Source: ref. 5)**

implying that more rapid total population growth is associated with more rapid megalopolis growth.

As noted previously in this section, megalopolises that are exhibiting low rates of population growth are found exclusively in the more developed regions, where both total and urban population growth rates are very low. However, if one limits the analysis to megalopolises of the less developed regions, the statistical relationship of city growth to total and urban growth is still apparent, although not as strong (see figure 2). A simple regression indicates that the national population growth rate explains 47 per cent of the variation in megalopolis growth rates in the less developed regions. That other forces must also be involved in explaining the growth of megalopolises is obvious just by noting the range of city growth rates within countries containing more than one megalopolis. For example, population growth rates among Indian cities during 1970–1980 ranged from 2.7 per cent and 3.3 per cent per year in Calcutta and Bombay to 4.5 per cent in Delhi and 5.5 per cent in Bangalore. None the less, the rela-

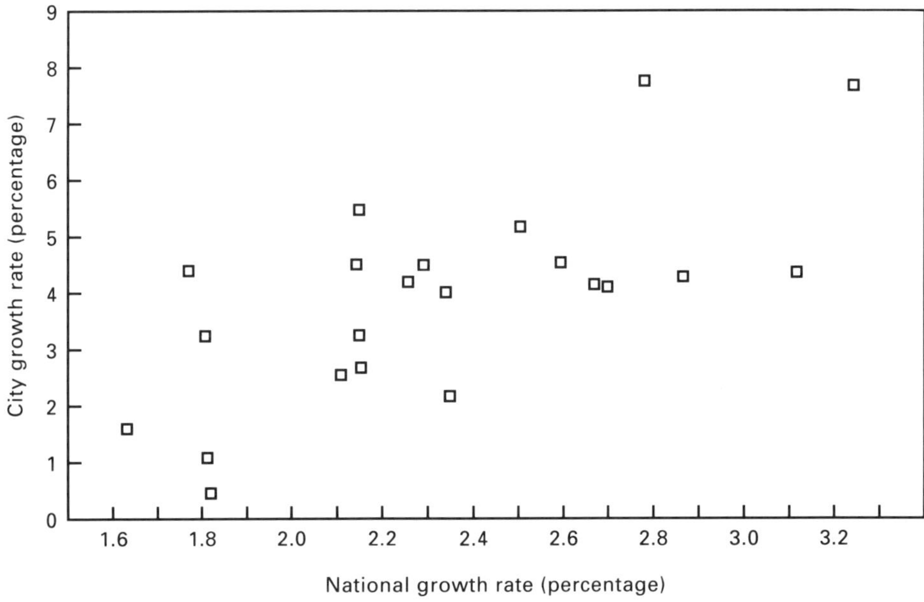

Fig. 2 **Cross-sectional relationship between national population growth rates and mega-city population growth rates, less developed regions only, 1970–1980 (Source: ref. 5)**

tionship between megalopolis and national population growth rates is quite remarkable, given that these megalopolises generally comprise only a very small proportion of the national populations.

Conclusions

Concomitant with world population growth and urbanization, the number of very large cities has increased rapidly during the last 40 years. In 1950, only New York and London could be called megalopolises, but by 1990, 20 cities had reached 8 million population or more. Not surprisingly, such large cities are increasingly found in the less developed regions, particularly in Asia, where populations are large and have grown rapidly.

Current growth rates of megalopolises vary widely. Some megalopolises, particularly those in the more developed regions, have recently been exhibiting rates well under 1 per cent per year, whereas others have been growing over 4 per cent per year. The speed at which megalopolises are growing can be explained by many social, economic, and political factors. However, the demographic context is extremely significant. In fact, nearly half of the variation in the growth rates of megalopolis populations in the less developed regions can be explained by the speed of national population growth.

References

1 Kelley, Allen C., and Jeffrey G. Williamson. *What Drives Third World City Growth? A Dynamic General Equilibrium Approach*. Princeton: Princeton University Press, 1984.

2 Paxton, J., ed. *The Statesman's Year-book: Statistical and Historical Annual of the States of the World for the Year 1989–1990*. New York: St. Martin's Press, 1989.

3 United Nations. *Estimates and Projections of Urban, Rural and City Populations, 1950–2025: The 1982 Assessment*. New York: United Nations, 1985.

4 ———. *United Nations Urban Agglomeration Chart 1990*. New York: United Nations, 1990.

5 ———. *World Urbanization Prospects 1990: Estimates and Projections of Urban and Rural Populations and of Urban Agglomerations*. New York: United Nations, 1991.

2

Demographic issues and data needs for mega-city research

Sidney Goldstein

G.H. Crooker University Professor and Professor of Sociology, Population Studies and Training Center, Brown University, Providence

In 1979, just over 10 years ago, a paper on "Research Priorities and Data Needs for Establishing and Evaluating Population Redistribution Policies" was prepared for the UN/UNFPA Workshop on Population Distribution Policies in Development Planning held in Bangkok [12]. Since then, the urban population of developing countries has increased by 43 per cent, from 972 million (1980) to an estimated 1.385 billion (1990) [35]. Concurrently, and despite rural-to-urban migration, the number of persons living in rural areas has grown by 15 per cent, from 2.342 billion to 2.702 billion. The faster growth of the urban population reflects the combined effects of natural increase, net migration, and annexation and reclassification. As a result, the level of urbanization in developing countries has risen from 29.3 per cent (1980) to an estimated 33.9 per cent (1990). The urbanization level is projected to reach 39.5 per cent by the end of the twentieth century and to pass 50 per cent by 2015.

These changes in the size of the urban population have been paralleled by equally dramatic changes in the urban structure. In 1980, less developed countries accounted for 521 cities of more than 250,000 persons; of these, 119 contained more than 1 million persons [30] and 22 had more than 4 million. United Nations estimates for 1990 indicate that 657 cities exceed 250,000 persons; of these, 187 contain more than 1 million population, and 33 cities, just 50 per cent more than in 1980, are in the 4 million and over class.

During the 1980s, the United Nations made concerted efforts to improve and to collate national data for assessing the urbanization process, stimulated in part by the growing recognition of the importance of urbanization in the overall development process; partly by the concern with the rapid growth of urban population and in the number of large cities; and in part by the call for improved data emerging from the 1984 Mexico City Population Conference [31]. These efforts have resulted in a series of impressive reports devoted to assessment of the interrelations among migration, urbanization, and development [28, 29]; to the patterns and prospects of world urbanization over the period 1950–2025 [34–35]; and to in-depth assessment of the demographic, social, and economic conditions of a growing number of mega-cities [32]. Yet, all too often, concerted efforts by the United Nations, other research agencies, and individual scholars to improve our understanding of urbanization itself, as well as its causes and consequences, have been seriously limited because the quality of demographic data available for the assessment of rural-urban population redistribution, the structure of the urban hierarchy, and changes associated with migration into and out of urban and rural places have not improved dramatically for many countries or for purposes of regional and worldwide comparative analysis. Serious obstacles continue to hamper attempts to assess the impact of population movement on urban growth itself and the effect of such migration, of overall urban growth, and of city size on the development process and on inequalities in the quality of life between urban and rural places and between big and small urban locations.

Among the major obstacles are limitations inherent in the existing conceptual treatment of urban/rural places and of population movement as a demographic process. The effect of conceptual weaknesses are compounded by the consequent lack of appropriate data and noncomparability among available data sets. Such problems exist at the national and international levels. They detract from our ability to evaluate urbanization and mega-city growth in relation to national development efforts and often preclude comprehensive assessment on a regional or worldwide scale. Even when data are available, the wide range of variation in national definitions, classification systems, and measurement complicates efforts to undertake comparative analyses. Such assessments are essential for a comprehensive evaluation of the reciprocal relations between urbanization and migration on the one hand and development on the other, as well as of the comparative effectiveness of different policies on population redistribution.

When my 1979 evaluation of research priorities and data needs was prepared, the United Nations had just completed its 1977 monitoring report [26]. Based on a survey of 158 governments, the results suggested widespread and serious concern with distribution problems; 70 per cent of the less developed countries reported their spatial distribution to be entirely unacceptable, compared to only 17 per cent of the more developed countries. The 1989 monitoring report [36] indicates that the problems associated with spatial population distribution persist. Of the 131 governments of less developed countries responding to the inquiry, 54 per cent reported their spatial distribution as requiring major changes, and an additional 38 per cent desired minor change. Only 8 per cent regarded the situation as satisfactory. Paralleling this evaluation, 60 per cent of all the developing countries already had policies designed to slow rural-to-urban or urban-to-urban population flows, and in 13 per cent more, the policies were intended to reverse the direction of movement. Only 5 per cent of the countries had policies designed to accelerate the ongoing pattern of migration, and 22 per cent had no policy.

In response to the views held in the late 1970s and early 1980s, the 1984 Mexico City International Conference on Population recognized that the collection and dissemination of statistics on population distribution must be advanced, including the development of concepts and methods. In particular, the Conference recommended that in formulating population distribution policies, governments should "take into account the policy implications of various forms of population mobility (e.g., circular, seasonal, and rural-rural and urban-urban, as well as rural-urban), to consider the direction, duration, and characteristics of these movements" [31, p. 157]. While some improvement has occurred in the quantity and quality of information on population movement, the changes have not kept pace with the increasing recognition of the importance of urban growth and migration in many developing countries, and particularly the emergence of so many megacities. Serious deficiencies still characterize the conceptualization and measurement of urban and rural population distribution and of population movement.

Adding to the frustration of limitations in the quality and quantity of the available basic data on the urban/rural populations of many countries and on internal migration is the still limited degree to which available data are exploited for analytic purposes. A variety of reasons may account for this, including the lower priority that concerns about urbanization and migration may have in the policy setting of the nation; the greater difficulties in obtaining funding for such research; the lesser number of experts interested in and trained to do research on migration and urbanization; the greater difficulty in undertaking migration research due to the multiplicity of locations, many with unique socio-economic characteristics for which information is frequently lacking; the politics and funding shortages associated with efforts to effect changes in distribution that often argue for ignorance of facts being better than their comprehension and the status quo better than change. Many of these same considerations may, in fact, also account for the failure to achieve improvements in the quality and quantity of data on urbanization and migration and greater standardization of basic concepts.

Sources and limitations of data

Undertaking research on urbanization and population movement in developing countries presents major challenges. While virtually all countries distinguish between their urban and rural populations and many make data available by size of urban place, the definitions of what constitutes an urban place and the urban population in a given country are often inconsistent, not only over time but even at given points in time. As a result, wide variations characterize national statistics on the number of urban places and the size of individual locations, as well as on the size of the aggregate urban population. The measurement of migration also confronts serious conceptual issues with respect to who qualifies as a migrant. The problems of comparability that stem from the considerable variations that exist in the type and quality of data among countries is compounded by the dearth of direct information on population movement in a number of countries.

The 1984 International Conference on Population recognized that migration was the least developed area of current demographic statistics. It therefore recommended that "governments may consider undertaking a comprehensive programme of migration statistics, in line with national priorities, focusing on such areas of concern as (1) internal migration, (2) urbanization, and (3) international migration. . . . To this end, Governments should consider ways of strengthening their national population censuses, sample surveys or administrative record systems in order to obtain needed migration data and estimates" [29, p. 33].

The extent of reliance on the specific data sources recommended by the United Nations for research on urbanization and migration varies. A 1975 United Nations [25] evaluation indicates that of the 121 countries that had investigated migration to some extent, 85 relied exclusively on field surveys (including censuses) as their data source, 12 on population registers (mostly European countries), and 24 used a combination of the two. Developing countries used field surveys more frequently than did developed countries; about 85 per cent of the former and only half of the latter depended exclusively on field surveys.

Detailed evaluation of the strengths and limitations of censuses, registers, and special surveys as sources of data on the urban population and on migration have been undertaken elsewhere [22, 14, 10, 1]. The evaluation of these alternative sources can therefore be largely restricted here to highlighting the data requirements considered necessary for evaluation of the demographic structure of mega-cities and population movement to such locations.

Population registers are often considered superior sources of place of residence and migration data because, theoretically, they provide information on every resident and on every residential move within the country, and they do so on a continuous basis. Because of their universal coverage, they allow analysis by a variety of geographical, political, or administrative units, including mega-cities. They often also include information on a range of individual characteristics that allow comparison of the permanent residents of mega-cities with the in-migrants and out-migrants, thereby making possible the assessment of the selective impact of migration on the size and composition of mega-cities. Moreover, to the extent that a registration system requires notification from persons who move into a given city for more than a minimum time, even though they intend to maintain their permanent residence elsewhere, the system, unlike many censuses and surveys, provides the possibility of identifying temporary migrants living in the mega-city. It thereby allows evaluation of the impact of temporary movement on the de facto population. If temporary movers constitute a large proportion of the daily population of mega-cities, the opportunity to assess their numbers and characteristics adds considerably to our understanding of the dynamics of demographic change in cities. The accuracy of the information about such movers obviously depends, however, on the extent to which they actually register, and here there may be serious deficiencies.

Registers also have some obvious disadvantages. The institution and maintenance of accurate registers requires a high degree of administrative sophistication and of public cooperation. Yet the means and motives for achieving these features are often lacking in less developed areas. For example, a study of migrants to Bangkok [3] found that the majority did not register their move because, among other reasons, they did not intend to become permanent residents of the metropolis. A 1984 study of Shanghai showed that about half of the temporary migrants living in households in the metropolis were not registered even though Chinese regulations required registration within three days of movement into the city [11]. Furthermore, since registration data are based on legal specifications of who is a resident of a given location, they may yield enumerations that differ widely from counts based on other criteria that may be more relevant to an assessment of a mega-city's size and composition. Also, some residents fail to update the information covering their socio-economic characteristics. Caution needs to be exercised, therefore, as later examples from China will indicate, in using such data sets. Overall, it appears unlikely that population registers will be widely instituted in the foreseeable future in those less developed countries that do not already have such a system in place.

Censuses and sample surveys have different advantages and limitations for providing data on the urban structure and migration. The census, like the register, obviously provides the type of geographical coverage that allows separate tabulation of statistics for cities of varying size; these can range from the metropolis at one extreme to small cities and towns at the other. Data for subdivisions within mega-cities can also be obtained, providing proper codes are incorporated into the coding system. Data for census tracts, city districts, or other statistically designated units are examples of breakdowns that can be used in intra-urban ecological comparisons to provide rich insights into the structure of the city and into changes over time.

On the other hand, the census lends itself less well to obtaining in-depth information about a particular subject, given the limited space and time available in this method of data collection and the need to encompass a broad range of topics. The superficiality of the census in this regard can be overcome only by the opportunities offered by sample surveys for in-depth probing, especially when they focus on a narrow set of topics. For example, the small number of questions on migration that can be included in a census contrasts sharply with the wide coverage that can be given this subject in an ad hoc survey that concentrates on population movement [10, 14].

The obvious disadvantage of the survey is the need, generally, to restrict its sample size, so that the number of cases available for meaningful analysis are too few, especially when the characteristic or the event under investigation occurs relatively rarely in the population. Concentrating the sample in particular locations, such as mega-cities, and employing stratified sampling may help to overcome this problem even while introducing other limitations.

Another obvious problem characterizing the census is the infrequency with which it is taken, usually decennially and sometimes quinquennially. The speed with which urban change occurs in many countries and the changing rate and composition of population movement to mega-cities make reliance on a census for assessing change and evaluating policies frustrating if not dangerous. The greater frequency with which surveys can be undertaken and the resulting currency of the information obtained makes the sample survey an attractive supplement and possible alternative to the census.

In contrast to a good registration system, however, both the census and the survey are usually restricted to persons living in the city of enumeration at the time the data are collected [18]. As a result, they generally give only one side of the migration picture and do not allow full evaluation of the impact of migration on the population of the mega-city under investigation. Moreover, these sources often do not encompass temporary residents of the city. Only through special methods [13] can coverage be obtained for those who have left an area or those temporarily resident in it.

Issues of definition

A host of decisions face any effort to collect the residence and migration information needed for demographic research on mega-cities. Which criteria should be used in classifying the population as urban or rural? Assuming there is a choice, as there is in some countries, which boundaries of the city (the inner city or the extended city) should be used in counting the mega-city population? How should migration be defined – in terms of birthplace, residence at some fixed point in the past (e.g., five years or one year), or duration of residence? Should efforts be made to identify temporary migrants; if so, how should distinctions be made between temporary movers and migrants taking up permanent residence? How important is it for planning and policy purposes to distinguish between repeat migrants and those making only one move into the city? Which socio-economic and demographic characteristics of the migrants and the resident population are relevant for analytic purposes? Which reasons for migration should be identified? How should those who move as family members rather than on their own be classified – according to the prime mover's reason or simply as secondary movers? How is the adjustment of migrants to life in the community of destination best measured – by comparison with the non-migrants at destination, with the non-migrants at origin, with the migrants at alternative destinations, or with the migrants themselves at an earlier point in time? What criteria should be used for measuring adjustment – housing, jobs, income, health, utilization of local facilities, attitudes? Does adjustment vary depending on the rural/urban origin of the migrants and, if so, how? How can the cost be assessed of absorbing the permanent migrants versus the temporary migrants into the urban structure?

The very nature of these questions emphasizes that effective research on mega-cities and on the role of migration in affecting their size and composition must include a basic concern with the relevance of concepts and data to policy questions, including problem identification, goal setting and monitoring, and evaluation. Several areas of research must thereby receive concurrent attention. The way in which the mega-cities themselves are delineated must be clarified. Concepts of population mobility must be refined to allow for identification of all forms of movement: those that contribute to problems associated with changes in the size and composition of mega-cities and those forms of mobility that may help such locations to cope with their problems. The types of data needed to measure these concepts must be determined and the most appropriate sources of such data identified. The residential categories (spatial units) for which such information should be made available need to be carefully reviewed. Lastly, research must be designed to assess the success of previous efforts to control the natural growth of mega-cities and population movement to them and to identify the underlying factors that have accounted for the success or failure of specific policies designed to affect growth.

Taken together, the general deficiencies that often characterize urban/rural and migration data and those that arise in specific efforts to assess the need for and success of policy efforts call for a concerted effort to reassess research perspectives and priorities and to improve data collection systems. The needs are particularly pressing with respect to mega-cities.

Problems of boundary changes

Countries vary considerably, not only in how they define urban and rural places, which affects the international comparability of statistics on urbanization, but also in how they delineate cities. The particular criteria used have special relevance for mega-cities. Some include only the densely populated, inner core of the city; others liberally overextend and incorporate populated suburban districts and rural areas that are "tied" to the city by one or more criteria (e.g., residence of commuters, supplier of food, or potential settlement area for expansion). Depending on how extended the city boundaries are and how they are changed over time, both comparability with cities in other countries and comparability for any single city over time may be seriously impeded.

This type of problem is illustrated by data for Bangkok. Until 1972 the city of Bangkok consisted of built up "urban" districts within the province of Phra Nakhon; the number of these districts changed over time. For some analytic purposes, Bangkok was combined with its twin city across the Chao Phraya River, Thonburi, to form Greater Bangkok. By 1970, Bangkok *per se* encompassed 1.9 million persons; together with Thonburi, it included 2.5 million. Over the previous several decades the boundaries of Bangkok had been changed to reflect the expanding residential areas. Data were not generally available, however, to allow evaluation of how much of the intercensal changes was due to population growth within the previous boundaries and how much was attributable to annexation of new areas. As a result, more analyses that attempted to decompose Bangkok's growth into its components, i.e., natural increase and migration, treated all of the population living in the annexed areas as though they were migrants even though some may have lived there all their lives or for a period longer than that over which migration was being measured [27]. Since a number of the non-migrants in the annexed areas may have been engaged in agriculture and have had characteristics different from the migrants and the population within the earlier boundaries of the city, their addition to the city population would add a rural component and affect other features of the city's population. The resulting changes might not be easily explainable without recognition of the effects of the annexation process on the statistics.

The problem was compounded when, in 1972, the Thai government decided to merge the two adjoining provinces of Phra Nakhon and Thonburi into a single city, referred to as the Bangkok Metropolitan Area. Since then data have been presented in Thai statistics only for the combined provinces. For comparability with earlier census data, statistics encompassing the entire populations of both provinces had to be merged. The inclusion of additional agricultural population in the newly created metropolitan area affected both the rural-urban composition of the city's population and the characteristics of the population on other variables. Moreover, whereas movement between the two provinces had earlier been treated as inter-provincial movement, after 1972 all such movement was regarded as residential change within the city, even though the outlying parts of both provinces, but especially Thonburi, remained quite rural and constituted a very different type of origin for migrants to the truly urban part of the metropolitan area.

Most obvious was the effect on the city's size. In 1980, the Bangkok Metropolitan Area contained 4.70 million people in contrast to the 2.50 million counted in the combined cities of Bangkok and Thonburi in the 1970 census. If both provinces containing these two cities are considered in their entirety, as was done in 1980, the 1970 population enumeration rises to 3.08 million, indicating an intercensal growth of only 1.62 million instead of 2.20 million. Thus, approximately 27 per cent of the decennial change in the combined cities' population is a function of boundary change.

A by-product of change in population resulting from boundary alterations is the impact on a city's position in the urban hierarchy. This can be illustrated again by the situation for Bangkok. The Thai capital has been the most primate city in the world. In 1970, it was 22 times greater than Chiangmai, the second largest city in Thailand. Reflecting the boundary changes in 1972, the 1980 census showed Bangkok to have become dramatically more primate, with a primacy ratio of 46. Much of this gain was an artifact of the changing boundaries, but unless this is taken into account, serious errors of interpretation could result. In turn, other boundary changes in Thailand in 1982 have drastically reduced Bangkok's primacy level: As a result of annexations to the north-eastern municipality of Nakhon Ratchasima, which in 1980 reported a population of 89,000, its 1985 population just exceeded 200,000, resulting in its displacing Chiangmai as Thailand's second largest city. A by-product of this change was a decline in Bangkok's primacy ratio to 27, a level similar to that in 1970 [24].

These examples are not cited to argue against the political decisions that lead to boundary changes; rather, they serve to illustrate that such changes can have a substantial impact on statistics relating to mega-cities and can, in turn, seriously affect analyses based on the available data, particularly if the analyst is not aware of the underlying reasons for the changes. Such problems can easily arise, particularly if data are "fed into" data banks in order to be used comparatively or in the aggregate together with statistics from many other locations. One can easily imagine the types of interpretations that could emerge from an analysis that indiscriminately used the data for Bangkok and other cities in Thailand in the period 1970–1990.

Such a situation argues first for extreme caution in the use of all data on cities and towns and full awareness of the definitions employed and their comparability over time. It also places a responsibility on the administrative offices responsible for generating and publishing such data to alert consumers about changes in definitions and boundaries. Most important, it argues strongly for coding and tabulating urban and rural data in terms of small spatial or statistical units so that these small units can be used either aggregatively to construct larger units that are comparable over time or to remove data covering annexed areas from a city's total statistics in order to approximate the city as it was earlier. Such small-unit data would also facilitate international comparisons by allowing greater comparability in the criteria employed in establishing city boundaries. They would also allow development for analytic purposes of larger statistical areas, such as "urbanized areas" or "metropolitan areas," which are not limited to political boundaries. Individual nations could concurrently continue to employ whatever criteria best serve their purpose.

Delineating mega-cities and their populations

Having data coded for small areal units within the larger metropolis would serve still another useful purpose, even for mega-cities whose boundaries remained stable for long periods of time. Such cities do not remain stable internally. As Richardson [20, p. 55] has stressed, submetropolitan geographical data are of major importance for such cities, given their polycentric evolution and the fact that so many mega-cities embrace several political jurisdictions. The rapid changes in the internal structure of mega-cities, which very much influence the role they play in the larger national development efforts, argue strongly for developing census, vital statistics, and even survey data sets that allow attention to the subunits of the city while also allowing modifications in city boundaries to facilitate comparisons over time and space.

What constitutes a mega-city? Taking note of the sharp rise in the number of giant cities, it is fairly simple, even though somewhat arbitrary, to decide that 3, 5, or 8 million persons should be the minimum population for an urban location to qualify as a mega-city. This suggests the strong need for more attention to the basic concept of mega-city. Ideally, a more clearly delineated set of criteria, based on such variables as size, financial resources, industrial/commercial structure, political role, educational facilities and scientific personnel, service function, and position in the world system, should be considered for classifying selected cities as mega-cities. Otherwise, the unusual situation may arise such that a city like London does not qualify as a mega-city. For example, under the 1980 UN mega-city criterion of 8 million population, London was dropped because it had declined to 7.7 million, whereas cities like Moscow, Bombay, and Rio de Janeiro did qualify. Use of criteria in addition to population size seems likely to insure greater comparability over time and across space in what really constitutes a mega-city.

It is obviously easier to rely on areas encompassed by specified political boundaries because such areas are usually administered by a single authority and are more likely to have relevant data sets collected and compiled for them. Yet, such political units, whether they be cities, metropolitan areas, or combinations of districts or counties, may not accurately represent the full area encompassed by the mega-city. Indeed, the United Nations itself recognizes this problem in its compilation of data for urban places [35, pp. 1, 18]. It is illustrated even more clearly by the arguments posited by T.G. McGee [17] that a new pattern of intense urban-rural interaction has evolved involving the emergence of a number of mega-urban regions that include major cities, peri-urban zones, and an extensive zone of mixed agricultural and non-agricultural activities. These regions are organized along arterial transport routes that facilitate the extreme mobility of people and goods.

While growing evidence pointing to the collapse of the traditional spatial/distance features of what constitutes a city favours rethinking our basic urban concepts, practical considerations undoubtedly will continue to justify our use of the more traditional units. But even here, it is not so simple for planners or scholars to decide the basis on which the area encompassed by a city and its resident population are to be determined. That there is considerable room for differences in determining city size is evidenced both in the varied practices of individual countries and in the statistics assembled by the United Nations based on these local practices. The data for Shanghai illustrate how the varying criteria used by different government agencies can affect the comparability of the statistics of a given location.

In *Prospects of World Urbanization, 1988* [35] Shanghai is identified as having a 1985 estimated population of 12.06 million. In *China Statistical Yearbook, 1988* [7], Shanghai is credited with a 1987 total population of 7.22 million and a non-agricultural population of 7.11 million. In *China Urban Statistics, 1986* [5], the total population of Shanghai for 1985 is listed as 6.98 million for the city only, and 12.17 million for the city including the counties under its jurisdiction. Which of these statistics provides the correct population of Shanghai? What accounts for the differences among them? The answer lies in the fact that not all of the population living in places in China designated as urban are necessarily counted as urban. As a result, the population enumerated as urban may vary, and sometimes considerably so, depending on the source of data, the definition of resident, and the areal boundaries employed.

Each individual in China is officially registered at a specific place of residence. A permanent change in residence requires permission from the appropriate authorities in places of origin and destination. An individual who moves is considered a permanent resident of the location at destination only if the move involves a change in household registration. In any enumeration based on the household register, only persons who are registered in the cities and towns of China are counted as residents of urban locations; this is equivalent to a *de jure* enumeration system. The omission from the registers – and the statistics based on them – of temporary migrants, i.e., those living in urban places but not officially registered there (de facto residents), distorts the data on the size and composition of urban places as well as the data on the population in the places of origin of the temporary migrants.

In partial recognition of this situation, the 1982 Chinese census counted as residents those people who had lived in a given locality for more than one year even though they were registered elsewhere, as well as those who were absent from their place of registration for more than one year, and persons whose registration status had not yet been settled. This practice was continued in the 1987 *One Per Cent National Sample Survey* [6], except that a six-month minimum residence period was employed. The same six-month criterion was scheduled to be used in the 1990 census. Use of these criteria obviously yields a different count than does the registration system.

Complicating the question of who is a resident of an urban place has been reliance on the official source of an individual's grain supply. A person with urban registration is entitled to purchase grain from State outlets (commercial grain), whereas rural registration requires dependence on one's own production or on other rural sources (for example, commune before 1980). The former group is operationally defined as non-agricultural, and the latter as agricultural, although many of the "agricultural population" are in fact engaged in non-agricultural activities, especially since the rural reforms introduced in the late 1970s. Furthermore, the agricultural population also includes persons living within city boundaries but engaged in farm activities; conversely, persons classified as non-agricultural may be living in rural areas. Such criteria result in enumerations far different from those of the census and the 1987 *National Survey*. Under this system, the city population again more closely resembles a *de jure* rather than a de facto count, with only those having an urban registration and therefore entitled to receive commercial grain counted as urban residents.

This distinction takes on special importance as new cities are created that incorporate large areas with village populations and as the volume of temporary migration to mega-cities increases. The size and composition of the urban population based on urban boundaries are likely to increasingly diverge from those based on registration and source of grain. Knowledge of which criteria are being used is essential for any correct use of the data.

Still another basis for delineating China's urban, and particularly city, population contributes to the wide variation in the size of particular cities. Since the late 1950s, State policy has allowed cities, and especially mega-cities, in China to control adjoining rural counties, particularly as a way to maintain the critical balance between population and arable land [16, p. 15]. A number of city boundaries have therefore been officially extended to include both inner city and suburban districts (often referred to together as the city proper) and the rural counties officially designated as part of the city. As a result, in 1982, for example, the extended cities encompassed 227 million persons, almost 60 per cent more than the 145 million in the cities proper.

The variations in the enumerations of Shanghai's population illustrate the confusion that can arise from the use of such variable criteria. Shanghai consists of 12 city districts (the city proper) and 10 counties that were added to the municipality in 1958. If the city's population is defined in terms of the city proper, it numbered 6.98 million persons in 1985; but this number increases to 12.17 million if Greater Shanghai's boundaries are used instead. If Shanghai's population is considered to comprise only those persons holding urban (non-agricultural) registration, then the city proper population is reduced to 6.87 million and that of Greater Shanghai to 8.43 million. The municipality's population size, therefore, under varying legal definitions, ranges between 6.87 million and 12.17 million, a difference of 77 per cent. Moreover, none of these figures includes many of the estimated 1 million and more persons who are temporary residents in the city and who do not meet the minimum residence period for inclusion in the enumerations. The problem is illustrated by the fact that the United Nations cites 13.4 million as Shanghai's 1990 population, evidently relying on the broadest set of criteria. Yet using these same criteria, Chongqing, with 14.5 million in 1987, not Shanghai, is China's largest city, and it does not even appear on the UN list of mega-cities, nor do a number of others with 8 million or more residents under the same criteria as used for Shanghai [8].

The range of variation in Shanghai's population is less than in other cities because Shanghai has an unusually large percentage (98 per cent) of its city proper population classified as non-agricultural. Guangzhou, for example, has a lower proportion of its population (78 per cent) so classified. The city proper includes 3.29 million persons and the counties 3.81 million, for a total population of the extended city of 7.10 million if both agricultural and non-agricultural persons are included. If the enumeration is restricted to non-agricultural persons, then the city proper's population drops to only 2.57 million. The range of 4.53 million between the lowest and highest counts represents a differential of 176 per cent.

These data for Shanghai and Guangzhou illustrate why it is essential to specify the criteria used – whether the enumeration encompasses the city proper or the extended city, the non-agricultural population exclusively or the total population resident within city boundaries. Inclusion of the rural counties and of the agricultural population living in the cities inflates the size of the urban population, raises the national levels of urbanization, and changes the socioeconomic and demographic composition of both the urban and rural populations.

While the situation in China is not necessarily typical of other countries, the variety of criteria employed in delineating the urban population generally and the populations of individual cities attests to the way that definitional considerations can significantly affect city populations and, in turn, affect the results of analyses using data based on particular definitions. Moreover, given China's size and its percentage of world population (about one-fifth of both the world's total population and its urban population under China's newest definitions), the particular set of Chinese data used by the United Nations and other international agencies in comparative and cumulative statistics can very much affect the picture of urbanization that emerges, not only in the particular country or region but also worldwide. The same considerations hold for other large countries, such as India [2], that have their own system of delineating urban places and drawing the boundaries of large cities.

Migration and mega-city development

To the extent that the fertility of many developing countries has already declined and is likely to continue to do so, and because fertility levels are generally lower in urban than in rural areas [33], migration takes on increased importance as a component of demographic change; it plays a particularly important role in mega-cities, where fertility levels may be the lowest. As a process affecting the size and composition of urban populations, migration is, however, much more complex than the traditional published census type of information suggests. For many persons, the most recent move is only the last of a series of moves, often involving a stepping-stone process from rural areas to towns and smaller cities to larger urban places; for others the move may be quite direct and lead to permanent residence in the mega-city. For still others, movement may be circular or involve commuting between the mega-city and smaller towns or rural places.

Too often, when migration data are collected and analysed, concepts and measures employed in developed countries have been used uncritically in less developed countries. In many instances, migration is restricted to permanent moves that involve the crossing of boundaries that generally encompass large areal units, such as provinces or states. This practice ensures the exclusion of most short-distance moves and those that are temporary. Often, the use of provincial boundaries even precludes measurement of migration into and out of mega-cities because their boundaries may not coincide with provincial borders. Moreover, the extent of circular/repeat migration and of short-distance migration is far greater than revealed by censuses [4]. Such mobility often constitutes a very high percentage of all moves, particularly for mega-cities, and has significant implications for the mover, for the places of origin and destination, and for development in general. Reflecting this, the United Nations Expert Group on Population Distribution, Migration, and Development [28] recommended:

> The formulation of policy requires an in-depth understanding of the types of migration flows exhibited by a given population and of the interrelationships existing between them. For example, knowledge of the trends in the different types of movements, such as circular migration, seasonal migration, or migration leading to a long-term change of residence, or about the extent to which commuting is a substitute for migration, or about the causes leading to the different types of migration movements is essential for the sound formulation of policy. Governments should therefore promote research aimed at advancing this understanding.

Full evaluation of migration, therefore, requires separate attention to movement that leads to a permanent change in rural/urban residence and to mobility that is temporary. Both may affect the size, structure, and dynamics of mega-cities, but quite differently. First, it is most important to recognize that the number of persons enumerated as resident in mega-cities generally refers only to individuals who are either officially registered as residents (in those countries that maintain population registers) or, under census and survey procedures, to those who have lived in the city for some minimum period of time (e.g., six months or a year). As such, the census and register counts may not only differ from each other, but both may also differ significantly from the de facto count of persons who are functioning on a daily basis as members of the community. To the extent that there are substantial numbers of temporary migrants, however defined, official counts may give misleading information on city size and on the number of persons whose daily needs for food, housing, transportation, and other services must be met, even though they do not reside in the city on a permanent basis.

The impact of various forms of migration

The potential impact of temporary mobility goes well beyond the question of its effect on the size of the city's population and infrastructure. Whether migrants to a mega-city live there for a short or a long time has serious implications for their ties to the community and to their rural places of origin; for the nature of the interaction with kin networks; for the extent and nature of the services needed in the mega-city; for the types of burdens their particular characteristics place on its infrastructure and whether these are similar in quantity and type to those imposed by permanent in-migrants [21]; and for the role of the moves in the social and economic development of the city. Concurrently, evaluation is needed of the extent to which the flow of funds and ideas from the mega-city that are engendered by circulation constitute a critical component of modernization in smaller urban places and rural areas.

Temporary migration may help to adjust labour supply and demand without the social dislocation that large-scale permanent migration may entail. It may also allow for the provision of services to mega-city residents through the informal sector that are in short supply otherwise. The high turnover rates inherent in high levels of temporary migration may also mean that self-correcting factors operate in the migration process, so that the net results are not as injurious to the cities or to the individual migrants as is often implied by the literature on overurbanization [15]. Within these general concerns, the gender, age, marital status, education, labour force status, and occupation of the migrants and whether they move alone or with family become important considerations.

To date, the implications of various forms of mobility for the urbanization process and for the growth of cities have been largely speculative. Systematic collection and analysis of data designed specifically to test these varied relations for mega-cities have been rare. Policy makers and researchers have begun to recognize that the process of population movement is very different from that usually portrayed by the traditional analysis of limited census data. Planning and policies based on such distorted perceptions of the relation between population movement and mega-city growth and functioning may therefore yield erroneous results. In fact, (1) mega-city populations may be much more fluid than usually assumed; (2) population movement to mega-cities takes on multiple forms and is not limited to permanent migration; (3) motives are not just economic but often have a strong social component; (4) links between mega-cities and both rural and other urban places are often stronger than assumed; and (5) the nature and degree of adjustment and assimilation are often better than hypothesized.

Evaluating redistribution for policy formulation

All of these possibilities have particular relevance for policies designed to affect population movement and the growth of mega-cities. Therefore, data collection and research efforts should encompass the broadest possible concept of population movement in order to allow for identification and assessment of the different types of movement, ranging from permanent migration at one extreme to daily commuting at the other, with provision for intervening categories such as circulation, onward or repeat movement, and seasonal migration. One must be able to ascertain who moves and from where, what form the movement takes and why this form was chosen, and what positive and negative impacts the different forms of movement have on the mega-city and on the movers and their families.

As part of this evaluation, attention should also be given to how changes from reliance upon one form of movement to another affects demands for housing, education, health facilities, transportation, and other services. Particularly relevant here is the assessment of the comparative costs and benefits (economic, social, and psychological) of permanent migration compared with temporary migration and commuting, in order to ascertain how greater reliance on one form of movement over another would affect the quality of life in mega-cities and lead to greater economies in governmental provision of services.

Careful attention must also be given, on the individual level, to the absorption and assimilation processes as they relate to migration to mega-cities. Is it the migrants or the natives of the city who are disproportionately in poverty, in squatter settlements and slums, in the tertiary sector? In particular, evaluation is needed of how migrants adjust to life in mega-cities, whether "maladjustment" contributes to high rates of return and onward movement, and whether the adjustment process of permanent migrants differs significantly from that of persons who plan to stay only temporarily in the city.

Disproportional attention has been given in migration research to male migrants and to heads of households. In part, this focus reflects the importance of economic variables in migration and the consequent belief that decisions to move are largely made on the basis of the economic activities of male household members, particularly the male household head. Yet, there is growing evidence that, increasingly, women are migrating to mega-cities in their own right and that decisions about who moves are often family decisions rather than those of individual household members [9]. In the analysis of census data and the development of migration surveys, more attention must be given to female migrants as well as to family members other than heads of households. This need becomes more urgent as employment opportunities in mega-cities increase for women, as the flow of information about such opportunities improves, as educational opportunities for women expand, as norms about family control of female members change, and as migration itself assumes growing importance in affecting the status of women. Assessment of the changing labour force structure of cities and the division of labour between men and women as well as evaluation of the changing household structure and of urban fertility would be misleading without full attention to female migration in all its forms.

The impact of fertility and mortality on mega-city growth warrants special attention, including assessment of changing birth and death rates, differentials among the various segments of the population, and the implications of these processes for the future age composition and labour force supply as well as demands on educational, health, and other facilities. The relation between migration to mega-cities and the fertility of the migrants warrants particular attention. Since migrants tend to be concentrated in the reproductive ages, whether their fertility contributes disproportionally to city growth is of particular interest. So, too, are such questions as whether the fertility of the migrants differs significantly from that of the non-migrants and whether the observed difference can be attributed to the impact of residence in the city.

Full assessment of such questions requires data that allow distinctions to be drawn not only between the fertility of migrants and that of non-migrants but also between the fertility of permanent residents of the city and that of women who come into the city just to deliver their babies. Similar concerns apply to mortality data; it is important to be able to distinguish between deaths of residents and those of persons who came to the city to take advantage of health facilities. If the effect of natural increase on city growth is to be clearly ascertained, data on births and deaths must be available by place of usual residence of the person to whom the event has occurred in addition to place of occurrence.

A number of countries have introduced policies intended to control the rate of mega-city growth, particularly through the control of movement to mega-cities. The effectiveness of such policies must be more fully assessed, and such assessment should include the impact of both direct and indirect policies, successful and unsuccessful ones.

The necessity for evaluative research on redistribution policies has been recognized in United Nations deliberations. The report of the Expert Group on Population Distribution, Migration, and Development, just prior to the 1984 International Conference on Population, recommended that,

> in view of the concern repeatedly expressed by Governments with regard to population distribution and migration . . . , Governments and the international community should support and promote the collection of data and the undertaking of analyses relevant to the formulation and evaluation of policies on population distribution and on international migration.

Moreover,

> since the monitoring of trends is essential for the formulation and evaluation of policies, countries are urged to make every effort to improve the quality, timeliness, quantity and comparability through time of the information they gather on the migration process, including its causes and consequences. In particular, countries that already collect relevant information on either internal or international migration, but that do not publish it on a regular basis, should take the necessary measures to improve its timely availability. [29]

Often, concerns about the growth rates of mega-cities lead to policies to control such growth through channelling population to smaller locations and alternate growth centres and through rural development strategies that will help to retain potential migrants in rural areas. To better understand the similarities and differences between migration to mega-cities and that to smaller places, the topics identified as important for research on population movement to mega-cities should also be pursued in terms of the extent of their differential impact on places that vary in size, function, location, and type. Even though current attention focuses on mega-cities, full understanding of the dynamics of population change in such places and of the likely effectiveness of policies to control their growth is not possible without comparative assessment of medium-size and smaller locations in the urban hierarchy. Even within the mega-city group, comparisons are essential among cities that are at different stages of development; have different political, economic, and social structures; and are linked in different ways and degrees to other cities within their own country and internationally. Particular attention needs to be given to evaluation of the comparative features of declining and growing cities. Why do some no longer qualify as mega-cities while others move into this category, often rapidly and unexpectedly? The need for comparative research argues strongly for the need for greater standardization of definitions and measures. Otherwise, comparative research will continue to be plagued by inconsistencies that preclude meaningful evaluation. Such comparative research could well serve to help us decide where, in fact, the lines should be drawn between mega-cities and other cities.

Data collection and analysis

To undertake the types of analyses and evaluations outlined, a variety of data sets is needed. Some sets are available in existing sources; others require refinements; and still others require generation of new bodies of information.

The census will undoubtedly remain an indispensable instrument for measuring the size and composition of mega-city populations and for ascertaining the role of migration in changes in size and composition. Everything possible should be done, therefore, to insure that the census encompasses the total population living in the cities, including both *de jure* and de facto residents, while concurrently distinguishing between these two groups so that they can be separated for analytic purposes. Direct questions on migration are also important, including information on duration of residence, registration status (for countries with registration systems), origin, and reasons for move. The questions asked must, to the maximum degree possible, make possible analysis of different types of movement (permanent migration, temporary migration, and commuting) to allow comprehensive assessment of the functioning populations of mega-cities, including especially their labour force, school population, and aged residents, i.e., all those who may make use of and impose burdens on the infrastructure.

The restricted space available in censuses, and the fact that they are generally taken only once every 10 or 5 years, means that censuses can be of only limited use in providing data necessary for the evaluation of the dynamics of mega-city growth and change. Efforts must be made to obtain data that complement the advantages offered by the census by being more comprehensive and more frequent; these efforts may include registers, omnibus surveys into which relevant questions can be incorporated, and ad hoc surveys directed at particular topics of concern.

Vital statistics records need to distinguish clearly between events occurring to usual residents of the city and events occurring to those entering the city for limited periods to take advantage of its care-giving facilities. As far as possible, such records should also ascertain the migration status of the registered persons and do so in a way that is consistent with other data systems. Only in this way will it be feasible to calculate correct rates, to ascertain the contribution of natural increase to city growth, and to evaluate the impact of migration on natural increase.

The value of administrative and other record systems for assessing and monitoring population distribution among cities, towns, and rural places and redistribution among them must be continuously reviewed. In a number of countries, population registers, tax rolls, social security and other insurance files, school enrolment statistics, and health records have substantial potential as sources of information on the size of either the total population of mega-cities or of selected segments of the population. They also can be a rich source of data on the volume, composition, and direction of population movement. Their utilization in conjunction with data on the labour market, on health, educational, housing, and other facilities should prove valuable in the assessment of the impact of changing population size and composition as well as of migration on the quality of life in the city. Research should also use the opportunities afforded by technological advances associated with remote-sensing devices to assess changes in population distribution, density, housing conditions (including squatter settlements), and environmental changes within mega-cities.

Given the complexity of population movement and the need to explore all its dimensions, comprehensive evaluation of population movement requires specialized surveys that focus exclusively on movement and related factors or in which attention to movement is a major component. Because migration may be a relatively rare event in the general population, consideration should be given to the use of a multiplicity approach [13]; this would increase the number of migrants encompassed by a survey and enhance the possibility of covering individuals who have migrated out.

A full migration survey should reconstruct migration histories, ascertain the economic and social characteristics of the movers before and after migration, and determine the motives for movement and why the mega-city was chosen as the destination. Attention should be given, too, to the adjustment process and to the uses that the migrants and the non-migrants make of the city's facilities. Particularly essential are questions to ascertain intentions with respect to future movement, both within the city and out of it, of the previous in-migrants and the natives. Using such a broad approach, a series of comparative migration surveys in various mega-cities of the world would provide valuable insights on how behaviour and attitudes of both migrants and non-migrants are related to the characteristics of the mega-city.

It is essential that in all such surveys the sample include not only migrants who have become permanent residents of the city but also temporary migrants, commuters, and non-migrants. The latter provide an important standard against which the behaviour and attitudes of the migrants can be compared; they also are essential to the assessment of the ways in which migration and commuting complement or create conditions that conflict with the structure and dynamics of change characterizing the native population of the city. For example, do migrants and commuters fill gaps in labour force needs, or do they compete with natives for limited vacancies? What demands do these different groups place on school facilities, housing and health services? How well do they integrate residentially, socially, and politically? Such comparisons and evaluations require that comparable data for migrants and non-migrants be obtained, including life-history matrices that encompass information on a range of demographic variables, usually including fertility, mortality, and mobility behaviour as well as changes in such characteristics as labour force status, occupation, marital status, education, and home ownership.

Several kinds of surveys can serve as models: The yearly surveys undertaken in Bangkok Metropolis (e.g., ref. 23) on migration to the metropolitan area in the preceding two years is an example of one type of ad hoc migration survey that serves the planning needs of a mega-city. The CASS Migration Survey [19], encompassing 74 cities and towns in China has so far been undertaken only once, but it provides a model of an attempt to assess comparatively both in- and out-migration for urban places of different size. If repeated, it could become a valuable source of information for planning and policy purposes. The various questionnaire, sampling, and tabulating manuals prepared by ESCAP [37] should prove particularly valuable in any effort to develop surveys focusing on the urban population generally or mega-cities in particular.

All data collection and tabulation efforts in any particular country should grow out of cooperative activities among the national statistical agencies, the major research institutions, and the groups responsible for local planning and for policy formation, implementation, and evaluation. Use should also be made of the advice and expertise available from international agencies. Such cooperation is essential to ensure that the information needed as the basis for planning and for policy formation and evaluation will, in fact, be obtained, and that the relevant government agencies will be made aware of key questions raised and the insights provided by ongoing research.

If research on the demographic structure of mega-cities and the impact of migration on this structure is to prove useful in the formulation and evaluation of population redistribution policies, data collection systems must incorporate attention to not only demographic variables, including migration, but also the related social, economic, and political indicators that can serve as measures of the quality of life in mega-cities and of the success or failure of particular policies. Too often, the relevant indicators of development and modernization are not available to allow their integrated use with demographic statistics.

To achieve these goals, efforts should be initiated to utilize all available data to develop systems of geo-coding. This would involve compiling, for the sub-areas of mega-cities, a comprehensive set of indicators on population characteristics, environmental and economic conditions, infrastructures, and other relevant variables for as many points in time as possible. Together with census data for small areas, these data files covering the small areal units can, in turn, serve as building blocks for delineating the characteristics of larger units and for the mega-cities as a whole, particularly as these cities undergo boundary changes. Availability of such integrated sets of contextual information for small areas would facilitate evaluation of causes and consequences of change in the structure of mega-cities and facilitate comparisons among different cities and of the same city over time.

Assessment of mega-cities is not restricted to the present. Much of the analysis that takes place is used for anticipating and planning the future of such cities. For this purpose, post-censal estimates and population projections are essential ingredients of the planning process. The importance of the migration component in such estimates and projections argues strongly for the need for both adequate migration data and improved methods for estimating and projecting migration. As the United Nations Expert Group on Population Distribution, Migration, and Development recognized,

> to assess the potential impact of migration on the redistribution of the population and to evaluate the performance of population distribution poli-

cies, national planners need flexible and realistic demographic models that, by incorporating migration variables explicitly, permit the simulation and forecasting of its demographic consequences. [29]

Concurrently, it must be recognized that any projections made may affect decisions that can, in turn, directly or indirectly affect the volume and composition of population movement. The complexity of the interrelations emphasizes the need for close monitoring of all elements in the growth and redistribution process.

In all future data collection efforts, every effort should be made to ensure that data become available quickly for analytical purposes. Steps should also be taken to ensure easy and full access to these data by scholars and policy makers, especially by means of the preparation and distribution of public use tapes. The considerable lag that often characterizes access to basic data and the great difficulty encountered by many scholars and graduate students in gaining access to such data serve as major impediments to their rapid and full exploitation for planning purposes and for the formulation and evaluation of policies relevant to urban growth and population movement.

Conclusion

Despite the growing attention given to the role of mega-cities in the urbanization and development processes of developing countries, serious deficiencies related to conceptual issues and data needs continue to confront researchers engaged in demographic research on such cities. These include such basic concerns as accurate delineation and measurement of the size and composition of mega-city populations; others relate to interest in the demographic processes affecting mega-city growth, the dynamics of the labour force, and the linkages between mega-cities and smaller urban and rural places.

For all these issues, population movement in all its forms is a key variable. Particularly essential is refinement of concepts dealing with (1) the urban/rural dimensions of population distribution, especially as these relate to classification of who is to be counted as a resident and a functioning member of the population of mega-cities, and (2) the various forms of population movement that affect short-term and long-term populations of mega-cities, including permanent in-migration, circular or repeat migration, and commuting. Such distinctions are essential as the basis for ascertaining what forms of movement characterize mega-cities, what function they perform for individuals and for cities, how they relate to city growth through natural increase, and how they affect the burdens imposed on the cities' infrastructure in the face of growing populations.

In turn, refinement of concepts must be accompanied by fuller exploitation of existing data sets and development of new data sources where existing sources are inadequate. Censuses, registration statistics, and ad hoc surveys, together with a wide array of administrative records and statistics, provide opportunities for obtaining more comprehensive and continual data on the size, composition, and processes of change characterizing mega-cities. Because each source has its own strengths and weaknesses, the different sources must be used in complementary fashion. In all attempts to exploit and generate appropriate data, special efforts must be exerted to undertake comparative research in order to assess the effects of differences, both within and between countries, in population scale, in the internal structure of mega-cities, and in socio-economic conditions and levels of development. Such comparative evaluation is essential to the formulation and revision of policies, both direct and indirect, affecting mega-city growth, the rural/urban distribution of population, and the nature of the urban hierarchy.

As was true in 1979 [12], the agenda of research needs remains long, complex, and challenging. It is obviously not intended to be fully implemented in any given location or by any specific time. To do so would overwhelm both researchers and planners with the task of collecting and analysing data sets that go well beyond what many need and what most can realistically use. Priorities need to be established. These must vary, however, by the status of the data collection systems already extant in given places; by local needs as determined by perceptions of problem areas involving mega-cities and population distribution generally; by policy efforts to cope with them; and by the personnel and financial resources available to assess existing data and to develop and utilize new collection and analysis systems.

If there is one message that emerges from this review, it is that more refined concepts and a firmer data base are essential for realistic assessment of the demographic condition of mega-cities and their role in the larger development process and for formulation and evaluation of policies affecting them and urbanization generally. As a corollary, in all efforts to assure adequate information as the basis for policy formulation, highest priority should be given to (1) fuller and more effective exploitation of existing data, with new materials being collected only when and where significant gaps are identified; (2) as high a level of standardization in definitions and measures employed as possible in order to insure maximum opportunities for comparative research; and (3) more effective combined use of quantitative and qualitative data, especially in the form of comparative case-studies, such as those developed in the United Nations series on population growth and policies in mega-cities; these should be comparative over both space and time. Only through a research agenda that takes full and concurrent account of conceptual, data, and policy concerns will the insights necessary for development of more effective policies be gained and the basis established for having mega-cities play as effective a role as possible in the urbanization and development processes generally, and in reducing inequities in the quality of life within such cities and between them and other urban places and rural areas.

Acknowledgements

This paper was prepared for a symposium on the Mega-city and Mankind's Future: Population Growth and Policy Responses, held at the United Nations University, Tokyo, 22–25 October 1990. It draws selectively on material contained in Sidney Goldstein, "Research Priorities and Data Needs for Establishing and Evaluating Population Redistribution Policies," in *Population Distribution Policies in Development Planning*, G.J. Demko and R.J. Fuchs, eds. (New York: United Nations, 1981), pp. 193–203. Much of the work for this paper was undertaken while the author was a Scholar in Residence at the Rockefeller Study and Conference Center in Bellagio, Italy.

References

1 Bilsborrow, Richard, A.S. Oberai, and Guy Standing. *Migration Surveys in Low-Income Countries*. London: Croom Helm, 1984.

2 Bose, Ashish. "Basic Data Needed for the Study of Migration: A Case Study of the Indian Census." In Sidney Goldstein and David Sly, eds. *Basic Data Needed for the Study of Urbanization*. Liège: IUSSP, 1975, pp. 71–93.

3 Chamratrithirong, Aphichat. *Recent Migrants in Bangkok Metropolis: A Follow-up Study of Migrants' Adjustment, Assimilation, and Integration*. Bangkok: Institute for Population and Social Research, Mahidol University, 1979.

4 Chapman, Murray, and R. Mansell Prothero. *Circulation in Population Mobility*. London: Routledge and Kegan Paul, 1985.

5 China. State Statistical Bureau. *China Urban Statistics, 1986*. Hong Kong: Longman Group (Far East) Ltd., 1987.

6 ———. *Tabulations of China 1% Population Sample Survey, National Volume*. Beijing: Department of Population Statistics, State Statistical Bureau, 1988.

7 ———. *China Statistical Yearbook, 1988*. Beijing: State Statistical Bureau, 1989.

8 ———. *China Urban Statistics, 1988*. New York: Praeger, 1990.

9 Fawcett, James T., Siew-Ean Khoo, and Peter C. Smith. *Women in the Cities of Asia*. Boulder, Colo., USA: Westview Press, 1984.

10 Findley, Sally E. *Migration Survey Methodologies: A Review of Design Issues*. IUSSP Paper no. 20. Liège: IUSSP, 1982.

11 Goldstein, Alice, Sidney Goldstein, and Shenyang Guo. "Temporary Migrants in Shanghai Households, 1984." Unpublished paper, Population Studies and Training Center, Brown University, 1990.

12 Goldstein, Sidney. "Research Priorities and Data Needs for Establishing and Evaluating Population Redistribution Policies." In G.J. Demko and R.J. Fuchs, eds. *Population Distribution Policies in Development Planning*. New York: United Nations, 1981, pp. 193–203.

13 Goldstein, Sidney, and Alice Goldstein. *A Test of the Potential Use of Multiplicity in Research on Population Movement*. Washington, D.C.: National Center for Health Statistics, 1979.

14 ———. *Surveys of Migration in Developing Countries: A Methodological Review*. Paper no. 71. Honolulu: East-West Population Institute, East-West Center, 1981.

15 Gugler, Josef. "Overurbanization Reconsidered." *Economic Development and Cultural Change* 31 (October 1982): 173–198.

16 Koshizawa, Akira. "China's Urban Planning: Toward Development without Urbanization." *Developing Economics* 16 (March 1978): 3–33.

17 McGee, T.G. "Urbanisasi or Kotadesi? Evolving Patterns of Urbanization in Asia." In Frank J. Costa, Lawrence J.C. Ma, Ashok K. Dutt, and Allan G. Noble, eds. *Urbanization in Asia*. Honolulu: University of Hawaii Press, 1989, pp. 93–108.

18 Nicholson, Beryl. "The Hidden Component in Census-Derived Migration Data: Assessing Its Size and Distribution." *Demography* 27 (February 1990): 111–119.

19 Population Research Institute, CASS. *China Migration of 74 Cities and Towns Sampling Survey Data, 1986 (Computer Tabulations)*. Beijing: Population Research Institute, Chinese Academy of Social Sciences, 1988.

20 Richardson, Harry W. "Efficiency and Welfare in LDC Mega-Cities." In John D. Kasarda and Allan M. Parnell, eds. *Third World Cities: Problems, Policies, and Prospects*. Newbury Park: Sage Publications, 1993, pp. 32–57.

21 Rondinelli, Dennis. "Balanced Patterns of Urbanization in Developing Countries: The Concept and Reality." Paper prepared for International Workshop on Urbanization and Population Distribution Policies in Asia, East-West Population Institute, Honolulu, 1989.

22 Tekse, Kalman. "The Measurement of Rural-Urban Migration." In Sidney Goldstein and David Sly, eds. *The Measurement of Urbanization and Projection of Urban Population*. Liège: IUSSP, 1975, pp. 143–210.

23 Thailand National Statistical Office. *Survey of Migration into Bangkok Metro-*

polis, the Vicinity of Bangkok Metropolis, and Khon Kaen Province, 1985. Bangkok: National Statistical Office, 1986.

24 Tritasavit, Phiraphol. "Urbanization and Population Distribution: The Role of Regional Cities Development in Thailand." Paper prepared for International Workshop on Urbanization and Population Distribution Policies in Asia, East-West Population Institute, Honolulu, 1989.

25 United Nations. *Statistics of Internal Migration: A Technical Report*. New York: United Nations, 1975.

26 ———. *World Population Trends and Policies—1977 Monitoring Report*. Vol. 2, *Population Policies*. Population Studies, no. 62. New York: United Nations, 1978.

27 ———. *Patterns of Urban and Rural Population Growth*. ST/ESA/Ser.A/68. New York: United Nations, 1980.

28 ———. *Population Distribution, Migration and Development*. ST/ESA/Ser.A/89. New York: United Nations, 1984.

29 ———. *Report of the International Conference on Population*. E/Conf.76/19. New York: United Nations, 1984.

30 ———. *Estimates and Projections of Urban, Rural, and City Population, 1950–2025: The 1982 Assessment*. ST/ESA/Ser.R/58. New York: United Nations, 1985.

31 ———. *Review and Appraisal of the World Population Plan of Action*. New York: United Nations, 1986.

32 ———. *Population Growth and Policies in Mega-Cities*. Population Policy Papers, nos. 4–8, 10, 12, 13, and 34. New York: United Nations, 1986–1990.

33 ———. *Fertility Behavior in the Context of Development: Evidence from The World Fertility Survey*. New York: United Nations, 1987.

34 ———. *The Prospects of World Urbanization, Revised as of 1984–85*. ST/ESA/Ser.A/101. New York: United Nations, 1987.

35 ———. *Prospects of World Urbanization, 1988*. ST/ESA/Ser.A/112. New York: United Nations, 1989.

36 ———. *World Population Trends and Policies—1989 Monitoring Report*. Population Studies, no. 103. New York: United Nations, 1990.

37 United Nations Economic and Social Commission for Asia and the Pacific (UNESCAP). *National Migration Surveys*. Manuals I–VII. New York: United Nations, 1980.

3

Labour force change and mobility in the extended metropolitan regions of Asia

T.G. McGee

Director, Institute of Asian Research, The University of British Columbia, Vancouver

Introduction

Today most scenarios of the future of Asia accept the inevitability of Asian societies experiencing an "urban revolution," in which a majority of the Asian population will soon be living in places defined as urban. In Asia a near doubling of urban population is expected in the period between 1980 and 2020, as an estimated 462 million people are added to the urban population. This will bring about an overall urbanization level in Asia of almost 50 per cent.[1] Such a large increase has raised predictable fears concerning the size of cities that will be needed to accommodate this increase and the problems that will be posed for the creation of urban infrastructure, housing, and the creation of productive employment. While one would not wish to underemphasize these problems, there is also a more optimistic scenario emerging that results from a more careful evaluation of the concepts upon which these assumptions concerning future urban growth in Asia are based.

The predictions of the preceding paragraph are, of course, largely based on assumptions concerning the growth of population in places defined as urban. These estimates are calculated on growth rates reflecting performance in previous decades that, when projected forward, appear to suggest a successful shift to urbanized societies and repetitions of patterns of developed countries. As Ginsburg has commented about urbanization in the United States, "This condition reflects the progression of the . . . space economy to a state of what one might consider 'maturity'; that is, to a condition whereby areas possessed of substantial comparative advantage . . . would be drawn effectively, through improved transportation networks, into the national geographic structure."[2]

While not denying that these processes are operating in the Asian context, the purpose of this paper is to suggest that this model of the "urban transition" needs careful evaluation, which, in this investigation, involves in part the discarding of the mental baggage of concepts and ideas that are part of the so-called body of urban theory that has grown out of the Western experience of the urban transition.[3]

Three main components of that Western experience are ubiquitous. First, there is a fundamental divide between rural and urban. This dichotomy is portrayed *spatially, sectorally* in terms of agriculture and non-agriculture, *politically* in administrative organization, and *ideologically* in the way policy is formulated for rural and urban areas. Second, the process of urbanization, in which a majority of a country's population comes to live in places defined as urban, is unilinear and inevitable. Third, the process of urbanization is a necessary part of the process of economic growth. In some versions of this theory, not only is it an inevitable part of economic growth, it is the growth of cities that is the crucial independent variable that causes economic growth. I do not need to repeat the arguments that are used to support this Western-derived theoretical position, for there is more than ample literature on the subject. But it is necessary to reiterate that this body of theory and its assumptions are the major explanatory tool applied to processes of urbanization in Asia and therefore dominate the views of the future Asian city. I would throw out the challenge that this body of urban theory should be evaluated most carefully as it is applied to the experience of urbanization in Asia. Indeed, I would argue that there are very different sets of conditions operating in Asia to those that occurred in the Western industrialized countries in the nineteenth and twentieth centuries.

To elaborate further the conventional view of the urban transition is inadequate in three respects. First, it is too narrow in its view that the widely accepted spatial separation of rural and urban activities will persist as urbanization continues. Second, it is inadequate in its assumption that the urbanization transition will be inevitable, because of the operation of "agglomeration economies" and comparative advantage, which are said to facilitate the concentration of the population in linked urban places. The emergence of such a system was described by Jean Gottman in 1961 as a megalopolis, which, when applied to the north-eastern United States, included a population largely concentrated in the urban and suburban areas but interspersed with areas of low population density used for intensive agriculture and as leisure spaces by the population of the megalopolitan areas.[4] In many parts of Asia, the spatial juxtaposition of many of the larger city cores within heavily populated regions of intensive, mostly wet-rice, agriculture based on a mixture of "skill-orientated" and "mechanical" technological inputs[5] has created densities of population that are frequently much higher than the suburban areas of the West. This permits demographic densities similar to urban areas over extended zones of intensely cultivated rural areas located adjacent to urban cores. The considerable advances in transportation technology, particularly in relatively cheap intermediate transportation technology such as two-stroke motor bikes, greatly facilitate the circulation of commodities, people, and capital in such regions, which in turn creates large mega-urban regions.

Third, the Western paradigm of the urban transition draws its rationale from the historical experience of urbanization as it has occurred in Western Europe and North America in the nineteenth and twentieth centuries, which is clearly not neatly transferable to the developing countries' urbanization process. The uneven incorporation of these Asian countries into a world economic system from the fifteenth century onwards created divergent patterns of urbanization that reflect the different interactions between Asian countries and the world system.[6] For example, the British, French, and Dutch also developed the productivity of wet-rice agriculture in South-east Asia.[7] In a similar manner, Japanese rule in Korea and Taiwan further accentuated the monocultural rice characteristics of parts of these countries as sources of supply for Japan's pre-war empire. Geopolitical events meant that both these countries emerged into "fragile" independence with high rural densities and low levels of urbanization. On the other hand, British intervention in Malaysia created an urban system orientated to the production of export products on the west coast, away from the heavily populated rice-bowls of Kedah and Kelantan, limiting the possibilities of the emergent mega-urban region.

Because of these inadequacies, it is suggested that the concept of the urban transition needs to be positioned within a broader paradigm of the transition in the "space economy" of countries. This would include: (1) a heightened sensitivity to the historical elements of the urban and agrarian transition within specific countries; (2) an appreciation of the ecological, demographic, and economic foundations of the urban and agrarian transition; (3) an investigation of the institutional components, particularly the role of the State in the development process; (4) careful evaluation of the transactional components within given countries including transport, commodity, and population flows; and (5) a broad understanding of the structural shifts in the labour force that are reflecting economic change. Essentially, such an approach attempts to investigate the manner in which particular sets of conditions in one place interact with broader processes of change.

Population growth, structural change, labour force absorption, and urbanization in Asia

The issues raised in the preceding discussion are central to the discussion of the relationships between population growth, structural change, labour force absorption, and urbanization in Asia. The major question must be whether Asian countries can experience a structural transformation in their economies that is associated with an "urban revolution" and the successful absorption of the labour force into their urban economies during this transition.

At the regional scale the prospects suggest difficulty. In the short term between 1985 and 2000, the Asian countries are expected to increase their population by an estimated 633 million.[8] While the overall population growth rates are declining, the decline is insufficient to make a major difference in the number of people who will enter the labour force in the next few years. Over the slightly longer period between 1980 and 2000, Hauser and Gardiner estimate some 536 million people will be added to the urban population of Asian countries,[9] while the overall urbanization level will grow from 17 per cent to 27 per cent.[10] From these data it is clear that the urban growth in the region will be insufficient to absorb either the population increase or the shift of people from rural areas, suggesting that population growth will continue in rural areas. However, the analysis of the Asian situation at the regional level is of limited value except in exercises concerned with global comparisons, for there are major differences between the various regions.

Table 1 **Urbanization trajectories for selected Asian countries 1965–1987**

Country	Popul. (1987) (mn)	Average annual pop. growth rate (%)		Urban pop. as percentage of total pop.		Average annual urban pop. growth rate (%)		Proportion of labour force in: Agric.		Industry		Services	
		1965–1980	1980–1987	1965	1987	1965–1980	1980–1987	1960	1980	1960	1980	1960	1980
Japan	122.1	1.2	0.6	67	77	2.1	0.8	33	11	30	34	37	55
Hong Kong	5.6	2.0	1.6	89	93	2.1	1.7	8	3	52	57	40	40
Singapore	2.6	1.6	1.1	100	100	1.6	1.1	8	2	23	39	69	59
Taiwan[a]	19.6	2.7	1.4	30.4	52.3	2.7	1.5	56	20	11	33	33	47
Rep. of Korea	42.1	2.0	1.4	32	69	5.8	4.2	66	34	9	29	25	37
Malaysia	16.5	2.5	2.7	26	40	4.5	5.0	63	50	12	16	25	34
Philippines	58.4	2.9	2.5	32	41	4.2	3.8	61	46	15	17	24	37
Thailand	53.6	2.9	2.0	13	21	5.1	4.9	84	76	4	9	12	15
Sri Lanka	16.4	1.8	1.5	20	21	2.3	1.2	56	54	13	14	31	32
Bangladesh	106.1	2.8	2.8	6	13	6.4	5.8	87	74	3	11	10	15
Myanmar	39.3	2.3	2.2	21	24	3.2	2.3	68	67	11	10	21	23
India	797.5	2.3	2.1	19	27	3.9	4.1	73	71	11	13	16	16
Indonesia	171.4	2.4	2.1	16	27	4.8	5.0	74	58	8	12	17	30
Pakistan	102.5	3.1	3.1	24	31	4.3	4.5	61	57	18	20	21	23
P.R. China	1,068.5	2.2	1.2	18	38[b]	2.3	11.0	75	62	15	25	10	13

Source: World Bank, *World Development Report* (1989).

a. Data drawn from Republic of China, *Statistical Yearbook of the R. O. P.* (1987). The urban population is defined as population in locations of 100,000 persons and more.

b. Data drawn from the World Bank 1989 *World Development Report*. The dramatic increase of China's urbanization level may be attributed in part to the statistical reclassification of Chinese cities rather than the rapid growth of urban population. See Lawence J. C. Ma and Gonghao Cui, "Administrative Changes and Urban Population in China," *Annals of the Association of American Geographers*, 77 (1987), no. 3: 373–395.

Table 1 presents data on selected Asian countries grouped according to urbanization trajectories. Type 1 presents the Asian countries in which the urbanization process is largely completed. In this respect, the figure for Taiwan may be regarded as somewhat low. Type 2 presents countries that are newly industrializing. In this respect, the situation in Thailand has changed so rapidly in the last decade that the 1980 data are of limited value. Third, there are the type 3, largely South Asian, countries, where rates of population increase remain high, urbanization levels are changing little, and the proportion of the labour force in agriculture has remained fairly constant. Finally, there is China, whose patterns of economic development and urbanization are somewhat different from those experienced in the other trajectories, particularly in terms of the fluctuations in levels of urbanization.

These variations reflect a number of factors, such as the patterns of structural change (table 2) and the economic conditions of these countries. But in terms of the relationship of urbanization and labour force absorption, there are three clear groupings. First, among the higher income countries that are found in type 1 and 2 trajectories, where urbanization and the growth of manufacturing have been quite rapid, there has been a significant decline in agricultural employment. The only exception to this generalization appears to be Thailand, but this situation has changed rapidly, as is illustrated by the case-study.

For the other group of countries, a major part of labour force absorption was carried out in the agricultural sector and rural areas in the period 1960–1980, as was the case in China. This has led to increased population pressure on agricultural resources, which is indicated by increasing densities in cultivated areas. While there is little doubt that significant improvements in agricultural technology and production, together with the development of new land and the improvement of old land, have led to increased agricultural productivity, it is not sufficient to prevent an increase in the number of people in the poverty sector in the rural areas of these countries, even though the proportion may be falling. Numerous studies attest to the growth of lawlessness, etc., which would seem to create the conditions for a substantial rural exodus, which is certainly occurring, but at not a sufficiently fast enough rate to lower greatly the numbers of people in rural areas.

Another important option is the movement of labour from farm to non-farm sectors within rural areas. In attempting to assess this facet

Table 2 **Selected Asian market economies: Structural contrasts in distribution of GDP, grouped by urbanization trajectories, 1960–1987**

	Agriculture			Industry			Manufacturing			Services		
	1960	1980	1987	1960	1980	1987	1960	1980	1987	1960	1980	1987
Type 1												
Japan	13	4	3	45	43	41	33	30	29	42	53	57
Hong Kong	4	2	0	39	31	29	26	26	22	57	67	70
Singapore	4	1	0	18	37	38	12	26	29	78	62	62
Taiwan	28	9	6	29	46	47	22	42	39	43	49	49[a]
Rep. of Korea	37	16	11	20	39	43	14	28	30	43	45	46
Type 2												
Malaysia	36	23	—	18	30	—	9	18	—	46	47	—
Philippines	26	22	24	28	36	33	20	24	25	46	42	43
Thailand	40	22	16	19	28	35	13	19	24	41	50	49
Type 3												
Sri Lanka	32	27	27	20	27	27	15	15	16	48	46	46
Bangladesh	57	47	47	7	14	13	5	7	7	36	39	39
India	50	33	30	20	26	30	14	16	20	30	41	40
Pakistan	46	31	23	16	25	28	12	17	17	38	44	49
Indonesia	54	26	26	14	39	33	8	13	14	32	35	41
Myanmar	33	48	—	12	13	—	8	9	—	55	39	—
Type 4												
P.R. China	39	33	31	38	47	49	30	37	34	23	20	20[b]

Source: The World Bank, *World Development Report* (1989)

a. Data from the Council for Economic Planning and Development, Republic of China, *Taiwan Statistical Databook* (1988).

b. The data are for the years 1965, 1985, and 1987.

Table 3 **The share of off-farm income of farm households in East Asia**

	Period		
Country	1965	1975	1980
Japan	54	66	79
Taiwan	27 (1966)	48	66
Rep. of Korea	16	16	20

Source: Compiled from Oshima, 1984; tables 1, 2, and 3 (see note 13).

of the employment transition, there are serious statistical problems. Most employment data suggest that approximately 20–30 per cent of the rural workers throughout Asia may be regarded as being employed in non-agricultural activities as a major source of income. It may also be concluded that this proportion is increasing.[11]

The importance of off-farm employment in these processes of structural change is well illustrated by the experiences of Japan, Taiwan, and South Korea, all of which had reached full employment, experiencing rising real wages and higher rates of gross domestic product, by the early 1980s. The growth of RNA resembles to some extent the overall economic development. Table 3 shows the dramatic increase of off-farm income that resulted from accelerated industrialization and the implementation of the "Green Revolution" in rural areas.

Other, more important aspects of agricultural transition in these countries were the diversification in farm activities, along with agricultural development. The successful land reform programme and related developments (including irrigation facilities) in Taiwan, for example, activated multiple cropping, intercropping, and diversification of farm activities to include the raising of vegetables, fruits, livestock, and poultry. Further, the agricultural diversification provided a fundamental basis for the development of food processing, manufacturing, and eventually export expansion in the 1960s.[12] The nature of agricultural transformation in East Asia did not adversely affect peasants by causing displacement and landlessness as in South Asian countries.

The rural economy in the East Asian NICs thus expanded and provided employment opportunities for farm and non-farm households outside agriculture. Many workers found employment (part- and full-time) in rural industries, and others commuted to nearby towns for employment during the slack season. However, as Oshima indicates, the agricultural incomes remained significant even when the off-farm incomes were overtaking the farm incomes in Japan in the 1960s, and in Taiwan and South Korea in the 1970s.[13] Such integrated rural economic growth was associated with a rapid fall in the rate of unemployment in rural areas.

The increased income levels of farm and non-farm households also increased the domestic savings and the domestic demand for non-farm products in East Asia. The development in Taiwan, South Korea, and Japan are examples of this trend. For example, in Taiwan the ratio of domestic saving to net investment increased from 48.6 per cent in 1951 to 111.1 per cent in 1971. Individuals, corporations, and the government, which invested in industrial activities, including rural industries, contributed towards this change.

Uneven spatial development in South Korea was due partly to past as well as present economic policies. In the past, Japan emphasized development of mainly the southern part of Korea, while rural areas remained largely undeveloped. In recent decades (1960s–1970s), government policies have been focused mainly on heavy industries and export-oriented growth. Some of the "rural industrial estates" (e.g., Saemul factory system) were located closer to the urban centres. As a result, the growth of non-farm activities was significantly lower in South Korea compared to other East Asian countries.

In Japan, the small- and medium-size industries are located in the small towns. Well-developed transportation systems enable subcontractors to move their goods and also provide more mobility to the male members of the farm household who commute to the towns for part-time and seasonal employment. Women have taken over some farm activities that were formerly done by males. A significant recent trend in Japan is the movement of small- and medium-size industries to rural areas in search of cheap labour.

A middle grouping of countries, particularly Malaysia, Thailand, and, to a lesser extent, the Philippines, has also been exhibiting similar patterns, with the process most developed in Malaysia, where it is now estimated some 40 per cent of rural household income comes from non-farm sources. In a recent study in Malaysia, the author and Malaysian colleagues found no village in which more than 30 per cent of village income was derived from agricultural sources.[14]

In the South Asian countries and in Indonesia, particularly Java, the employment conditions in rural areas were influenced by rapid growth of the labour force and uneven performance of the economy.

Table 4 **Relative contribution to family income of different income sources in rural India, 1970–1981**

Gross cropped area (ha)	Estimated families with no cropped land (%)	Total income (Rs)	Shares in total income			
			Crops	Agric.	Others[a]	Total
0	41	1,865	—	37.7	62.3	100
Less than 1.0	15	1,630	39.0	27.0	34.0	100
1.0–2.5	21	2,450	59.0	14.0	27.0	100
2.5–4.5	12	3,640	81.0	5.0	14.0	100
4.5–6.5	5	4,550	81.0	3.5	15.5	100
6.5–8.5	2	5,580	89.0	2.0	9.0	100
8.5–10.5	2	6,710	92.0	1.0	7.0	100
10.5–14.5	1	8,480	95.0	0.3	4.7	100
14.5+	1	14,330	97.0	0.4	2.6	100
All cases	100	2,650	52.0	17.0	31.0	100

Source: International Labour Organisation, *Promotion of Employment and Income for the Rural Poor Including Rural Women Through Non-farm Activities* (Geneva, 1983), table 4:42.
a. Other income sources include remittances, pensions, divided income, rents, and income from non-farm activities.

In these economies, rural non-agricultural activities were dominated by part-time and seasonal work. Here the limited amounts of new cultivatable land and population pressures created a situation in which the poor have no option but to seek additional or alternative occupations outside agriculture. In India, for example (table 4) the lower-income groups have a higher proportion engaged in RNA than the higher-income groups. This is further illustrated by Islam in his study of 11 villages in six Asian countries: Bangladesh, India, Sri Lanka, Thailand, Pakistan, and Indonesia (study based on ILO/ARTEP country studies). Some of the major findings relevant to our discussion are as follows.[15]

First, the overall inverse relationship between farm size and non-farm income is confirmed; that is, the higher the land size the lower the RNA income. But the exceptions to this are the households with relatively large farms and also with a high proportion of non-farm income. This is because families owning large farms have high incomes and are therefore able to penetrate the organized sector of the rural economy and find relatively prestigious occupations there. Second, the *decline of self-employment* resulting from increased wage employ-

Table 5 **Share of different categories of RNA in selected South and South-East Asian countries, circa 1980s**

Country	Manufacturing	Construction	Sub-sectors: Trade & commerce	Sub-sectors: Transportation	Services	Other
Bangladesh	43.3	3.9	26.4	3.6	12.2	10.6
India	39.0	4.9	15.0	5.4	33.1	2.6
Malaysia	21.4	7.1	19.0	7.1	38.1	7.3
Pakistan	32.4	14.2	20.9	8.8	21.3	2.4
Philippines	28.6	8.8	17.0	9.5	32.0	4.3
Thailand	34.5	9.5	23.6	7.2	25.1	0.1

Source: Extracted from Mukhopadhyay and Lim, 1985: table 1.2:10 (see note 11).

ment has been noted throughout the villages under Islam's study. This decline is evident in the cross-country statistical analysis as well.[16]

The structure and the growth of rural industries, too, illustrate the nature of RNA growth in these countries. Structurally, the rural non-farm activities are dominated by *manufacturing* activities based on *food processing* and other basic activities. The manufacturing sector consists of a large proportion of the total RNA in the reported countries, with the exception of Malaysia and the Philippines, where the service sector is equally important in terms of total RNA (table 5). In the manufacturing sector, tobacco and beverage manufacturing appear to be the most important activities in the rural industries in Malaysia (61.7 per cent) and India (47.5 per cent). Textile and footwear manufacturing is more dominant in Bangladesh (58.2 per cent), Pakistan (39.6 per cent), and the Philippines (46.4 per cent). These two broad categories of manufacturing sectors together comprise 75 per cent or more of the total RNA in Bangladesh (81 per cent) and India (75 per cent). The continuing high proportion of employment in these manufacturing categories may be an indication of adherence to traditional rural industries in South Asia.

South-East Asian countries show a different pattern of rural industrialization, where *non-traditional* manufacturing activities have shown a rapid increase. For example, metal production in Malaysia (11 per cent of total manufacturing) and machinery and equipment in the Philippines (13 per cent) account for a significant proportion of rural employment.

The *service sector* appears to be prominent in the rural economy of

South and South-East Asia (table 5). In recent years, it has grown rapidly in many developing countries, and it has been suggested that increasing open unemployment, underemployment, and poverty in less developed countries have led to a "low" productivity type of service occupation. There are indications that in the Philippines, it is the informal sector – e.g. small-scale trading – and domestic and personnel services that form an important segment of RNA. In countries like Sri Lanka, where free education is available, educated rural poor seek government-related service employment. Undoubtedly service sector occupations have proved to be important sources for employment absorption in the rural areas of much of South and South-East Asia.

While this growth of rural non-agricultural activities is not the only factor influencing the patterns of urbanization and labour force absorption, it is a very important factor in the Asian context. From the point of view of the arguments presented in the latter part of this paper, it is important to emphasize that the proximity to urban centres is a major factor in increasing the proportion of non-agricultural incomes in "rural households." A large number of studies have shown that greater opportunities for linkages in marketing and employment increase the proportion of non-farm income in these regions. This permits increased household income, investment in agriculture, diversification, the growth of small industry, and creates growth regions that are attractive to both indigenous and foreign capital. The State's investment in public infrastructure provision such as electricity and transportation greatly facilitates this process.

In effect, it may be argued that because of the operation of these processes in many parts of Asia, the process of rural-urban transition is being slowed by the "holding" of populations in areas defined as "rural." But in effect, these "holding areas" are rapidly becoming giant urban regions. To understand this process, one needs a careful re-evaluation of the prevailing paradigms of the urban transition.

A model of the spatial economy transition

Since it is clear that the rural-urban paradigm is confusing the issue of urbanization and labour force absorption, it is necessary to spell out in some detail the definitional components of this broader view of the spatial economy transition.

In figure 1 a model is presented of the spatial configuration of a hypothetical Asian country that, for the purposes of this exercise, I

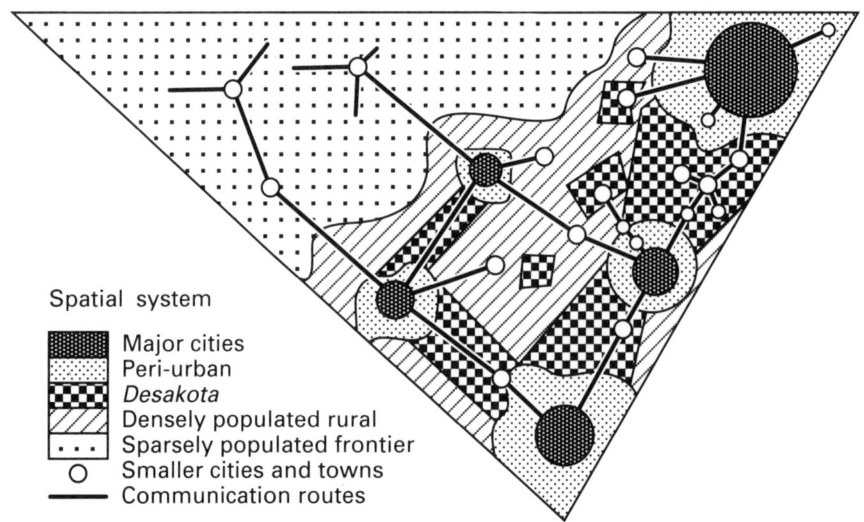

Fig. 1 **Spatial configuration of a hypothetical Asian country**

have labelled Asiatica Euphoria.[17] In this example, five main regions of the spatial economy are identified. They are: (1) the major cities of the urban hierarchy, which are often dominated in the Asian context by one or two extremely large cities; (2) the peri-urban regions, which are areas surrounding the cities and within a daily commuting reach of the city core. In some parts of Asia these regions can stretch for up to 30 kilometres away from the city core; (3) the regions labelled *desakota*,[18] which are regions of an intense mixture of agricultural and non-agricultural activities that often stretch along linear corridors between large city cores. These regions were previously characterized by dense populations engaged in agriculture generally dominated by wet-rice cultivation; (4) densely populated rural regions, which occur in many Asian countries, particularly in those practising wet-rice agriculture; and (5) sparsely populated frontier regions, which, in many Asian countries, offer opportunities for land colonization schemes and various forms of agricultural development.

The model of the spatial economy is, of course, not static and will change as the economy changes. The pace and characteristics of this settlement transition vary from country to country, reflecting the features of socio-economic change at the macro level. From the point of view of the arguments that are presented in this paper, it is the role that the growth of metropolitan cores and the *desakota* process play in this transformation that is of major importance. Thus, what one is observing in this transition is the emergence of mega-urban regions that often incorporate two large urban cores linked together by fast arterial transportation routes. These regions include the major cities, peri-urban zones, and an extensive zone of mixed rural-urban land use along arterial routes. These mixed economic activities may also occur in villages in these zones that are less accessible. Travel time from any point in this region would probably be no more than three to four hours, but in most cases is considerably less.

It should be stressed that this model of the transition of the spatial economy is not intended to be universally applicable but to fit the situation where one (or more) urban core is located in densely settled peasant rural areas.[19] There may also be cases where the urban core(s) is located in a lightly populated region of plantation agriculture, as is the case of Kuala Lumpur in Malaysia. This contrast between the two agro-economic systems as they are reflected in socio-economic systems, export trade, and class relations is not a new theme. It has been utilized by Baldwin for a theoretical exposition of patterns of development in newly settled regions; by Dowd to explain the differences in the settlement patterns of the American west and south; and by Morse to explain the different urban systems that evolved in the "hacienda" and "plantation" regions of Latin America.[20]

It must be emphasized that these writers are not suggesting that a particular urban system results from a pre-existing agro-economic system, but rather that the existence of these agro-economic systems provides the possibility for certain urban systems and regions to change.

In the Asian context, the existence of high-density, mostly wet-rice growing regions adjacent to large urban cores offers an opportunity for a particular form of mega-urban region to emerge; their existence does not ensure the inevitability of the emergence of such regions. They will result from the policies of private and public sectors, the form of economic growth, the position of the urban core relative to international connections, etc. Thus, for instance, in the case of the Republic of South Korea, with a precondition of high-density rice regions, the government adopted a strategy of concentrating on industrialization rather than agriculture, which led to slow growth of rural income and a rapid release of surplus rural population into urban-based industrialization. As a result, South Korea became characterized by a metropolis-dominated urban hierarchy. On the other hand, in a region of similar pre-existing rural densities such as Yogyakarta

Table 6 **Growth of core areas[a] in selected Asian countries**

Country	Year	National population (1,000)	Core pop. (1,000)	Core share of pop. (%)	Real gross dom. prod. 1975[c]	Percentage of labour force in		
						Agriculture	Industry	Services[b]
Taiwan	1956	9,311	1,818	19.5	678	56	11	33
	1970	14,693	3,736	25.4	1319	—	—	—
	1980	17,969	5,700	31.7	2443	20	33	47
Rep. of Korea	1960	24,989	5,194	20.8	633	66	9	25
	1970	31,435	8,879	28.2	1123	—	—	—
	1980	37,489	13,302	35.5	2011	34	29	37
Malaysia (West)	1957	6,279	1,103	16.1	872	63	12	25
	1970	8,810	1,630	18.5	1281	—	—	—
	1980	10,945	2,346	21.4	2305	50	16	34
Philippines	1960	27,088	4,147	15.3	790	61	15	34
	1970	36,684	6,449	17.6	912	—	—	—
	1980	47,914	9,639	20.1	1010	46	17	37
Thailand	1960	26,258	2,567	9.8	434	84	4	12
	1970	34,397	3,676	10.7	802	—	—	—
	1980	44,278	5,547	12.5	1169	76	9	15
Pakistan	1961	42,880	2,135	3.0	418	61	18	21
	1972	65,309	3,607	5.5	575	—	—	—
	1981	83,782	5,353	6.4	659	57	20	23
India[d]	1961	424,336	12,246	2.9	413	73	11	16
	1971	528,918	16,647	3.1	464	—	—	—
	1981	638,141	23,107	3.5	497	71	13	16
Indonesia (Java only)	1961	63,060	6,705	10.6	366	75	8	17
	1971	76,086	9,200	12.1	385	—	—	—
	1981	91,270	13,027	14.3	785	58	12	30

Bangladesh	1961	50,840	5,096	10.0	363	87	3	10
	1974	71,479	7,612	10.6	365	—	—	—
	1981	87,052	10,049	11.5	434	74	11	15
Sri Lanka	1963	10,582	2,207	20.9	960	56	13	31
	1971	12,690	2,672	21.1	759	—	—	—
	1981	14,850	3,088	20.8	838	54	14	32
People's Republic of China[e]	1981	1,100,000	138,390	12.5				

a. Defined in appendix I of Vining, 1986 (see note 21).
b. W. Armstrong and T.G. McGee, *Theatres of Accumulation* (London: Methuen, 1985), p. 90.
c. Adjusted for terms of trade, 1975 international prices.
d. India core consists of three urban agglomerations of Calcutta, Greater Bombay, and Delhi (Vining, 1986; see note 21).
e. China core consists of (1) Shanghai-Nanjing-Hangzhou, (2) Hong Kong–Guangzhou, (3) Beijing-Tianjin-Tangshan, and (4) Shenyang-Dalian.

in Java, in a slow growth situation, there are only limited possibilities for drawing off surplus rural population to urban centres in other parts of the country, and the rural inhabitants engage in an intense mixture of non-agricultural and agricultural activity that permits survival but does not greatly increase income.

The emergence of the extended metropolitan region in Asia

In the remainder of this paper the major aim will be to concentrate on the features of these extended urban regions, paying particular attention to the emergence of regions of most rapid change. In order to do this, it is necessary to examine the statistical patterns of growth within the broader Asian context.

Using data provided by a number of sources, table 6 attempts to present some statistical information on these regions.[21] Much of this material is taken from Vining, who documented the process of population redistribution towards what he labels the core areas of 44 less developed countries. While his definition of core areas as "the regions containing and surrounding the country's most important and dominant city (in a few cases, cities), which is generally but not always the capital city" (p. 4), is certainly not coterminous with the areas I would describe as *desakota* zones, the actual administrative definition of these cores that he takes from the census is broad enough to encompass sizeable parts of them – for instance, Jabotabek, which includes areas with all the features of the *desakota* zones. Generally, these core areas are too narrowly defined spatially to fit neatly with zones of *desakota*, which may extend over large areas between two urban centres, but I have taken the data presented in his analysis in order to give some overall picture of the emergence of *desakota* zones in Asia.

Utilizing Vining's analysis, table 6 indicates the growth of core population between 1960 and 1980 for 11 Asian countries. Data for Hong Kong and Singapore are not presented in this table because, as city-states, they do not fit into a *desakota* definition. However, particularly in the case of Hong Kong, one may argue that a *desakota* zone is now emerging, stretching from Hong Kong through Shenzhen Special Economic Zone and the Pearl River delta to Guangzhou and south to Macau.[22] Some might argue the same process is occurring between Johore and Singapore.

Generally, the table shows that core areas have continued to increase their share of total population most markedly in the nations of

Korea and Taiwan, which have experienced rapid industrialization and increases in the GDP, but also in the case of the Philippines, Malaysia, and Thailand, where the industrial transformation has been less marked. In the countries that have large populations (the exception is Sri Lanka) and have experienced modest growth until recently, the growth of the cores is relatively slower. It must be stressed that almost two-thirds of the core population in developing countries is located in Aisa.

The location of these regions in Asia, grouped into three main types, are shown in figure 2. In the first rank are those areas that have experienced a rapid transformation of the spatial economy in terms of rural to urban shift in population, although agricultural land use may remain persistent. Japan and South Korea provide the most prominent examples.[23]

Second are regions that have experienced a rapid change in their economic features in the last 30 years. Examples are the Taipei-Kaohsiung corridor of Taiwan, which has experienced a declining proportion of people in agriculture, to 20 per cent from 56 per cent between 1956 and 1980, and a concurrent growth of industrialization. Speare et al.[24] have estimated that the growth of small-to-medium-size industries in rural areas slowed the growth rate of cities by 6 per cent in the 1960s and 1970s. At the same time, this region was characterized by a decline of staple crops as a proportion of total agricultural value of production. Thus, over the last 30 years, while the production of rice has increased considerably, the share of rice as a proportion of gross agricultural receipts has dropped from 50 per cent in 1950 to 34 per cent in 1980, and at the same time, other agricultural products have increased from 20 per cent to 36 per cent, and vegetables and fruits, from 7 per cent to 20 per cent. More recently, there has been a rapid increase in fish farming (prawns), chicken rearing, and other forms of capital-intensive agribusiness. This has led to a significant change in the patterns of female employment, with a decline from 52.5 per cent (1965) in primary industry to 16 per cent in 1980, and an increase in secondary industry, from 18.2 per cent to 43.7 per cent.[25] Rather similar patterns are being exhibited in the Bangkok-Central Plains region of Thailand and in the four major coastal zones of China. These zones, constituting only 12.5 per cent of China's population, accounted for 46.3 per cent of the value of industrial production and 13 per cent of the value of agricultural output in 1986.[26]

Third is a type of region that, while it bears some spatial and eco-

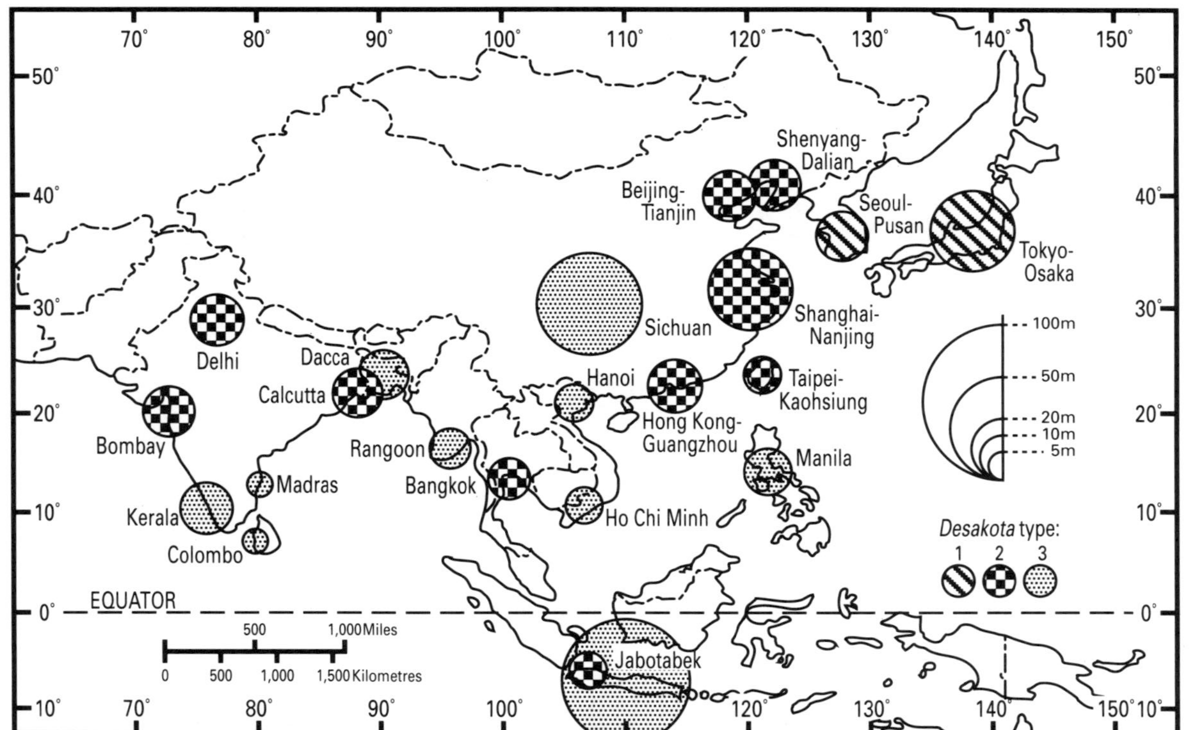

Fig. 2 **Core areas in Asia (Miller cylindrical projection, scale approximate) (Source: N. Ginsburg, B. Koppel, and T.G. McGee, eds., *The Extended Metropolis Settlement Transition in Asia* [Honolulu: University of Hawaii Press, 1991], fig. 1.2, p. 12)**

nomic resemblance to type 2 above, is characterized by the changes that occur because of high population growth and slower economic growth. This results in the persistence of underemployment and self-employment in unpaid family work and enterprises. In such a situation, there may be a juxtaposition of elements of types 1 and 2 producing a highly dualistic economic structure. Thus technological inputs in agriculture may cause labour shedding and an increase in non-agricultural activities in the rural areas adjacent to urban cores. This phenomenon has been recorded in regions such as Kerala and Tamil Nadu. While there is often some growth of small industry and other income opportunities, these regions are characterized by the persistence of low incomes, which reflects the slow structural transition in the allocation of labour. In some cases, regions continue to absorb population into agricultural areas, as, for example, in Sichuan basin, where non-agricultural employment has remained fairly static over the last 40 years, while the population has almost doubled in size.[27]

To summarize, these regions have six main features:

1. They have been, or are, characterized by a large population engaged in smallholder cultivation of mostly rice that, in the pre–World War II period, had considerable interaction through accessible transportation routes.
2. They are generally characterized by an increase in non-agricultural activities in areas that have previously been largely agricultural. These non-agricultural activities are very diverse and include trading, transportation, and industry. This increase in non-agricultural activity is characterized by a great mixture of activities, often by members from the same household. Thus, one person may commute to the city to work as a clerk, another engage in farming, a third in industry, and another in retailing in the *desakota* zone. This creates a situation in which the economic linkages within this region may bc as important as the dominance of the large cities in the megalopolis that draw the surrounding regions into their orbit.
3. They are generally characterized by extreme fluidity and mobility of the population. The availability of relatively cheap transport such as two-stroke motor bikes, buses, and trucks has facilitated relatively quick movement over longer distances. Thus, these zones are characterized by both commuting to the larger urban centres and also intense movement of people and goods within the zones.
4. These zones are characterized by an intense mixture of land use, with agriculture, cottage industries, industrial estates, suburban

developments, and other uses existing side by side. This has both negative and positive effects. Agricultural produce, particularly if it is industrial crops, has a ready market. On the negative side, the waste from industrial activity can pollute and destroy agricultural land. On the whole, these zones are much more intensely utilized than the megalopolis. Writing of land use in this zone, Gottman commented on the amount of woodland and recreational areas that exist. In the *desakota* zones of Asian countries, population pressures place greater demands upon the available space.

5. Another feature of these zones is the increased participation of women in non-agricultural labour. In part, this is associated with demand for female labour in industry, domestic service, and other activities, but it is also closely related to changing patterns of agricultural production in the *desakota* regions. Generally, agricultural production shows a shift from single-crop cultivation (principally rice) to a diverse production of livestock, vegetables, fruits, etc., sometimes for national interregional production.
6. Finally, these zones are to some extent "invisible" or "grey" zones from the point of view of the State authorities. Urban regulations may not apply in these "rural areas," and it is difficult for the State to enforce them despite the rapidly changing economic structure of the regions. This feature is particularly encouraging to informal sector and small-scale operators, who find it difficult to conform to labour or industrial legislation.

Features of the extended metropolitan regions in Asia

From the point of view of this paper, it is the regions shown on the map as type 2 *desakota* zones that are of major significance for the urban future of Asia. While one may legitimately argue that the experiences of South Korea and Japan in accomplishing the urban transformation should be utilized in developing policy responses for other countries in Asia (for they started with somewhat similar ecological prerequisites), for the purposes of this paper, I shall take their experiences as given. Type 3 *desakota* regions, characterized by high-density populations, low rates of economic growth, and problems of labour absorption, present another set of problems that, at present, are not being resolved by processes such as those of the extended metropolitan regions of *desakota* type 2. For this reason they, too, are not discussed in this paper.

What then are the features of the extended metropolitan regions shown on the map as *desakota* type 2? First and of most importance, it must be emphasized that these extended metropolitan regions include both the urban core(s) and surrounding areas, which include large numbers of small- and medium-size urban centres. The morphology of these regions is quite variable, although linking corridors between the major urban foci are often of major importance. For instance, in the case of the four major extended metropolitan regions of China, the existence of these corridors has led to their description by Zhou as interlocking metropolitan regions. What we are describing here are often very large integrated urban regions that provide the settlement framework for economic growth.

A second feature of these extended metropolitan regions is that they are the major focus of economic growth in their countries. The historical juxtaposition of the port cities, which almost universally remain at the core of regions, and the densely crowded population of the regions has created the necessary precondition of global linkage and readily available surplus labour, which, in turn, have encouraged a rapid growth of industrialization. In 1986, the four main extended metropolitan regions of China contained 12 per cent of the population, produced 46 per cent of the value of total industrial output, and 13 per cent of the agricultural output. In the extended metropolitan region of Bangkok, similar figures were recorded. In the period between 1970 and 1980, while the population of the Bangkok Metropolitan Region grew from 13 per cent to 14 per cent of Thailand's population, 58 per cent of Thailand's non-agricultural economic growth was generated here. Similar figures exist for the Jabotabek region of Indonesia, the extended metropolitan region of Manila, and the Calcutta metropolitan region. It is obvious that these regions are of major importance to the economy of their countries.

Thirdly, it is necessary to stress the significant role of transportation in the emergence of these regions. Historically, many of these regions had well-developed systems of regional transportation in which water transport was important; but increasingly land transport and fast highway and railway linkages have become important. They are important because they permit an intense transactional environment of people, commodities, and information to grow. This is greatly facilitated by the creation of arterial linkages through the region that collapse time and space.

Fourthly, there are intense changes occurring at the demographic and household levels, such as declining birth rates, increased employment of women, and growing household income from a multiplicity of sources, often including a mix of agricultural and non-agricultural activities.

Finally the dynamism of these regions presents a large number of problems of environment and mixed land use that are an important challenge to policy makers. In the next section, I illustrate these features with reference to the extended metropolitan region of Bangkok.

The emergence of the extended metropolitan region: The case of Bangkok

One way in which to make these processes clearer is to illustrate them by the example of one city region – the Bangkok Metropolitan Region.[28] The urbanization of the Bangkok region has been occurring for more than 200 years, during which time it has developed from a small royal capital city to a primate city that is now 1 of the 15 largest metropolitan centres in the world. The primacy of Bangkok in Thailand is spectacular. It is 45 times the size of the next populous city, Chiang Mai. In the last several decades, Bangkok urban growth has been spreading into the surrounding provinces of Nonthaburi, Pathum Thani, Samut Prakan, Samut Sakhon, and Nakhon Pathom. These areas, combined with the Bangkok Metropolitan Area (BMA), form a region of 7,639 sq km known as the Bangkok Metropolitan Region (BMR).

The BMR is the heart of the Central Plain. The Central Plain has been characterized as a "rice-bowl," and since 1855, with the signing of the Bowring Treaty with Britain, the plain has become a significant region of rice export. Rice cultivation expanded extensively as new lands opened. Government expenditures on irrigation and flood control began to increase slowly.[29] By the early 1900s, the Central Plain had been integrated into the global market as rice became a significant export and cash crop. Rural cottage industries were phased out to open more paddy land, and for the first time, commercial, bureaucratic, and political penetration came at the village level.[30] As the Central Plain developed through Green Revolution technology, sophisticated irrigation schemes, and double cropping, the benefits that accrued tended to flow to Bangkok. The revenues derived, combined with steep rural taxes, constituted a one-way rural-to-urban capital flow. Surplus capital, based on the productivity in the rice-bowl, built Bangkok's import-substituting industrial economy. With the coming of the late 1970s, Thailand's economy changed. The agricultural sector's share of GDP began to decline, while the manufacturing sector's share increased sharply. As Bangkok became more congested, the government began attempts to decentralize industry. Substantial investment, promotion, and subsidies were directed to any industrial unit that would locate outside of Bangkok. Owing to the proximity of the port and the extensive transportation networks, industries began to flourish *en masse* on the periphery of Bangkok. The creation of the new port zone in the south-eastern region of the BMA also encouraged this trend. In increasing numbers, the local villagers shifted from agricultural activities to industry. Large tracts of land were sold by farmers to speculators and industrialists. The socio-economic character of the adjacent rural provinces began to transform rapidly.[31]

Population

Population growth in the BMR since 1960 is summarized in table 1 in the Appendix of this paper. The population of the BMA stood at 5.7 million in 1988, and that of the BMR was 8.5 million in that year. Thus, the BMR represented 15.5 per cent of the total population of Thailand in 1988. Population growth in the BMR has been slowing down in recent years and now averages 3.3 per cent per annum. However, three of the adjacent provinces show a steady increasing growth and are proceeding at considerably higher rates than the BMA. Thailand as a whole grew at a modest 2.5 per cent per annum between 1970 and 1989, which indicates a considerable fall in fertility.

The level of urbanization, expressed as the proportion of the population of the BMR living in "urban" places, increased from 71.5 per cent in 1970 to 81.5 per cent in 1986. Table 2 shows the rate at which the "urban" population of the BMR (by province) increased between 1970 and 1986. Particularly notable is the flourishing annual urban growth in the provinces of Nonthaburi, Pathum Thani, and Samut Prakan. Pathum Thani, for instance, grew by 37 per cent (from 242,000 to 332,000) between 1970 and 1980; during this samc period, its urban population grew by 248 per cent. Nonthaburi experienced an even more dramatic increase. By 2001, the population of the BMA is projected to grow by 36 per cent, and the urban population of the five adjacent provinces, by 124 per cent.

The population recorded for the BMR shows that its population had reached 9.1 million in 1991, and is forecast to reach 11.5 million in 2001. This represents an increase of 3.4 million over 15 years. As table 3 demonstrates, the BMA and adjacent provinces are expected to grow considerably faster than Thailand as a whole. Thus, the primacy of the BMR will increase from 15.5 per cent to nearly 18 per cent in 2001.

As in most metropolitan regions, density varies as a function of proximity to the central business district. All built-up areas of the BMR have densities of over 300 persons per sq km. Thailand as a whole has 100 persons per sq km. Table 4 shows how densities in the BMR changed between 1980 and 1986. While the densities in the BMA have grown modestly (12 per cent) on average, densities in the five provinces have increased substantially.

As the BMR becomes a strong economic force, migration becomes an increasingly substantial factor. The BMR exerts the strongest pull on migrants from all over Thailand. Ninety per cent of the country's net interregional migration between 1975 and 1980 came to the BMR.[32] The BMA clearly receives most migrants, the largest group arriving from adjacent provinces. A trend since 1975 has been an accelerated migration from the BMA to Nonthaburi and Pathum Thani. This migration is merely a normal metropolitan response of suburbanization.

Rural-urban migration in many Asian metropolitan regions is often associated with urban unemployment, poverty, and slums. In Bangkok, this is generally not the case. The 1981 survey of migration indicates that migrants to the BMR are highly motivated and their unemployment rates were only 2.3 per cent in Bangkok and 3.5 per cent in the adjacent provinces. Furthermore, unlike in other Asian cities, in Bangkok, natives are more likely to fall under the poverty line than are migrants. Also unique to Bangkok is that housing has grown faster than population. In 1974, there were 552,000 housing units, and by 1984 this had risen to 902,000. This amounts to an average increase of 5 per cent per annum; population grew at only 3.5 per cent per annum. Table 5 shows migration by origin and destination in the period 1975–1980. What is evident is that the BMA receives the lion's share, nearly 80 per cent of all BMR net migration. Also of importance is the dramatic net increase in the provinces of Nonthaburi, Samut Prakan, and Pathum Thani, all receiving the majority of their migrants from Thailand's north-eastern provinces.

Economy

Bangkok's domination does not lie solely in its large population but also exerts a major influence on the national economy. Between 1970 and 1983, half of all national growth was due to economic activity in the BMR. In fact, 58 per cent of all non-agricultural economic growth in the same period was generated in the BMR. Table 6 shows the gross national and regional products for 1970 and 1983 (in millions of baht). It indicates the sharp increases in manufacturing product for all of Thailand and especially the BMR. Although agricultural productivity increased substantially, its percentage share showed a marked decrease. Nevertheless, in 1983 the BMR accounted for 43 per cent of the nation's GNP, up from 34 per cent in 1970. Thus, by economic measures (and demographic), the BMR's primacy increased during the 1980s. The future success of Thailand's international competitiveness in the world market lies in the performance of the BMR.

Within the BMR, the constant sustained economic growth, averaging 8.6 per cent annually between 1970 and 1983, has shifted emphasis from the BMA to the adjacent provinces. Although the BMA's dominance is still substantial, there has been a marked growth in the share of the regional total GRP in favour of Samut Prakan and Pathum Thani (table 7). As the BMA's share fell from 80 per cent in 1970 to 75 per cent in 1983, the combined share of Samut Prakan and Pathum Thani increased from 11 per cent to 18 per cent, averaging 12.5 per cent growth annually. Table 8 shows a sectoral breakdown. All provinces, with the exception of Nakhon Pathom, cut their agricultural share of GRP in half between 1970 and 1983. This, of course, was compensated by major increases in manufacturing and in other sectors. Note that for the BMR, only 3.4 per cent of total GRP constitutes agriculture and mining. Even in non-"urban" provinces such as Pathum Thani, Samut Prakan, and Nonthaburi, less than 15 per cent of total GRP comes from the primary sector.

Liberal national trade and investment policies in Thailand in the 1980s have stimulated this vast expansion in the industrial and service sectors. Much of the growth is directed to the adjacent provinces. Policy decisions to decentralize industry to locations outside the BMA have spurred this dramatic growth, especially in Samut Prakan and Pathum Thani. These two provinces accounted for 22.7 per cent and 10.4 per cent, respectively, of all manufacturing output in the

BMR between 1970 and 1983, and between them, over 25 per cent of all manufacturing growth in Thailand.

A broadly similar sectoral pattern emerges from employment statistics. Within the BMR, 70 per cent of the region's employment was in the BMA in 1984. Table 9 portrays employment by sector and province. In Pathum Thani, for instance, 60 per cent of the population resides in "rural" settlements, yet only 74,000 of the 262,000 economically active population (or 28 per cent) are engaged in primary sector employment.[33] It is this unique combination of "rural" settlement-non-agricultural employment that has caused many geographers to question this newly emerging phenomenon in the mega-urban regions. Pathum Thani, in particular, fits the *desakota* model as it is clearly a region where rural and urban distinctions are blurred. Is it merely a stage of transition en route to full urbanization, or could this intensive mixture of agriculture and non-agriculture on a predominantly rural plain persist?

Two important aspects of this employment transformation are worth noting. First, there are an estimated 130,000 workers from rural areas migrating to the BMR annually on a seasonal basis during the dry season (January–July). The pattern of seasonal unemployment is crucial, since most of those temporary migrants are from poorer regions in the north and north-east, where irrigation facilities are poor, hence limiting cultivation to the rainy season and to a single crop. Second, many new job opportunities, especially in factories and the informal sector, are taken by females. In Pathum Thani, 41 per cent of all economically active females were in either the manufacturing, service, or commerce sectors in 1980. In contrast, in 1970, less than 20 per cent of economically active females were engaged in these three sectors. This rapid rise of females in off-farm employment has probably led to falling fertility rates and dependency ratios.

The distribution of land use in the BMR offers some interesting insights. Despite the economic "urban" nature and industrial strength of the provinces in the BMR, only a tiny fraction of total land is developed (residential, commercial, industrial, government). In Pathum Thani, roughly 3 per cent of total land is built up, and the remaining 97 per cent is in agricultural usage or is unused (for either urban or agricultural purposes). Similar proportions characterize land use in the other four adjacent provinces.

The data in table 10 show per capita gross regional provincial product for all regions, Pathum Thani, and Thailand as a whole. Only the central region, which contains the BMR, topped the national average growth. The strength of Pathum Thani cannot go unnoticed, as in the period 1981–1985, GRP per capita grew nearly three times the national average, or an impressive 16.25 per cent annually. In fact, Pathum Thani, with 4.5 per cent of the BMR's population, accounted for 13 per cent of all its provincial product growth in that time period; Bangkok, with 70 per cent of the region's population, accounted for only 10 per cent. These statistics underscore the emerging modern industrial base that is prospering in the extended metropolitan region of Bangkok. These characteristics point to the industrialization of areas beyond Bangkok. The metro-shadow subregion plays in increasingly crucial role in the world market. The adjacent provinces are clearly within a territory that is in economic unison with Bangkok.

Transportation

Mega-urban regions are characterized by a well-developed infrastructure of roads that permits a heavy flow of commodities and people. Regions at a distance of 30–70 km from the core city would never have been able to develop without efficient transport networks leading to the markets. In Thailand, road, rail, and waterway networks all converge on Bangkok. It is no surprise that as time progresses, the population becomes more mobile and routinely travels greater distances.

In Thailand, road transport is the most important of the three modes and carries more than 50 per cent of all passenger and freight traffic. Water transport provides important freight service, but its role is declining. The Chao Phraya River, leading from the north to Bangkok, has always been an important route for rice barges coming from the Central Plain rice-bowl. Rail transport services mainly middle- and long-distance passenger and freight traffic. Outside Bangkok, and particularly in the adjacent provinces, the highway network is well developed, with few problems. Highways leading to Bangkok have steady flows of traffic, especially transport trucks, which run 24 hours a day. However, in the past, overemphasis has been placed on major highways, while distributor and feeder roads have been neglected. Hence, there is major growth of extensive ribbon development in the urban shadow subregion. The stretch of the Rangsit Highway immediately north of Bangkok, with 82,700 vehicles passing a day, is clearly one of the most heavily used highways in Asia. Much of the traffic is comprised of transport trucks coming and going to the many factories that line the road, and also trucks shipping produce from the north to Bangkok.

There is every reason to believe that transport routes within the adjacent provinces will become more intensively used over time. The present development pattern is characterized by large portions of land being held idle by speculators close to main arterial routes. Partly to blame is certainly the lack of access roads, discouraging development between main arterial highways. The Sixth Plan of the Bangkok Metropolitan Regional Development Proposals calls for improving these interstitial road networks to pry open new areas. Such development will further integrate the nearby provinces with the conurbation.

Traffic congestion in Bangkok is extremely serious. As proof of this claim, the Japan International Cooperation Agency recently published a report that claimed the costs of Bangkok's jammed roads may amount to 60 per cent of the capital's regional product. Bangkok is the largest city in the world outside of China without a rapid mass transit system. However, by the mid-1990s, the Second State Expressway System (SES) should be in use. It was approved by the Cabinet in 1985 despite its astronomical cost. However, by 2001, it is expected that 740,000 automobiles will be in use in the BMR (in 1986, there were about 245,000). Thus, even with the SES, congestion will be much worse than today. It is worth noting that ownership rates of automobiles in the BMA are much higher than in the adjacent provinces, but this is changing as growth rates outside of Bangkok are increasing rapidly. This is shown by the recent emergence of automobile dealerships in the nearby provinces.

This case-study of the emergence of the Bangkok Metropolitan Region illustrates the importance of such regions in the economic growth and labour absorption strategies of Asian countries. In the conclusion of this paper, I discuss the implications of the emergence of these regions for future Asian urbanization.

Implications of the emergence of *desakota* regions for future Asian urbanization

I think it is important to spell out the implications of the emergence of these *desakota* zones for the future of Asian urbanization. First, there is the argument that such zones are economically productive, "catalytic" regions for economic growth and therefore economic growth should be encouraged. In fact most economic evidence supports this view, and the emergence of these regions with an increasing diversity of economic activity and economic growth presents many problems to planners. The mixture of activities often creates serious environmental, transportation, and infrastructural problems, particularly if such regions are treated from the perspective of a "conventional" city planning mind-set. In such a conventional approach, the capital requirements for infrastructure alone seem totally out of reach to most national governments in Asia. On the other hand, the very mixed, decentralized, intermediate and small scale of economic organization and the persistence of agriculture offer exciting prospects that involve recycling, use of alternative energy sources, etc., which are difficult to introduce into conventional city space. The challenge to planners is how to take advantage of the "growth feature of these regions" and yet prevent and solve the costly side-effects of growth within these regions and the problems of regional inequality that will emerge as they grow.

A second implication concerning the "sustainability" of these regions is even more important if one accepts the rather gloomy predictions that are presented if the unilinear model of Western urbanization is utilized. As many writers have often observed, if the cities of China and India alone were to reach the levels of energy consumption of New York or London, the demand on world fossil energy sources would not be possible to fulfil. Similar arguments can be presented with respect to food supplies for cities. Many writers have commented on the likely food demands of large Asian cities and problems that future growth poses to national food supplies. The increase of food imports from outside these countries is a viable option, but the opportunity to keep a high level of national food self-sufficiency through increasingly intensive productive agriculture in these *desakota* regions is very attractive. Finally, the extraordinary range of activities in these regions offers many opportunities for employment for all employable household members, which will enable increased household income and consumption.

It is of course a legitimate question to ask how persistent these widely spread regions of *desakota* will be. Will the processes of concentration ultimately triumph and lead to a reassertion of the conventional city? For the reasons already expressed, particularly those relating to the collapse of space-time and the mix of transportation technology that is available, I believe such regions should be remarkably persistent.

This assertion has important implications for planning and policy formation for such regions. There would appear to be five priorities for most Asian countries. First, the governments will have to make significant decisions with respect to the recognition of the viability of these regions. If these regions are as important in economic growth as has been suggested, then hard decisions will have to be made by governments against fostering small-town development and rural industrialization in outlying areas.

Second, governments will need to improve access in these zones of intense interaction. In this respect, one may argue that the building of fast, major arterial routes in these regions, such as the Shinkansen, the Seoul-Pusan highway, and the Taipei-Kaohsiung freeway, was very crucial in the case of Japan, Korea, and Taiwan. The network of pre-existing feeder roads flows very easily into these fast, central transportation routes. Governments should also take every advantage of pre-existing systems of communication, such as water routes, and encourage flexibility in transportation modes.

Third, governments will have to adopt careful monitoring of environmental and land-use problems in these regions so as to keep "conflict problems" to a minimum. In this activity, the development of "fast" systems of data collection is crucial, as is the development of responsive, decentralized implementing agencies.

Fourth, governments will need to develop policies that cope with the human resources of the region. The highly flexible labour regimes that exist in the region, the varying types of work, and the maximum input of a majority of the households place considerable strains on the central social institutions such as the family, as well as on the educational and cultural institutions that characterize these regions.

Finally, it is necessary to address the activities of the private sector and its role in these regions. It must be clear from the previous discussion that it is the existence of private capital pursuing labour that has largely stimulated developments in these regions that occur within an envelope of state and international policy decisions. From the point of view of private capital, these regions are attractive because of cheaper labour, cheaper land, and a more flexible work environment. In these regions, capital is deployed in an extraordinarily diverse set of ways: capital intensification in chicken rearing; subcontracting of production processes; industrial estates and upper income housing estates, etc; and the "planning trick" will be to make these regions continue to be attractive to capital, and the economic and social features of the population begin to change with increasing wealth. This is a facet that I believe is particularly challenging. But what seems important to me is that the fundamental features of the regions, which include flexibility in economic and political organization, persistent mobility in the flows of these transactive networks, and a constant acceptance of "change," be incorporated into the planning process.

What I envisage are large, persistent *desakota* regions in many Asian countries in which flexibility, mobility, and change are constant elements. In planning for such regions, it seems to me that the physical planning and design response will involve radically new departures in ways of thinking. For instance, shopping for basic commodities might incorporate the elements of the "periodic markets" traditionally part of such regions. In this case, permanent supermarkets are not required but simply mobile units. One could extend such thinking to entertainment, education, and virtually any sphere of service activity. These regions are, after all, an amalgam of the pre-existing high densities and juxtaposed technology that permit such regions to survive and flourish.

Of course, not all Asian countries are going to be characterized by such regions. For instance, Singapore is clearly an exception, and I doubt if peninsular Malaysia is developing in this way. It is hardly surprising that their cities and surrounding regions are much more illustrative of the Western experience. It is also clear that the growth and features of these *desakota* regions vary dramatically between different Asian countries. The emergence of *desakota* regions offers an alternative to the Western city-centred urban transition. The challenge is to grasp the meaning of this development and plan for the future.

Appendix

Tables to accompany Bangkok case-study

Table A–1 **Total population of the BMR and its growth rate classified by province in 1970, 1980, and 1988 (Unit: 1,000)**

Province	Total population			1970–1988 annual average growth rate (%)
	1970	1980	1988	
Bangkok Metropolitan Area (BMA)	3,185	4,815	5,717	3.5
Samut Prakan	341	503	789	3.8
Nonthaburi	278	383	596	3.4
Pathum Thani	242	332	435	3.3
Samut Sakhon	208	256	341	2.4
Nakhon Pathom	434	545	631	2.1
Total BMR	4,688	6,834	8,509	3.3
Whole country	35,633	46,718	54,961	2.2
BMR/whole country (%)	13.2	14.7	15.5	

Sources: National Statistical Office (NSO); National Economic and Social Development Board (NESDB).

Table A–2 **Urban population of BMR Province, 1970–1986 (Unit: 1,000)**

Province	1970	1980	1986 (urban/total %)	1970–1986 (growth rate, % p.a.)
Bangkok Metropolitan Area (BMA)	2,953	5,773	100.0	4.3
Nonthaburi	51	176	37.3	8.0
Pathum Thani	54	170	41.9	7.4
Samut Prakan	133	322	51.4	5.7
Samut Sakhon	79	113	38.5	2.3
Nakhon Pathom	80	119	19.4	2.5
Total BMR	3,350	6,673	81.5	4.4
Whole kingdom	8,017	14,848	28.2	3.9
BMR/whole kingdom (%)	41.8	44.9		

Source: *1980 Census*, NESDB, 1986.

Table A–3 **Population growth by province, 1986–2001 (Unit: 1,000)**

	Total population			Growth rate (% p.a.)	
Province	1986	1991	2001	1986–1991	1986–2001
Bangkok Metropolitan Area (BMA)	5,772	6,477	7,850	2.3	2.1
Nakhon Pathom	614	672	796	1.8	1.7
Nonthaburi	473	556	782	3.3	3.4
Pathum Thani	406	478	681	3.3	3.5
Samut Prakan	625	739	1,002	3.4	3.2
Samut Sakhon	294	331	430	2.4	2.6
Total BMR	8,185	9,253	11,541	2.5	2.3
Thailand	52,654	57,196	65,138	1.7	1.4
BMR/Thailand (%)	15.5	16.2	17.7		

Source: NESDB, 1986.

Table A–4 **Average population densities in the BMR, 1980 and 1986 (Unit: person per sq. km)**

Area	1980	1986
Bangkok Metropolitan Area (BMA)	3,285	3,680
Saturated urban areas	33,654	32,261
Slow-growing urban areas	21,250	23,811
Fast-growing urban areas	3,152	4,138
Transitional urban areas	965	1,234
Rural areas	265	311
Other five provinces		
Samut Prakan	560	697
Nonthaburi	585	723
Pathum Thani	218	266
Samut Sakhon	315	362
Nakhon Pathom	252	285

Source: After Isarankura Watana, "Emerging Rural-Urban Linkages: The Bangkok Metropolitan Region," *Regional Development Dialogue* 11 (1989), no. 2: 56–82.

Table A–5 **Migration by origin and destination, 1975–1980**

Region and type of migration	Province of destination						Total
	Bangkok	Nonthaburi	Samut Prakan	Nakhon Pathom	Pathum Thani	Samut Sakhon	
In-migration from:							
Central	46,114	4,608	4,554	1,841	6,131	599	63,847
East	35,260	2,477	5,430	1,049	2,463	689	47,368
West	39,022	2,500	3,620	8,186	1,600	3,392	58,320
North-east	131,819	5,059	11,635	3,939	4,130	2,300	158,882
North	47,895	3,362	4,554	2,193	2,286	912	61,202
South	36,978	2,732	1,683	1,247	492	378	43,510
Total	337,088	20,738	31,476	18,455	17,102	8,270	433,129
Out-migration to:							
Central	13,756	1,157	667	730	1,526	235	18,071
East	19,964	990	3,670	1,427	946	884	27,881
West	14,125	1,007	685	7,839	640	1,638	25,934
North-east	23,729	742	942	1,136	599	334	27,442
North	24,373	1,086	798	1,197	488	445	28,387
South	15,546	573	866	1,358	256	540	19,139
Total	111,493	5,555	7,628	13,687	4,455	4,076	146,894

Net-migration from:							
Central	32,358	3,451	3,887	1,111	4,605	364	45,776
East	15,296	1,487	1,760	378	1,517	−195	19,487
West	24,897	1,493	2,935	347	960	1,754	32,386
North-east	108,090	4,317	10,693	2,805	3,571	1,966	131,440
North	23,522	2,276	3,756	996	1,798	467	32,815
South	21,432	2,159	817	−111	236	−162	24,371
Total	225,595	15,183	23,848	4,770	12,687	4,194	286,277

Source: NESDB, 1986.

Table A–6 **Gross national and regional product, 1970 and 1983 (Unit: 1 million baht, 1972 prices)**

	1970				1983			
Sector	Thailand	%	BMR	%	Thailand	%	BMR	%
Agriculture	48,332	32.2	3,517	6.9	80,940	23.6	4,881	3.3
Mining	2,555	1.7	77	0.1	4,367	1.3	135	0.1
Manufacture	23,320	15.5	14,456	28.4	71,948	21.0	54,550	36.5
Construction	8,705	5.8	4,080	8.0	15,843	4.6	8,550	5.7
Utilities	1,638	1.1	362	0.7	7,393	2.1	1,499	1.0
Transport	9,195	6.1	5,590	11.0	23,608	6.9	12,548	8.4
Trade	26,524	17.7	6,665	13.1	55,591	16.2	21,058	14.1
Banking	5,800	3.9	4,049	7.9	24,330	7.1	17,716	11.8
Dwellings	3,000	2.0	1,448	2.8	5,152	1.5	2,987	2.0
Public Admin.	6,476	4.3	4,891	9.6	14,399	4.2	4,561	3.6
Services	14,541	9.7	5,838	11.5	39,306	11.5	20,083	13.5
GNP/GRP	150,086	100.0	50,973	100.0	342,877	100.0	148,568	100.0

Source: NESDB, 1986.

Table A–7 **Gross provincial product, 1970 and 1983 (Unit: 1 million baht, 1972 prices)**

Province	1970	%	1983	%	Growth rate (% p.a.) 1970–1983
Bangkok Metropolitan Area (BMA)	40,713	79.9	112,435	75.2	8.1
Nonthaburi	968	1.9	2,489	1.7	7.5
Pathum Thani	1,900	3.7	8,285	5.5	12.0
Samut Prakan	3,671	7.2	18,546	12.4	13.3
Samut Sakhon	1,912	3.8	3,151	2.1	3.9
Nakhon Pathom	1,809	3.5	4,672	3.1	7.6
Total BMR	50,973	100.0	149,578	100.0	8.6

Source: NESDB, 1986.

Table A–8 **Percentage distribution of gross provincial product by sector, 1970 and 1983 (Unit: 1 million baht, 1972 prices)**

	Agriculture, mining		Manufacture		Other sectors		Total
Province	1970	1983	1970	1983	1970	1983	1970, 1983
Bangkok Metropolitan Area (BMA)	1.4	0.7	28.3	31.9	70.3	67.4	100.0
Nonthaburi	37.9	15.3	22.4	26.9	39.7	57.8	100.0
Pathum Thani	33.8	9.8	47.1	58.4	19.1	31.8	100.0
Samut Prakan	13.5	4.5	49.6	59.5	36.9	36.0	100.0
Samut Sakhon	52.3	24.9	17.5	33.2	30.2	41.9	100.0
Nakhon Pathom	30.6	31.0	15.1	23.2	54.3	45.6	100.0
Total BMR	7.0	3.4	30.2	36.3	62.8	60.3	100.0

Source: NESDB, 1986.

Table A–9 **Employment by sector and province, 1984 (Unit: 1,000)**

Province	Agriculture, mining	%	Manufacture	%	Other sectors	%	Total	%
Bangkok Metropolitan Area (BMA)	132	5.4	610	25.0	1,697	69.6	2,439	100.0
Nonthaburi	60	41.4	13	8.7	73	49.9	146	100.0
Pathum Thani	74	28.3	113	43.2	75	28.5	262	100.0
Samut Prakan	46	17.0	131	48.8	92	34.2	269	100.0
Samut Sakhon	60	64.9	12	10.1	30	25.0	102	100.0
Nakhon Pathom	149	62.6	30	12.7	59	24.7	238	100.0
Total BMR	521	15.1	909	26.3	2,026	58.6	3,456	100.0

Source: NESDB, 1986.

Table A–10 **Per capita gross regional, provincial product – 1981 and 1985**

	1981	1985	Percentage increase over period
BMR	46,891	59,003	26
BMA	54,207	68,532	26
Pathum Thani	29,046	47,809	65
Central region	13,327	16,749	26
Eastern region	21,968	25,603	17
Western region	20,230	21,047	4
North-eastern region	6,581	8,124	23
Northern region	11,064	13,353	21
Southern region	13,446	15,358	14
Thailand	13,469	20,263	50

Source: *Statistical Yearbook of Thailand*, 1985–1986.

Notes

1. See United Nations Centre for Human Settlements, *Global Report on Human Settlements* (New York: Oxford University Press, 1987), p. 53. Please note that these data include data for western Asia, which are not always included in Asian data. However, the western Asian population is only a small part of the total for Asia.
2. Norton Ginsburg, "The Urban Transition: Reflections on the American and Asian Experience" (Lecture delivered at the Chinese University of Hong Kong, January 1988), p. 4.
3. Some of these ideas were first put forward by me in an address at the International Conference on Asian Urbanization held at the University of Akron in April 1985. This address has now been published as: T.G. McGee, "Urbanisasi or Kotadesasi? The Emergence of New Regions of Economic Interaction in Asia," in L. Ma, A. Noble, and A. Dutt, eds., *Urba-*

nization in Asia* (Honolulu: University of Hawaii Press, 1989), pp. 93–108. An enlarged and revised version of that paper is available in N. Ginsburg, B. Koppel, and T.G. McGee, eds., *The Extended Metropolis Settlement Transition in Asia* (Honolulu: University of Hawaii Press, 1991).

4. Jean Gottman, *Megalopolis: The Urbanized Northeastern Seaboard of the United States* (Cambridge, Mass.: MIT Press, 1961).
5. This division between "skill-orientated" and "mechanical" technological inputs is used to buttress Bray's provocative arguments concerning the distinctive role of Asian wet-rice agriculture in the agrarian development processes in Asia. She argues persuasively that this agro-economic system has created very different conditions from the "Western model." This position is certainly central to some of the arguments of this paper, but its acceptance does not rule out the application of the "mechanical" technological input (as reflected by capital replacing labour in these regions), as can be seen in the growth of agribusiness in the chicken industry in such areas as the central plains of Thailand, etc. See Francesca Bray, *The Rice Economies: Technology and Development in Asian Societies* (Oxford: Basil Blackwell, 1986).
6. This argument is presented in much greater detail for Latin America by Richard Morse, "Trends and Patterns of Latin American Urbanization, 1750–1920," *Comparative Studies in Society and History* 16 (1974): 416–477, and "The Development of Urban Systems in the Americas in the Nineteenth Century," *Journal of Interamerican Studies* 17 (1975), no. 1: 4–26.
7. See C. Baker, "Economic Re-organization and the Slump in South and Southeast Asia," *Comparative Studies in Social and Economic History* 23 (1981), no. 3: 325–349.
8. See United Nations, *World Population Prospects, Estimates and Projections as Assessed in 1982* (New York: United Nations, 1985).
9. Ibid.
10. This calculation is based on a definition of urban that utilizes cities in excess of 100,000 population. See P.M. Hauser and R.W. Gardiner, "Urbanization, Urban Growth and Intermediate Cities: Trends and Prospects" (Paper prepared for the East-West Population Institute Workshop on Intermediate Cities, Honolulu, 1980).
11. See "Rural Non-farm Activities in the Asian Region: An Overview," chap. 1 in S. Mukhopadhyay and C.P. Lim, eds., *Development and Diversification of Rural Industries in Asia* (Kuala Lumpur: Asian and Pacific Development Centre, 1985).
12. See S.P.S. Ho, "Economic Development and Rural Industry in South Korea and Taiwan," *World Development* 10 (1982), no. 11: 973–990.
13. H. Oshima, *The Significance of Off-farm Employment and Incomes in Post-war East Asian Growth*, Asian Development Bank, Staff Paper no. 21 (Manila, 1984).
14. See T.G. McGee, Kamal Salih, and Mei Ling Young, *Silicon Island: Penang, Malaysia. Industrialization, Labour Force Formation, and the Household Response* (Vancouver, B.C.: University of British Columbia, Institute of Asian Research, 1989).
15. See R. Islam, "Non-farm Employment in Rural Asia: Dynamic Growth or Proletarianization?" *Journal of Contemporary Asia* 14 (1984), no. 3: 306–324.
16. See P. Gregory, "An Assessment of Changes in Employment Conditions in Less-developed Countries," *Economic Development and Cultural Change* 28 (1979), no. 4: 673–700; and G.T. Harris and B.A.Z. Rashid, "The Employment Performance of Developing Countries During the 1970s," *The Developing Economies* 24 (1984), no. 3: 212–287.
17. The diagram that is presented in this section was constructed by Dr. M. Douglass of the Department of Urban and Regional Planning, University of Hawaii, during the course of some extended evening discussions on the subject of the "urban transition." I am very grateful to him for his constant probing of my ill-formed ideas that formed the basis of earlier presentations of this idea. See M. Douglass, *Urbanization and National Urban Development Strategies in Asia, Indonesia, Korea, and Thailand*, University of Hawaii, Department of Urban and Regional Planning, Discussion Paper no. 8 (Honolulu, 1988).

18. The use of a coined Indonesian term formed from the two words *kota* (town) and *desa* (village) was originally adopted after discussions with Indonesian social scientists because of my belief that there was a need to look for terms and concepts in the languages of third world countries that reflect the empirical reality of their societies. This also stems from a belief that the language and concepts of Western social science, which have dominated the analyses of third world societies, lead to a form of "knowledge imperialism." In this text I have used the term *desakota*, which can be used interchangeably with *kotadesa*.
19. The term "peasant" in this context applies not only to farmers who own their land but also to tenants operating small units of farm land.
20. See Robert E. Baldwin, "Patterns of Development in Newly Settled Regions," *The Manchester School of Economic and Social Studies* 24 (1956): 161–179; A. Dowd, "A Comparative Analysis of Economic Development in the American West and South," *Journal of Economic History* 16 (1956), no. 7: 558–574; and Richard Morse (see note 6 above).
21. This table utilizes data cited by Daniel R. Vining, "Population Redistribution: Towards Core Areas of Less-developed Countries, 1950–1980," *International Regional Science Review* 10 (1986), no. 1: 1–45, and other articles in this volume.
22. Graham E. Johnson, "1997 and After: Will Hong Kong Survive? A Personal View," *Pacific Affairs* 59 (1986), no. 2: 237–245; and Han Boacheng, "Industry Booms on the Zhujiang River Delta," *Beijing Review* 22/28 August 1988: 18–23; and François Soulard, "La formation d'un corridor de développement économique dans la région du delta du Zhujian, Chine" (M.Sc. thesis, Université de Montréal, Quebec, 1989).
23. See Yujiro Hayami, *A Century of Agricultural Growth in Japan* (Minneapolis: University of Minnesota Press, 1976). Otohiko Hasumi, "Rural Society in Postwar Japan," *The Japan Foundation Newsletter* 12 (1985), no. 5: 1–10 and no. 6: 1–7. Norihiko Nakai, "Urbanization Promotion and Control in Metropolitan Japan," *Planning Perspectives* (1988) 3: 783–810. See also John Lewis, "The Real Security Issue: Rice," *Far Eastern Economic Review* (19 June 1981): 70–71.
24. Alden Speare, Paul K.C. Lin, and Ching-lung Tsay, *Urbanization and Development: The Rural-Urban Transition in Taiwan* (Boulder, Colo.: Westview Press, 1988).
25. See Daniel Todd and Yi-Chung Hsueh, "Taiwan: Some Spatial Implications of Rapid Economic Growth," *Geoforum* 19 (1988), no. 2: 133–145; and Jack F. Williams, "Urban and Regional Planning in Taiwan: The Quest for Balanced Regional Development," *Tijdschrift voor Economische en Sociale Geografie* 79 (1988), no. 3: 175–187.
26. See various Chinese statistical yearbooks.
27. I am grateful to Rex Casinader and Wang Yaolin, Ph.D. candidates in the Department of Geography at the University of British Columbia for information on developments in South India and Sichuan.
28. I am grateful to Charles Greenberg, Ph.D. candidate in the Department of Geography, UBC, for carrying out the research that is incorporated in this section.
29. See Takaya Yoshikazu, *Agricultural Development in a Tropical Delta: A Study of the Chao Phraya Delta* (Honolulu: University of Hawaii Press, 1987).
30. See World Bank, *Thailand Rural Growth and Development* (Washington, D.C., 1983).
31. See Thirauet Pramuanratkern, "The Impact of Urbanization on a Peripheral Area of Bangkok, Thailand" (Ph.D. diss., University of Washington, 1979).
32. See National Economic and Social Development Board (NSEDB), *Bangkok Metropolitan Regional Development Proposals: Recommended Development Strategies and Investment Programs for the Sixth Plan*, Bangkok, NESDB, 1986.
33. In Thailand in 1986 70 per cent of the economically active population was engaged in primary sector activities.

4

The impacts of current global adjustment and shifting techno-economic paradigm on the world city system

Fu-chen Lo

Senior Academic Officer, United Nations University, Tokyo

Introduction: Cities and the world economy

The population explosion and massive rural to urban migration in the developing countries during the post–World War II period are among the key determinants of the rapid growth of the third world mega-cities. In addition, policies and measures to promote economic development and industrialization in the developing countries have been transforming predominantly agricultural and rural societies to more industrialized and urbanized societies in a relatively short period. The growth and structural transformation of mega-cities are integral parts of national development. Furthermore, global economic integration, increased international trade, capital flows, telecommunication, new waves of technologies, and shifts in the comparative advantage of production continue to play a central role in integrating national territories and shaping the spatial organization of national economies at the world level. At the centre of this global economic

I would like to acknowledge the able assistance of N. Dana in the preparation of this paper. The views expressed in this paper are the author's own and do not necessarily represent the opinion of the affiliated institution.

integration and structural adjustments is the interlinkage of mega-cities and other major metropolises, which form a world city system.

The rise and stagnation of OPEC cities; the debt burden of Latin American metropolises; the collapse of commodity prices and stagnation of import-substitution industries in African urban centres; and the rising role of Tokyo and other Asian cities as new, dominant trade and financial centres in East Asia and the world economy clearly demonstrate how the major metropolitan centres in the world have been affected by the current global economic adjustments occurring in the recent past. As will be highlighted later, the new wave of techno-economic paradigm is in the process of replacing the old production paradigm and reshaping the major metropolitan centres in both developed and developing countries, a process that will continue in the decades to come.

Lewis Mumford wrote in 1961 that the "megalopolis is fast becoming a universal form, and the dominant economy is a metropolitan economy, in which no effective enterprise is possible without a close tie to a big city." Whether they should be called megalopolises, mega-cities, or world cities, their role at the world or national levels is increasingly associated with their economic capacity and external linkages as the world economy has increased its interdependency during the post–World War II period. During the 1980s, the world economy underwent a series of economic upheavals that have changed the configuration of mega-cities and defined new conditions for their transformation in the early twenty-first century.

Uneven growth under current global adjustments

Regionalization of the world economy

The global adjustments that took place in the early 1980s continue to transform the world economy into a pattern of uneven growth among the major economic blocs. East and South-East Asia are leading with the highest growth rates, while the US, EC, and the rest of the world remain at much lower levels. The process of uneven growth and regionalization of world economic development is not a short-term phenomenon; it is mid-term to long-term in scale and structural in nature.

One of the key issues in the world economy today is the unresolved third world debt problem. The third world debt amounts to US$1.2 trillion. Since 1984, there has been a net capital outflow from the third world to the industrialized countries. Despite numerous efforts at debt rescheduling and negotiations, the net capital outflow to the industrialized countries had reached, by 1988, US$40 billion a year, and it is likely to continue for some time. In Latin America alone, the overall debt servicing ratio was 43 per cent. The Latin American NICs, namely Brazil, Mexico, and Argentina, undertook heavy investments in the import substitution industries and rapid expansion of the public sector during the commodity boom of the 1970s. The debt to GNP ratio in these countries reached 75 per cent, yet the composition of manufacturing exports still remained at below 40 per cent. Inflation, lack of fresh capital inflow, and heavy debt burden may require a decade of structural adjustments in Latin America.

In Africa, the debt to GNP ratio reached 55 per cent in 1988. The sub-Saharan countries in particular have been most seriously affected by widespread poverty and economic stagnation.

The OPEC and Middle East bloc have also been experiencing a negative current account balance since 1982. On the other hand, the share of OPEC bloc oil production has also dropped to less than 40 per cent against the share of non-OPEC bloc production. This trend has been further aggravated by a sharp devaluation of the US dollar against other major currencies in the early 1980s.

Apart from the aggravated situation in Africa, Latin America, and other major primary commodity exporting countries, the prolonged shadow of the US twin deficits remains another key issue. This economic problem has not only caused increasing pressures towards greater protectionism in the US but also weakened the US economy as a major market and source of development capital for the third world countries, in particular for the Latin American bloc. As a major debtor, the US has been a black hole draining savings from Japan, Europe, and other surplus countries against the needs of the developing countries. The debt issue and revitalization of the US economy through technological change are expected to take more than a decade to resolve.

In Europe, the 12 member countries of the EC are in the process of forming a single market by 1992 by integrating a combined population of 320 million and a GNP of US$4,200 billion under its umbrella. As a single entity, the EC will be a powerful economic bloc compared to the rest of the world. In anticipation of a free internal market in the EC in the near future, a fresh flow of direct foreign investment has already been generated from the non-EC countries, particularly from Japan as it attempts to secure a foothold in the EC market. It is also expected that full economic integration of the EC will not be completed by 1992, as it may require a much longer time for internal adjustments within the bloc and in each member country. Intra-European trade shares have steadily increased, from a 45 per cent level in 1970 to over 70 per cent in 1988. With the recent opening of the East European bloc, restructuring of Eastern European economies will continue to drain capital flows within Europe rather than allow such funds to meet the needs of the rest of the world.

In view of this new trend of regionalization of the world economy, the Asia-Pacific countries tend to be more economically complementary rather than competitive. The economies of East and South-East Asia, which comprise Japan, the Asian NICs, ASEAN, and China, are at different stages of economic development. The shifting comparative advantage and the potential of a large market are positive contributory factors for future regional economic restructuring. The structural interdependency developed in the past decades, particularly in East and South-East Asia, has been further strengthened with the current global adjustments [11, chap. 5]. In spite of the slow growth of the world economy in the 1980s, East and South-East Asia have become the highest growth regions in the world.

Under the current trends in the regionalization of the world economy, North America, the new Europe, and East and South-East Asia may form a tri-pole development in the 1990s. UN and other projections clearly indicate a pattern of uneven growth among the major economic blocs in this period, with East and South-East Asia leading with a growth rate of over five per cent, while the US and EC remain at two to three per cent.

Excess supply of commodities and third world stagnation

The current third world debts and economic stagnation are largely attributed to the collapse of prices of oil and other primary commodities in the early 1980s. As shown in figure 1, relative prices of manufacturing goods increased against sharp declines in the petroleum price index and the non-fuel commodity price index. As most of the developing countries are heavily dependent on commodity exports for their foreign exchange earnings to support their industrialization, the collapse of commodity prices has led to serious economic crises in Africa, Latin America, the OPEC bloc, and other commodity exporting developing countries.

As shown in table 1, shares of fuels and non-fuel primary commod-

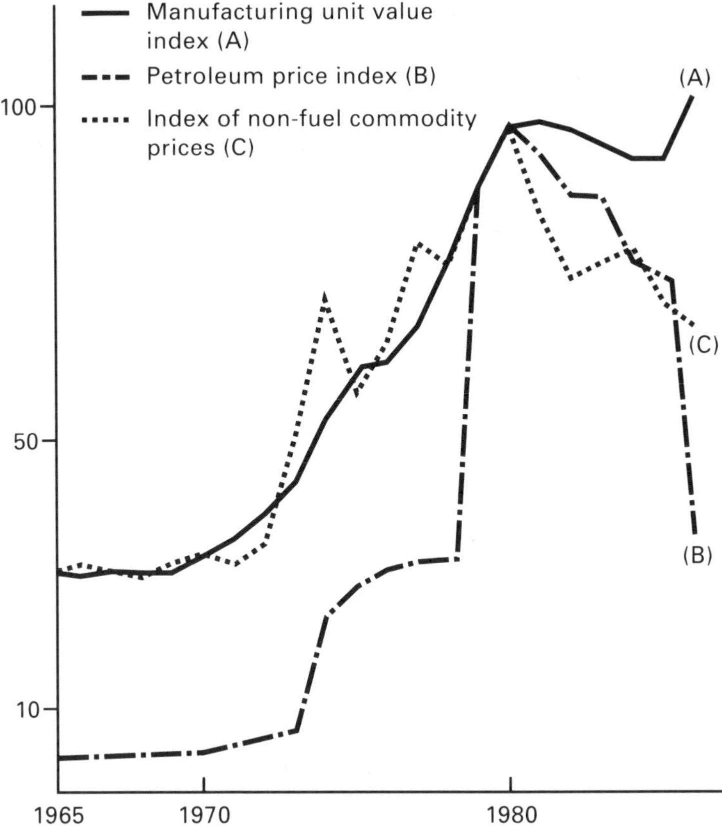

Fig. 1 **Relative prices of manufacturing goods, petroleum, and non-fuel primary commodities (1980 = 100) (Source: ref. 11, chap. 13)**

ities in world trade declined from 43.5 per cent in 1980 to 28.4 per cent in 1987. This trend is reflected in the sharp declines in the imports (9 per cent) of developed countries and exports (25 per cent) of developing countries. This has dramatically changed North-South trade relations and worsened terms of commodity trade and the external debt repayment schedules for those countries now facing serious debt problems.

Most seriously affected are the African countries. As their industrialization started much later than that of Latin America and Asia, more than half of the African countries have over 90 per cent dependency on primary commodity exports (see figure 2). Yet their import substitution industries remain at an infant stage and are not ready to replace commodity exports. The Latin American bloc has a

Table 1 **Percentage share of trade of fuel and non-fuel primary commodities**

	World trade			Import of developed countries			Export of developing countries		
	Fuels (1)	Non-fuel primary commodities (2)	Total (1) + (2)	Fuels (1)	Non-fuel primary commodities (2)	Total (1) + (2)	Fuels (1)	Non-fuel primary commodities (2)	Total (1) + (2)
1980	23.7	19.8	43.5	27.0	19.8	46.8	60.8	19.4	80.2
1983	20.9	18.7	39.6	22.8	18.6	41.4	50.1	20.5	70.6
1987	11.4	17.0	28.4	10.8	17.1	27.9	31.3	24.1	55.4

Source: Ref. 9.

Fig. 2 **Share of primary export in total export in Africa (Source: UNCTAD, *Africa's Commodity Problems: Towards a Solution* [UNCTAD, 1990])**

more serious debt problem due to rapid industrialization and heavy expenditures in the public sector expansion during the period of commodity boom and intensive external borrowings.

What may be considered as a structural problem is the trend of long-term decline of material inputs in the developed economies. For instance, in Japan it was estimated that only 50–60 per cent of resource inputs is required to produce the same level of GNP in comparison with 1980. A declining share of material inputs in products has been spreading across most of the high value trade manufacturing products, including automobiles, machinery, and electronic goods.

Micro-electronics and communication, robotics technology, biotechnology, and new materials have gradually become the fast growth and dominating sectors in the developed countries and in some of the newly industrialized economies. And those sectors are basically resource saving in nature.

In view of these structural changes, commodity trade may increase in the course of increasing South-South trade, but the world economy may be in a process of entering into a period of gradual disintegration of the commodity economy and of the industrial economy in the long run.

Changing comparative advantage and new economic configurations

The trade patterns that emerged among East Asian countries and between them and the United States and the European Economic Community were the result of the rapid industrialization of the 1970s and early 1980s in the Asian countries. Two basic processes occurred during the period: (1) adjustments at the global economic level: the changing comparative advantage in manufactured goods among the advanced industrialized countries, i.e. the US, EC, and Japan, and (2) adjustments in East and South-East Asia leading to their changing comparative advantage. This includes the shift from light manufactures to durable consumer goods and machinery products in the Asian NIEs and from raw material exports to manufacturing exports in ASEAN. Also evident is the emerging division of labour among Japan-NIEs-ASEAN with the creation of a new industrial belt within the global economy. The emergence of this area has been induced by worldwide structural adjustments and industrial relocation.

These adjustments follow the changing dynamic comparative advantage of the US, EC, and the East Asian countries in different sectors in the industrialization process. The resultant pattern has been described as one conforming to the changing comparative advantage, or the so-called flying geese pattern of development (figure 3). In this industrialization process, latecomers appear to have successfully adopted a strategy of entering into sectors in which they have a rising comparative advantage in some cost terms and importing technology from an already mature economy whose competitive advantage in that industry seems to be on the decline (see also figure 8). They later begin to invest in new industrial products using new

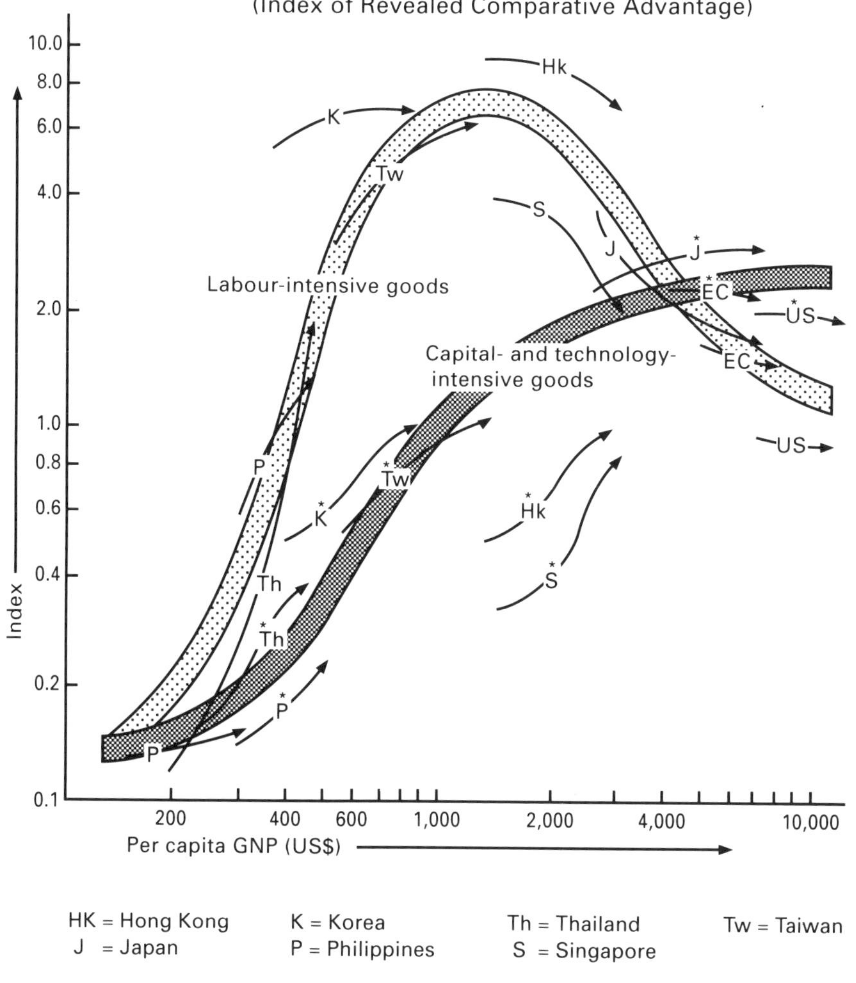

Labour-intensive goods consist of: SITC 611, 612, 613, 631, 632, 633, 651, 652, 653, 654, 655, 656, 657, 662, 663, 664, 666, 667, 691, 692, 693, 694, 695, 696, 697, 698, 812, 821, 831, 841, 842, 851, 891, 893, 894, 895, 896, 899.

Capital- and technology-intensive goods consist of: SITC 512, 513, 514, 515, 521, 531, 532, 533, 541, 551, 553, 554, 561, 571, 581, 599, 621, 629, 641, 642, 661, 671, 672, 673, 674, 675, 676, 678, 679, 681, 682, 683, 684, 685, 686, 687, 688, 689, 711, 712, 714, 715, 717, 718, 719, 722, 723, 724, 725, 726, 729, 731, 732, 733, 734, 735, 861, 862, 863, 864, 892.

Fig. 3 **Changing comparative advantage for manufactures of ASEAN, NIEs, Japan, US, and EC (Source: Toshio Watanabe)**

technology and know-how for which they have the innovative edge. This industrial restructuring and shifts in position of the economies involved in the global specialization and division of labour are not always smooth and involve frictions in adjustment and competition. The flying geese pattern is discernible in the case of heavy industries, whose production focus seems to have shifted from the US to Japan in the 1970s, at the same time as a similar shift in pattern appears to have occurred in the light manufactured goods industry from Japan to the Asian NIEs.

The situation in the late 1970s and early 1980s, however, has reached a stage whereby within the East Asian industrial belt, the NICs and ASEAN have become competitive with Japan for different items in light manufacturing and in exports to the US and elsewhere. As a result of this, and as a result of the oil shocks and adjustments in the post 1973–1983 period, when Japan began to develop and adopt resource-saving technology, Japan has relocated "sunset industries" to the NICs, as in the case of non-durable consumer goods, electrical products, etc. At the same time, food processing, textiles, etc., have been relocated from the NIEs to ASEAN. In the 1990s, the NICs and ASEAN have had to depend on cross-Pacific trade, namely to the US and EC, to sustain their export drive in consumer and light industry. From the mid-1980s, Japan has also become a major importer of the manufacturing exports of the NIEs and ASEAN.

This shift was made possible by the global restructuring that took place particularly in the US and EC. The pent-up demand for consumer goods in the world's largest market, rising labour costs inducing the relocation of off-shore production facilities, and the availability of cheap labour in East and South-East Asia, as well as active promotion of foreign investments, have contributed to rapid growth in manufactured exports from East Asia to the US and EC. International relocation of industry through this product life cycle is well illustrated by Vernon (see figure 8). Hall and others have attributed the decline of Western European cities in the 1970s to the product cycle theory [5].

While the flying geese pattern of industrialization has been applicable to light manufactured goods, it has not proceeded to intermediate goods and heavy industries. As a result, the situation is complementary and trade in East Asia has been increasing. This structural interdependency can be seen in figure 4. From the figure, one can see that the strongest ties in Japanese inter-industrial linkages

Induced countries	Japan						USA					
Inducing countries / Industrial sector	India	Malaysia	Philippines	Singapore	Thailand	Korea	India	Malaysia	Philippines	Singapore	Thailand	Korea
Food, beverages, tobacco	○											
Textile and leather products	◯	◯	◯	○	○	◯	○	○	○			○
Lumber and wood products				◯						○		○
Pulp, paper products, printing	◯	◯		◯	○	○				○		○
Chemical products	◯	○		◯	◯	⊕				○		○
Petroleum refining												
Rubber products			◯		○	⊕			○			○
Non-metallic mineral products				○								
Metal products	⊕	○	⊕	⊕	◯	⊕						◯
Machinery	⊕	◯	○	◯	◯	⊕	○	○		◯		◯
Transport equipment	⊕	◯	◯	⊕	⊕	⊕			○	○		○
Other manufacturing industries	◯	○	◯	◯	○	◯			○			○
Construction	◯	◯	○	◯	○	○				○		

⊕ Inducement coefficient of more than 0.4.
◯ Inducement coefficient of between 0.2 and 0.4.
○ Inducement coefficient of between 0.1 and 0.2.

Fig. 4 **Production of Japan and the United States induced by industries of East and South-East Asian countries (Source: S. Furukawa, *International Input-Output Analysis* [Tokyo: Institute of Development Economics, 1986])**

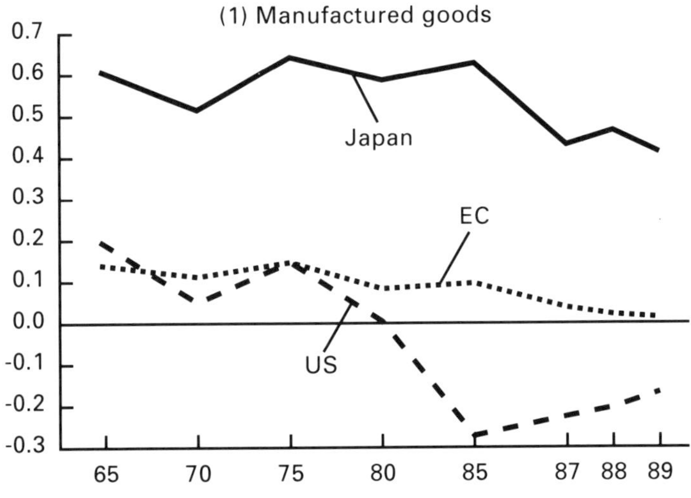

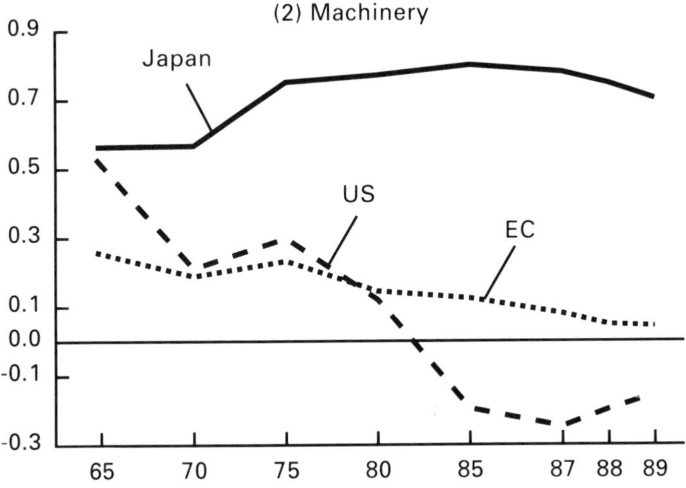

Fig. 5 **Trends of international comparative advantage of trade (trade specialization coefficients) (Source: ref. 9)**

are with the NICs and ASEAN in chemical products, metal products, machinery, transport equipment, and construction. The growth of this trade constitutes the major distinguishing feature of trade in the region. The trade in intermediate and heavy industries between Japan and the rest of the East Asian countries appears to have increased in recent years, in contrast with the 30 per cent decline in US inter-industrial linkage with the NIEs and ASEAN [7, chap. 1].

The role of transnational corporations in this trade and investment activity in the region has strengthened further the globalization of production in East Asia. The importance of technology, finance, and market channels can be increasingly observed from the activities of TNCs. In some industries, it becomes clear that effective transfer of technology does take place, as well as an increase in the spin-off effects of direct foreign investment in the host economies. Enhanced intra-firm division of labour and the new decentralized forms of organization of production have been intensified within the East Asian countries as illustrated by the increasing momentum of the flows of direct foreign investment in recent years.

By comparing the trade specialization coefficients of Japan, the EC, and the US (figure 5), Japan's superior performance in all manufactured goods and machinery is clearly indicated relative to that of the EC and US. The US has shown a negative index (as net impor-

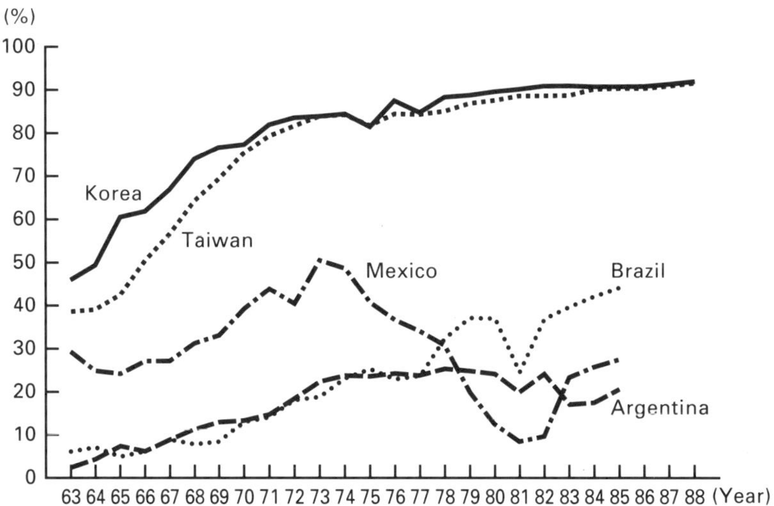

Fig. 6a **Percentage share of manufacturing export: Korea, Taiwan, Argentina, Brazil, and Mexico (Source: ref. 9)**

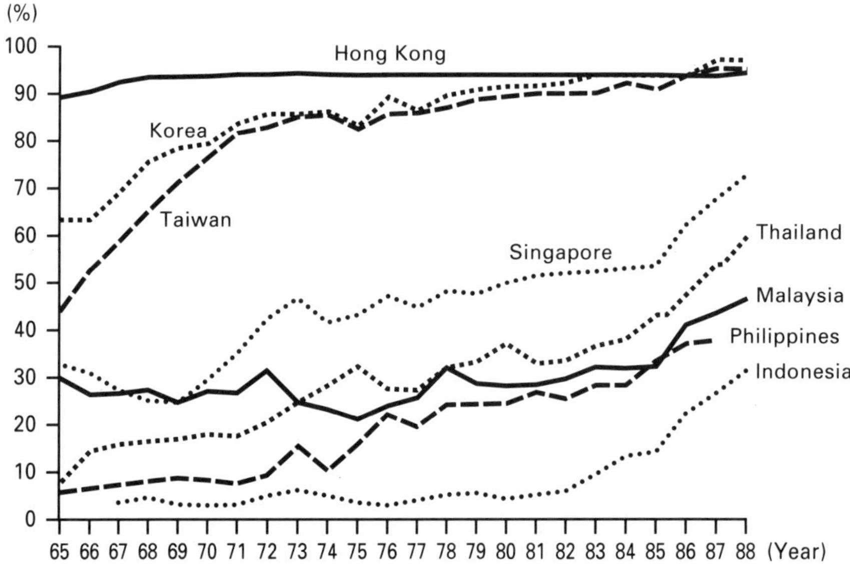

Fig. 6b **Percentage share of manufacturing export: Asian NIEs and ASEAN**

ter) from the early 1980s in both categories. The EC as a whole has maintained a position of net exporter with a declining trend. During this period, the US has been suffering with the twin deficits and has reduced US-Latin American trade and investments considerably, a clear sign of economic disintegration between the two. In Europe, intra-regional trade shares have steadily increased from 45 per cent in 1970 to over 70 per cent in 1988. In view of the gradual economic integration of a new Europe, it is expected that this trend will strengthen in the future. Thus, only in East Asia has inter-industrial linkage been strengthened, between Japan and the East Asian high growth economies, as the consequences of current global adjustments.

Emerging pattern of a world city system

The emerging pattern of a world city system based on current global adjustments and national economic performance can be summarized as in table 2. Latin American and African cities are plagued by the high debt, high inflation, and a high dependency on primary commodities. These cities face immense difficulty in financing structural adjustment and urban infrastructural expenditure. Stagnation of commodity prices has also led to massive rural to urban migration, escalating pressures to expand the stock of urban infrastructure. Heavy

Table 2 **Grouping of major world cities by regional/national economic performance**

High debt, high inflation, high primary export economies	Medium growth (2–4%) economies	High economic growth (4% and over) economies
	USA	Japan
	New York	Tokyo-Yokohama
	Los Angeles	Osaka-Kobe
	Chicago	
	San Francisco	
	W. Europe	
	London	
	Paris	
	Milan	
	Rome	
	Rhein-Ruhr	
	Berlin	
	Madrid	
	E. Europe	
	Moscow	
	St. Petersburg	
Latin America	South Asia	NIEs
Buenos Aires	Bombay	Seoul
Lima	Calcutta	Taipei
La Paz	Delhi	Hong Kong
Santiago	Madras	Singapore
Caracas	Karachi	ASEAN
Bogotá	Dacca	Jakarta
Mexico City	Middle East	Bangkok
São Paulo	Istanbul	Kuala Lumpur
Rio de Janeiro	Teheran	China
Africa	Baghdad	Beijing
Lagos	ASEAN	Tianjin
Kinshasa	Manila	Shanghai
Cairo		Guangzhou
Nairobi		
Accra		
Abidjan		
Algiers		

external lending and sluggishness in commodity export earnings are further aggravating financing future urban development. This spiral of stagnation is casting a dark shadow over immediate recovery of cities in these countries.

In the medium growth group lie a whole range of cities from both developed and developing countries. The cities in the United States and Western Europe have been suffering from the trend of deindustrialization of the 1970s accompanied by a continuous decline of blue-collar jobs in the traditional industrial centres. It is also evident that structural changes in those metropolises correspond with the increasing importance of the service sector. Lately a new trend of information processing and high-technology industries has begun to serve as the new impulse for future growth. But this does not necessarily hold for some of the old metropolises. In Europe, the opening of Eastern European cities and the initiation of a larger integrated EC market are expected to stimulate the revitalization of European industries with an increasing role for high technology. These new trends are likely to induce a structural adjustment in European cities.

The major cities in South Asia and in the Middle East are traditionally more inward looking, thus less affected by the current global adjustments, and have maintained moderate growth.

In contrast, the cities with high economic growth rates have been highly concentrated in the East and in South-East Asia. These cities are in nations that have had phenomenal expansion in their share in world trade and production. The share of Japan's GNP in the world GNP rose from 4.1 per cent in 1960 to 13 per cent in 1990. Tokyo has quickly emerged as a world financial centre as Japan has assumed the role of the largest creditor in the world. Many Asian economies have also experienced two-digit growth in the recent past. Trade and inter-industrial linkages, together with a massive flow of capital among Japan, the Asian NIEs, and ASEAN, have led to rapid growth and structural transformation of Asian cities. A network of Asian cities is expected to form a new growth corridor in the world city system.

Shifts in successive techno-economic paradigms and the impact on world cities

Long waves and world cities

In recent years there has been a revival of interest in the long waves of economic structural changes. Schumpeter and Kuznets have studied 40–60 year cycles of long waves of economic fluctuations with historical data that are often known as Kondratieff cycles (see figure 7). Innovation is seen as the fundamental impulse that sets and keeps the economic engine in motion. In the Schumpeterian model, clusters of basic innovations appear prior to a long wave upswing. Each long wave is dominated by an underlying techno-economic

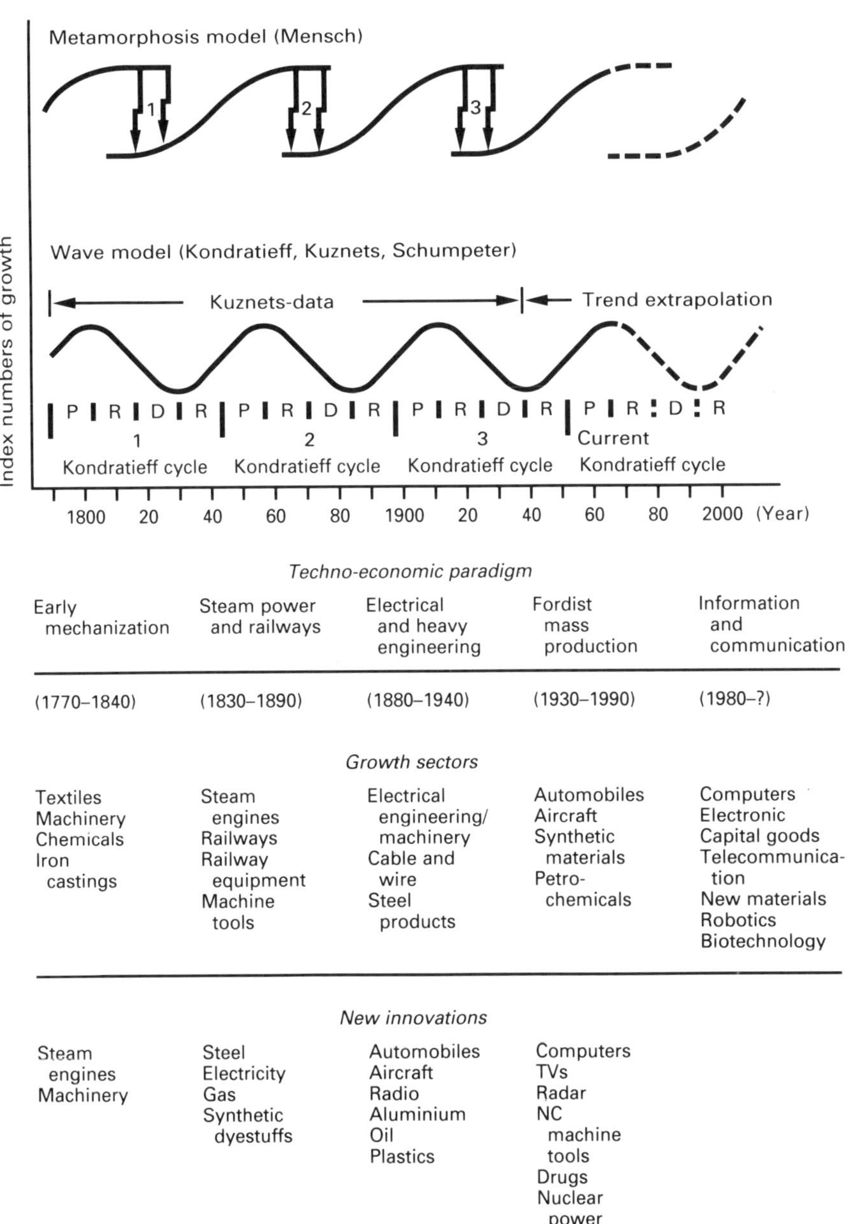

		Techno-economic paradigm		
Early mechanization	Steam power and railways	Electrical and heavy engineering	Fordist mass production	Information and communication
(1770–1840)	(1830–1890)	(1880–1940)	(1930–1990)	(1980–?)
		Growth sectors		
Textiles Machinery Chemicals Iron castings	Steam engines Railways Railway equipment Machine tools	Electrical engineering/ machinery Cable and wire Steel products	Automobiles Aircraft Synthetic materials Petro-chemicals	Computers Electronic Capital goods Telecommunica-tion New materials Robotics Biotechnology
		New innovations		
Steam engines Machinery	Steel Electricity Gas Synthetic dyestuffs	Automobiles Aircraft Radio Aluminium Oil Plastics	Computers TVs Radar NC machine tools Drugs Nuclear power	

Kondratieff cycles: Shifting of techno-economic paradigm 1770–1980 (Source: C. Freeman, ed., *Design, Innovation and Long Cycles in Economic Development* [London: Frances Pinter, 1986])

Fig. 7 **Waves of successive techno-economic paradigms since the Industrial Revolution (Source: ref. 8)**

paradigm that pervades the entire economy and provides the overall scope for productivity increases.

In the first long wave from 1770 to 1830, clusters of innovation in the steam engine, iron casting, textiles, and mechanization brought with them the factory organization and the emergence of British supremacy in trade and international finance. The State apparatus was small and there was rapid expansion of retail and wholesale trade in new urban centres. The dissolution of feudal and medieval monopolies was substituted with industry competition based on a *laissez-faire* economy. There was minimal State regulatory control and cities began to flourish as new urban centres with the expansion of factories and retail and wholesale trade.

In the second Kondratieff wave from the 1830s to the 1890s, railway and steam power were the dominant technologies and overcame the limitations of water power. The extension of mechanization and factory production provided the impetus for market growth. Britain continued to lead during this wave and was joined by France, Germany, and the USA. The rise of the middle class and the growth of the transport and distribution sectors flourished further due to the *laissez-faire* economic regime. Modern urban centres in the major industrial countries emerged during this period interconnected by railways and seaports.

In the third wave from the 1880s to the 1930s, Germany and the US took over the lead from Britain in applying electrical and heavy engineering and steel technology in overcoming the limitations of iron as an engineering material. An important phenomenon was the rise of mega-cities such as London and New York as the world cities for the major commodity markets as well as for banking and capital-finance. The world cities became the headquarters of the newly emerging giant firms. Specialized large R&D departments in companies and the growing importance of university scientists and engineers and specialized middle management became the main features of the national system of innovation. As a consequence of developments in the tertiary sector, the major city was the driving force in the growth of department stores, chain stores, the entertainment and tourism sectors. The concept of the city was no longer limited to just meeting the needs of producers of goods and services, but rather, with the new techno-economic paradigm, it had to provide the resources to perform its new role as the management centre of its diverse constituents and the gradual expansion of markets all over the world.

Crossroads of the old and new waves

Mensch, one of the leading Kondratieff revivalists, argues that the metamorphosis model of cycles of structural change takes place when the economy has evolved through a series of basic innovations that take the form of successive S-shaped cycles (see figure 7). Growth ends as former growth industries reach their levels of saturation of their respective life cycles; the take-off of a new paradigm is the result of the introduction of basic innovations.

By the fourth Kondratieff wave of the 1930s to 1980s, with the rise of Fordist mass production as the dominant paradigm, Britain had lost its preeminence to the US and Germany, with Japan emerging as a latecomer. The major world cities in the industrial countries became the growth centre for super and hyper consumer markets, research and development, financial services, and information technology. Fordist mass production was based on full standardization of components. The US had the advantage in cheap energy resources with the requisite technology to tap mass markets. Increasingly, these world cities were the centres of hierarchical control of multinational affiliates around the globe. The speed and flexibility of air and automobile transportation allowed the world city greater power and influence over government and business.

The fourth wave coincided with the post–World War II industrial development of most of the third world countries. This was also the era of mass production and consumption. The availability of relatively cheap and abundant resources witnessed a massive build up in production capacity. The economies of both the North and South were becoming increasingly interdependent, with cross-border movements of raw materials, goods, capital, and technology. The major cities began to assist in the process of globalization and integration of national economies.

Many of the developing nations entered their industrialization phase when Fordist mass production was already well established in the United States and other developed countries. Many products had already entered into the mature stage of their life cycle (see figure 8). These countries embarked on import substitution industrialization financed through the export earnings of primary products, oil, timber, and other natural resource exploitations. Many of these import substitution industries suffer today from the technological obsolescence based on high resource consumption and production methods of the old paradigm. Furthermore, the sharp decline in the relative

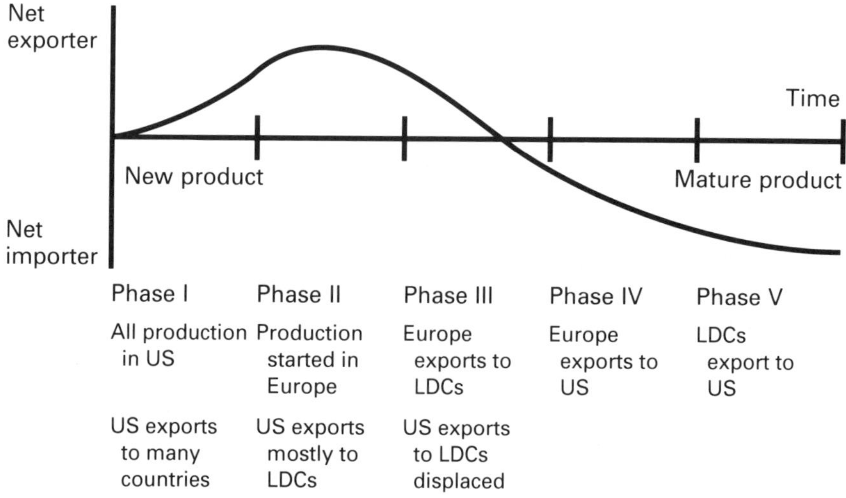

Fig. 8a **Vernon's product life cycle (Source: L.T. Wells, ed., *The Product Life Cycle and International Trade* [1972])**

prices of commodities *vis à vis* manufactured goods in the mid-1980s has further aggravated the import substitution industrialization strategy of many developing countries based on the old paradigm. The crossroads of the old and new paradigms is evident in many industries where there is increasing technological fusion of the past and emerging paradigms. The innovative combination of traditional mechanization with electronics is producing a new generation of factory automation, robotics, and numerical control machine tools. In office automation, the digitalization of telecommunication has rejuvenated traditional products such as cameras, business machines, mobile telephones, and other telecommunication equipment. A similar attempt is being made in the introduction of new materials and robotics in the automobile industry. These streams of new technologies are beginning to transcend a broad cross-section of industries in the old Fordist mass production paradigm. Developing countries trapped under the old regime are becoming less competitive, while Japan and the new Asian NIEs are very focused on the next generation of technologies.

The emergence of the new paradigm

It has been argued that the fifth Kondratieff cycle emerged in the late-1980s to 1990s with clusters of new innovations in computers,

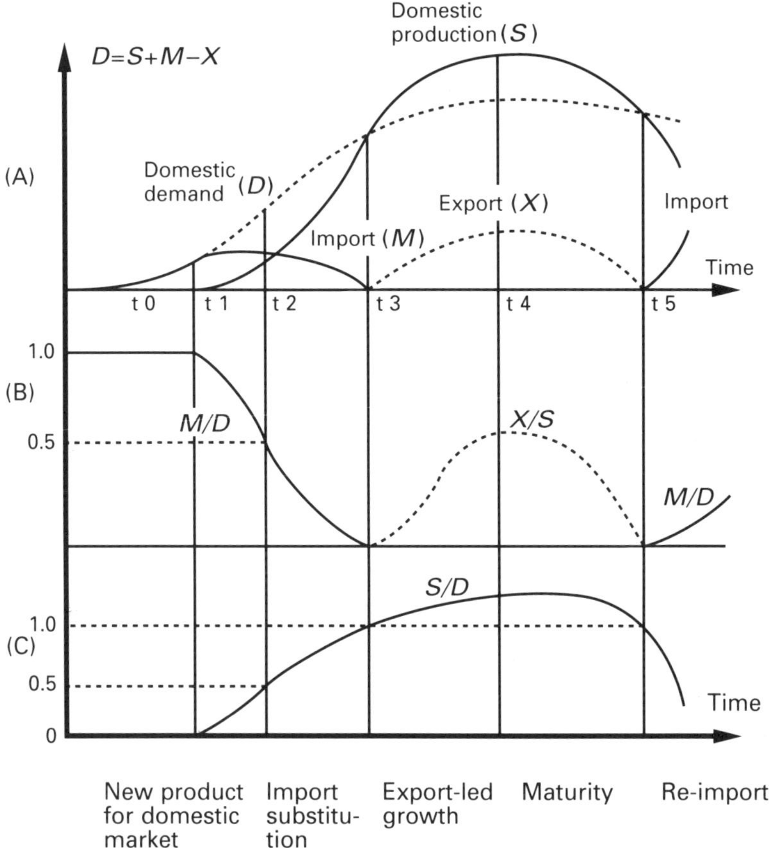

Fig. 8b **Akamatsu-Yamazawa's flying-geese theory (Source: I. Yamazawa, *Economic Development and International Trade: The Japanese Model* [Honolulu: East-West Center, 1990])**

electronics and telecommunications, new materials, biotechnology, and robotics entering as the leading growth sector in the world economy. The new paradigm is basically resource saving in nature and it also provides the capability of maximizing the diseconomies of scale and flexibility in production permitted by micro-electronic "chip" technology.

The level of technological change is increasingly seen as the main determinant of structural change. The current microelectronics-new materials paradigm has challenged the Fordist mass production paradigm of massive resource utilization, especially high energy consumption, and scale economies of standardization. The application of micro-electronics has minimized energy consumption and permitted flexible manufacturing and has created new mega-supplies and demands in many sectors and invigorated many mature and declining sectors. This can be observed in many industries, as in the Japanese consumer electronics industry. Innovation and continuous technical change are used to create new growth markets as mature products decline (see figure 9). The commercialization of many more new innovations based on this new techno-economic paradigm awaits the economic incentives to create new mega-demands. According to a recent UN forecast [13], it is estimated that the potential from information technology will increase 10 times more in the next 10 years than in the past decades. World demand for computer services, for information technology systems is estimated to grow 15–20 per cent per year during the period 1986–1995. Interestingly, the newly industrializing economies are projected to double their semiconductor production by the year 2000. Most notably, the Asian NIEs are investing heavily in high technology industries in the new techno-economic paradigm and are beginning to take a visible share in world trade (see figure 10).

Those mega-cities that have shown greater potential to tap the new, rapidly growing knowledge intensive industries have been able to rise in global prominence. In particular, Japan and its mega-cities have demonstrated that they have the social and institutional ability to exploit this new paradigm and as such have assumed a new leadership role under this order. Japanese policies in mega-city management have ensured the necessary infrastructural investments and also enjoy support by regional policies that lay great stress on the development of "technopolises" providing science, education, communications, and transport infrastructure. Tokyo, Osaka, Nagoya, Kita-Kyushu, and other cities have consistently sought to strengthen technological and managerial capabilities to serve their new knowledge-intensive industries. The future power of a mega-city will be in its capacity to identify and formulate policies on the basis of new technologies that are likely to transform the existing paradigm.

The city system and the shifting techno-economic paradigm

As stated, during the 1980s and early 1990s, the world economy was experiencing a series of economic structural adjustments that have changed the configuration of mega-cities and defined new conditions for their transformation in the early twenty-first century.

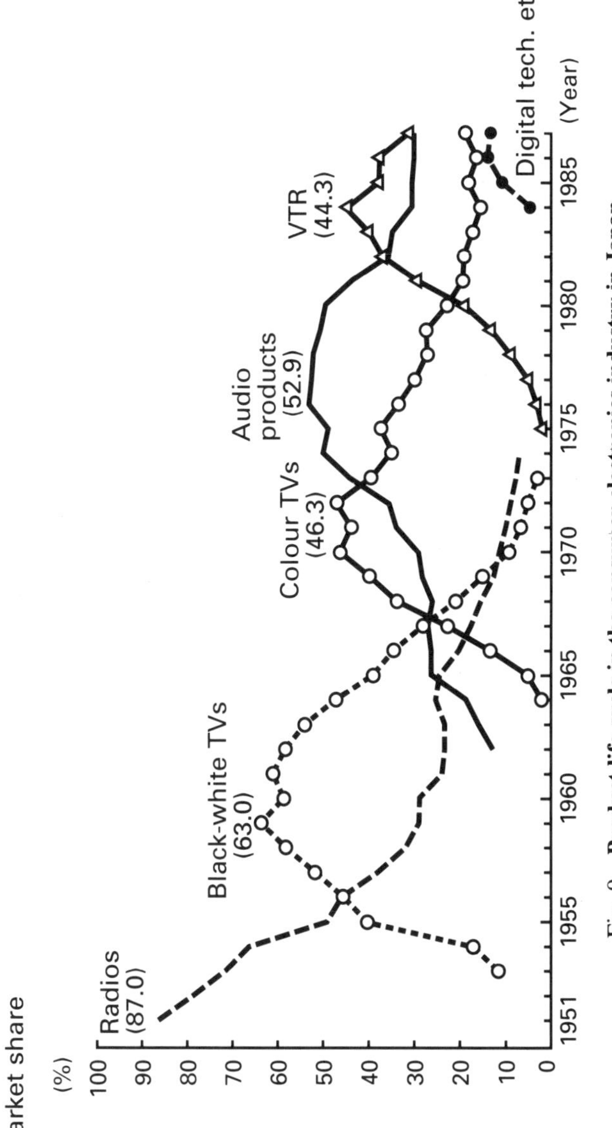

Fig. 9 **Product life cycle in the consumer electronics industry in Japan**

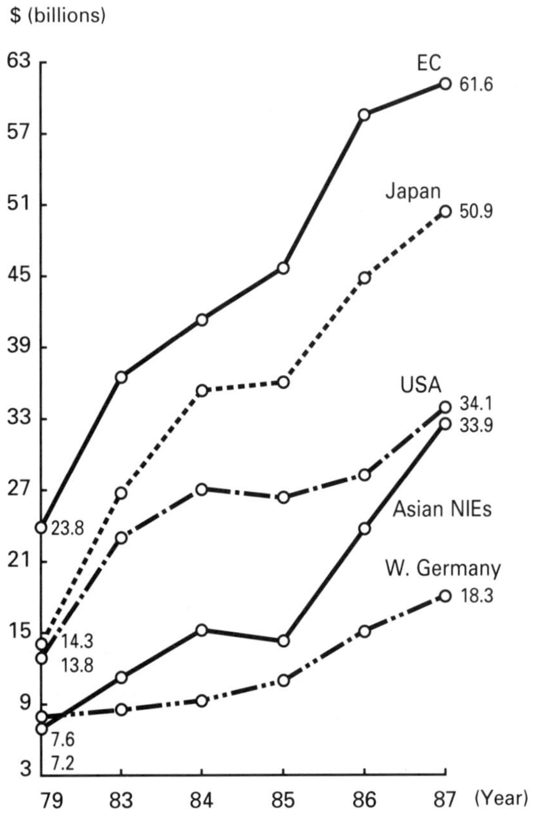

Percentage share of major exporting countries

	1979	1987
EC	35.9	28.5
Japan	20.8	23.6
USA	21.6	15.8
Asian NIEs	10.9	15.7

Fig. 10 **Trend of electronics exports from EC, US, Japan, and Asian NIEs (1979–1988) (Source: GATT, "International Trade")**

The evolution of technology and product life cycle poses new challenges to the mega-city's economic growth. Supply side policies of identifying industries with innovation and growth potential must be supported with investments in new infrastructure and services. The mega-city in this context can be characterized by three trajectories: (1) the traditional mega-city, (2) network world city, and (3) dominant world city.

The traditional mega-city services the traditional manufacturing and agricultural sectors, which are often domestic market oriented. Among the cities in this trajectory are most of the ones in South Asia and in the centrally planned economies, which pursue very inward looking industrial policies. They are less affected by the cyclical turns of the world economy and the advances in science and technology. In the traditional mega-city, the tertiary sector is organized through vertical and hierarchical organizational forms mostly to meet market needs within national boundaries. But even some of the traditional mega-cities are beginning to respond to the shifts in the techno-economic paradigms. Despite inward looking strategies, New Delhi and Bombay are participating in India's increasing software exports, which have been growing at 40 per cent annually in recent years.

In the network world city mode, the city views the world as one open market and coordinates R&D, production, and marketing to achieve efficiency in the global industrial system. Many world cities in developing countries are host to branches of transnational corporations as well to their domestic transnationals engaged in international trade and finance. Such firms are clustered in one or a few world cities in each developing country. The core industries include the Fordist mass production assembly type industries in consumer goods, household electronics, automobiles, etc., either induced under an import substitution policy or as part of direct foreign investments. Increasingly, transnational corporations have created borderless regional and global operations to take advantage of their fast growth and dominant role in global trade and production.

The network world cities are greatly affected by the shifts in the techno-economic paradigms. With European integration occurring with momentum, the European world cities may tend to strengthen their networks more on a regional basis. The fast growing East Asian economies are very dependent on world trade and as such their cities are very outward orientated despite being highly integrated with Japan. However, Latin American and African cities are tied to their primary commodities and debt burden, which make them less integrated with the fast growing sectors in the world city system. Furthermore, with the liberalization of capital and currency markets, the trade in this sector far exceeds by multiples of 10 the value of international trade in goods and services. In addition to the gradual separation of the commodity economy and the manufacturing economy since the 1980s, it is also evident that there is a departure in the separation of the "money economy" from the "real economy." World cities that are part of the world financial markets are gaining increasing prominence in the world city system through currency trade, transfers of short-term and long-term capital, and other forms of portfolio investments around the world financial markets.

Our third mode, the dominant world city, is mostly located in the developed countries, but examples can also be expected to emerge in a few newly industrializing countries. The dominant world city has some fundamental characteristics. First, it has become established as a predominant centre of new innovations and technological diffusion. Secondly, it serves as the environment for the conglomeration of global, central managerial functions, including headquarters of multinationals and international organizations. Thirdly, it is a dominant world financial centre. And fourthly, it acts as the focal point of a network of other world cities. In the wake of new technologies that promote flexibility and transmission of information with great speed, these cities divest from complete centralization in management. Network relationships with autonomous regional and national organizations enable speedy decisions that quickly seize economic opportunities. The centre provides consultative and expert services to its network. In the current economic environment, simple control and dissemination structures may be obsolete and incapable of responding to changing demand and technological conditions. As such, it may be increasingly difficult to define the boundary of a mega-city by just national jurisdiction; rather, it may be more appropriate by its interactions with international networks.

As the world economic gravity has shifted from Pax Americana to a tri-pole development, the role of the dominant mega-cities in Europe, the US, and East Asia has also been adjusted accordingly.

Each one of the mega-city modes described could evolve into a higher order and adjust to the structural changes in the global economy. The rise of OPEC cities and some major cities in developing countries as a result of the commodity boom in the mid-1970s and early 1980s has led to their integration into the financial and commodity capitals of the world. However, their inability to respond to new technologies and knowledge intensive industries, coupled with a subsequent downturn in primary commodity prices, have restricted these cities from evolving into the world city type. These cities seemed only to react to changes in relative factor prices to spur their growth and influence in the world city system. Similarly, Latin American and African mega-cities have been driven by their reliance on their import substitution industries, resource exploitation, and export-crop agricultural economies and have been seriously affected by the current global adjustments. However, the cities of East Asia, as a result of the expansion in their export oriented economies, have been able to move into the global mode. There is intense scanning of global markets and technologies by industrial organizations in East Asian cities through joint ventures and inflows of direct foreign investment. These cities had to serve their higher order needs by organizing and coordinating their vast economic and political relations. Tokyo is emerging as a dominant world city where complex and heterogeneous activities are organized in a systems approach and at the same time having the flexibility and spontaneity permitted by the new micro-electronics and information intensive paradigm. Each mega-city is dynamically interacting and evolving and the strategic allocation of mega-city resources can alter the direction and speed of its evolution.

References

1 Dogan, Mattei, and John D. Kasarda, eds. *The Metropolis Era*. Vols. 1 and 2. Beverly Hills, Calif.: Sage Publications, 1988.

2 Economic Planning Agency. *World Economic White Paper* (Sekai Keizai Hakusho; in Japanese). Tokyo: Government Publication, 1989.

3 Friedmann, John, and Goetz Wolff. "World City Formation: An Agenda for Research and Action." *International Journal for Urban and Regional Research* 6 (1982), no. 3: 309–404.

4 Hall, Peter. *The World Cities*. New York: McGraw Hill, 1977.

5 ———. "Urban Growth and Decline in Western Europe." In *The Metropolis Era*, vol. 1. *See* Dogan and Kasarda above.

6 Kuznets, Simon. *Economic Change*. New York: W.W. Norton, 1953.

7 Lo, Fu-chen, and Narongchai Akrasanee, eds. *The Future of Asian-Pacific Economies: Emerging Role of Asian NIEs and ASEAN*. New Delhi: Allied Publishers, 1991.

8 Mensch, G. *Stalemate in Technology*. Cambridge, Mass.: Ballinger, 1979.

9 Ministry of International Trade and Industry. *MITI White Paper* (Tsusan Hakusho; in Japanese) Tokyo: Government Publication, 1990.

10 Rostow, W.W. "Kondratieff, Schumpeter, and Kuznets: Trend Periods Revisited." *Journal of Economic History* 35 (1975): 719–753.

11 Shinohara, Mayohei, and Fu-chen Lo. *Global Adjustment and the Future of Asian-Pacific Economy*. Tokyo: PMC Publication, 1989.

12 United Nations. *Prospects of World Urbanization*. Population Studies no. 112. New York: United Nations, 1989.

13 ———. *Overall Socio-economic Perspective of the World Economy to the Year 2000*. New York: United Nations, 1990.

14 Van Duijin, J.J. *The Long Wave in Economic Life*. London: George Allen and Unwin, 1982.

15 Vernon, R. "International Investment and International Trade in the Product Cycle." *Quarterly Journal of Economics* 80 (1966): 190–207.

5

Technology and the city

George Bugliarello

President, Polytechnic University, Brooklyn, New York

Abstract

The city is a product of technology, and the rapid evolution of today's city as a highly concentrated centre of services has been made possible by technology.

The potential ability of a city to have direct access to any other city or region in the world, through transportation and telecommunications technology, gives today's city an unprecedented economic and social power, but at the same time, it is changing the population dynamics of the city.

Technology advances have an ever increasing impact on virtually every facet of today's city – from transportation and telecommunications to pollution, housing, water supply, and entertainment. As a rapidly changing and complex technological entity, every major city is in urgent need of a technology policy to guide the key aspects of its socio-technological interactions. The most important aspect of that policy should be the fundamental reshaping of the structure and organization of the city to respond to its new function and its new needs.

Introduction

The concentration of population is the essence of a city. That concentration was made possible, historically, by agriculture and by the development of technologies – however primitive they may have been at the beginning – for supplying the city with water, for eliminating waste, for transporting goods, for building dwellings, and for defence. As cities became more extensive, the spectrum of urban technologies extended to the provision of energy, the communication and storage of information, as well as the conveyance and transportation of city dwellers.

Different degrees and kinds of technological development influenced and continue to influence the evolution of cities [4]. The industrial revolution favoured the concentration of industry in the cities as sites of population needed to operate industry's plants. It also favoured the creation and growth of cities near the sources of energy required by industry to transform materials.

The invention of railroads favoured the development of cities connected by rail networks, just as, from ancient times, the invention of ships and sails had favoured cities with harbours or easy access to harbours and the construction of roads had favoured cities with easier road access to and from other cities and the countryside. Highways and railroads in various combinations have made possible the extended "linear" agglomerations of populations that are encountered in both the developing world and mega-city corridors, like that linking Washington-New York-Boston in the United States.

At the turn of the nineteenth century, the streetcar – as an urban adaptation of the concept of railroads – made possible the shifting of industry to the outskirts of cities and also created the first circle of modern suburbs. The automobile extended that circle very considerably, first in the American cities and now, albeit not always to the same extent, in cities in other continents. At the same time, the creation, in the second half of the nineteenth century, of effective water supply and waste-water treatment works led to very rapid and large increments in the population of most cities, which in the case of large cities began to be much greater than it had been historically for the largest urban concentrations of ancient times.

The population concentrations in the cities led in turn to the invention of technologies like the elevator, which further encouraged that concentration by making tall buildings possible. It also led, already in earlier times, to the creation of a host of services and other infrastructural elements – from hospitals to schools, universities, shops, hotels, restaurants, professional offices, etc. – that became essential and permanent elements of the urban fabric. It can be said that most of these elements of our life are creatures of the city, even if later they spread beyond the city.

The last three major chapters in the relation of technology with the city concern the invention of nuclear weapons, the development of commercial aviation, and the creation of modern information and telecommunications technology. The invention of nuclear weapons has completely and instantaneously destroyed any value the cities might have had in the case of war as a protective device for its dwellers (a value not always certain even in previous times, however, for which examples abound, from Carthage in the Punic Wars to Sevastopol in the Crimean War, to cases of city defences overtaken by a determined besieger and, often, of ensuing slaughter of the city's inhabitants). It is remarkable, however, that the exposure of cities to nuclear weapons has not had any influence on urban development, urban planning, and urban architecture in the past 45 years of the nuclear age.

Far greater have been the impacts of aviation and of information and telecommunications technologies. Aviation has given great impetus to the growth of cities – Atlanta in the US, for example – that were inaccessible to sea transport, transforming them *ipso facto* into international cities. Today, every city with an airport has become part of an international network of cities, the more so if it has direct, non-stop international airline connections. Aviation has also had a direct impact on urban development, by favouring the creation near the airports of new concentrations of infrastructural elements – offices, shipping facilities, housing – as well as of high value added manufacturing. At the same time, the high noise of airport operations, the heavy surface traffic they generate, and their ever growing need for greater space often have made airports into environmentally undesirable neighbours, creating at times serious conflicts as in the case of Narita in Japan.

The ubiquitous presence of information and telecommunication technology is much more difficult to fathom in terms of its impact on the cities. Information and telecommunications have become indispensable ingredients of the urban infrastructure and, even more than aviation, have given every city instant international access and hence a basic international dimension. On the other hand, they have not yet produced on a sufficiently large scale a shift toward the technically feasible work "at home" or in decentralized suburban centres that would have relieved, as it was hoped or theorized, the flow of commuters and the congestion of urban centres. Yet, the current impacts are already very significant. Service operations such as data processing often are being moved to locations far away from the cities they serve – at times even offshore – or have been moved, as in the case of New York City, away from the high priced city core to the outer boroughs of the city. Also, the ability of a city to attract and retain business – the business of a city being overwhelmingly in the service sector of the economy – depends in ever greater measure on the quality of its telecommunications infrastructure [7]. The competition between New York, London, and Tokyo, as well as eventually other cities, to be the leading financial centre depends on many factors but is strongly affected by the power, availability, flexibility, and robustness of the telecommunications infrastructure of each of those cities [6].

In many cities of the economically developing world, however, the picture is somewhat different. The service activities in the city, albeit strong and inevitably growing in importance, are flanked by a strong manufacturing sector, which draws on the city's large concentration of population – as was the case, earlier, for most cities of the developed world.

The two faces of today's cities

The potential ability of a city to have direct access, through aviation and telecommunications technology, to any other city or region of the world and the never abating concentration, in the city or around the city, of the most sophisticated intellectual, cultural, and service activities are giving today's city an unprecedented economic and social power. That power is evidenced by the attraction by today's metropolitan areas (cities plus suburbs) of a very large fraction of the total population of a country.

At the same time, the city – particularly the large city – has also become a major focus of problems in our society. This is so for a variety of factors, ranging from the city's own management inadequacies to its dependence on higher government jurisdictions (with often insufficient resources allocated to the city's infrastructural and social needs), to the magnet the city represents for immigrants and job seekers and the shelter it offers, however inadequately, to the indigent. As a result, today many large cities throughout the world have old and inadequate infrastructures, are congested and polluted beyond tolerable limits, and possess a mass of hard-core and marginalized unemployed. Furthermore, in the measure that a city is dependent on technology, it is vulnerable to failure of technology – to major disruptions in power supply, transportation, and telecommunications. It is also vulnerable to the actions – such as strikes – of those who operate these technological systems, as well as to sabotage.

Thus the paradox of the large city is that, while its attraction for business, culture, and the professions is unsurpassed, the city is also unsurpassed in concentrating within itself the most difficult social problems of our time – poverty, disease, alienation, despair, neuroses, as well as social unrest and failures of complete technological systems. These problems are not necessarily created by the city or the technologies embodied in the city, but are more evident in the city and exacerbated by it.

The response to this paradox has usually been the shift of a substantial portion of the white-collar population to the suburbs, while the urban core retains only the most affluent, as well as the poorer segment of the population, which is tethered to the services the city offers, however imperfectly.

These population shifts, made possible by transportation and telecommunications technology, aggravate the economic plight of the cities in that a large mass of higher income citizens resides outside the cities' administrative jurisdictions and thus weaken fiscally the cities where they work or to which their work is intensively connected.

Technology and the city in the future

In the future, technology will continue to influence crucially the structure, function, and demography of cities. This influence will demand that critical choices be made for all cities, but particularly for the mega-cities, in the developed as well as in the developing world. For instance, only by strengthening the transportation and telecommunications infrastructure will it be possible to counteract the paralysing traffic congestion. Such strengthening requires the critical study of a series of trade-offs: rail versus road; train versus aeroplane; concrete (that is, further construction in the urban core) versus electronics (that is, decentralization through telecommunications); land versus water transport; addressing the problems of the handicapped by modifying elements of the infrastructure (e.g. creating ramps) versus creating new kinds of self-propelled vehicles.

To go into some issues in greater detail, in transportation the current trends in air transport techno-economics (large planes, greater network efficiency) contribute to making the cities into transportation hubs, creating, at the same time, the need to reinforce the ground infrastructure much beyond its current capacity. The same is true for the development of high speed trains, which can operate economically only between major centres of population.

The growing concentration of population in metropolitan areas (albeit ever more in the suburbs of those areas) reinforces these trends and the need for strengthening the transportation infrastructure within metropolitan areas. To the extent that cities will succeed in doing so, they will be able to counteract the growing threat of congestion. But they will succeed only partially unless new kinds of urban personal vehicles, new intermodal transportation systems, and new command and control systems for traffic are developed.

Cities, as destinations and loading points of much freight volume, will also benefit from better intermodal links and more advanced naval architecture (currently at a plateau). Economy, comfort, and environmental reasons will favour in certain regions with high ratios of coast length to land surface area the development or resurgence of maritime passenger and freight transport.

Telecommunications will contribute to containing congestion by encouraging the trend toward suburban relocation of offices and industrial plants – and associated shifts of residential patterns. Less likely will be major shifts of the workforce toward rural areas, although they would be technically possible because of the existence of telecommunications. In addition, telecommunications will be an instrument for enhanced commercial competition between cities, so that the strength of the telecommunication infrastructure, the quality of life, and the tax burdens will be major factors in the ability of a city to compete.

Water supply will be an increasingly difficult problem for large metropolitan areas, particularly in their suburbs, where population dispersion is more likely to lead to mining the aquifers rather than resorting to water storage reservoirs and centralized supply systems. Major efforts will have to be made by metropolitan areas to guarantee for themselves a water supply adequate for their populations. Hence we can expect the development of a new set of highly ambitious public works to capture and convey water from far away – particularly in mega-cities in arid climates. These efforts will have to be coupled with strong conservation measures that will employ very advanced technology at the user's level.

Energy and power supply, another weak spot of the cities, will continue to keep cities – but for very few exceptions – tributary to distant sources of energy and will require major advances in conservation technology, not only in terms of user practices but also in the design of buildings. This should lead in turn to new forms of urban architecture, in which, as in the case of a home appliance, the total operating cost of a building over its foreseeable lifetime receives much more weight than is the case now. (Suffice it to think of the energy costs of very tall buildings or all-window buildings designed in an era of cheap energy.)

Pollution, in all of its various forms, will tend to increase with the population and with the spread of the city. Cities will have to make a major technological effort to make that increase more linear rather than exponential – a difficult challenge, as the very spreading of a city changes, for instance, the microclimate of the region, reducing its powers of recuperation. A more ambitious and long-range technological effort should be focused on making a city as autonomous as possible in terms of waste treatment, through a combination of conservation measures, recycling, and *in situ* treatment. The modern odyssey of New York City garbage barges roaming the seas in search of an accepting disposal site is a harbinger of this need. A particular form of pollution that many cities will have to address and that will become an ever more significant determinant of the quality of city life is noise. Reduction of noise is synergistic with the reduction of air pollution and the addressing of congestion. It demands a rethinking of the interaction between transportation needs and the other functions of the city, such as housing, business, and leisure activities, and it also demands the redesigning of urban vehicles, construction equipment, emergency signalling devices, intersections, etc.

Entertainment and cultural facilities also present a significant technological challenge. One of the key attractions of the city – in spite of the electronic media – is the ability to offer live programmes made financially possible by large audiences. The design of these facilities will need to become increasingly integrated with transportation systems and with the fabric of the city (as in the case of Madison Square Garden in New York, built on top of a major railroad station).

In brief, technology will contribute ever more, with these and other tangible and intangible elements, to a multiplication of the number of mega-cities and to an increase in the population concentration of most urban areas. Technology will also make the cities, more and more, into centres and capitals of the service economy. There are, however, some sociological dangers in making a city exclusively into a service centre, as manufacturing activities – of a kind that makes sense – not only give impulse to creativity and entrepreneurship but also provide jobs in many larger cities for the vast population of the disenfranchised, who otherwise would be unemployable.

Perhaps the most essential future contributions of technology to the city revolve around the concept of system, with all that it implies, and the making available of unprecedented sensing, communication, information, and feedback (as well as "feed-forward") capabilities for managing systems. The concept of system is necessary to guide the much needed integration of supply and services, as well as the integration with systems of other cities [5]. Sensing, communication, information, and feedback capabilities are keys to systems integration and to the effective economic performance of city systems. They also reinforce the function of the city as a centre for services with worldwide, real time connections through global networks of computers and humans. These "hyperintelligent" global connections now on the horizon [2] are going to drastically affect the business dynamics, education, and social dynamics of the city. They will accelerate the trend to locate offices operating at a distance from the main office, as is exemplified in New York City by Citicorp and some elements of Metrotech, a complex of facilities catalysed by a university (Polytechnic University) that has attracted, at a very short distance from the financial district of Wall Street, a considerable segment of the technological operations for that district. They will also make possible "24 hour" international design teams operating in real time around the clock [2], as well as the easier coexistence of a city's culture with a world culture.

The most significant impact of the concept of system, however, is that it underscores the importance of the multiple socio-technological interfaces in the city – that is, of the interfaces between technologies and social systems or social forces. These interfaces are the locus of major opportunities, but also of major problems. The opportunities are exemplified by what happened, historically, when technology and social forces reinforced each other in the development of water supplies or of urban rail [4]. The problems of the socio-technological interface in the city are exemplified by our failures in health care, housing, or education to effectively use technologies already well developed in order to make a major impact on problems that are among the most vexing in many cities. Taxation, zoning, urban jurisdiction, and subsidies for services are other examples in various areas in which the socio-technological interface will play an ever increasing role.

From a technological viewpoint, in the future, the city will be increasingly a centre for the development of new technologies responding to the needs of rapidly growing urban concentrations. The city is truly a new technological frontier, in which the *users* of technology are going to play a far greater part than they do today in technological innovations.

Toward a redefinition of the mega-city

Customarily, any city with a population above an arbitrarily established threshold (usually several millions) is defined as a mega-city. Such a definition, however useful for demographic purposes, leaves much to be desired. It does not reflect the great variety of urban focuses that may be associated with a given population concentration. Neither does it reflect the truly unique features that differentiate functionally a mega-city from other cities.

A socio-technological view of the city suggests a functional approach to defining a mega-city (and, for that matter, other kinds of cities) by focusing on the relation between size (demographically and spatially) and other features, characteristics, and functions of the city.

For instance, just to list a few parameters, in terms of population, what percentage does the city represent of the total population of the country? Athens, with one half of the population of Greece, is certainly a mega-city in terms of its share of population, even if it may not exceed a standard global threshold. (This suggests the *relativity* of the mega-city concept.)

In terms of wealth generation, what percentage of the gross national product is generated by the city?

In terms of institutions, be they involved in health care, education, culture and entertainment, or finance, what is their concentration and significance with respect to the rest of the country? The abundance of certain institutions, such as major museums, stock exchanges, research universities, or tertiary health care centres, is also a functionally defining characteristic of a mega-city.

In terms of transportation and telecommunications, what is the fraction of a country's transportation networks that is centred in the city?

In terms of congestion, what is the average commuting time for workers in the city from their residence to their place of work, or the time to cross the city?

Clearly no one characteristic is sufficient to define a mega-city, or any other kind of city. Yet, taken together, characteristics of this type respond more effectively to our need to understand and define the mega-city than a simple demographic figure. Thus an important area of research on mega-cities should be concerned with the systematic comparative study of these and other pertinent characteristics.

Demography and technology

It is appropriate at this point to underscore the relationship in the city between technology and demography. Technological factors affect both positively and negatively the population in a metropolitan area; those that increase it positively include sanitation (a highly technological process); hospitals; jobs made possible by technology – in agriculture, industry, and services – facilities for handicapped, old-fashioned databases (such as libraries), vertical transportation (elevators), and horizontal transportation (railroads, streetcars, buses, taxis, etc.). Factors that tend to decrease the population in a metropolitan area include new kinds of data banks (that is, electronic distributed data banks that allow for decentralization of the repositories of information such as libraries or record offices that are so critical an element of modern life); reduction of fertility through technical or social means (except when cultural or social factors work against it); the hostile environment of the city in comparison to the more benign one of the countryside; and epidemics that find in the city a high concentration of potential victims.

It should also be noted that several of these factors are ambiguous. Information, for instance, helps to both concentrate and disperse. Transportation does the same.

A number of technological factors, directly or indirectly, tend to increase the quality of life – by increasing life spans and providing a more affluent and comfortable and hence healthier life. There are others, however, that tend to decrease the quality of life in the city by providing a more fertile ground for crime and by engendering anomie because of the psychological imbalance between the human scale and the massive scale of the city.

Finally, a modest technological investment often has a major impact on the demography of a city. Technology does not have to be very "high-tech" in order to have such an impact. Consider, for example, the impact of asphalt paving, or streetcars, housing, water filtration, sewers. These are all technologies that have been around for a long time.

The city as an ecological device

Pollution and the difficult problems of water supply and waste disposal tend to obscure the fact that the modern city is also a very crucial ecological device.

In the first place, the city concentrates population that otherwise, if spread over the countryside, would do irreparable ecological damage. For instance, the population of New York City, if evenly spread over the state of New York, would increase by nearly one-third the population density of the countryside. This would create new demands for transportation facilities, new encroachments on natural resources, greater mining of aquifers, etc., as well as nearly intractable problems in living with waste, given the absence of concentrated centres of production and collection.

Secondly, the cities, as they concentrate the population from the countryside, experience major reductions in birth rate with respect to the countryside. This is generally so throughout the world, except when cities have a core of alienated, unemployed, or undereducated population with a high rate of unwanted pregnancies.

In the third place, the cities, with their high concentration of waste production and the potential for recycling, have the best potential for innovative solutions to the treatment of waste.

These factors suggest the possibility of establishing as a goal for cities a high degree of self-reliance with their own waste problems. In turn, national and international environmental policies, as well as population policies (where they exist), should take into account these important ecological functions of cities and provide incentives to the cities to continue to carry out such functions.

Technology policies for the city

The concept of a technology policy for a city is generally far removed from the thinking of city governments and electorates. Yet, as a complex technological entity, the city requires the guidance of a technology policy for the coordinated and synergistic development of its technological systems and for its technological interactions with the rest of the world [3]. Mega-cities have populations that exceed those of many countries that have technology policies as a matter of course. Even smaller cities would benefit from the development of such policies, as the investment in their technological systems can exceed that of many large corporations.

A city's need for a technology policy becomes even more evident and pressing as one considers not only the city proper as an administrative jurisdiction but also the city with its surroundings. Thus, in the case of New York City, one must also consider portions of New Jersey, Long Island, and southern Connecticut – a region of over 20 million inhabitants – which together form the New York City metropolitan area. The gross regional product of the region exceeds the gross national product of Canada, China, Brazil, or Sweden – all countries with well-developed science policies and science policy mechanisms.

Clearly, the technology policy of a city must be geared to the city's geopolitical and economic environment. There are, however, constants in technology policies that are valid for all cities that are determined to use technology to their best advantage in the future. These constants include:

1. Identification of "critical masses" of technological needs within the city in areas such as health care, education, transportation, business, culture, or housing.
2. Encouragement of innovation and entrepreneurship to respond to these needs.
3. Development of policies to create more effective multi-modal transportation systems, to increase the efficiency of transport within the city, reduce pollution, and counteract the disastrous impact of the growing number of cars.
4. Encouragement of alternate energy-efficient low-pollution urban vehicles. Such a development can capitalize on the great concentration and relatively short travelling radii of vehicles in cities.
5. Development of more effective user charges, taking advantage of new technologies such as bar codes to make it possible for the specific users of a major element of the infrastructure, such as a highway or bridge, to pay as they go. This, in turn, will provide incentives for innovation in the infrastructure by providing better means for a direct return to the innovator-entrepreneur.
6. Adoption of total quality approaches. These approaches have

been very successful in industry and can find a fertile ground in improving the operation of a city's infrastructure and municipal bureaucracies, to the greater satisfaction of the public.

7. Addressing, in general, the greatest need of a city as a technological entity – namely the most effective integration of its various infrastructural systems, resorting also extensively to communication, command, and control approaches (including sensors and satellite technology). The goal is to enable the various systems of a city to perform on demand more effectively, to better control and schedule the delivery of water, power, gas, waste collection, health care, and other services, and to better identify emergencies and trouble spots.
8. Provision of incentives for faster construction. This is one of the most urgent needs in cities where a growing population and an aging or inadequate infrastructure constantly under construction or repair are causing a dramatic increase in traffic jams. The duration of construction and repair jobs in most cities is much too long, leading to economic losses because of the time wasted by people in traffic and the long-term alienation and exodus they cause of the most affluent.
9. Encouragement of new designs and materials for the city infrastructures and dwellings to reduce costs and improve effectiveness.
10. Establishment of consortia with other cities that will give greater incentives to the producers of the new technologies needed by the cities. This is necessary because most cities, standing alone, do not have the resources for the creation of major new technologies, such as a new and efficient urban car.

A new view of the city

In its 6,000 year history the city has evolved from a centre of trade and artisanship (Nineveh, Venice) to one of manufacturing (Liverpool, Pittsburgh) to one of services (London, New York, Tokyo).

The modern mega-city is above all a centre of services. This is so in the developed world and is beginning to be so also in the developing world. However, neither the form nor the organization of the city [1] has corresponded yet to this last historic evolutionary phase. A new view of form and organization is needed, based on both the characteristics and the opportunities that being a centre of services entails. Those characteristics and opportunities are beginning to be better understood only now, given the speed with which the transformation to being almost exclusively a centre for services has occurred, and given also the speed with which technology is influencing that transformation. For instance, we are beginning to understand that:

1. As a major centre of population, the city is bound to exert a major socio-political influence – one that will make the cities somewhat akin to the city-states of the Middle Ages and that demands the development of a city's technology policy.
2. The city has a potential for becoming a centre of new technological opportunities because of the concentration of needs, the presence of "critical masses" of needs for artifacts – such as computers, incinerators, or traffic signals – and critical masses of population in need, such as patients in virtually every category of disease.
3. The city is becoming a complex and most influential element of a global hyperintelligence network. Some elements of that network are already in existence, influencing much of the business that is transacted in the city (e.g. stock exchanges, work of corporate headquarters, media, design and consulting organizations). The hyperintelligent network has the potential for extending the web of relationships among cities and between cities and the rest of the world, for influencing education, and for creating new world views.

These and other major potentials of the city as a centre of services made possible by technology need to be reflected in the organization and physical plans of the city – by, for instance,

1. The creation of new complexes of techno-commercial activities next to a major area of services. Examples are Metrotech in New York and the Medflex facility now being planned in Chicago to concentrate the activities that support the operation of the very large medical centre of that city. The creation of these complexes of techno-commercial services has not been taken into account thus far in planning for future cities. Yet it can have a very beneficial impact on the efficiency of services, in the generation of jobs and new technological and business activities, and in the physical renewal of the city (including the creation or rehabilitation of housing and the reorientation of the transportation infrastructure to serve these new needs).
2. The creation of new "high-tech" and manufacturing districts in the city to respond to the opportunities that the city offers to supply its own needs in a variety of areas as outlined earlier.

3. Similarly, the creation of new centres for software to supply the very large software needs of the service sector and also to take advantage of the large population in the city that has or can acquire software skills.
4. The orientation of the education system to serve more directly the city's needs (such as service jobs, upper level training for the kind of entrepreneurship that responds to the needs of the city, and management of hyperintelligent networks.)
5. The creation of a strong technology policy and development office at the top echelon of city government, with three key tasks. In the first place, to help the city marshal its technological and scientific resources, including universities, research laboratories, and other pertinent institutions. Secondly, to coordinate the technological aspects of the myriad of systems and services within the city administration. Thirdly, and most importantly, to serve as a catalyst for socio-technological innovation.

Conclusion

The rapid evolution of today's city as a highly concentrated centre of services has been made possible by technology. Yet, technology as a system with its own dynamics, its own possibilities, as well as its own constraints, is rarely in the forefront of the consciousness of administrators and citizens. Rare is the city that has technology advisory mechanisms, commissions on technology, etc., and rare are the planning agencies that have the same level of expertise in assessing the impact of telecommunications as that of architectural designs, transportation, and recreational or shopping districts. Lacking, furthermore, is an integrated set of statistics about the functional characteristics of the city that may help to better define and compare mega-cities around the world.

Thus, the modern city is at a crossroads regarding its future. It can continue to operate as an extrapolation of its past, endeavouring, with increasing difficulty, to patch up its structures and operations so as to try to cope with a new dynamic it cannot control. Or the city can take bold steps to project itself into the future and be in command of this newest phase of its evolution. It can do so only by reshaping itself fundamentally in all of its elements and functions from infrastructure to organization, from education to economic development.

References

1 Bacon, Edmund N. *Design of Cities*. New York: Penguin, 1967.

2 Bugliarello, George. "Toward Hyperintelligence." *Knowledge: Creation, Diffusion, Utilization* 10 (September 1988), no. 1: 67–89.

3 Mayor's Commission for Science and Technology. *Science and Technology in New York City for the 21st Century*. New York: Polytechnic Press, December 1989.

4 National Academy of Engineering. R. Hanson, ed. *Perspectives of Urban Infrastructure*. Washington, D.C.: National Academy Press, 1984.

5 ———. Jesse H. Ausubel and R. Herman, eds. *Cities and Their Vital Systems. Infrastructure Past, Present, and Future*. Washington, D.C.: National Academy Press, 1988.

6 New York City Partnership. *The $1 Trillion Gamble: Telecommunications and New York's Economic Future*. New York: New York City Partnership, June 1990.

7 Office of Technology Assessment. *International Competition in Services*. Washington, D.C.: US Government Printing Office, 1987.

Part 2
Economic and social consequences of mega-city growth

6

The redistributive role of mega-cities

Laurent Davezies and Rémy Prud'homme

The authors are respectively Director/Professor and Professor, Observatoire de l'Économie et des Institutions Locales (L'OEIL), University of Paris XII, Créteil

Introduction

It is very difficult to use the concept of mega-city, which seems to refer to a specific and different concept than "large" or "largest" cities. Mega-cities should be defined more by their weight in the world than in their countries. For example, it is possible to propose a concept of "agglomerations of 10 millions and above," including cities like Mexico, São Paulo, or Shanghai, but also, in developed countries, Los Angeles, New York, or Tokyo. But, what could be the lessons from a comparison between such different cities? Whatever the field of analysis, what differentiates them seems more important than what makes them comparable. Many authors state how difficult it is to use the notion of city size (population, area, output, etc.), but despite these difficulties, there are obvious examples: some cities in the world are now giants, Mexico City, for example, which has more than 15 million people.

Are such absolute giants relative giants too? It is not so clear. Table 1 shows that the relative weight of the biggest cities in national urban populations is not so important.

The weight of giant cities like Mexico City, Shanghai, Calcutta, and São Paulo appears in fact to be less important than the weight of

Table 1 **Weight of the biggest cities in national urban population (selected countries, 1980)**

Lower income	13	Intermediate lower	34	Intermediate higher	27	Higher income	19
Lagos	17	Cairo	39	São Paulo	15	London	20
Shanghai	6	Bangkok	69	Buenos Aires	45	Paris	23
Calcutta	6	Istanbul	24	Seoul	41	Tokyo	22
Jakarta	23	Bogotá	26	Teheran	28	New York	12
		Santiago	26				
		Mexico City	32				

Source: *World Development Report 1989* (Washington, D.C.: Oxford University Press/World Bank, 1989).

most of the primate cities in countries of the same income classes. Mega-cities are very different, because they are the product of two effects: (1) an economic effect and (2) a national size effect.

These two effects play different roles: the former effect, as it is possible to see in table 1, is that the primacy index, in most countries, grows with economic development and, after a certain level, begins to decrease. It is another statement of the Williamson law [11] on regional disparities. The share of the primate city in urban population in the 1980s went from 13 per cent in lower income countries to 34 per cent in the lower intermediate income countries; 27 per cent in the upper intermediate income countries, and 19 per cent in the higher income countries. The size of cities like Mexico City (32 per cent) is the product of this effect.

The latter effect, i.e. national size effect, is related to the size of the country. The weight of urban population of primate cities in lower intermediate income countries like Lebanon (79 per cent), Jamaica (66 per cent), or Senegal (65 per cent) do not produce mega-cities because these countries are not populous. Contrarily, mega-cities in higher income countries are produced by large, populous countries like Japan or the United States.

So the size of primate cities is a function of the level of development of a country and also of the size of the country, as shown in figure 1. So what produces and what constitutes a mega-city depend on the mix of these two effects.

Another topic of academic and political focus today is the speed of growth of the largest cities. Looking at the available data, it is interesting to observe that, in the last decades, the biggest growth has not been experienced by the biggest cities (mega-cities). Looking at the largest cities of the developing countries in 1980, it is possible to show that the larger the city is today, the lower its rate of population growth was in the 1950–1980 period (although immigration in the biggest agglomerations, such as Shanghai, Beijing, or Moscow, was administratively restricted). This suggests that the problem of tomorrow will be less the problem of the development of current "mega-cities" but more the problem of future mega-cities (figure 2).

The data in figure 2 can be interpreted to suggest that the joint effect of the rapid increase of national populations – or increasing opening of borders within some regions (national effect) – in developing countries and the low pace of development (economic effect) will be that many current secondary cities (at the world scale) will soon be very large cities. So an analysis for the future of mega-cities has to

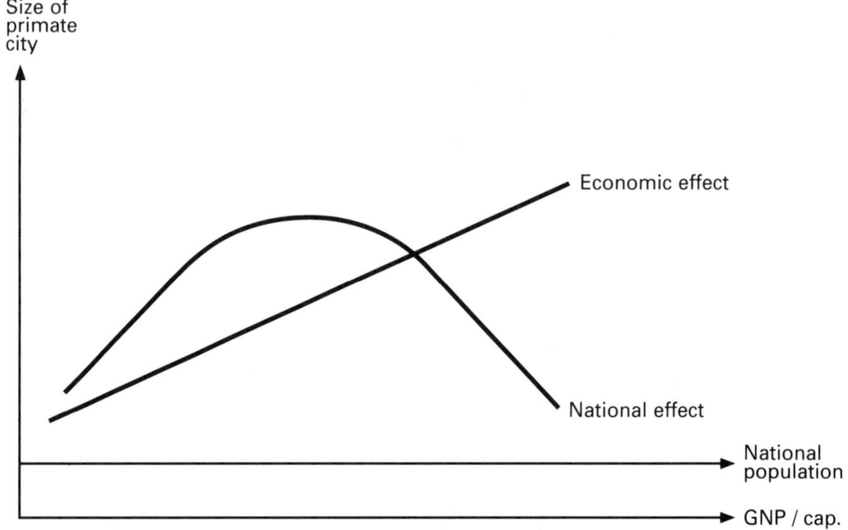

Fig. 1 **The primate city size as a function of national population size and level of development of the country**

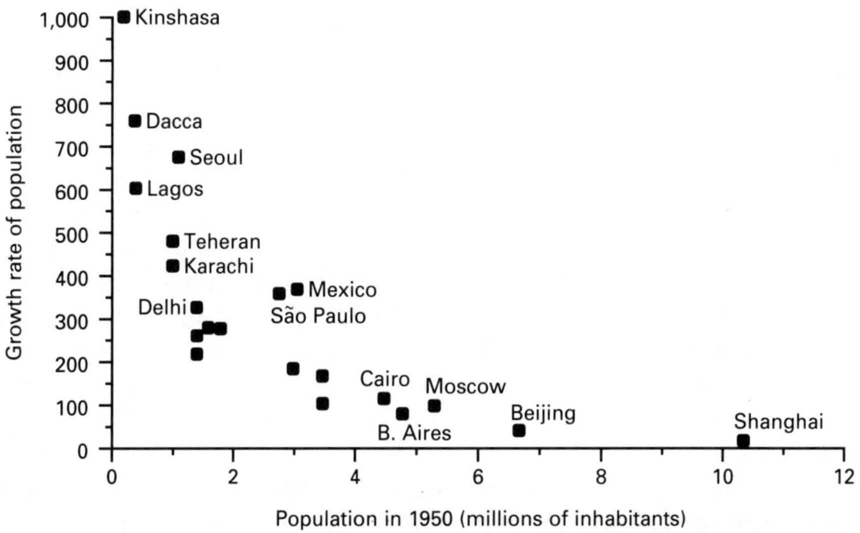

Fig. 2 **Population growth between 1950 and 1980 of the current largest cities of the developing countries (Source: United Nations, *Urban and Rural Population Projections 1950–2025: The 1984 Assessment* [New York, 1986])**

give attention to all the primate cities of large countries, particularly in the developing countries. In 1980, there were 125 developing metropolises, each accounting for more than 1 million inhabitants. In 2000, according to United Nations estimates, there will be 300 cities of 1 million in the world.

There is a common view regarding this strong urban concentration in both developed and developing countries. Politicians and academics agree generally that big cities are too big and that policies should aim at reducing them. Urban and regional policies in most of these countries have tried and continue to try to stop or reverse the growth of the largest cities. The rationale for these policies is that these cities are dead weight that hinder development, exploit the rest of the country, which would be far better off if the size or the growth rate of these cities could be reduced.

During the 1980s, a change in this way of seeing these large cities began to emerge. For more and more people, but still few, large cities, far from being a burden on the economy, are "locomotives" that drive their countries as a whole along the path of progress. Higher earnings in large cities merely reflect higher productivity, which in turn implies "agglomeration economies." Manufacturing, commerce, banking, and services, which represent the most dynamic sectors of the economy, are concentrated in large cities, which are development poles benefiting to the rest of the country.

We shall not attempt here to assess these arguments on the natural trends of the private sector economy – which are often more ideological than quantitative – and thus close the discussion. We shall rather focus on the public part of the economy (between 25 and 50 per cent of the GNP in most countries) and continue this discussion with an analysis of a phenomenon general for all the primate – and particularly the large primate – cities: their redistributive role.

As Musgrave [6] has explained, public policies have three tasks or functions: allocation, stabilization, and redistribution. There is a huge literature about each of these functions, and particularly about the redistribution between people or between households. But not much attention has been paid to the spatial redistribution produced by public policies. There is agreement among politicians and journalists that the large cities gain in the game of public policy, but little serious research has been done on this subject.

We shall examine what kind of redistribution mechanisms between large cities and the rest of the country are produced by public policy. The most important and perceptible expression of public policies is national budgets. There are many other public policies producing spatial transfers: public pricing, protection of selected sectors, and credit policy are examples. All of these policies produce a disequilibrium and transfers between the agents and also between large cities and other parts of the respective countries. In a later section of this paper, we shall make a brief survey of recent or current changes in the economies and policies in most of the countries of the world in order to understand what kind of impacts these changes could have on these redistributive mechanisms.

Budget induced transfers

Every national budget collects and spends money throughout the country. On average in the world, national budgets represent a quarter of the gross national product. This means that very important amounts are collected and distributed, producing important transfers, because there is no reason why the gains of a given area would be equal to the contributions of that area. Do the contributions of primate cities exceed their gains? and if so, by how much?

In an effort to answer these questions, four studies were undertaken at L'OEIL (Laboratoire d'Observation de l'Economie et des Institutions Locales, University of Paris XII) that endeavoured to determine budget receipts and expenditures between the primate city and the rest of the country in the cases of Côte d'Ivoire, France, Morocco, and Thailand.

The concept of city used in these four studies was that of agglomeration. Table 2 shows the weight of these four primate cities in their countries. The fiscal year used for the studies was 1984 for Côte d'Ivoire [5] and France [1], 1987 for Thailand [7], and 1982 for Morocco [4]. A specific methodology was elaborated in a previous study of the 1976 fiscal year in France [3]. It is important to note that, for each of these studies, we used the accounting data of the year for recurrent items (taxes, wage expenditures, etc.) and created five or ten year mean figures for non-recurrent items (investment expenditures) to give a more general answer to the question and to avoid producing conclusions biased by a too specific fiscal year.

These studies make the same methodological choices in dealing with the important conceptual and statistical problems. The conceptual problems lie mainly in the definition of what is a "contribution" to and what is a "gain" from the national budget.

What is contributed by an area is not what is actually paid and

Table 2 **Demographic weight of Abidjan, Bangkok, Casablanca, and Paris in their respective countries**

	Primate city		Rest of country		Total
	Millions	%	Millions	%	Millions
Côte d'Ivoire (1984)	1.7	18.0	7.8	82.0	9.5
Thailand (1987)	7.3	13.6	46.57	86.4	53.9
Morocco (1982)	2.5	12.0	18.5	88.0	21.0
France (1984)	10.0	18.2	44.9	81.8	54.9

Note: The agglomerations of the primate cities are defined as follows:
Abidjan: *Communes* of Abidjan, Treichville, Plateaux, Adjamé, Marcory, Koumassy, Yopougon, Abobo, Port-Bouet, and Attecoube.
Bangkok: Greater Bangkok defined as Bangkok Metropolitan Area plus three provinces: Nonthaburi, Pathum Thani, and Samut Prakan.
Casablanca: The 1982 *willaya* of Casablanca
Paris: The *région* Ile de France.

collected in the area. The corporate income tax, for instance, is collected at the place where the headquarters of a corporation is located, and available accounting data show that a major part of that tax is collected in primate cities: such figures are meaningless and must simply be ignored.

The corporate income tax is supported partly by capital owners, by wage earners, and by product buyers, so the burden of this tax could be allocated between the areas proportionally to their share of private capita or to wages paid or to goods purchased, or proportionally to a combination of these criteria. So there is not only one answer to the question of the incidence of a tax in an area.

It is even more difficult to identify the gains of an area. At least, two notions must be distinguished: the notion of flow and that of benefit. According to the flow concept, the "gains" of an area are the amount of money spent from the budget in this area: wages paid, purchase from enterprises in the area, etc. According to the benefit concept, the gains of an area are the share of services produced by budgetary procedures and that benefit this area. For many budgetary expenditures and for each of the concepts, there are often several meaningful criteria.

These conceptual difficulties are compounded by statistical deficiencies. Even when we know what concept we want to utilize, the statistical data necessary, particularly in developing countries, are not available, and it is often necessary to resort to proxies.

Table 3 **Coefficient of dispersion of the evaluations of the weight in the national budget of the primate cities in Côte d'Ivoire, Thailand, Morocco, and France**

	Contribution	Gains (benefit)	Gains (flow)
Abidjan	0.01	0.03	0.001
Bangkok	0.04	0.06	0.03
Casablanca	0.001	0.002	0.0004
Paris	0.009	0.002	0.03

Sources: For Côte d'Ivoire, ref. 5; for France, ref. 1; for Thailand, ref. 7; for Morocco, ref. 4.
Note: The national budgets were divided into:
60 items of revenue and 70 items of expenditure for Côte d'Ivoire;
147 items of revenue and 94 items of expenditures for Thailand;
61 items of revenue and 80 items of expenditures for Morocco; and
60 items of revenue and 303 items of expenditures for France.

The combination for all the budgetary items of the conceptual choices and of the statistical proxies produces an enormous number of possible evaluations of the weight of the large cities in national budgets. It was impossible to calculate all of them, so we preferred to make, for each country, three samples of 100 random combinations for, respectively, (1) the share of revenue contributed by the primate city, (2) its share of "benefit" gains, and (3) its share of "flow" gains. These calculations produced, for each city, a set of estimates of these different amounts. If, for each of these 100 calculations, the range of estimates was very large, this procedure would not mean much. Fortunately, it turned out not to be large. The dispersion coefficients (standard error divided by mean value) of these estimations are all very low, as shown in table 3.

With such a low disparity of all these sets of results, it was relevant to use the median result of each to give a synthetic answer to the question of the weight of the primate city in the national budget. The results are quite striking (table 4). In each of these very different countries, the contribution of the primate city largely exceeds the gains, whether evaluated in terms of flow or of benefits.

In each of the countries studied, the transfers financed by the primate cities in terms of flow are smaller than the gains in terms of benefit. This is easy to understand: in terms of "flow" allocation, the wages of civil servants are allocated to their place of work and housing, so the capital cities get a lot of money from this budget expenditure. This is still true for Abidjan, which is no longer the capital city of Côte d'Ivoire but still concentrates a lot of administration. The difference between the flow and the benefit gains is less important for

Table 4 **Budget induced transfers: Abidjan vs. Côte d'Ivoire (1984), Bangkok vs. Thailand (1987), Casablanca vs. Morocco (1982), Paris vs. France (1984)**

	Abidjan	Bangkok	Casablanca	Paris
Contribution to the budget as a % of budget	54.2	41.1	33.8	26.1
Gains (benefits) from the budget as a % of the budget	25.3	28.2	18.0	19.3
Gains (flow) from the budget as a % of the budget	34.0	34.5	20.6	21.1
Transfer (in local currency)				
benefit total	−152 GF	−30.3 GB	−5.9 GDh	−76.0 GFF
per capita	−88 KF	−4.1 KB	−2.4 KDh	−7.6 KF
flow total	−121 GF	−15.6 GB	−4.9 GDh	−55.6 GFF
per capita	−70 KF	−2.1 KB	−2.0 KDh	−5.5 KF
Transfer (in current US$)				
benefit total	−347.8 M	−1,169 M	−979.5 M	−88,695.6 M
per capita	−201.0	−158.0	−398.0	−870.0
flow total	−276.9 M	−602.3 M	−813.5 M	−6,361.5 M
per capita	−163.0	−81.0	−332.0	−629.0
GDP per capita of the country in US$ (1987)	689	899	719	15,708

Sources: On transfers: for Côte d'Ivoire, ref. 5; for France, ref. 1; for Thailand, ref. 7; for Morocco, ref. 4. On GDP: *World Development Report 1989* (Washington, D.C.: Oxford University Press/World Bank, 1989).

Notes: Abbreviations of the national currencies are defined as follows:
F = Franc CFA of Côte d'Ivoire (US$1 = 436.96 F in 1984)
B = Baht of Thailand (US$1 = 25.9 B in 1987)
Dh = Dirham of Morocco (US$1 = 6.023 Dh in 1982)
FF = French Franc (US$1 = 8.74 FF in 1984).
K = thousand, M = million, G = billion.

Casablanca, because the primate city of Morocco is not the capital city of the country.

It appears that primate cities heavily subsidize the rest of their countries. The amount transferred between the primate city and the rest of the country via the national budget represents, in terms of the benefit concept, 5.3 per cent of the gross domestic product in Côte d'Ivoire, 2.5 per cent in Thailand, 6.5 per cent in Morocco, and 1.7 per cent in France. In the flow approach, this transfer represents 4.2 per cent in Côte d'Ivoire, 1.3 per cent in Thailand, 5.5 per cent in Morocco, and 1.3 per cent in France.

It is possible to argue that these transfers are produced by all the cities and are not a monopoly of primate cities, and that Bouaké in Côte d'Ivoire or Rabat in Morocco also produce a big amount of transfers to the rural areas of their countries. It is probably true, and it would be interesting to calculate these transfers. In the case of France, we studied the allocation of the national budget between the 95 departments of the country and calculated the amount of transfers between these departments. There are large cities in France, like Marseilles, Lyons, or Lille, and the Paris agglomeration accounts for only 24 per cent of the urban population of France. But Paris by itself produces 68 per cent of the "flow" budget induced transfers and 90 per cent of the "benefit" transfers (between 5,500 and 7,500 FF per Paris citizen). By comparison, the two biggest urban agglomerations of France after Paris, Marseilles (considered as the Bouches du Rhône Department) and Lyons (Rhône Department) comprise in total 7.5 per cent of the French urban population and represent as a whole only 1.7 per cent of the "benefit" of interdepartmental transfers, or 0.2 per cent of the "flow" of interdepartmental transfers (between 50 FF and 420 FF per citizen).

These findings are not surprising. They are explained by the fact that in every country, the primate city has a higher income per capita than other parts of the country. Budgetary expenditures per capita do not vary, or vary weakly, as a function of income. Most of the national budget is allocated to general social purposes, such as education, security, general administration. Investment expenditures, which could be more geographically selective, represent generally a small share of the budget, particularly in developing countries, and because of strong agricultural or regional policies, are quite equally allocated among regions (in per capita expenditures).

On the revenue side of the budget, the situation is very different. In all countries, the revenue collected is a function of the income,

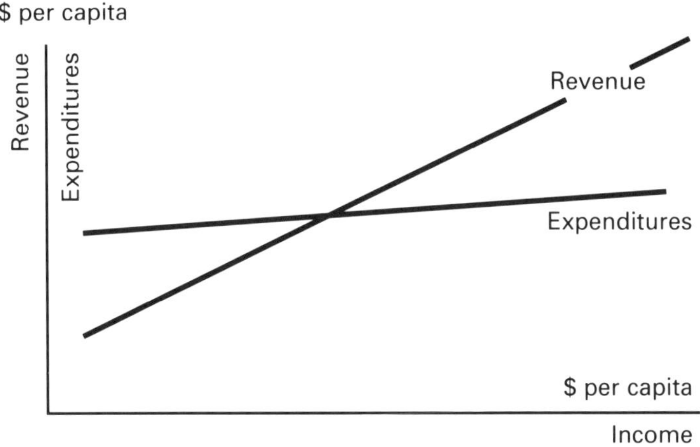

Fig. 3 **Mechanism of spatial redistribution of public funds**

even with a regressive tax system. The higher income per capita of the biggest cities means that each contributes more than what it receives from the national budget. In lower income countries, there is also an important difference in the revenue collected in and out of the urbanized areas, which can be explained by the difference of the rate of recovery of taxes.

The general mechanism of spatial redistribution induced by the national budget works as shown in figure 3.

With these four case-studies there is too little material on which to build a strong general theory on the level of induced budget transfer as a function of (1) the level of development, (2) the primacy index, or (3) the tax and expenditure structure. More simply, these results show that the large concentration of urban population (even in capital cities that are usually considered to get a large benefit from this status) finances more than it consumes of public funds and is thus an important producer of interregional or social redistribution of income. And this point is verified in both developed and developing countries.

Pricing policy induced transfers

National budgets are the main or the most apparent mechanism of redistribution of income from large cities. But some public policies or decisions that do not necessarily have budgetary implications can also produce important income redistribution between the largest cities and their respective countries' other areas. These policies are mainly pricing policies. Government intervention in pricing is to be found in both public and private economies. In most countries, national public agencies operate large public services as public monopolies. The difference between the administrative price of these services and their real cost produces important transfers. The national government can also modify the relative prices of goods and services on the market through, for example, commercial protection policies or price regulation policies.

There is very little research on these subjects, and it is very difficult to give a quantitative measure of each of these phenomena, but it is important to have these flows in mind and to understand their general direction.

Public price induced transfers

Electricity, gas, railroad transportation, air travel, mail, telephone, and telecommunications are examples of services often – if not usually – produced and sold throughout a country by large public enterprises. These institutions usually have a monopoly, as well as an obligation, to service the entire territory. The goods and services they sell have a cost and a price. The important point here is that this cost will often vary spatially: it will be lower or higher in the large city than in the rest of the country. These goods and services are sold at a price, which may or may not be the same in every part of the territory. In many cases and in many countries, the price is similar in every part of the territory: it is then said to be "perequated." There is no a priori reason to think that, in a given part of a territory, the cost and the price of a given service will be equal. In many cases, they are not. When they are not (and when the accounts of the public enterprise providing the service are balanced), some consumers or some areas are paying for others. Are the large cities benefiting or not from such transfers?

It is difficult to give a well-grounded answer to this question, because public price policies vary among countries and also because of conceptual difficulties. The issue of spatial transfers induced by public price policies is even more complex than that of transfers from the national budget. First, it is difficult to define what the cost of delivering a service in a given area should be: Should it be the marginal cost, which varies greatly over time for many of the services considered (such as electricity or telephone)? Should it be the cost of today or the cost of tomorrow (which may be different because of technological progress and/or the induced additional demand over time)? Then, in many cases, such as transportation and telecommunications, the service is not associated with one point in space, but with two: which of the two areas pays the price is difficult to tell. Finally, even if the conceptual problems were settled, the practical difficulties of arriving at figures would be very great. We shall only attempt a cursory discussion of the most important cases.

For electricity, the situation varies from one country to another and, within a country, from one voltage level to another. In France [10], at the beginning of the 1980s, the price of high voltage electricity varied between regions and with respect to production and distribution costs. Paris had the highest price of high voltage electricity in France (around 2 per cent more than the average price) because of transportation costs. But for low and medium voltage, the price is perequated throughout the country. The question is whether the cost of delivering the electricity in Paris is higher because of the transportation costs or whether it is lower because distribution and collection costs are inversely related to density. There is no clear answer to the question.

In Tunisia the situation appeared (in 1973) to be clearer: the only two power plants in the country were both located near Tunis. The price of electricity was perequated throughout the territory. Tunis by itself consumed 40 per cent of this electricity, but, because the cost of transportation was 12 per cent higher in the rest of the country than in Tunis, this perequated price induced a heavy net transfer from Tunis to the rest of the country [8]. Another mechanism of implicit redistribution in developing countries from the large city to the rest of the country lies in the organization of user fee collection: it is easier – or, in certain countries, the only possibility – to collect fees in the largest cities. In Mali, for example [2] the cost of electricity is recovered only in the main city of Bamako, and most bills remain unpaid in the rest of the country. This would also induce transfers from the capital city to the countryside.

Mail distribution most probably gives rise to positive transfers from the largest cities to the other areas of their respective countries. Prices are generally identical for all types of trips. Costs are not, however. The cost of moving a letter from one part of a large city to another is much less than the cost of moving a letter from a city to a small village, which is less than the cost of moving a letter from a small village to another. Generally, the large city pays more for the cost of this service.

The case of telephone service is more important because the amounts involved are substantial. Prud'homme and Savy [10] give an estimate in the case of France of the difference between long distance and local calls in 1980. The price of an intra-urban call was, on average, 23 per cent lower than its cost, and the interurban call price was 233 per cent higher than its cost. The intra-urban calls were heavily subsidized by interurban calls. It is difficult, because there are no detailed consumption data, to form conclusions as to the amount and the direction of the transfer between Paris and the rest of France. In many developing countries, where the telephone is very concentrated in cities, this point is very important and should be evaluated, particularly in countries where the telecom administration is a part of the general administration directly subsidized by the national budget. For example, the city of Tunis, in 1984, accounted for 20 per cent of the Tunisian population, 52 per cent of the telephone consumers, and 66 per cent of telephone service consumption.

The same kind of mechanism is to be found in railroad transportation. In many countries, the companies operating railroad freight or passenger transportation are public entities, with administrative and perequated prices. The cost per kilometre is very different from line to line, however, so the fixed price means the more utilized lines subsidize the less utilized ones.

The general mechanism of redistribution induced by public service prices comes from the fact that public entities very often ignore the large economies of scale produced by large cities. There are probably many good political reasons to maintain such redistributive systems (if one considers that all or most of them transfer from high density to low density areas, which is not verified), but very few to ignore them. We shall see later that as these mechanisms are ignored, the current modifications of public services management in most countries could induce important and involuntary alterations to these mechanisms.

Pricing policy induced transfers

A number of government decisions change relative prices and produce a different allocation of resources inducing important transfers. The spatial dimension of these transfers is generally unknown. There are very few studies on this point. Here and there, in research or policy papers, it is possible to find a reference to mechanisms producing pro-urban or anti-urban biases, but no definitive assessment of this issue seems available. It is, however, a very important field of analysis of the evolution of large cities: depending on whether the large city population grows with and because of its increasing economic efficiency or because it benefits from administrative protection or price distortions, very different conclusions are arrived at. Because external economies are very hard to measure and to portray, there is often the conclusion that large cities are subsidized by the other parts of their respective countries and that they don't pay their real costs and that this fact should explain a large part of the immigration flows into large cities. We saw that this is not true for public funds, for which large cities pay more than they receive, nor for public prices, for which urban economies of scale are often not credited to cities. It is more difficult to draw conclusions for general policies and their impacts on the market and on relative prices.

Let us examine two such policies: the regulation of agricultural product prices in developing countries and import substitution policies.

The regulation of agricultural product prices has a direct implication for transfers between rural and urban areas. A variation in the price of these products has direct implications for the income of both rural and urban households (and thus on migration flows). In developing countries, many governments, for social purposes, penalize local agriculture through their tax policy and encourage imports of food products. This policy increases the purchasing power of urban households and lessens the income of rural ones. On the other hand, in developed countries, governments subsidize agriculture. The OECD estimates that net transfers from consumers and taxpayers to farmers in the OECD zone were US$280 billion in 1988. It is obvious that, in developed countries, large cities heavily subsidize rural areas through agricultural prices.

Import substitution policies are used by governments, particularly in developing countries, to develop local industries. This protection is effected through tariffs or quotas on imported industrial goods. The impact of such protection is an increase in the price of industrial goods and an increase of the quantities produced. Table 5 provides a plausible illustration of this impact.

In this theoretical example, it is possible to observe that the protection of industrial goods produced locally increases in their prices and

Table 5 **Impacts on prices and quantities of protection policy on local industry**

	Industrial goods	Agricultural goods	Total
Before protection			
World price (per unit)	100	100	
Quantities	20	20	
Value	2,000	2,000	4,000
After protection; price effect:			
Nominal price	150	100	
Quantities	20	20	
Value (nominal price)	3,000	2,000	5,000
Inflation rate			+25%
Deflated price	120	80	
Value (real price)	2,400	1,600	4,000
Transfer (tax or subsidy)	+400	−400	0
Transfer (in %)	+20%	−20%	0
After protection; quantity effect:			
Price (real)	120	80	
Quantities	24	16	

Sources: Côte d'Ivoire, ref. 5; France, ref. 1; Thailand, ref. 7; Morocco, ref. 4.

in quantities but also decreases in relative prices and in quantities of agricultural products. Thus, the protection of industrial goods can be considered as a subsidy to industry financed by a tax on agriculture. There is a net transfer from rural to urban areas, where most of the industries in developing countries are located.

The two examples discussed of policies introducing price distortions between rural and urban production and inducing transfers from the countryside to the cities are observed in developing countries. Such policies have generally disappeared in developed countries, and, contrary to developing countries, the freer international competition in industrial goods and the protection of agricultural goods induce in these countries transfers in the opposite direction, from urban to rural areas.

Impacts of recent economic and policy changes

As seen in the previous sections, large cities are producing substantial transfers of income for the benefit of the rest of the countries where they reside. In a given country, developed or developing, the national budget is the main mechanism of redistribution. Perequated price policies can also induce important transfers, generally financed by large cities. Relative price implications of policies are more complex and quite unclear, but it seems that generally, they produce a pro-urban bias in developing countries more than in developed.

The recent and current changes associated with the structural adjustment have and will have implications for these mechanisms, weakening some of them and strengthening others. We shall try to make a rapid overview of these changes: first, changes related to the national budget, second, changes related to public service price policies, and finally, changes related to macroeconomic policy.

The evolution of many factors can determine changes in the amount of transfers induced by the national budget between a large city and the rest of the country. The first is the evolution of the large cities themselves. Among others, the weight of the budget in the national income and the structure of the tax system, which are both changing in many countries, can have important implications for the extent of transfers produced by large cities.

Are the transfers increasing with city size? There is no general answer. If it is clear that generally, the more people living in a city, the more money they transfer totally, it is not clear that this transfer, on a per capita basis, will increase or decrease with an increasing city size. It is even possible to imagine that, other things being equal, both per capita and total transfers begin to decrease. As long as the average productivity of urban dwellers is higher than that of the rest of the country, income will remain higher in the city. An increase or decrease of this difference will induce an increase or decrease in transfers. This evolution, which could be interesting to look at in various cities, depends probably on the national economic situation.

In a developing country, a large city receiving large numbers of poor and unskilled immigrants joining a large unemployed urban population can experience a decrease of the average income of households and, as a consequence, a decrease of the per capita transfers to the rest of the country. This will be the case if, at the same time, (1) the more productive activities in the city do not counterbalance this low productivity and (2) the other parts of the country do not experience an equal or stronger decrease of income. In such a case, the large city, as some authors say about African cities, is becoming, so to say, more rural. Transfers do not go to the people in the country but people come to the city to get directly public advantages. Another large city, which can employ the immigrants and draw out of this crowd of new citizens new external economies and more productivity, will be richer and will produce more per capita transfers. There are no comparable time series data available on income in largest cities, particularly in developing countries, and it is not possible today to determine clearly if one rapidly growing city is getting richer or poorer and as a consequence producing more or fewer transfers.

In developed countries, where the largest cities have experienced over the past 15 years a demographic stagnation or decline, it is possible to have an idea of the evolution of income – and productivity – in the large cities through the evolution of land prices. With the comeback of economic growth after 1985, it is possible to observe a strong urban recentralization in industrial countries. The case of Tokyo is widely known, and other studies in European countries show that urban land prices, particularly in the largest cities, are growing more rapidly than anywhere else. This means that the preference for central locations is very strong and increasing for firms and households. This evolution makes the largest cities richer and richer. The per capita transfers are growing with this growing wealth of large cities. But the overall extent of transfers, all other factors being equal, could decrease because of the demographic decline of some of these cities (though the latest censuses in industrial countries suggest that there is probably a new demographic turn benefiting the large cities).

The weight of the national budget in the national income is another important factor in the degree of transfer. The more money going through the budget, the more that is redistributed. Recent and current evolutions in the relative amount of national budgets are very different in the world, because this weight is a function of two factors. First, the weight of the national budget is a function of the level of development of the country (Wagner Law). Second, the evolution of the weight of the budget is a function of macroeconomic policies. The combination of these two trends makes the evolution different in developing countries and in developed countries.

Developing countries, if they experience economic growth, spend more money in public funds to get more services and infrastructure. So the weight of the national budget in the GDP is generally increasing in these countries: for example, in India, between 1977 and 1986, the share went from 23.5 per cent to 31 per cent, and in Zimbabwe in that period, it rose from 39.4 per cent to 46.2 per cent. It can safely be predicted that, in these countries, the number of transfers financed by the largest cities will increase. It is possible to imagine too that some countries experiencing a hard recession could have, with a constant amount of public funds, an increase in the weight of the budget, financed by a deficit. In this case, there will not be more absolute transfers, but rather the maintenance of their previous level with an increase in the relative weight of these transfers in household income.

In the developed countries, on the other hand, where national public funds reached a ceiling in the 1970s, the general tendency after 1980 was to reduce their relative importance. Between 1983 and 1987, for example, such reductions went from 38.3 per cent to 36.9 per cent in the United States, from 60.6 per cent to 55.6 per cent in Austria, from 49.5 per cent to 48.3 per cent in France, and from 47.3 per cent to 42.1 per cent in the United Kingdom. A reduction of the weight of the national budget makes it less redistributive, even if the absolute number of transfers continues to grow because of growth in the GNP.

Another important evolution for redistributive mechanisms is the current tendency, in most countries, to decentralize some central government functions to lower levels of administration. Decentralization does not always mean an automatic decentralization of taxes. In countries like Italy or the Netherlands, most of the taxes are still collected by the central government (local governments collect only 10 per cent of their total tax revenue) and it is only the expenditure decisions or choices that are decentralized, the central government sharing global or specific grants to local governments. But, in many countries, decentralization does mean the transfer of national taxes and/or of taxation power to local or regional authorities. The redistributive machine between urban and rural areas or between rich and poor regions is, by definition, a national machine. Local taxes are collected and spent in the same area and induce only redistribution at the local level; there is no transfer between rich and poor areas, between large cities and the rest of the country.

It is difficult to give comparative quantitative measures of the decrease in central government revenue linked to the rise of local taxation in developed and developing countries. Data are not yet available because of the huge statistical, but also conceptual, problems of general definition of local revenue components (the IMF is supposed to offer such data in the near future in its *Government Finance Statistics Yearbook*). It is likely that the share of taxes collected by local governments is still very low in most of the traditionally centralized countries. In France, for example, after years of decentralization efforts, local taxes, which were 14.5 per cent of national taxes in 1975, were only 18.8 per cent in 1986. But if this increase is still not very important, it is important to know that its cost is less spatial redistribution, and particularly from large cities.

A last evolution is related to the evolution of the structure of national budgets. The more progressive the tax system, the more it feeds the redistribution mechanism. The income tax or the corporate income tax are, in all countries, the most income-related taxes. During recent years it is possible to observe in most developed countries a regular decrease of the marginal rate of the income tax and of the rate of the corporate income tax. This means again a weakening of the redistributive mechanisms of the national budget. Contrarily, in the developing countries, there were few changes in the rates of taxes on income and profits. What is quite surprising is to observe that there was the same kind of evolution of the share of these taxes in total government revenues in both developed and developing countries. Between 1982 and 1987, the share of taxes on income and profit went from 41.2 per cent to 40.1 per cent in the industrial countries and from 24.68 per cent to 22 per cent in the developing countries: this similar trend is explained by less tax on more income in the industrial countries and the same tax on less income in the developing countries (in Africa, the share of these taxes fell from 47.5 per cent to 39.5 per cent during this period).

In the area of public services prices, there is also an evolution that has implications for their redistributive function. In both developed and developing countries, there is a general tendency to improve the management of public services by privatization (linked to a growing international competition in services like telecommunications) or at least by a better consideration of marginal costs. Economic or financial thinking takes precedence over political action. This evolution is quite new and has not had important implications until now, but in the future, all experts agree that the best services at the lowest prices will be produced and consumed in areas with large economies of scale. The cost of services like transportation, telecommunication, energy distribution, and mail is a function of the density of consumers and is lower in (or between) large cities than elsewhere. In many countries, services in low density areas such as secondary railroads diminish, while services in high density areas, like airports, tend to grow better and cheaper. We saw in an earlier section that the transfers induced by large public services were often the result of the non-consideration of economies of scale in pricing. It is likely that in the future these transfers will decrease.

Last, regulation policies, such as commercial protection or regulation of food products, are less and less used by governments. The external shocks of the 1980s revealed in most countries structural problems and the need to change their structures. Structural adjustments in the developed and developing countries, in market-oriented and socialist countries, have been and are now a main objective in these countries. Structural adjustment is a modification of relative prices, of the structure of government expenditures, a reorientation of activities by policy reforms (public finances, monetary policy, institutions, sectoral policies). The economic rationalization of economies induces a more important role of the market in the determination of relative prices and the surrender of many administrative distortions. This suggests that many non-voluntary or voluntary transfers are now to decrease: in developing countries, the deregulation of food prices is going on quickly (in Africa, for example, in Mali, Niger, Nigeria, Uganda, Somalia, Senegal). This means that discrimination against rural areas is now decreasing. Protectionist and import substitution policies are also tending to disappear in many developing countries. The global result tends, in the short term, to curtail the advantages of large cities and to reduce the rate of protection of their economies. Large cities in developing countries will have, in the future, fewer policy induced advantages at a time when they have very few comparative advantages in a more competitive world. In the developed countries, by contrast, the adjustment benefits more the large cities: most commercial protections have been or are being abandoned (at least at the regional level and more and more at the GATT level), liberating the productivity advantages of the largest cities as innovation poles. The protection of farmers is, at the same time, decreasing. The total amount of subsidies – US$280 billion in 1988 – was US$245 billion in 1989. The current GATT negotiations indicate a greater tendency in this direction by means of a more competitive international organization of food product trade and by fewer subsidies to agriculture.

Conclusion

The large cities, and particularly the largest cities, subsidize heavily the other parts of their respective countries through the national budget and through many national public services. Most of the economic or sectoral policies that were introducing a pro-urban bias, particularly in the developing countries, are now being abandoned or are about to be. Does this mean that the more large cities there are the more transfers that will be produced to the benefit of the other parts of the particular countries? It is not sure. In certain developing countries, through the combination of economic growth and an increase in the share of the budget in the GDP, the relative degree of transfer by large cities will probably increase; but, for others, if there is weak economic growth or a recession (because of economic difficulties or demographic dynamism) and thus a low level of taxes collected, it is possible that some largest cities will become poorer and distribute less to the rest of the country. In developed countries, the evolution of the relative amount of transfer also depends on economic growth, which will or will not be able to compensate for the diminution of both national budget weight and the rate of taxes on income and profit. Decentralization, privatization, and deregulation trends could have also a negative impact on transfers between the largest cities and the rest of their respective countries. In the end, it is likely that more large cities will finance more transfers mainly in the intermediate-income countries that are experiencing real economic growth, and less likely in both the poorest and the richest countries.

References

1 Davezies, L. *La redistribution interdépartementale des revenus induite par le budget de l'Etat 1984*. Rapport pour la DATAR, OEIL, Institut d'Urbanisme de Paris. April 1989. Polygraphié 30 p + annexes 60 p.

2 ———. "*Les mécanismes financiers publics nationaux et locaux au Mali.*" Communication au Séminaire sous-régional sur les méthodes et instruments de planification urbaine et les supports méthodologiques de l'urbanisme opérationnel tenu à Bamako en mai 1985, IUP, Université de Paris XII, Créteil, polygr., 15 p.

3 Davezies, L., C. Larrue, and R. Prud'homme. *Les Départements qui payent pour les autres, essai sur la répartition spatiale des fonds budgétaires et de la Sécurité Sociale*. Paris: DATAR, September 1983. Polygr., 225 p.

4 Davezies, L., B.H. Nicot, and R. Prud'homme. *La place de Casablanca dans le budget de l'Etat marocain*. Rapport de consultants, diffusion restreinte. February 1985. Polygr., 20 p. + annexes 43 p.

5 Davezies, L., B.H. Nicot, P. Pouliquen, and R. Prud'homme. *La contribution des grandes villes au développement: Abidjan subventionne-t-elle le reste de la Côte d'Ivoire?* Centre de Nations Unies pour les Etablissements Humains (Habitat). January 1987. Polygr., 40 p.

6 Musgrave, R., K. Case, and H. Leonard. "The Distribution of Fiscal Burdens and Benefits." *Public Finance Quarterly*. July 1974.

7 Nicot, B.H., and N. Letrung. *The Share of Bangkok in the National Budget of*

Thailand. Consultant report for the World Bank. Restricted distribution. OEIL/IUP, 1989. 65 pp.

8 Prud'homme, R. *Urban Public Finances in Developing Countries: A Case Study of Metropolitan Tunis*. World Bank report. Washington, D.C., January 1975.

9 ———. "Does Paris Subsidize the Rest of France?" In F. Ewers, *The Future of the Metropolis*, 285–295. Walter de Gruyter & Co., Berlin and New York: 1986.

10 Prud'homme, R., and M. Savy. *Rapport du Comité Aménagement du Territoire* (pour la préparation du huitième Plan). Paris: Documentation Française, 1980. 144 pp.

11 Williamson, J. "Regional Inequality and the Process of National Development: A Description of the Patterns." *Economic Development and Cultural Change*. 1965, 13 pp.

7

Economic impacts of third world mega-cities: Is size the issue?

Andrew Marshall Hamer

Principal Sector Economist, The World Bank, Washington, D.C.

Introduction: An urban economist's perspective on the facts

The diversity of the developing world's mega-cities makes it difficult to generalize about appropriate urban development strategies. Yet, this brief discussion cannot be cluttered with numerous exceptions. Thus, stylized facts are presented that provide useful generalizations that abstract from any specific case-study or piece of evidence. The views expressed are personal ones. Though some opinions are buttressed by analytical work sponsored by the World Bank, none of the conclusions is necessarily endorsed by the World Bank.

If one were to differentiate the urban economist's perspective toward urban development from the perspectives often prevalent among other disciplines – such as urban planning, urban sociology, urban geography, or urban demography – one would have to focus on two or three critical areas of disagreement, all linked by a common thread: whether or not third world mega-city development is doomed to systemic failure or not. One issue is the degree of rationality involved in individual, household, and enterprise behaviour. Here the urban economist is more likely to conclude that that evidence suggests an absence of pathological behaviour and the essential soundness of micro-responses to the incentive structure in place. A second issue involves governance, i.e. the types of institutions, policies, and regulations called for, given conclusions about micro-level behaviour. Here the urban economist lays stress on affordable, replicable solutions that tend to involve indirect public policy levers to fulfil a set of limited objectives. One can contrast this with social engineering/micro-management approaches, which seek to impose "order" on an "unruly" urban world. Here the agenda for government planners is distressingly long and rather far removed from any "hands on" understanding of how to build up, operate, and maintain a city. Finally there is the inevitable issue introduced by the time frame used, given the ongoing process of structural adjustment. Certain countries in Africa and Latin America, and the mega-cities within them, are experiencing historically atypical problems created largely by macroeconomic mismanagement. If an urban centre were viewed from a short-term perspective, certain problems that are related to structural adjustment could be mislabelled as evidence of systemic failure. The urban economist tends to reject this view and focus on long-term trends in urban performance.[1]

Mega-cities: A framework for discussion

Re-examining the meaning of size

Surveying the top 10 mega-cities of the developing world (see table), one could argue that size, and its implications, are in the eye of the beholder. For, in most cases, the relevant size can be defined to include a wide spectrum, from the traditional core city of 100–200 sq km to a region of 2,000–10,000 sq km and more. One has to ask if, in the abstract, these numbers contribute very much to our understanding of issues and options; if, in fact, they do little more than alarm the uninitiated and create an assumption of unmanageability. Furthermore, the growth rates of the constituent parts of these mega-cities differ widely from one another, with low or even negative growth rates in the densest core and higher growth rates at the low density periphery [5, 6, 34, 37–49, 56]. What we have are polycentric clusters of identifiable and separate cities and towns that require both regional trunk infrastructure and effective local urban management, in much the same way that a province or a small country might need.[2] And would anyone be alarmed to hear that there are small countries or provinces with an urban population of 10–20 million? In short, to treat the totality of these residents as members of one city, even if we

Population (in millions) and area size (sq km) for selected mega-cities

City region	Population I (United Nations)	Size I	Population II (US Census Bureau)	Size II	Population III (City core)	Size III	Population IV (Mega-region)	Size IV
Mexico	17.3	2,100	17.0	2,100	3.3	150	ca 21	14,500
São Paulo	15.9	6,000	14.9	6,000	NA	NA	NA	NA
Shanghai	12.0	6,200	6.7	500	5.9	ca 100	14.4 (1988)	6,186
Calcutta	11.0	1,400	10.5	1,400	4–5	ca 150	NA	NA
Buenos Aires	10.9	3,900	10.8	3,900	3.0	200	NA	NA
Rio de Janeiro	10.4	6,500	10.1	6,500	5.6	1,200	12.8	43,300
Seoul	10.3	600	13.7	4,400	NA	NA	ca 15	11,700
Bombay	10.1	400	10.1	400	3.3	100	NA	NA
Beijing	9.25	16,800	5.6	2,700	2.4	100	9.25	16,800
Jakarta	8.0	650	8.1	650	1.5	100	ca 12 (1988)	6,700

Sources: World Bank files; United Nations, *The Prospects for World Urbanization*, revised as of 1984/1985 (New York, 1987); US Bureau of Census, *World Population Profile 1985* (Washington, D.C., 1986).

use the prefix "mega-," is to pervert the common sense definition of what a "city" is. Size *per se* is not the issue; instead, it is mismanagement at both the regional and local levels, and wrong-headed national urbanization policies promoted by physical planners with visions of optimal geography and very little sense of economics.

Why do mega-cities exist?

Economic development and urbanization are joint products of a wealth-creating process that generates large urban regions where per capita output exceeds the national average by a factor of 2–5 times, though some of this advantage may be due to distortions in the macroeconomic environment.[3] Maximizing economic growth, a key objective for most countries that are poor, is facilitated, up to the time middle income status is reached, by a concentrated "city-states" model of urbanization [30, 33, 53, 21, 54].

By focusing activity in a relatively small portion of the nation's landscape when national income is low, governments reap the so-called *urbanization* economies of agglomeration, which create an inverse relationship between production costs per unit of output and population size for many economic activities. Simultaneously, these "city-states" conserve investments in regional trunk infrastructure for transport, communications, power, and water supply. In such agglomerations, one can cost-effectively gather a labour force with a wide array of skills, a large number of suppliers, diversified financial and commercial services, venture capital, access to information on foreign markets and technologies, as well as the social amenities (health, education) needed to attract managerial talent. It is in these places that a low-income economy can reap the benefits of a rapid diffusion of new skills and technologies. At the same time, the local market will place concentrated purchasing power at the doorstep of the business community. In effect, the mega-city becomes a giant supermarket with the greatest array of choices in the country.

With the passage of time, and given the resources economic development makes available, as well as strenuous efforts to decentralize decision-making and resource mobilization, a systematic extension of regional trunk infrastructure and the emergence of vibrant secondary centres can occur.[4] Many of these cities will then develop around the exploitation of a resource-based industry or at a strategic transport node. Eventually, in a broad range of economic activities, urbanization economies begin to give way to *localization* economies of agglomeration, where individual clusters of particular industries and services reap cost reduction benefits from being close to producers of similar products, without requiring the simultaneous presence of a broad array of other economic activities. Since localization economies are quickly exhausted for many of the beneficiary clusters, as these grow in size, smaller cities (with their lower costs of land, labour, and disamenities) can often provide suitable locations. In those centres, firms experiencing localization economies can become competitive with mega-city firms performing similar activities but forced to absorb the high land, labour, and disamenity costs of sharing locations with many other sources of employment. Thus, population size, *per se*, becomes less important in determining the profitability of a broad range of economic activity [13].[5] At this point, the macroeconomic framework in place is a key determinant of the speed of spatial transformation. If efforts are not made to decrease central government influence in business decisions, decentralization tendencies may be strongly opposed by "rent-seeking" behaviour encouraging a continued presence near the centre of national power. In particular, decentralized development will be facilitated by a liberalized macroeconomic environment that guarantees: (1) that price controls, interest rate controls, and exchange rate controls are dismantled; (2) that the tax and trade regimes are reasonably transparent and honestly administered, allowing for a minimum of bargaining; (3) that the tariff structure in place does not favour the premature emergence of import substitutes whose capital intensity and technology content would require mega-city locations; (4) that individuals, businesses, and cities have access to long-term finance mechanisms across all regions that encourage them to divert funds from consumption to save and invest and to service debt repayments while accumulating long-lived assets; (5) that public corporations, where they exist, operate essentially as business enterprises and are responsible for their own hiring, firing, pricing, and location policies, as well as meeting performance targets; (6) that inter-governmental fiscal arrangements, including grants and transfers, are predictable and reward local mobilization of extra resources, discouraging a "hand-out" mentality; (7) that local authorities are given wide discretion in mobilizing resources, programming expenditures, and adapting urban development standards and regulations to local conditions; and (8) that local-level public sector career incentives and technical assistance are consistent with those required to allow local planning, implementation, maintenance, and financing of local development.[6]

In the transition from the "city-state" model to a decentralized one, World Bank work suggests that deconcentration within a metropolitan region is the most cost-effective way to cut the costs of doing business while reaping the benefits of urbanization economies. In suburban and ex-urban locations, one can escape many of the consequences of rising congestion, pollution, land and labour costs while reaping both the emerging economies of localization and the residual economies linked to population size [7, 19]. The advantages of deconcentration over wholesale decentralization may be sufficiently strong to forestall the emergence of a highly competitive network of secondary centres until national income per capita reaches US$4,000 per capita, expressed in 1980 purchasing power parity terms [21].[7] The expansion of mega-cities is, therefore, not easily contained. The one consolation for enthusiasts of decentralization is that overall growth rates of those agglomerations are falling sharply over time and are generally not expected to exceed three per cent per annum between 1985 and 2000 [50, 51].[8]

Mega-city outcomes: What's inevitable, what's not?

What proves most interesting when examining case-studies across mega-cities – with regard to income distribution, poverty, access to services, and housing – is the *great variety of outcomes,* a fact that immediately suggests that country-specific factors and governance issues are more important than size in almost all cases except where certain environmental issues are involved.[9] That is to say, the river basin or air shed capacity of a given land area on which a mega-city is built may be limited enough so that the mere concentration of people raises negative externality issues that require pricing or regulation action. That one factor aside, among mega-cities, there are examples[10] of:

- rapid growth in average per capita incomes (Bangkok, Beijing, Shanghai, Tianjin, Seoul) and virtual stagnation in the same indicator (Calcutta);
- narrow and wide disparities in household income classified by deciles;[11]
- variable levels of poverty (with little in China's mega-cities, in Bangkok, and Seoul); with the percentage of the population that is poor lower than in rural areas; because the wealthy are more concentrated in mega-cities than elsewhere, rural income distributions are more equal than urban ones;

- housing markets that generate non-slum units with low price to annual household income ratios (Bangkok, 2–3:1) and housing markets that clearly do not (China's mega-cities, 8–10:1) – with many outcomes in between;
- cases with widespread slums and cases where these are no longer a significant problem (Seoul, Bangkok, Beijing, Tianjin);[12]
- public utilities that provide near universal access to public services like water or solid waste collection (Seoul, Beijing, Shanghai) and utilities that do not.

While work *across mega-cities* allows one to conclude that size *per se* is not a decisive variable, less analysis has been done comparing (and documenting) outcomes across cities within a given country. For Korea [57] the "outcomes" are better in Seoul than elsewhere. Much the same appears to be true in Brazil [7] and Thailand [2] when São Paulo and Bangkok are compared to secondary centres in their countries. Mixed results appear in other studies, such as one that examines Indonesian cities [29, 35]. Even these studies do not control for cost of living differences. What can be said, then, is that existing evidence does *not* allow analysts to conclude that households living in mega-cities are worse off than households residing in secondary cities. For business activity, whose attraction to mega-cities is discussed in the preceding section, there is little question but that a large number of enterprises prefer to locate in mega-cities rather than elsewhere.[13]

When one examines the economic impacts of mega-cities on households more carefully, there is further reason to suspect that "disorderly" outcomes in the housing sector or in access to public services is not due to concentrations of poor residents but rather to an inadequate policy and regulatory framework. In Bombay, for example, roughly two-thirds of the population belongs to the poor (15 per cent) or low-income (50 per cent) household categories. Yet careful studies of slums like Thawari reveal that 70 per cent of the households belong to the middle income or upper income groups.[14] In Bangkok, studies of the slum population suggest that earnings per employed person are above the metropolitan average, and that only 10–20 per cent of slum households have incomes below the poverty line [2]. In fact, the average income of slum households is about twice the poverty line. In Jakarta, 80 per cent of the housing stock is supplied by the so-called "informal" sector that evades the regulatory system, while only 17 per cent of the population falls below the poverty line [35]. In China's mega-cities, the link between income and the quality/quantity of housing, or the quality of public services, is weak; with considerable evidence that higher than average household income does not translate automatically into good housing and public services [59].

If this trend can be documented more fully, then one can argue that potentially beneficial economic impacts are being blocked by public policy, producing a greater number of suboptimal outcomes than household incomes would suggest are possible. The hypothesis put forward here is that the income base is present in mega-cities to finance near universal access to "adequate" housing and public services.

The poverty problem – even if one focuses on it after acknowledging that the poor are *not* representative of the mega-city population – can be viewed from a less pessimistic perspective than is currently fashionable [58].[15] Much poverty is temporary and related to life-cycle factors when viewed from the perspective of individual households, be they migrants or "natives." In general, the poverty problem in cities is not a migrant problem but a "native" problem, and is thus not susceptible to city-size controls. Furthermore, migration, when it occurs, is sensible and not an irrational form of behaviour that leads to poverty outcomes, in the main. Again, size controls do not appear appropriate.

The revulsion caused by low-income households in mega-cities has fostered a "myth of marginality" whereby these communities are seen as a "disorderly agglomeration of unemployed loafers, abandoned women and children, thieves, drunks, and prostitutes" [31]. In turn, this view has been buttressed by the hypothesis that urban labour markets function in a perverse manner. The so-called Harris-Todaro model postulates that a high-wage manufacturing sector, with a relatively limited number of jobs in any mega-city, acts as a beacon to potential rural-urban migrants, who are, in turn, blamed for most mega-city and urban population growth [12]. These migrants are assumed to relocate in large numbers in the hope of winning an employment lottery that entitles them to a secure, high-paying urban job. While waiting for a winning "ticket," these migrants crowd into slums and experience prolonged, if not permanent, periods of underemployment and unemployment. According to Harris-Todaro, migrants are relegated to residual jobs that pay little and have minimal social value.

In fact, the evidence available on urban labour markets in developing countries suggests that the Harris-Todaro hypothesis is derived from poor or incomplete data [58]. Immigrants are, on average, rapidly assimilated into urban labour markets, with earnings linked not to their migrant status but their human capital endowment. The earnings of the migrant labour force are high enough, on average, to justify the decision to migrate, given the level of income that could be expected had they remained in the rural sector. In fact, the so-called "informal" labour market, viewed as a dumping ground by Harris-Todaro, yields a distribution of income rewards that overlaps to a significant extent with that of the so-called high-wage "formal" sector. Migrants appear well aware of this and move in response to considerable information provided through kinship networks about "formal" and "informal" sector jobs. They come because, on average, their personal attributes (above-average education, relatively young age) are best utilized in an urban environment.[16] The very poorest, least educated rural workers remain largely immobilized in the countryside [1, 3, 22, 25, 55]. The poor who stay behind benefit from tighter rural labour markets and remittances. There is, thus, little evidence that poverty in the sending areas is worsened by migration. In addition, there is no evidence that migration causes the incomes of city natives to fall [58].

The fact that no mega-city has managed to achieve high marks in all relevant areas of economic performance does not rule out widespread improvements. Furthermore, and foreshadowing the comments made in the next section on public policy, international experience shows that the *size* of mega-cities cannot be regulated through direct public sector prohibitions and controls on the movement of people or the procreation of children. The temporary exceptions to this rule, found among the authoritarian political systems during their traditional command economy phase, proves the point: as soon as those systems begin to change in the direction of a market economy (which is the context within which most third world mega-cities operate), then the new options available to individuals, households, and enterprises weaken the effectiveness of direct controls so seriously that other solutions to mega-city problems must be pursued. Thus, *whatever the economic impacts of mega-cities, the policy levers are not size related.*

Public policy agenda: Toward an affordable, self-regulated mega-city

Whatever policy recommendations are made, they must pass two tests: (1) they must be consistent with the constraints imposed by the macroeconomy in place at the time and (2) they must be implementable.

National spatial policy options for government

What can a national government do to accelerate the transition to a world of decentralized development with a more "balanced" spatial structure? It can systematically reinforce the forces promoting the expulsion of selected economic activities from mega-cities and help reshape mega-city economic expansion away from standardized industries and towards services and high technology and customized production industries. Among the various measures government can take, other than those already cited, one would be the scaling back of subsidies to the mega-city *as a whole,* making it pay its own way, *on average.*[17] This means removing rent controls and subsidies on public transport and water supply, as well as systematically reducing capital investment grants for individual mega-city projects. In addition, it means promoting local tax options, including vigorous development of property taxes, sales taxes, and business and vehicle licence fees. In the final analysis, one reason that economic activity in developed countries does not automatically locate in New York, London, Paris, or Tokyo is that, for many activities, the economic benefits do not justify the very high costs. The cost structure acts as a filter, drawing in primarily high productivity work and related consumer services and expelling the rest. This mechanism has a distinct advantage: it fosters spatial relocation by businesses and households without requiring additional government intervention [8]. By way of contrast, the Chinese mega-city, for example, exists within an environment of massive subsidization (in kind) that doubles the average total income per household and creates very large disparities[18] in average incomes (4:1) between mega-city regions and the rural sector [9]. This has forced the public sector to devote considerable effort to control population movements and deny most migrants access to in-kind privileges (near-free housing, medical care, permanent employment, retirement benefits, food subsidies, etc.), thus creating a type of second-class citizenry in the Chinese mega-city.

A necessary implication of greater financial self-reliance on the part of mega-cities, through the use of user fees and local taxes, is a heightened concern for *affordability*. Two decades of World Bank and other research across the developing world suggest that land use standards and the level of infrastructure service can be cut in half, taking prevailing high quality norms as the starting point, while preserving most of the expected benefits [20, 11, 32]. *The capital costs of urbanization can therefore be tailored to the income and effective demand of each mega-city's population.* Once households and businesses are willing to pay for a given level of service, there is little left to argue about. The issue then shifts away from a concern that mega-cities may absorb an inordinate level of capital to supply infrastructure and towards a concern about putting in place a system of infrastructure financing and decision-making that yields appropriate service levels.

Similarly, government at the national and local levels must establish a regulatory framework, with incentives and penalties, to tackle the disamenities that emerge with growing size, particularly pollution and congestion. In this regard, there are well-established and cost-effective precedents for instituting better traffic management and at-the-source pollution abatement procedures without resorting to futile and costly efforts to control city size.

Can the government go further and pursue an even more activist set of policies? International experience suggests the answer is no. The force-fed redirection of urban growth to secondary centres is too expensive to replicate widely, particularly in a poor country. In addition, governments are ill-equipped at dealing with the politicization of location decisions that accompany spatial promotion efforts; what usually occurs is the emergence of "pork-barrel" policies that give every special interest group (in regional terms) a piece of the subsidy pie.

Can the government instead repress and punish the mega-city? Yes, but at a cost – in terms of national output growth foregone – that is all too obvious to macroeconomic planners, who then set about to subvert these controls. The champions of controls are the cadre of physical planners, who cannot argue the issue in economic terms and are thereby reduced to a marginal role in the macroeconomic planning process. Were the physical planners to triumph, the result would probably be a mega-city like Calcutta. And Calcutta, with it economic *raison d'être* gutted through a combination of political misfortune and punitive policies, represents the type of mega-city containment "success" story that few other policy makers would care to replicate. As noted, even the exceptions prove unconvincing when examined closely. Within a modified command economy like China's, population controls were successfully blended with rapid economic growth in the early 1980s; since then, however, "temporary" migrants (referred to as part of the "floating" population of migrants and visitors) have arrived in large numbers and total 10–15 per cent of each mega-city's population, while growing on average by 15–20 per cent a year. Simultaneously, some of the growth spilled over the administrative barriers of the mega-cities, to emerge as "disorderly," unregulated peri-urban sprawl [9].

Dealing with urban poverty

What is government to do about urban poverty and the uneasy feeling its presence creates among the vocal élites in urban areas? Urban poverty is often rural poverty transferred from the countryside by rapid population growth and a rural economic and political environment unconducive to change. No urban system can tackle poverty in its midst in a decisive manner until the rural-urban transition has been largely completed and only a small portion of the population remains in the countryside (Seoul, Hong Kong, Singapore). Instead, at the national level, a commitment to eliminating macroeconomic distortions can lead to a decline in the number of urban poor. Prudent fiscal policies minimize the likelihood that a highly regressive "inflation tax" will burden the poor. Even if public sector spending falls, the residual spending in the social sectors can be retargeted toward basic health care, child nutrition, and primary education, thus improving the living standards of the poor. Trade protection and subsidized credit tend to benefit large, capital-intensive firms while discouraging small enterprises in the "informal" sector. Removal of these distortions tends to encourage the growth of employment opportunities, including those of the urban poor. Price reform, deregulating the official price of various goods, does not usually affect the poor, who must rely on the parallel, "black" market for such commodities. Failure to undertake these reforms can lead to increases to proportion of the urban population that is poor (e.g. Brazil), while vigorous implementation can cut the urban poverty population significantly (e.g. Indonesia) [58].

Housing markets and local public utilities are effected primarily by policies and regulations created at the national level. The national government's approach to subsidies will dictate outcomes at the local level. Governments may sensibly adhere to the following rule: where urban household incomes and access to public services or "non-slum" housing are highly correlated, and the critical obstacle is assessing the ability to pay of households, then programmes can be put in place that allow cross-subsidization between those households and business enterprises, along with better-off households in the same mega-city.

This, as noted, is rarely the case. Slums are often the refuge for a wide spectrum of households, classified by income; and they exist because of reasons linked to public policy and regulatory failures in land use and housing markets, making conventional solutions unaffordable. Lack of access to public services is also unlikely to be primarily an "inadequate" income issue. In fact, in cases such as piped water, it is *cheaper* to buy water from a public utility, even a financially independent one, than to purchase water from vendors. In addition, the failure to provide public services because of inadequate cost recovery indirectly contributes to depressing the incomes of the poor, by discouraging the emergence and growth of the small firms that can significantly affect the demand for unskilled and semi-skilled labour [19].

More generally, a "permissive" attitude toward subsidies almost always results in two unequitable outcomes:

1. subsidies get "hijacked" by politically connected civil servants, military personnel, and other middle-income households, with few benefits flowing to the poor; or
2. the subsidies are so widely redistributive in character that the poor absorb little of the impact of such policies. If these lead (as they often do) to restrictive access to public services, it is the poor who have the fewest low-cost alternative sources. Subsidization, for its own sake, is a double-edged sword, as far as the poor are concerned. Such blunt weapons should be retired and replaced by more fine-tuned solutions. The process of structural adjustment under way in many countries allows governments to sharply target subsidies to the poor while cutting the overall level of subsidies [58].

Beyond size: Getting a local management framework in place

Symptoms of disorganization include limited access to public services and urban infrastructure; existence of squatter settlements and unregulated subdivisions; prevalence of pollution and congestion; poor maintenance of urban assets; poor cost recovery and tax administration; price controls and untargeted subsidies; physical plans and regulations/standards that ignore affordability; a local government workforce that has few tools and fewer incentives to use them. All of these factors are interconnected. One cannot improve living conditions without addressing the issue of what government should do and should not do, and how it can finance its initiatives [11].

In order to build an affordable city, governments at the local level must improve their performance in four major areas:

1. develop a sectorally and territorially integrated capital budget;
2. simplify planning and administrative procedures to encourage private initiative;
3. intensify the utilization of existing urban assets; and
4. improve resource mobilization.

Sectoral and territorial integration of mega-city capital budgets requires the setting of investment priorities across sectors and locations, based on a region-wide assessment of demand, performed by core metropolitan agencies using minimum, affordable standards. Such programmes should be three to five year rolling plans, revised annually and accompanied by identifiable sources of financing for both construction and operations. The budget exercise should also provide an opportunity each year for core agencies to review policies that might obstruct the accomplishment of priority objectives. Finally, as financing sources are reviewed, it is possible to reconsider the level of tariffs for public services. Once these budgets are in place, line agencies can implement, operate, and maintain the investments, while the metropolitan region's core agencies can shift to coordinating, monitoring, and evaluation efforts, allowing future programming work to proceed on the basis of better information.[19]

With this focus on the short- and medium-term future, and with the use of investments in major trunk infrastructure to guide spatial development, the government has to work actively to cement a private-public partnership in carrying out the provision of urban services, including shelter provision. Regulations and licences affecting businesses, land development, and building construction require constant review to simplify and reduce the number of restrictions, particularly for those activities that fall under the rubric of the household or small business economy. Considerable effort should be devoted to developing an up-to-date cadastre that identifies the owners of land and property, with quick adjudication of disputed claims. Neighbourhoods that are certifiably low income should be allowed to reach standard norms through the use of progressive upgrading; restrictions on the use of properties – such as exclusion of business activities on residential premises, rent control, etc. – should be eliminated as unenforceable and detrimental to the welfare of the poor.

The private provision of services – including solid waste collection and disposal; bus and microbus transport; water supply billing and collection; property tax assessments, billing, and collection; road and building maintenance; and management contracts to operate other services – should be considered on its merits, without ideological biases about the "intrinsic" superiority of a public sector that is likely to be overstaffed, underpaid, and poorly motivated.

Since the supply of urban assets is likely to be considerably below levels to satisfy effective demand, local governments should turn their attention to getting the most of existing assets. It is absurd to have water supply systems with unaccounted for water rates of 30–40 per cent. Traffic management, greater attention to traffic safety, priority use of roads for public transport – all these types of measures can double the use of road surfaces in the face of increasing congestion. Private incentives to maintain existing rental housing stock can be strengthened through the abolition of rent controls.

A final requirement for better management is a predictable, growing level of revenues. Ad hoc central transfers of funds should be replaced by tax sharing formulas whose impact can be predicted in advance. Public utility customers, on average, should finance the full costs of such services as water and public transport. Property taxes should be the object of vigorous mining, as should the use of betterment taxes levied on the immediate beneficiaries of neighbourhood-specific infrastructure, since they form an equitable source of funds to cover investments in trunk infrastructure. The structure of other local fees should be reviewed, drastically pruned, and simplified, and be subject to vigorous collection efforts. Where possible, central governments should encourage local governments to take out (and repay) loans for municipal development on terms that would fit the long-lived nature of much local public infrastructure. Finally, blanket "negative revenues" (i.e. subsidies) open to all households should be progressively eliminated and replaced by cross-subsidies paid by the more affluent users of the same service that the poor would receive at reduced rates.

With these approaches in place, mega-cities can be turned into more manageable entities, capable of delivering services at a more rapid rate and bringing access to minimum levels of services to a higher percentage of the poor and the small businesses they operate or work for. Those that argue that the prescriptions outlined above may be politically painful are correct. However, failure to act because of a failure of nerve relegates those urban areas to suboptimal performance. That is a situation poor countries can ill afford.

The research agenda

The series of mega-city studies now being produced by the United Nations should be continued and lead to periodic (every 5 years) updates of each mega-city involved. This provides a useful way to monitor trends for a large number of variables and provides an antidote to alarmist literature. In addition, it disseminates the lessons – good and bad – that are otherwise likely to be missed. The cumulative effect of reading the whole set of reports is to make clear which public policy practices "work" and which almost certainly fail, sector by sector.

It would be useful to monitor the emergence of competing regional centres in countries with mega-cities that show potential of reaching large if not mega-city size. This would provide the policy makers with a clearer understanding of the mix of economic conditions and public sector policies that generate such centres. It would also provide an early alert, should that be necessary, of another giant "in the wings."

Specific topics appear to be better researched than others. Land and housing market behaviour is well understood by researchers working on mega-cities. Income distribution data, trends in poverty and its component parts, labour market studies, including unemployment and underemployment – work on these topics could all be expanded, since the existing degree of documentation is miniscule. There is also only a small body of data for relative performance (for these variables) across cities of different sizes.

Notes

1. The sections that follow, particularly those dealing with public policy, focus on Asian outcomes more often than not. This reflects the author's present comparative advantage, not a belief that such outcomes cannot be documented elsewhere.
2. In effect, a mega-city of 10 million can be seen as a collection of contiguous cities of several hundred thousand to one or two million inhabitants.
3. For an example, the Bangkok Metropolitan Region has 16 per cent of the nation's population and accounts for 43 per cent of GNP [2]. That this is not unusual is confirmed by World Bank data suggesting that similar outcomes are found in Metro Manila, Karachi, the Federal District of Mexico, Greater São Paulo. Government statistics in China reveal much the same result for places like Shanghai, Beijing, and Tianjin [4].
4. This is particularly clear in large countries that have a varied resource base and a sizable population. The emergence of secondary centres has not been extensively documented in a case-study manner. The evidence from Brazil is discussed in Hamer [7]. Decentralized

urban development is also evident in Mexico, India [17], China, Korea [57], and, more recently, in the Philippines [36]. Worth watching are developments in Indonesia [10, 29].

5. Although self-evidently true, much of the relevant literature overlooks the fact that at *all* times big and small cities coexist and that, therefore, there are always economic activities in which efficiency does not depend on local population size. With economic development, what changes is the mix of activities for which this holds true.
6. Some of these items are discussed further in the section below.
7. Purchasing power parity (PPP) rates represent the local purchasing power of a currency, expressed in US dollars. For developing countries the PPP value of a currency far exceeds its foreign exchange value.
8. The references cited earlier on intra-mega-city growth rate differentials, by city, also bear out the secular decline in aggregate growth rates. These declining growth rates are closely linked to the fall in national population growth rates and do not, by themselves, imply a loss of economic competitiveness on the part of mega-cities.
9. The continuing series of Population Policy Papers issued by the United Nations Department of International Economic and Social Affairs provides much of the data for this section. They have been supplemented by unpublished World Bank data, as necessary, particularly in the case of income distribution.
10. The discussion that follows assumes that household incomes, *per se,* do not provide a meaningful measure of "outcomes" or "impacts" if access to public services is limited and if prevailing housing units are generally "unsatisfactory."
11. Whether measured in terms of the ratio of the top decile's average household income to the bottom deciles or in terms of the relation of each of those decile averages to the mega-city median household income, the narrowest ratios are found in Chinese mega-cities (top:bottom ratio equal to 3:1), Seoul (8:1), Bangkok (10:1), and Indian mega-cities (10:1). Elsewhere, in São Paulo, Mexico City, and Metro Manila, for example, top:bottom ratios of 20:1 or more are common. (Source: World Bank unpublished data).
12. An obvious, if excluded variable, is unemployment (and underemployment). The existing data are so suspect, given the absence of unemployement issuance schemes, that further discussion must await better information.
13. This theme recurs in the literature produced by economists. See, for example, comments on Korea [57]: "Even allowing for its rising land and infrastructure costs, Seoul still represents the lowest overall cost location for many types of industries"; on Indonesia [10]; on Brazil [7]; on Thailand [2].
14. Personal communication, Deepak Satwalekar, Housing Finance Development Corporation (Bombay), April 1990.
15. The report provides extensive documentation for the points made below. For purposes of presentation, it is not cited after each statement of fact or interpretation involving poverty.
16. Even the Calcutta pavement dwellers are better off, on average, than their rural counterparts [58].
17. See the next subsection for a discussion on the link between this statement and the urban poor.
18. Typically, in developing countries, the ratios vary from 1.5 to 2.5.
19. For an example of such an exercise, see ref. 2.

References

1 Banerjee, B. "Some Aspects of Rural-Urban Migration in India: A Case Study of Delhi." Ph.D. diss., Oxford University, 1981.

2 *Bangkok Metropolitan Region Study, Intergrated Major Investment Programs*

for the 6th Plan (1986), Draft Final Report. National Economic and Social Development Board, Bangkok.

3 Bloom, D.E., and R.B. Freeman. "Population Growth, Labor Supply and Employment in Developing Countries." In D.G. Johnson and R.D. Lee, eds. *Population Growth and Economic Development: Issues and Evidence*. Madison: University of Wisconsin Press, 1987.

4 China. State Statistical Bureau. *China: Statistics Abstract: 1989*. Beijing: China Statistical Information and Consultancy Service Centre and International Centre for the Advancement of Science and Technology, 1989.

5 Chun, D.H., and K.S. Lee. *Changing Location Patterns of Population and Employment in the Seoul Region*. World Bank Water Supply and Urban Development Department Discussion Paper no. 89. Washington, D.C., 1985.

6 Dogan, M., and J. Kasarda, eds. *Megacities*. Vol. 2 of *The Metropolis Era*. Newbury Park, Calif.: Sage Publications, 1988.

7 Hamer, A. *Decentralized Urban Development and Industrial Location Behavior in São Paulo, Brazil: A Synthesis of Research Issues and Conclusions*. World Bank Staff Working Paper no. 732. Washington, D.C., 1984.

8 ———. "Decentralized Urban Development: Stylized Facts and Policy Implications." In R.J. Fuchs, G.W. Jones, and E.M. Pernia, eds. *Urbanization and Urban Policies in Pacific Asia*. Boulder, Colo.: Westview Press, 1987.

9 ———. "Four Hypotheses Concerning Contemporary Chinese Urbanization." In Kwok, R.Y. et al., eds. *Chinese Urban Reform: What Model Now?* London: M.E. Sharpe, 1990.

10 Hamer, A.M., A.D. Steer, and D.G. Williams. *Indonesia: The Challenge of Urbanization*. World Bank Staff Working Paper no. 787. Washington, D.C., 1986.

11 Hamer, A.M., and J.F. Linn. "Urbanization in the Developing World: Patterns, Issues and Policies." In E.S. Mills, ed. *Handbook on Regional and Urban Economics*, vol. 2. Amsterdam: Elsevier Science Publishers, 1987.

12 Harris, J., and M. Todaro. "Migration, Unemployment, and Development: A Two-Sector Analysis." *American Economic Review* 60 (1979), no. 1.

13 Henderson, J.V. *Urban Development: Theory, Fact and Illusion*. New York: Oxford University Press, 1988.

14 Kahnert, F. *Improving Urban Employment and Labor Productivity*. World Bank Discussion Paper no. 10. Washington, D.C., 1987.

15 Kannappan, S. "Urban Employment and the Labor Market in Developing Countries." Washington, D.C.: The World Bank, 1983. Unpublished.

16 ———. "Urban Labor Markets in Developing Countries." *Finance and Development* 26 (1989), no. 2.

17 Kingsley, G.T., J.P. Telgarsky, and B. Walter. *India's Urban Challenge: Trends and Implications*. Washington, D.C.: The Urban Institute, 1989.

18 Kwon, Y.-Y. "Population Decentralization from Seoul and Regional Development Policy." In H.W. Richardson and M.-Y. Hwang, eds. *Urban and Regional Policy in Korea and International Experience*. Seoul: Kon-Kuk University Press, 1987.

19 Lee, K.S. *The Location of Jobs in a Developing Metropolis*. New York: Oxford University Press, 1989.

20 Linn, J. "The Costs of Urbanization in Developing Countries." *Economic Development and Cultural Change* 30 (1982), no. 3.
21 MacKeller, F.L., and D.R. Vining. "Population Concentration in Core Regions of LDCs: Updates from the Post-1980 Censuses and a Regression Analysis." Paper presented at the annual meeting of the Population Association of America, Baltimore, 1989.
22 Mazumdar, D. "Rural-to-Urban Migration and Labor Markets." In R.J. Fuchs, G.W. Jones, and E.M. Pernia, ed. *Urbanization and Urban Policies in Pacific Asia*. Boulder, Colo.: Westview Press, 1987.
23 Mills, E.S., and C. Becker. *Studies in Indian Urban Development*. New York: Oxford University Press, 1986.
24 Mohan, R. *Work, Wages and Welfare in a Developing Metropolis*. New York: Oxford University Press, 1987.
25 Montgomery, M. "The Impacts of Urban Population Growth on Urban Labor Markets and the Costs of Urban Service Delivery: A Review." In D.G. Johnson and R.D. Lee, eds. *Population Growth and Economic Development Issues and Evidence*. Madison, Wis.: University of Wisconsin Press, 1987.
26 Moomaw, R.L. "Have Changes in Localization Economies Been Responsible for Declining Productivity Advantages in Large Cities?" *Journal of Regional Science* 26 (1986), no. 1.
27 ———. "Agglomeration Economies: Localization or Urbanization." *Urban Studies* 25 (1988), no. 2.
28 Motlu, S. "Urban Concentration and Primacy Revisited: An Analysis and Some Policy Conclusions." *Economic Development and Cultural Change* 37 (1989), no. 3.
29 *National Urban Development Strategy Project (1985), Final Report*. Jakarta, Directorate of City and Regional Planning; Directorate General for Human Settlements; United Nations Development Programme, United Nations Centre for Human Settlements.
30 Parr, J. "A Note on the Size Distribution of Cities over Time." *Journal of Urban Economics* 18 (1985), no. 2.
31 Perlman, J. *The Myth of Marginality: Urban Poverty and Politics in Rio de Janeiro*. Berkeley: University of California Press, 1976.
32 Richardson, H. "The Big, Bad City: Megacity Myth?" Paper presented at the meeting of the American Association for the Advancement of Science, San Francisco, 1988.
33 Rosen, K., and M. Resnick. "The Size Distribution of Cities: An Examination of the Pareto Law and Primacy." *Journal of Urban Economics* 8 (1980), no. 2.
34 Shanghai City Planning and Design Institute. "Shanghai: Development Scenarios, Phase I Report, Shanghai Metropolitan Transport Project." Shanghai, 1989.
35 Struyk, R.J. et al. *Housing Policy Studies Project Final Report (Draft)*. Jakarta: The Urban Institute and Hasfarm Dian Konsultan, 1989.
36 Tiglao, R. "All That Glistens Is Not in Manila." *Far Eastern Economic Review*, 17 July 1990.
37 Townroe, P. "Spatial Policy and Metropolitan Economic Growth in São Paulo, Brazil." *Geoforum* 15 (1984), no. 2.

38 United Nations. *Population Growth and Policies in Mega-Cities: Bombay*. New York, 1986.
39 ———. *Population Growth and Policies in Mega-Cities: Calcutta*. New York, 1986.
40 ———. *Population Growth and Policies in Mega-Cities: Seoul*. New York, 1986.
41 ———. *Population Growth and Policies in Mega-Cities: Metro Manila*. New York, 1986.
42 ———. *Population Growth and Policies in Mega-Cities: Delhi*. New York, 1986.
43 ———. *Population Growth and Policies in Mega-Cities: Dhaka*. New York, 1987.
44 ———. *Population Growth and Policies in Mega-Cities: Madras*. New York, 1987.
45 ———. *Population Growth and Policies in Mega-Cities: Bangkok*. New York, 1987.
46 ———. *Population Growth and Policies in Mega-Cities: Jakarta*. New York, 1989.
47 ———. *Population Growth and Policies in Mega-Cities: Mexico City*. New York, 1990.
48 ———. *Population Growth and Policies in Mega-Cities: Cairo*. New York, 1990.
49 ———. *Population Growth and Policies in Mega-Cities: São Paulo*. New York, 1990.
50 ———. *The Prospects of World Urbanization, Revised as of 1984–85*. New York, 1987.
51 ———. *World Population Trends and Policies: 1987 Monitoring Report*. New York, 1987.
52 U.S. Bureau of Census. *World Population Profile 1985*. Washington, D.C., 1986.
53 Vining, D.R. "Population Redistribution Towards LDC Core Areas, 1950–1980." Philadelphia: University of Pennsylvania, 1984.
54 Wheaton, W., and H. Shishido. "Urban Concentration, Agglomeration Economies and the Level of Economic Development." *Economic Development and Cultural Change* 30 (1981), no. 1.
55 Williamson, J.G. *Migration and Urbanization in the Third World*. Harvard Institute for Economic Research Discussion Paper no. 1245. Cambridge, Mass., 1986.
56 World Bank. *The Mexico City-Region: Issues and Perspectives, Special Sector Report*. Washington, D.C., 1984.
57 ———. *Korea: Spatial Strategy Review*. Washington, D.C., 1986.
58 ———. *World Development Report 1990: Poverty*. Washington, D.C., 1990.
59 ———. *China: Urban Housing Reforms: Issues and Implementation Options*. Washington, D.C., 1991.

8

Social and welfare impacts of mega-city development

Aprodicio Laquian

Director, Centre for Human Settlements, The University of British Columbia, Vancouver

As the world faces the prospect of being half urban by the turn of the century, concern over the social and welfare impacts of living in very large cities is increasing. In both developed and developing countries there is a feeling that the quality of life in mega-cities is deteriorating. In the 47 mega-cities expected to have populations of 5 million or more by the year 2000, there is a search for policies and programmes to cope with worsening social and welfare problems. While here and there there are some positive developments enhancing the developmental role of cities, in general, future prospects do not seem too bright.

Mega-cities have more in common with each other than with their rural hinterlands whether they are located in developed or developing countries. This makes for easier comparability in an analysis of their social and welfare conditions. However, it is still true that most mega-city development is rooted in the specific economic, social, and cultural conditions in the country or region the mega-city is in. The distinction in conditions is particularly sharp between developed country cities like New York, London, or Tokyo and developing

The views presented in this paper are those of the author and do not represent those of the United Nations Population Fund (UNFPA).

country cities such as Mexico City, Lagos, or Calcutta. While very large cities might be heavily influenced by so-called mega-trends, the particular problems they face arise from their specific conditions.

Mega-trends in social change

The past couple of decades have seen the emergence of basic social changes in urban affairs that may be described as mega-trends. The most important of these are: (1) the rapid spread of urbanism as a way of life despite the decline in metropolitan area growth; (2) further impoverishment of the urban poor in most mega-cities; (3) erosion of the capabilities of metropolitan governments to plan, finance, and manage urban development; (4) increase in social ills and urban pathologies; and (5) changing demographic structures, including aging, of large city populations.

The mega-trends cited above have had significant impacts on the social and welfare aspects of living in mega-cities. The impacts have been felt in cities whether they are in more or less developed countries. Some of the impacts of these mega-trends have had positive implications for social development; others have exacerbated urban ills. As stated by the United Nations *Human Development Report* [10], "what makes sense is to reinforce the creative and productive capabilities of the cities and to overcome their many social ills."

Spreading urbanism, declining metropolitan growth

Recent decades have seen a significant decline in population growth rates in metropolitan areas. As the table shows, all but 1 of the 47 mega-cities expected to have a population of 5 million or more by the year 2000 have shown reduced rates of population growth. (The only exception to the trend is Lagos, Nigeria, where the annual rate of population growth is expected to increase from 3.39 per cent in 1970–1985 to 3.54 per cent in 1985–2000.) The decline is most marked in third world cities, but those in more developed countries, despite their already low growth rates, have decreasing populations too.

Some urbanists originally thought that the declining rates of population growth in mega-cities was a form of "urbanization reversal," a tribute to the rational decision-making of urban residents and migrants as well as urban planners and managers. It is becoming increasingly clear, however, that the decline is more of a statistical artifact than a real case of urban decline. To paraphrase Wirth's [11]

The world's urban agglomerations

	Population			Average annual rate of growth (%)			
				Total population		Urban agglomeration	
Agglomeration	1970	1985	2000	1970–1985	1985–2000	1970–1985	1985–2000
Tokyo-Yokohama*	14.91	18.82	20.22	0.97	0.48	1.55	0.48
Mexico City*	9.12	17.30	25.82	2.89	2.16	4.27	2.67
São Paulo	8.22	15.88	23.97	2.31	1.87	4.39	2.75
New York	16.29	15.64	15.78	0.99	0.80	−0.27	0.06
Shanghai	11.41	11.96	14.30	1.62	1.13	0.31	1.19
Calcutta	7.12	10.95	16.53	2.09	1.60	2.88	2.75
Buenos Aires*	8.55	10.88	13.18	1.62	1.31	1.61	1.28
Rio de Janeiro	7.17	10.37	13.26	2.31	1.87	2.46	1.64
London*	10.59	10.36	10.51	0.08	0.03	−0.14	0.09
Seoul*	5.42	10.28	13.77	1.71	1.41	4.27	1.95
Greater Bombay	5.98	10.07	16.00	2.09	1.60	3.47	3.09
Los Angeles	8.43	10.05	10.99	0.99	0.80	1.17	0.60
Osaka-Kobe	7.61	9.45	10.49	0.97	0.48	1.44	0.70
Beijing*	8.29	9.25	11.17	1.62	1.13	0.73	1.25
Moscow*	7.07	8.97	10.40	0.95	0.81	1.58	0.99
Paris*	8.34	8.68	8.72	0.50	0.30	0.26	0.03
Jakarta*	4.48	7.94	13.25	2.17	1.59	3.81	3.42
Tianjin	6.87	7.89	9.70	1.62	1.13	0.93	1.37
Cairo-Giza	5.69	7.69	11.13	2.33	2.06	2.01	2.46
Teheran*	3.29	7.52	13.58	3.01	2.52	5.51	3.94
Delhi*	3.64	7.40	13.24	2.09	1.60	4.74	3.88
Milan	5.52	7.22	8.15	0.45	0.15	1.79	0.81
Manila-Q.C.*	3.60	7.03	11.07	2.48	2.04	4.46	3.03

Chicago	6.76	6.84	7.03	0.99	0.80	0.08	0.18
Karachi	3.14	6.70	12.00	2.83	2.26	5.06	3.88
Bangkok*	3.27	6.07	10.71	2.31	1.61	4.13	3.79
Lima-Callao	2.92	5.68	9.14	2.67	2.33	4.43	3.17
Madras	3.12	5.19	8.15	2.09	1.60	3.39	3.01
Hong Kong	3.53	5.13	6.37	2.28	1.33	2.48	1.44
St. Petersburg	3.96	5.11	5.93	0.95	0.81	1.70	0.99
Dacca*	1.54	4.89	11.16	2.78	2.44	7.68	5.50
Madrid*	3.37	4.71	5.36	0.88	0.61	2.23	0.86
Bogotá*	2.37	4.49	6.53	2.15	1.87	4.24	2.51
Baghdad*	2.10	4.42	7.42	3.53	3.12	4.95	3.45
Philadelphia	4.05	4.18	4.36	0.99	0.80	0.21	0.29
Santiago*	3.01	4.16	5.26	1.61	1.37	2.16	1.58
Pusan	1.85	4.11	6.20	1.71	1.41	5.33	2.74
Shenyang	3.14	4.08	5.35	1.62	1.13	1.74	1.81
Bangalore	1.66	3.97	7.96	2.09	1.60	5.80	4.63
Caracas*	2.12	3.74	5.03	3.27	2.37	3.78	1.98
Lahore	1.97	3.70	6.16	2.83	2.26	4.19	3.41
Lagos*	1.44	3.65	8.34	3.39	3.54	6.18	5.51
Belo Horizonte	1.62	3.25	5.11	2.31	1.87	4.63	3.02
Ahmedabad	1.74	3.14	5.28	2.09	1.60	3.92	3.46
Hyderabad	1.80	3.12	5.13	2.09	1.60	3.67	3.30
Ankara*	1.27	2.90	5.20	2.22	1.88	5.52	3.90
Kinshasa*	1.23	2.69	5.04	2.86	3.09	5.21	4.19
Algiers*	1.19	2.66	5.09	3.05	2.88	5.34	4.32
Medan	0.64	2.09	5.36	2.17	1.59	7.93	6.28

Note: The concept of urban agglomeration has been used to the extent possible. For some countries, however, only data on the administrative city proper are available.
*Urban agglomeration contains the capital city.

observation, the rate of urbanization might be declining but urbanism as a way of life is on the increase (see also [2]).

Urbanism, as a social process, involves certain changes, such as the secularization of society, loss of primary group relationships, erosion of kinship ties and other traditional bonds, increased diversification in economic production and social functions, and differentiation between what one produces and what one consumes. With rapid urbanization, the spread of these social processes tends to jump the physical boundaries of the city proper and extend to formerly rural hinterlands. The technological revolution in information and communication in recent years has accelerated the spread of urbanism. In other words, since a person nowadays does not have to physically live within a statistically defined urban area to become "urban," quite a number of people have now moved to "rural" areas although they continue to enjoy all the benefits of urbanism.

The spread of urbanism is most obvious in the rapid growth of urban agglomerations. As the table shows, mega-cities like New York, Detroit, Manchester, and London, which had negative rates of growth in their urban agglomerations in 1970–1985, are showing positive rates of growth in 1985–2000. The growth of urban agglomerations is also observable in cities in centrally planned economies, such as Beijing and Shanghai. In these cities, strict adherence to planning regulations that artificially confined urban growth to administratively set boundaries has created urban sprawl, which is requiring adjustments of metro/region boundaries.

In technologically advanced countries, one effect of spreading urbanism is that urban citizens seem to be working longer hours as they are able to communicate decisions wherever they are and whenever they feel like it, instead of being controlled by the workplace or official working hours. Decisions can be made and communicated through computer networks, electronic mail, faxes, beepers, and cellular phones. Some jobs, therefore, are increasingly freed from the tyranny of geographical space. Information technology has made possible "moving jobs where people are," rather than "moving people where jobs are." This capability has had significant implications for urban forms.

The spread of urbanism will most likely have salutary effects on social development in the mega-cities of the future. Improvements in communication – the movement of ideas rather than persons and things – might help to ease urban ills such as congestion, traffic jams, and pollution. Positive effects in human socialization, education, and social control might also be achieved. In recent times, for example, the reduction of the world into a global village through television coverage and satellite hook-ups have helped to bring to most people's attention such events as Tiananmen Square, the breaching of the Berlin Wall, or the toppling of a dictatorship in Bucharest. In cities as varied as Hong Kong, Tokyo, and New York, quicker decisions are being made with the help of cellular phones, pagers, computers, and faxes, a fact directly related to higher productivity.

The information revolution, of course, might have negative impacts as well. With people working longer hours, the traditional division between home life and workplace is becoming blurred. Leisure and work hours are also losing most of their meaning. In the urban fast lane, the information-driven way of life can cause premature burn-out, psychological pressures, and poor mental and physical health. The new lifestyle might also further erode the family, as competing claims for one's time multiply with the rapidity with which decisions are communicated.

The urbanization of poverty

In mega-cities of both industrialized and developing countries, the gap between the very rich and the very poor seems to be widening. In 1980, the UNDP estimated that 40 million urban households were living in poverty; this was projected to increase to 72 million by the year 2000, a 76 per cent increase [10]. The polarization of affluence and poverty is seen in more developed countries as well. Moynihan [8] has estimated that more than half of the babies born in New York City by the year 2000 will be born to parents who are on welfare. He blames government policies that cut back welfare assistance for the further impoverishment of the already poor.

In developing countries, the global recession and economic difficulties in the 1980s have significantly weakened the capacity of central governments to respond to urban needs. Hyper-inflation, the debt burden, and the structural adjustments imposed on many developing countries have combined to make national survival more pressing than solving the problems of cities. High rates of rural-urban migration have continued to inundate mega-cities, merely transferring rural poverty to urban areas.

Urban infrastructures in most developing country mega-cities have not been able to keep up with expanding need. For example, in Nairobi, the per capita spending for water and sewerage fell from $28 in 1981 to $2.50 in 1987; expenditures for water and sewerage maintenance went down from $7.30 per person to $2.30 within the same period [10].

Not surprisingly, housing and social services have suffered the most. In Calcutta, about 3 million people live in shanty towns without potable water. Another 2.5 million live in under-served inner city areas. In Karachi, only a third of urban households have a piped water connection. In Bangkok, less than a third of the people have access to piped water; so many households have dug wells that the water-table has been causing the land to subside [10].

Pavement dwellers and the homeless used to be found mainly in third world cities like Bombay, Calcutta, and Madras. Now, an estimated 600,000 to 3 million people in America are homeless, with about 35,000–70,000 in New York and 6,000 in San Francisco. The conservative ideology and fiscal policies of the Reagan administration have severely cut back federal grants for social and welfare programmes.

The appropriations for subsidized housing of the Department of Housing and Urban Development was cut by 75 per cent during the Reagan administration, from $33 billion in 1981 to $8 billion in 1988. At the same time, this had the effect of dropping some 500,000 people from the welfare rolls. About 1 million flop-house rooms have been torn down in the United States since the 1970s [7].

The effects of these policies have been hardest on the mega-city poor. In Los Angeles, welfare payments have gone down by 33 per cent. In New York, programmes for the homeless have increasingly relied more on community philanthropy, providing shelters and soup kitchens for the homeless, transitional housing, and health care and counselling. While these efforts have been able to help a few, authorities and NGOs are finding that quite a proportion of the homeless are beyond their reach. It was estimated, for example, that about half of the women in transitional housing in New York have a drug problem [7].

The problem of the homeless in America has reached a point where President Bush himself has called it "a national shame." The problem seems to be intractable, as it involves so many sectors. As Wright [13] indicated, homelessness

> is simultaneously a housing problem, an unemployment problem, a demographic problem, a problem of social disaffiliation, a mental health problem, a family violence problem, a problem created by the cutbacks in social wel-

fare spending, a problem resulting from the decay of the traditional nuclear family, and a problem intimately connected to the recent increase in the number of persons living below the poverty level.

In the impoverishment of urban populations, women have been affected specially hard. In theory, urbanism is supposed to cut the traditional shackles that have relegated women to an inferior role in many third world societies. The promise of education, employment, access to social services, and exposure to the mass media associated with urban life has not been fully fulfilled. Research findings have shown that women do not play such an important role in deciding to migrate to cities, for example. When single women do migrate, their low education and lack of skills force them to take menial jobs as maids, waitresses, or factory workers. Some of them end up in prostitution, drug addiction, and crime. Even when women join the international migration streams, most of them take on low paying jobs such as servants, hotel chambermaids, and service industry workers.

A particularly difficult problem in many mega-cities is the increasing number of women who head single-parent households because of abandonment, divorce, unwanted pregnancies, and multiple spouses. Studies have shown that women who head households tend to have lower incomes and are more likely to be on welfare. Because of the need to earn a living and look after the children, women who head households find it extremely difficult to adequately fulfil both roles. With governments cutting back social and welfare assistance to disadvantaged women, they and their children eventually become part of the so-called urban poverty problem.

Weakening of metropolitan governments

In the mid-1960s, the metropolitan solution was hailed as the cure to mega-city problems. In such experiments as Greater Miami, Metropolitan Toronto, Greater London, the Bangkok Metropolis, and Metro Manila, metropolitan government provided the comprehensive planning, wider and stronger tax base, area-wide services, multiple tier representation and participation, as well as administrative efficiency that promised to cope with the problems of the mega-city.

Barely two decades after the flourishing of metropolitan approaches, however, the metropolitan solution is in retreat. In 1989, the Greater London Council was abolished. The Metropolitan Manila Commission was also virtually disbanded (although in this case, the reasons were due more to national politics than metropolitan disaffection).

What brought about the weakening of the metropolitan approach is a complex of factors rooted in ideology, economic recession, and civic reactions. The past two decades have seen the rapid growth of a conservative ideology that railed against big government, bureaucratism, and higher taxes, while at the same time hailing popular participation, private enterprise, and voluntarism – the "thousand points of light" call of President Bush. The Thatcher version of this ideology, calling on the traditional interests of smaller local units, weakened the Greater London Council until it was abolished. The increasing costs of providing metro-wide services, the growing assertiveness of local units, and the general ineffectiveness of some area-wide solutions have eroded metropolitan governments in many mega-cities as well.

The metropolitan solution was supposed to be the answer to local government fragmentation and irrational municipal competition. It is ironic that it has now been weakened by stronger demands for citizen participation and "issues-oriented civic politics" at the community level. As metropolises have become more fragmented, the push for urban reform has provided the justification for central governments to intervene and abolish the metro government tier that was originally expected to provide comprehensive area-wide solutions.

The pathology of the city

There are few areas where traditional religions and Communist ideology agree totally, and the city as the source of evil is one of them. Recent developments in urban pathology seem to bear out their dire prophecies about urban living as dehumanizing, corrupting, and degrading.

Even a cursory reading of recent headlines leaves one with the impression that mega-cities are falling apart. Inner city schools in New York City are braced for the entry into kindergarten of a generation of five-year-olds prenatally exposed to crack, "little monsters" with neurological, emotional, and learning problems put under the charge of poorly paid and ill-trained teachers. Bangkok and Manila admit that AIDS cases are badly underestimated even as tourism officials warn against alarmist statements that may scare the tourists away. Tokyo's rapidly aging workforce worry about future security at the same time that younger couples are faced with the pressure of caring for elderly parents in cramped, overpriced housing or evading their responsibilities and pursuing a consumer-oriented way of life.

Drug-related bombings and assassinations plague Bogotá, while gangs battle each other for turf in Miami, Boston, and Toronto. Riots break out in Berlin, Amsterdam, and London as squatters are evicted from dilapidated buildings or as ethnic conflicts erupt between Asians and Caucasians. A survey has revealed that more than two-thirds of New Yorkers feel unsafe to go out at night; thousands of families have been fleeing the inner city for the safety of the suburbs.

The number of killings in big cities across the United States soared in 1989 and 1990. Comparing the first six months of 1989 with the same period in 1990, the number of homicides increased by 45 per cent in New York, 56 per cent in Boston, 75 per cent in Seattle, 41 per cent in San Francisco, and 31 per cent in Memphis. The Federal Bureau of Investigation set the homicide rate in the United States at 8.4 per 100,000 population in 1988. However, the homicide rate in cities of 1 million or more rose by 7 per cent during the first six months of 1990 (compared to 1989), and the number of violent crimes rose by 6 per cent [4].

Violent crimes and homicides are related to drugs in most cities, both because of wars over turf and the violent actions of people under the influence of drugs or alcohol. Another factor at play is the availability of powerful guns, such as semi-automatic assault rifles, which are fast replacing handguns as the instrument for death. According to the police, both murderers and victims in big cities are falling into younger and younger age brackets. Blacks and ethnic minorities are also over-represented among both victims and perpetrators.

Recent urban pathologies include rising incidence of "hate crimes" or bias-related random violence. New York tabloids have sensationalized the phenomenon of "wilding," resulting in gang rape, assault on strangers, and random terrorism of innocent citizens. So-called "thrill killings" have been known in Bangkok and Manila. Ethnic and religious tensions in mega-cities are indicated by assaults and boycotts. Live television coverage has given urgency to urban violence, be it the shooting down of demonstrators in Beijing, tear gas attacks in Seoul, artillery duels in Beirut, or coup attempts in Manila. While there may be some positive images of mega-cities in some areas, in general, the mega-cities in recent times have been depicted as violent, decadent, and falling apart.

Changing population structures and aging

The population structure changes in mega-cities are following two contradictory patterns. In cities located in less developed countries, continuing in-migration and high fertility rates among recent migrants are making city populations younger. In technologically advanced country cities (and in some third world cities as well), the phenomenon of aging is already apparent.

The aging of urban populations (the increase of the proportion of people aged 60 and above) is most marked in industrialized societies. In earlier decades, the migration of young workers to urban areas kept the population structure relatively young. As the migrant workers have aged, however, and as urban fertility levels have declined, the proportion of elderly in city populations has increased. In Madrid, for example, there are more people aged 65 and above than those below 15. Even China, where only 5.7 per cent of the total population was aged 60 and above in 1989, the city of Shanghai already has more than 10 per cent of the population in the elderly category.

The main impact of population aging is an increase in the old age dependency ratio. In Tokyo, as in most European cities, aging workers become more dependent on more productive family members in their old age. While social security, company pension funds, and other schemes have been instituted in many cities, their benefits are only available to people employed in the formal sector. A great proportion of the unemployed, underemployed and self-employed, small business people, and housewives are not included in such schemes.

Even people in the formal labour sector have their problems. In the United States, it has become very apparent that company financed pensions are failing to fulfil their promise of old age security. A survey in 1990 found that, of the 6 million people getting pension checks from former places of employment, only 7 per cent rely on them for more than half of their incomes. Personal assets, savings, and social security payments have become the main sources of income in old age for most people. The main reasons for the failings of company pension funds have been high levels of inflation, decrease in the number of people employed in manufacturing and industry as small service jobs have proliferated, and the economic dislocations that have undermined the yields of fixed income investments.

While cities in industrialized societies are aging, in the less developed countries, continuing high rates of rural-urban migration are providing a steady stream of young people. By the year 2000, when half the world's population will be living in cities, half of that population will be aged 25 and below. In developing countries, 35 per cent of the population will be under 14. In Latin America alone, projections to the year 2020 point to almost 300 million urban minors, of whom 30 per cent will be extremely poor [1].

A specially acute problem in many mega-cities is the growing number of street children, estimated at 30 million worldwide by the Independent Commission on International Humanitarian Issues. While extremely difficult to define precisely, it is known that street children are minors to whom the street (in the widest sense of the word) has become a habitual abode. Authorities often make a distinction between children "of the streets," who have no adults for company, and those "on the streets," who are parts of kinship groups but are still forced to gain their livelihood, education, leisure, and growing up on the streets.

Street children are associated with massive rural-urban migration that has dumped millions of formerly poor farmers into urban areas. Poverty and other problems have eroded family ties so that the street children have been forced to fend for themselves. They survive mainly by odd jobs, stealing, prostitution, drug dealing, and other illegal means. Their education mainly takes the form of learning how to survive, of becoming "street wise," and aging beyond their years. Growing up beyond the pale of moral and legal norms, street children become a real problem, because even if they survive to adulthood, they are quite likely to lead deviant lives.

A search for solutions

While the mega-trends in urban developments cited above paint a rather bleak picture of the mega-city, there are many policies, programmes, and interventions all over the world that promise some solutions to urban ills. Some of these measures are peculiar to the economic and cultural conditions of some cities, others apply to various situations. Some of the more noteworthy of these interventions include: (1) investments in human capital to enable certain disadvantaged sectors to achieve self-reliance; (2) subsidies and support for social and welfare programmes; (3) strengthening of urban management; (4) reliance on non-governmental organizations for the implementation of certain programmes as well as on the use of local communities for achieving local action; and (5) special sector efforts to assist women, youth, and the elderly. Quite a number of these interventions have been tried in mega-cities, and analysis of the factors that influence success or failure can help tremendously in the search for workable solutions.

Investing in human capital

As the World Bank's *World Development Report* [12] pointed out, investments to improve education, health, and nutrition are needed to alleviate poverty in mega-cities or rural areas. A rapid rate of economic growth does not necessarily translate into increased investments in human capital that could solve social and welfare problems. Certain countries like China, Cuba, Costa Rica, and Sri Lanka have been able to combat poverty and raise social and welfare conditions for the broad masses of their citizens despite having low or medium level per capita incomes. In China, life expectancy is as high as 69.5 years, infant mortality rates have dipped to 32 per 1,000 live births, and literacy is more than 80 per cent – all this achieved in a country with a per capita income of $320 per year. Costa Rica has been able to reduce its mortality rate for children under 5 years of age from 112 per 1,000 in 1960–1965 to 24 in 1980–1985, while Sri Lanka achieved the same feat at much lower per capita income, reducing the under 5 mortality rate from 101 per 1,000 in 1960 to 35 in 1985 [12].

The experience in countries that have improved the social and welfare conditions of their urban populations reveals the importance of certain measures. Such measures include providing safe drinking water, improved sewage disposal, environmental sanitation, mass immunization against contagious diseases, and campaigns against parasitic diseases. Improvement of the health of mothers and children through provision of basic health services, affordable drugs, and access to medical facilities is very important. Family planning services, which make it possible for couples to space the births of their children, help achieve maternal and child health. They also prevent illegal abortions, one of the main causes of maternal mortality in developing country cities.

Many countries have also used low cost technologies popularized by international action, such as immunization, the use of oral rehydration therapy for diarrhoea, growth monitoring to improve health conditions, and breast-feeding. Safe motherhood campaigns have had tremendous impacts on health in developing countries. Such impacts have been achieved not so much by sophisticated technology but by the increased awareness and knowledge brought about by mass mobilization programmes.

Of course, health, education, and nutrition interventions in many developing countries still suffer from some misallocations and inefficiencies. For example, 70–85 per cent of total health spending in developing countries is still devoted to curative care. In urban areas, this translates into modern hospitals, specialized clinics, and high prestige medical centres of "international calibre." Educational investments also devote the great bulk of funds to school buildings and teacher salaries, usually in tertiary education. The misallocation of human investment capital is usually related to élitist policies that neglect the urban poor.

The social investment dislocations in mega-cities are particularly evident in housing. Despite the popularization of certain basic housing schemes such as sites and services and community upgrading, even the most low cost housing solutions are not accessible to the bottom 20 per cent of mega-city populations [5]. Policy makers still treat housing in an ambivalent way – unable to decide whether housing is a social welfare expenditure or an economic and productive investment. In most mega-cities, housing is left to the forces of the market and the abhorrence of subsidies makes it inaccessible to the urban poor. In planned economies, housing solutions have gone to the other extreme, where "guaranteed housing" takes up less than three per cent of household income but where housing standards and maintenance levels are so bad that massive dissatisfaction and housing shortages are the rule.

One of the most positive developments in recent years is the realization that housing is a basic need that requires subsidies and individual investments. Thus, public housing units are being sold in China and the USSR to recoup some of the public investments, while subsidized housing for the disadvantaged and the urban poor is being constructed in North America and Europe. While the pace of housing reforms in both market oriented and centrally planned economies still needs to accelerate to keep up with housing need, the growing pragmatism about basic housing is a positive development.

Subsidies and support for social and welfare programmes

While general social and welfare programmes are usually effective in alleviating misery and poverty, they may miss the poorest of the poor, who need the benefits from such programmes the most. In many mega-cities, authorities have come to realize that despite investments in human capital, there remain significant portions of the urban poor who miss out on the benefits. For these sectors – the extremely poor, the disadvantaged, and the infirm – some form of "safety net" has to be provided through subsidized programmes. This may include food rations, public employment, shelter, health facilities, and subsidized housing. An example of such approaches is the concept of "five guarantees" in China, which assures every citizen access to food, clothing, shelter, employment, and burial [6].

Subsidies and support may be generally provided to all citizens or they may be targeted to benefit only specific groups. Subsidized food in urban areas, a general feature in most developing countries, have been found to be extremely costly. However, many governments have supported such policies because they are politically very popular to those who count politically and because the administrative costs of a selectively targeted programme are extremely high. In the widely entangled societies in many developing countries where kinship and other ties predominate, the enforcement of certain criteria and qualifications for access to subsidized public welfare is extremely difficult because of widespread favouritism and corruption.

Special targeting of subsidies and support might work in cases where such subsidies are provided only to items usually consumed by the poor. For example, in Egypt, the government subsidizes mainly coarse flour and Brazil subsidizes cassava. Since these items are consumed mainly by the very poor, while those who can afford to prefer to consume better quality items, the subsidies reach those who need the items most.

In Sri Lanka, food stamps were targeted for families earning less than 300 rupees a month – about half of the total population. The administrative simplicity of the food stamp programme, compared to the cumbersome system of food rationing used before 1980, made the approach more effective. The government was also able to pass on the administrative savings from the new system to the poor beneficiaries.

While generalized subsidy programmes tend to have wider coverage, experience has shown that more precisely targeted subsidies have a more salutary effect on the welfare of the very poor. Some of the more frequently targeted beneficiary groups are poverty stricken female heads of households, nursing mothers, the aged, infirm, squatters and slum dwellers, recent migrants, etc. The more precise the identification of the target group, the more efficient the subsidies can be. The benefits of subsidies, therefore, tend to have a stronger impact on the social and welfare problems of the mega-city.

Strengthening of urban management

The weakening of metropolitan approaches in coping with mega-city problems highlights the need to strengthen urban management, especially in developing countries. Despite the many problems of mega-cities, they are still the engines of growth and economic spur to social development. Strengthening of urban management, in turn, requires such interventions as the decentralization of authority to appropriate urban units, improving municipal revenue, pursuing "enabling strategies" that tap the resources of the socially underprivileged, and launching environmentally sensitive interventions.

In most developing countries, the mega-city, which is usually the political and administrative capital of the country, is tightly controlled by the central government. While the mega-city benefits from higher infrastructure investments, greater concentration of educational, medical, and social facilities, and more welfare subsidies, mega-city management usually suffers from the heavy handed interventions of central governments.

Where mega-cities are not given sufficient political and administrative authority to manage local affairs, they become mere appendages to national systems of decision-making. They become overly dependent on central government revenues and grants-in-aid, which, because they are awarded on the basis of national political priorities and short-term considerations, do not allow for long-term and medium-term planning. Central government dominance hinders the development of human resources to improve urban management as career ladders are geared more to national rather than to municipal office advancement. Worst of all, the financial resource base of mega-cities is not fully tapped as tax shares and grants become more important sources of municipal finance. Local taxpayers are also loath to pay taxes if they do not see a direct relationship between what they pay and the benefits they enjoy.

Central city dominance transforms the primary urban centre into a magnet for rural-urban migrants. However, because social and welfare priorities are set at the national level, the urban poor might not be given enough attention by national politicians, who find rural residents more predictable in their voting support. The mega-city, therefore, becomes saddled with the unexpected results of central government social policies at the same time that it is denied the fiscal and human resources to deal with those problems.

Whether authority is delegated to the local municipalities or towns or to metropolitan political or administrative structures would depend on the particular historical and political situation in every country. Strengthening of municipal or metropolitan government tiers, however, is invariably positively related to improvement of social and welfare conditions. Public responsibilities and governmental authority need to be well matched. Local officials are generally more responsive to local social demands and needs, so they tend to look after local needs better than central government officials, whose political power base may lie in rural constituencies set apart from urban areas.

Non-governmental organizations and community support

Some of the most important resources in improving mega-city development involve non-governmental organizations and civic groups that perform such important social functions as articulation of interests, mobilization of indigenous resources, implementation of programmes, and monitoring and evaluation of the effects and impacts of programmes. In both developed and developing countries, NGOs perform an important integrating and mobilizing role in urban affairs. In some cases, NGO efforts supplement and complement governmental efforts for social and welfare development. In others, NGOs serve as pressure groups and critics to feed back community reactions to public efforts and even to stop programmes inimical to social and welfare goals.

NGOs have proven most effective in collaborating with governmental efforts. For example, police efforts to combat crimes against property in many North American cities have been significantly augmented by civic efforts such as "neighbourhood watch," where neighbours look out for each other's properties in an organized way. Civic efforts such as etching identification numbers on valuables carried out jointly by police and NGOs have been successful in curbing theft and the trade in stolen articles.

NGO efforts have also been most useful in mobilizing communities to safeguard the urban environment. An anti-littering effort in Bangkok called the "Magic Eyes" campaign has used a cartoon and the admonition that "magic eyes are watching you" to influence children 10–16 years of age and their parents to keep the city clean [9]. Similarly, the "cash for trash" programme in the Bronx borough of New York, which is now partially supported by the Department of Sanitation, has not only collected recyclable trash, it has created 20 full-time jobs in neighbourhoods and supplements the income of hundreds of poor people.

NGOs have even carried out projects generally perceived to be the responsibility of government. In the Orangi settlement in Karachi, some 700,000 low income people are the beneficiaries of NGO efforts to provide water pipes, septic tanks, and sewer systems in the unauthorized settlement. An NGO was organized in Orangi to plan, implement, and manage this system, by organizing communities into lanes of 15–20 houses and laying out the appropriate technology for the system. After three years, the community has had its own water and sanitation system, at costs almost 10 times lower than commercial or government set rates [10, p. 94].

Private businesses, working through NGOs, have assisted in making basic housing projects more successful in Metro Manila. One of the most difficult problems of poverty-stricken house builders in community upgrading and sites and services projects is a lack of a ready source of building materials that is within the capacity to pay of the builders. The "Freedom to Build" foundation in Metro Manila meets this need by selling lumber recycled from shipping crates, used galvanized iron, recycled nails and wires, recovered stones and concrete blocks, etc. These materials are obtained from housing demolitions, shipping companies, and various recycling sources. The effort, therefore, not only provides affordable building materials, it also helps to preserve the urban environment by recycling materials that would otherwise just add to the city's waste.

The positive roles of NGOs and communities have been recognized in urban management. Cohen has concluded, after reviewing the relationships between macroeconomic adjustments and the city, that urban management, especially the capacity to maintain and operate projects, is most important and that NGOs have an important role to play in this. He said that "relying on non-governmental responses to fill the need for service, whether through private enterprise in the market or through community action is . . . likely to be more efficient in services such as housing or on site sanitation than assuming that social engineering through top down public sector solutions can respond to a majority of the needs of the population" [3].

Assisting women, youth, and the elderly

In many mega-cities, some of the most disadvantaged groups include women, youth, and the elderly. Women who head urban households are particularly vulnerable as they try to fulfil the twin roles of income earner and home maker. The young, especially those living outside the traditional support net of the family, present enormous problems, especially as in no time at all, they join the ranks of the city's impoverished groups. The elderly are also victims of the weakening of family ties and, where they do not have sufficient savings, assets, or social security, find it difficult to survive in the mega-city.

Efforts to assist women are best carried out when they are young, and in the form of public and private efforts supporting formal schooling. Studies have shown that the number of years spent in school is one of the best predictors of women's welfare, whether this is measured in number of children born, capacity to earn money, or overall life expectancy. Unfortunately, in many cultures, parents prefer boys to girls as cultural traditions expect sons to support their parents in old age while girls join their husband's family. A most important intervention, therefore, is a public policy that provides free compulsory education to all young people, especially girls. This may even be supplemented in some countries by incentive schemes whereby parents receive financial rewards for every year that a girl is kept in school until the end of secondary education.

Urban programmes to improve the literacy rates of adult females, to train them in community organization skills that will enable them to participate in community decision-making, to provide them with credit and business skills to make it possible for them to earn their own income and with nursery and preschool services to allow them to enter gainful employment are badly needed in mega-cities. Of crucial importance, also, are programmes to allow women to control their own fertility so that they are able to have control over their own bodies.

In-school and out of school youth need special programmes to respond to their special needs. Governmental and NGO efforts to assist street children have been launched in many mega-cities with some success. Vocational schooling, counselling, and motivation are needed for disadvantaged youth, especially those who have lived outside the influence of the family for some time. The traditional institutions to deal with wayward youth (reformatories, orphanages, and jails) have been known to sometimes exacerbate the problem. Social and welfare efforts, particularly those carried out by communities and NGOs, have been particularly useful in many mega-cities. Such efforts include skills training, "Big Brother" programmes, counselling, drug rehabilitation, and shelters and hostels for the young.

As the population of mega-cities ages, the plight of the elderly is gaining greater attention. Traditionally, the elderly were looked after in the context of the family, especially in cultures that revered old age as being synonymous with wisdom. Increasingly, however, the elderly in mega-cities are left to fend for themselves as housing shortages, lower nuclear family income, and weakening kinship ties make it more and more difficult to rely on the family. In many mega-cities, public and NGO programmes have been initiated to help the elderly. Among the more innovative of these are:

1. Public programmes that offer incentives to families that agree to look after elderly members. These could include tax breaks, financial subsidies, or civic awards. In some Chinese cities, for example, young families are given financial incentives if they agree to "adopt" an elderly person and care for him or her even if that person is not related to them.
2. Homes for the aged that are integrated with communities have been set up in many North American and European cities. Typically small and looked after by professional staff, these homes do not isolate the elderly in large institutions. For as long as they are physically able to be up and about, the residents of these homes are able to participate in community affairs, do their shopping, and lead lives in tune with the pace and rhythm of urban life.
3. Health care for the elderly that relies on community assistance and mobile services instead of large hospital-like environments are especially appropriate. To be avoided are institutions with advanced technological services that isolate the elderly and only cater to their physiological and medical needs.
4. Home ownership arrangements where the elderly are able to live normal lives within a community context have been tried and should be encouraged.
5. Continuing education and leisure activities for the elderly that enable them to be intellectually, physically, and economically active for as long as they are able to are needed. In many cities, old people are encouraged to continue to be gainfully employed in such functions as community work, teaching, or imparting old traditions and craft skills to the young. In this way, the elderly are recognized and respected for what they can offer at the same time that they earn extra income.

Concluding remarks and research needs

The social and welfare needs in mega-cities of developed and developing countries have not received as much attention as programmes for comprehensive planning, urban management, or economic investments. However, as shown in this paper, recent mega-trends and macroeconomic changes have made social and welfare conditions in mega-cities significantly worse. As the world faces the prospect of becoming half urban by the turn of the century, there is a need to understand the dynamics of the mega-city better, and, based on careful research, such understanding may become the foundation of developmental policies. Some of the key research needs in mega-city development include the following:

1. Social impacts of macroeconomic developments on the mega-city. During the last 10 years or so, major developments external to the city have had profound effects on urban development. Some of these include the global recession in the beginning of the 1980s, structural adjustments in developing country economies, the debt burden, and increased problems with rural-urban and international migration. While the evidence has been mainly qualitative up to now, there is a widespread feeling that all these trends have worsened social and welfare aspects of urban life. To the extent that the macroeconomic data allow, careful studies should be carried out on the scope of the social changes correlated with macroeconomic developments. Mega-cities, although they usually form the core of national economies, usually do not have control over the larger forces that directly affect them. Such a study should explore central government and mega-city mechanisms that would help alleviate the social and welfare problems associated with macroeconomic changes.

2. The urbanization of poverty. Quantitative and qualitative indicators of urban life are tending to show the steady growth of poverty in mega-cities. Growing poverty in urban areas needs to be studied in both developed and developing country cities. In the former, studies should focus on the marked increase of the homeless, deteriorating housing conditions, the return of contagious diseases such as tuberculosis in areas where they were virtually eradicated in the past, and in rising drug use and crime rates. In the latter, urban poverty studies are needed on the continued growth of slum and squatter areas, more beggars and street dwellers, persistence of contagious diseases such as cholera, diarrhoea and other water-borne diseases, and the expansion of inner city slums occupied by third or fourth generation slum dwellers left behind by upwardly mobile individuals. Based on the results of these studies, more policy-oriented approaches may be formulated.

3. Changing role and status of women in mega-cities. The megatrends affecting mega-city developments have significant implications for the changing role and status of women. Studies of internal and international migration already show the differential participation of women in migration streams to urban agglomerations. Rapid changes in social relationships associated with urbanization, theoretically, break the traditional bonds that relegate women to inferior roles. However, case-studies and targeted studies are needed to find out if this hypothesis is true. There are qualitative studies suggesting that special groups of women (unmarried women with children, single women, elderly women) may be adversely affected in a more critical way by rapid social changes in urban areas. These studies have to be verified and, if found true, measures for alleviating and improving the conditions of these disadvantaged groups should be found.

4. Popular participation in mega-city development. The rhetoric of development is increasingly advocating the strengthened role of popular participation in urban life. Popular participation is variously defined to include communities and neighbourhoods, the private sector, civic associations and clubs, non-governmental organizations, and special interest groups. Most of the evidence on the positive role of popular participation, however, is qualitative and anecdotal. The so-called success stories are usually limited in scope, the cases written cover the initial period of euphoric success and neglect to include cases of long-term failures, and they fail to illustrate how popular participation could be institutionalized in such a way that the process of popular participation can become a predictable component of mega-city development. Most studies are also unique to a particular city or country; they neglect to isolate the general or common factors that may transcend cultural and historical particulars. Perhaps a more thorough study of popular participation based on analysis of an adequate number of cases would be able to provide some answers to the real (as against the ideological) importance of participation in metropolitan life.

Popular imaginings of the mega-city of the future dwell primarily on the technological marvels, such as anti-gravity trains, greenhouse agriculture, computerized home shopping, solar powered cars, etc. In contrast, research and thinking on the social and welfare aspects of mega-city life hark back to nostalgic ideals of the small community, the traditional family, the reliance on civic conscience and charity, the town meeting as the medium for community decision-making, and the resurgence of voluntarism and private enterprise. It is natural for a time-lag to occur before social changes catch up with physical technologies, but urban societies seem to be reverting to old norms instead of adapting to technological trends. What cannot be ignored, however, is the increasing deterioration of social life in mega-cities. There seems to be an inability to apply some of the near-magical innovations in science and technology to the human condition. If this incapacity persists, the future of the mega-city, and the future of the human species, might not be such a bright one.

References

1 Agnelli, Susana. *Street Children, A Growing Urban Tragedy*. Report for the Independent Commission on International Humanitarian Issues. London: Weidenfeld and Nicolson, 1986.

2 Anderson, Nels. *The Urban Community: A World Perspective*. New York: Henry Holt and Company, 1959.

3 Cohen, Michael A. "Macroeconomic Adjustment and the City." In *Cities* 7 (February 1990), no. 1: 49–59.

4 Hinds, Michael de Courcy. "Number of Killings Soars in Big Cities Across US." *The New York Times*, 18 July 1990, p. 1.

5 Laquian, Aprodicio A. *Basic Housing: Policies for Urban Sites, Services and Shelter in Developing Countries*. Ottawa: International Development Research Centre, 1983.

6 ———. "The Effects of National Urban Strategy and Regional Development Policy on Patterns of Urban Growth in China." In Jones, Gavin, and Pravin Visaria, eds. *Urbanization in Large Developing Countries: China, India, Indonesia and Brazil*. Canberra: Australian National University, in press.

7 Levitas, Michael. "Homeless in America." *The New York Times Magazine*, 10 June 1990, p. 45.

8 Moynihan, Daniel Patrick, quoted in *The New York Times*, 6 June 1990, p. 6.

9 Perlman, Janice. "A Dual Strategy for Deliberate Social Change in Cities." *Cities* 7 (February 1990), no. 1.

10 United Nations Development Programme. *Human Development Report, 1990*. New York and Oxford: Oxford University Press, 1990.

11 Wirth, Louis. "Urbanism as a Way of Life." *American Journal of Sociology* 41 (July 1938), no. 1: 1–23.

12 World Bank. *World Development Report, 1990*. Washington, D.C.: Oxford University Press, 1990.

13 Wright, James D., *Address Unknown*, quoted in Levitas, p. 90 (see ref. 7 above).

9

Impacts of mega-city growth on families and households

Eleonora Barbieri Masini

Professor, Institute of Social Sciences, Gregorian University, Rome

Economic development and urbanization

The nineteenth century can be called the century of urbanization of the industrialized countries. There is no doubt that there is a strong historical correlation between economic development and urbanization processes, as indicated in table 1.[1]

Prior to 1800, no European country had more than 50 per cent of its whole population living in urban areas. After 1850, the process of urbanization accelerated so rapidly that there is now no European country with under 50 per cent of its population in urban areas. This means that in the course of only one century, practically all European countries have moved from a prevalently rural to a prevalently urban situation with a high incidence of urbanization (47 per cent); the exceptions are Yugoslavia (46 per cent), Albania (34 per cent), and Portugal (30 per cent).

While in Europe urban development can be said to have started in the Middle Ages, in North America, urban development started from a very low level at the end of the eighteenth century and subsequently became one of the most intensive urban processes. In 1790, the United States was virtually an agricultural country, with only five per cent of its population living in urban areas. New York City had a

Table 1 **Percentage of urban population, 1990**

More developed countries	73
North America	74
Europe	75
North	85
West	83
South	68
East	64
Oceania	70
Australia	86
New Zealand	84
Latin America	69
Central America	61
Caribbean	55
Tropical South America	71
Temperate South America	85
USSR	66
Less Developed Countries	32
Asia	29
West	58
South	26
South-East	27
East	29
Africa	31
Northern	41
West	30
East	18
Central	37
Southern	53

Source: *World Population Data Sheet* (Washington, D.C.: Population Reference Bureau, 1990).
Note: World average 41 per cent.

population of just over 30,000. By 1900, the city had 3 million inhabitants and represented the greatest urban concentration in the world.[2]

If we move to the developing countries, we find a very definite confirmation of the historical correlation between economic development and urbanization. However, in these countries the process of urbanization is often so rapid that it precedes economic development, thus increasing social marginalization in the urban areas.[3]

According to Pizzorno, the process of urbanization in the developing countries can be described as a process of over-urbanization on the basis of the following observations:

– The level of urbanization in the developing countries is higher than that of urbanized countries with the same level of industrialization.

- The process of urbanization in the developing countries has increased more rapidly in recent years than in the economically advanced countries; quite the opposite can be observed in relation to increases in per capita incomes.
- In developing countries, migration flows to urban areas exceed the job supply.

In this brief correlation between economic development and urbanization, it is important to look at what is known as the process of megalopolization.

The 1990s: The period of megapolization

If the nineteenth century was the century of urbanization, the twentieth century can be described as the century of metropolization (cities with more than 1 million inhabitants) and then megapolization (cities with more than 8 million inhabitants).[4] In the previous century there were very few cities with a population that exceeded 1 million inhabitants. By 1900 there were 15 (London being one of them), and by 1950 115, with populations that ranged between 1 and 8 million inhabitants. In 1970 there were 252 cities with a population of over 1 million inhabitants, and 4 cities – New York, London, Tokyo, and Shanghai – whose populations exceeded 8 million inhabitants.

Megapolization is a distinctive feature of the second half of this century. By 1985 there were 11 cities with more than 8 million inhabitants (see table 2).[5] It is an extremely important trend, whose consequences appear to be irreversible, as very clearly evidenced by sociological analysis. Undoubtedly megapolization is much more than a purely demographic phenomenon; its many repercussions on society and lifestyles can be expected to be lasting.

Table 2 **Cities with 8 million or more inhabitants as of 1985 (in millions)**

City	Population	City	Population
1. Mexico City	18.1	7. Buenos Aires	10.9
2. Tokyo	17.2	8. Rio de Janeiro	10.4
3. São Paulo	15.9	9. Seoul	10.2
4. New York	15.3	10. Bombay	10.1
5. Shanghai	11.8	11. Los Angeles	10.0
6. Calcutta	11.0		

Source: Pedro Beltrao Calderon, *Sociologia dello sviluppo* (Sociology of development) (Rome: Editrice Pontificia Università Gregoriana, 1988), p. 215.

It is important to stress that megapolization is a qualitative jump that brings urbanization to the global level, overcoming the historical logic of nation-states and even of regions, and entering into a "world dimension."[6] This is now occurring in the second half of the twentieth century. A second aspect of this new trend concerns the concentration of a very high proportion of the inhabitants of a country in the urban area. Mexico City is an example: already in the 1970s one-fourth of all Mexicans lived in the capital city. These two specific characteristics are creating a new kind of urban aggregation, with new needs and demands that in turn have a global impact.

In addition to the above, there is also the fact that we do not have only one model of urban concentration that one can conceptualize.[7] When is a mega-city such? Is it only a quantitative issue? What distinguishes the mega-city from a metropolis? What specific characteristics does it have, beyond numbers? Maybe each city belongs to a different methodologically defined entity. What is the impact of migration – permanent or temporary or even of a commuting nature – on a large city where people need the infrastructures for travel, food, and so on but do not permanently sleep in the town? What is the connotation of a satellite town, taking into account its relations with the major town? What are the limitations of censuses, which frequently are incapable of capturing such differences?

These are just some of the issues that are now emerging. The mega-city issue will be central to the future of many countries and peoples[8] and has not been the object of research in its various aspects as it should have been.

The urban family

Although the family as a social institution has been greatly influenced by the process of urbanization, it is not easy to grasp to the full the extent of this influence, because of confusion between the influence of urbanization and that of industrialization. The influence that the city has had on the family is also differentiated depending on the level of income, the job of the family members – for example, whether the family is a craft family, a working-class family, a white-collar family, etc.

In any event the specific influence of the trend must also be related to (1) family size; (2) the function of the family in terms of it being a social institution and a social group; (3) the power structure and the interpersonal relations between the sexes; (4) the social role of the various members of the family within and outside of the household; (5) family habits, rituals, etc.

If we look at family size (an aspect that will be further developed in the case-studies to be presented in the next part of the paper), we can say in very general terms that families are very definitely becoming smaller. This trend has already occurred in the industrialized countries and can be expected to increase in the developing countries. The ideal family size, according to this trend, is from two to three children per family.

Another trend to take into consideration is the increasingly difficult relations between generations in the mega-cities, due to lack of space and co-residence. The space issue will become ever more complex as cities increase in size. The tendency to build smaller rather than larger houses has, and will obviously continue to have, an impact on family size and intergenerational relations, especially as life expectancy continues to increase.

Closely related to these issues is the importance of structures or infrastructures for people living alone, the aged who need specific services, or groups of aged who live in compounds with their own independence and at the same time some company and social relations but who are physically isolated from the rest of the community. For these kinds of needs, the "district" question seems to become an answer to different needs and would give a certain human dimension, even in a large town. This kind of vision, which seems mainly related to industrialized countries, may have a certain logic in the developing countries, where urbanization often precedes industrialization and similar isolation problems could develop in direct relation to the size of the city.

Another trend shown by research is that family relations can extend in cities even over four generations, though spread over the urban area. This trend seems to be re-enforced in the developing countries, where the responsibility of family members is directed towards the original rural society. In some studies it is claimed that the extended family and non-coresidence continue to exist.[9] This may well be the case with the increasing need of group support in the large cities of the developing countries.

In relation to function, the urban family has been studied mostly in relation to its disintegration. More recently, especially in the US, analyses have been geared to the need to solve crises in families. This kind of analysis has the great disadvantage of considering the middle-class US family and comparing it with pioneering families. The urban family and the decrease in its economic productive function are very much part of the analysis carried out between the two wars. After the Second World War, in analysing the family, particularly the urban family, the social function has become increasingly important. This kind of analysis takes into consideration the reproductive function of the family, as well as the different socio-economic categories of families, and more recently other functions, such as education, religion, health, and recreation in different kinds of families.

The analysis of the economic function of the family has also become more related to family consumption. While this must be seen as being very closely related to the industrialized world, all the other functions must be considered in terms of the impact of the city on developing country families. Consumption as a family function is already becoming important in many developing countries and will become increasingly so, although more in some than in others, influencing other aspects of life, such as production and lifestyles. Indeed, in the urban area the family is becoming a very different economic unit, with different requirements. In many cases it has become more affluent, in others poorer.

In relation to power structures within the urban family, the internal structure of the family and the relations within it, there is a tendency for a greater equality between parents and less authoritarian relations between parents and children. These trends have often been indicated as a move towards an egalitarian family, based on different elements. Again, it is necessary to diversify in analysing such trends, in terms of the developing and even the industrialized countries, as well as in cultural terms, at least in temporal terms, as the process is under way and is, in my view, irreversible.

The reasons behind the trend for a more egalitarian family are (1) the family is based on a better social and economic position of women, as well as their growing psychological independence (this point will also be further developed later); (2) the decrease of the reproductive role of the family in economic terms, with the consumption role increasing; (3) the reduction of the influence of religion in the family; (4) the change in traditional values, such as children's submission to the father; (5) the greater influence of other factors: school, television, peer groups, associations, etc.

Sociologists believe that the greatest change to have occurred in the family is the reduction in the authority of the husband and father.[10] This trend has undoubtedly become increasingly evident in the industrialized countries; however, with diversification, it is already very much present in the developing countries. In the industrialized countries it is especially noticeable in relation especially to migrant families, as shown by research.

Another important indicator of the influence of the city on relations within families is the accentuation of the division of age groups and classes within the family. The urban environment seems to create more problems with regard to the co-residence of different age classes. In turn, different institutions also tend or try to satisfy the needs of the various age groups, especially the younger ones, thus creating a subculture of the young, frequently with interests and roles that are in contradiction with the family itself. Professional activities also tend to create subcultures that make the relations between the different age groups more difficult. This means that centripetal forces in relation to the family are present in the city, thus rendering the family a weaker social institution.

With the ageing of the population, the subculture of the aged is once again a very strong centripetal move that may have very strong effects: whether the external institutions try to answer the needs of the older age group is quite another matter, but it is apparently centripetal.

Recent sociological studies indicate the existence of forces tending in the opposite direction that seem to be re-enforcing the family. These trends may be linked to the characteristics of cities, which tend to rationalize relationships and life activities and to bureaucratize almost all aspects of living, because of the complexity of city life. These two aspects, rationalization and bureaucratization, seem to reduce the space available to the individual to express emotions. The family seems to be the only area for such expression, which, in turn, can make the family extremely vulnerable as so many demands are placed on it.

This is the cause of the apparent contradiction between the psychological expectation from the family and the higher incidence of broken families and unhappy marriages. On the one side, material impersonality becomes stronger in cities and places on the family expectations that sometimes make it fragile because it is incapable of responding to them. We have extreme individuality of life in cities and, on the other side, we have the social expectations from the family.

As Elise Boulding puts it, "families are the primary agents of social change in any society."[11] She underlines the myth, which still exists, that in some societies families were "golden-age families" and the families of today are only pain and no devotion. Instead, the truth lies somewhere in between the past and the present, offering a third solution: the capacity of human beings to continuously live in change. Elise Boulding uses the metaphor "the family is a dance of growth," thus conveying the magic and the dynamics of the difficulties of family life.[12]

Mega-cities and the family in transition

Once the population of a city exceeds 8 million, families seem to start to encounter even greater difficulties than those already described. I shall try to examine the long-term effects of the mega-city on the family, as I believe that this is the only way to look at an issue that is inevitably long term, since it is based on values, lifestyle, and choices that all have a long-term dimension.

Family size seems to tend to follow the world trend of a two-child family. However, this is a process that is slower and more lengthy than the process of development of the mega-city. Mexico City, Rio de Janeiro, or even Calcutta are examples of this contradiction and emblematic of the situation.

The percentage of families actually co-residing may tend to become smaller in order to survive in a strongly oppressive environment such as the mega-city; however, the smaller family will still keep up the more extended relations with the parents or near relatives, if they live at hand, or even with distant cousins. A Nairobi case-study shows that when a cousin (i.e. someone from the same tribe) is in town, the relative living in the town is responsible for him or her. In any event, the size of houses is an important factor: it is very difficult for families to find or afford houses large enough to accommodate extended families.

The number of children per family seems not to decrease so easily in mega-cities, as in Mexico City or other mega-cities, as evidenced by the number of small children begging in the streets or making petty thefts, even in Nairobi, where almost 90 per cent of the population lives in slums.

What seems to be important in relation to family size in mega-cities is the type of support system that develops, whether in the slums, in the "barrios" of Bogotá, or in the "pueblos jovanes" of Lima, where women from different families support each other: one woman goes into town, into domestic service or to sell fruit juices and chickens, and the other stays at home to look after the children – a sort of substitute for family support.

The family in a way becomes a household, in the sense of supportive relationships, as in the Nairobi example, where blood ties are the ties that count, when even the family has been left behind in the village, or as in the case of Lima, where supportive ties substitute for the family.

The point is that in mega-cities, ties or bonds have to develop in different ways and not necessarily only within the family as usually conceived (parents, children, grandparents, parents, and grandchildren). What seems important is that ties should be capable of adapting to different situations and environments and being supportive in order to survive.

In other cases, women create ties between families in a situation of danger or extreme need: in Warsaw the women built schools for the children after the destruction brought by World War II. We can cite the women of Japan, and closer to our time, the women of Mexico City after the 1985 earthquake: first they guaranteed the survival of their wounded families and then revived the social structure in terms of solidarity. In a sense, these women and families acted, at a time of destruction and when the public authorities seemed unable to provide for them, to revive the social structure, which inevitably was affected. Moreover, the size of Mexico City (the population has now reached 20 million inhabitants – more than the entire population of Australia) obviously increased the magnitude of such a great disaster. In a situation of danger and distress, therefore, the family as a primary living unit expresses its great strength.

In this context we should recall that mega-cities are relatively recent developments. The different family configuration seems to spring from the search for protection and answers to emotional needs. This is more than evident in the urban environment, as briefly indicated earlier.

In the mega-cities we also find what we might call neighbourhood alliances: young married mothers alliances among the mothers of children attending a particular school; alliances in religious or even professional communities; and alliances within ethnic groups. The important point is to have some form of social support that may originate from an individual's activity or his or her role in the family or within specific institutions.

What seems to be emerging is a kind of service system that is more flexible and innovative, being geared to needs as they emerge and developed by the people themselves, the families and households. Of course such innovative spontaneous infrastructures are more difficult to manage than regional or municipal public infrastructures. They usually develop within the neighbourhood, or even within a single block. Being so decentralized, it is difficult to link such infrastructures as they are created to meet different needs, and hence the difficulty of seeing them in their long-term perspective.

Another point to consider is the time dimension as related to space. In the extended mega-cities people obviously need a lot of time to get from one part of the city to the other. This means making allowances that weaken the family or its structures: people find themselves having to leave the family unit. It means different relations also within the family. It can mean a greater gap in generational differences. Older people become more isolated and find themselves having to depend on public organizations or on the goodwill of younger people, as the younger people, once they have jobs and start working, are often far away from the family. Solitude is the great menace for members of the family.

Thus the mega-city can either keep the family together in terms of generations closing to the outside or separate it, with the older members of the family being left alone, unless cultural bonds emerge in some stronger way. For example, in Shanghai, where the Chinese family, with its strong sense of duty toward the older members of the family, in a way bridges the difficulties between generations that have been created by the mega-city, keeping the old people within the family, with specific functions, such as looking after the only grandchild.

If we turn to consider the function of the family in the mega-city in economic terms, it is without doubt increasingly related to consumption rather than to production. The only ties in terms of production can be related to the activities of the various family members: finding ways of survival and bringing back to the family the results of their labour.

In looking at the internal structure of the family and its interrelations in the mega-city, we see that the marginalization of age groups arises even more frequently in the mega-city than in other urban structures. The young find their peers in institutions that figure in their lives: school first and then other institutions, including even the media, sports, music, and so on. The next age group is absorbed in its work. As it becomes the older generation, it starts to be increasingly marginalized. The only limit to this process of marginalization is to be found in the cultural roots of many of the families. Here again I would cite the example of the older population of Shanghai, where old men have an interest in animals – birds, goldfish – or of Calcutta and Bombay, where the ever extended family still seems to survive.

The relations between men and women in the family can become further complicated by various factors: the need for both to find employment, or a high percentage of unemployment or underemployment among the men, which is relatively common.

This is something that has been shown very clearly in research conducted in Latin America. In Lima especially, women are forced to find ways for the family to survive, while the men have no job and often squander the little that the women manage to earn.[13]

In terms of family structures, the loss of paternal authority in the urban society is also very closely linked to the strength of cultural identity in mega-cities. From research conducted by the author in Canada,[14] the authority of the father in the Italian migrant family seems not to have changed too greatly, the main changes having occurred at the economic level. At the social level, decisions concerning the education and the marriage of the children, for example, are still subject to the authority of the father, with some influence of the mother on educational issues. In other words, when cultural identity ties are strong, the diminished authority of the father, mostly related to industrialized countries, seems to not occur.

Another phenomenon that is more noticeable in mega-cities is the higher incidence of women as heads of households: women who are separated, widowed, divorced, or single and working alone for the children. This is one of the most important trends that is leading to the increasing "feminization" of poverty and seems to be a characteristic of the urban environment.

Two case-studies: Buenos Aires and Bogotá

The United Nations University has conducted important field research involving eight developing countries (of which only two will be cited here). The topic of research, as related to urban areas, concerned the issue of changes in the household and in women's roles.[15]

The urban area research concerned the mega-city of Buenos Aires and also Bogotá, which, though not an actual mega-city, seems to contain points of relevance.

In the area of greater Buenos Aires, San Martín being the specific site, the research focused mainly on women and households, in which the women worked in the textile industry. The need for both the men and the women working emerged very clearly. When women were the only providers in the household, they controlled the finances. An interesting aspect was that women seemed to have what was referred to as "formal management" on matters related to everday decisions but not on extras, such as vacations, for example, repairs, etc.

What emerged very clearly was the very long hours spent in travelling to and from the factory every day and also the fact that the division of labour in the household in fact changed very little, even though the women worked outside the home. So much so that in Buenos Aires the women spent on average two hours a day on housework during the week, and four hours at the weekend; this of course in addition to working hours. Men seem to participate very little. Fieldwork has shown very clearly that this is a general trend in many countries and does not seem to undergo, through the years, any great change in urban areas.

Concerning work in developing countries and mega-cities, the young women tend to start work at the same age as their mothers did. In Latin America their very first job is usually domestic work (Bogotá and Buenos Aires being the cases presented here) or in the textile industries. It is also clear that women's work is still valued at a lower level than men's. This point is also shown in research in China, even if in the urban area the difference seems to be mitigated because state control is stronger.[16]

Marriage age changes very slowly in the developing countries, even in the mega-cities. Children are often born, and jobs found, before marriage. What is clearly indicated is that families, whether formally constituted or not, start a little later than in the recent past, but child bearing in the developing countries still starts at an early age.

The situation is undoubtedly different in the industrialized countries, where stable unions and child bearing are being gradually postponed, even to after the completion of the woman's thirtieth year. This is increasingly evident in cities such as London; however, it is not a global trend: in New York, for example, among the Hispanic and the black populations, the changes in age at first marriage and first child are less marked.

Changes in marriage patterns or in the age of the first stable union are also influenced by religious factors, as indicated in the past by research conducted by S. Agarwala.[17] Even if the data are not very recent, they seem to be important because they indicate how age at marriage among the Hindu population was very low and has not changed that much.

In India age at marriage for the Hindu population is still very low: 19 for males and 13 for females. As many of the mega-cities are in India, this kind of indication has to be taken into consideration, even though more research is needed. For Muslims, age at marriage is older for men – 21 – but only 14 for women. This too is changing, but the growing Muslim population in cities is an element to be taken into consideration. Christians tend to marry later, males at 24 and women at 17.5. There has been very little change in age at marriage of males, as indicated in the research carried out for the United Nations University in greater Buenos Aires and in Bogotá, and only a very slight change in female age at marriage (around 19).

According to Ogburn's analysis, the religious element and its influence on family size seems to be weakening. In the developing countries, however, I would say that this is not the case. This point must be taken into consideration, since most of the mega-cities are in the developing countries, where the religious aspect is very strong. The religious element can be expected to continue to have a marked influence among the immigrant populations of the industrialized countries: the so-called "third world in the first world."

In the two case-studies cited, Bogotá and Buenos Aires, it emerged very clearly that the religious factor still has an important influence on family size, age at marriage, age at the birth of the first child, child spacing, etc. As to the older cohort, to which I have already made some reference, to some extent this research and the other fieldwork undertaken have shown that this cohort seems to be separated increasingly from the rest of the family, with a polarization of the age cohorts. The debate on this issue is still very much open, as indicated by Nancy Foner,[18] who, taking into consideration urbanization and industrialization, claims that the modernization process seems to produce a decline in the status of the older cohort. According to this author, in the rewards system of the modernization process, the older generation certainly receives fewer rewards. Such rewards include esteem, influence, and the highly prioritized values of industrialized and industrializing society. As young people have greater access to economic roles, the roles related to rights, or even to political power, are superseded by those related to economic capacity, for example, or by the greater importance attributed to ideas, influenced by schools, political parties, etc. However, in the developing countries, where, as already mentioned, the process of urbanization sometimes precedes industrialization, the role of the older generation seems not necessarily to decline, remaining as it had been in the village. If the older cohort remains in the village itself as the head of the tribe or the family, it still keeps the valued role and the respect of the young in the village, or even within the mega-city. In some cases, for example in Africa during the period of colonization, the role of the elders was even enhanced. This may still hold true in the modern process of urbanization.

What may be the issue in mega-cities in relation to the role of the elder generation is that there may be manifold aspects to this role, which is not only economic. It is not easy to say if the authority of the elders is declining, holding fast, or even growing. Empirical research is needed in order to understand this issue, which is one that is culture bound. It might well be that, after an initial decline, it will come to the fore once again on the basis of values, which are re-evaluated and are, again, important when economic values alone are no longer sufficient. They may even be revaluated for religious reasons.

It is true that the gains of one generation or cohort, according to a set of values, are sometimes at the expense of another generation. To apply a single role to the process of megapolization in the various regions is, however, at the very least superficial. To be sure, too little research has been done.

Conclusions

What can be concluded in this paper is that although analysis of changes in the household and urban society as a whole may be partially applied to the mega-cities, not much has been done in terms of empirical research on this topic in relation to mega-cities *per se*. The dimensions of mega-cities, and the greater distances and dispersion that they entail, need to be carefully considered, bearing in mind, however, that the greater the dispersion, the stronger the need for the support of the family, in its emotional answering capacity, even as the sole holder of responses to such needs. Again, this will probably mean a greater vulnerability of the family and the household.

Such research would need to be diversified in ethnic and cultural terms. As an example, it would be necessary, in relation to Mexico City, Calcutta, or Rio de Janeiro, to investigate the different responses of ethnic groups to the impact of the mega-city. Taking Rio de Janeiro as a first example, recognizing the presence of different ethnic groups from the north-west or from the north-east, with different African backgrounds in some cases, conveys the importance of the possible differences in terms of reactions of households to the same types of trends in relation to culture. Special attention has to be paid to an understanding of the effects of migration on the family and on the household.

In addition to such research, indications for policy would also be related to the need for local governments or international organizations to first get at the basis of such dynamics, in terms of ethnic groups, related to religions and rights and different values, in order to understand how the family can be supported in the change. Institutional support is needed as well as lightening the burden of women, who often have a double role and are often also heads of households. It will also be necessary to provide well-directed support for the older generation, which will increase in the mega-cities.

In conclusion, I would stress the need for the support systems themselves also to obtain the necessary backup. More flexible, innovative infrastructures (such as child care, health clinics, tailored education and training) may well be more adaptable than the state initiatives and be better suited to rapid change. Frequently they are better accepted by the population. The family and the household are often at the core of such support systems and thus may be able to counteract the centripetal forces, described earlier, that seem to emerge in the urbanized family as a first reaction, and some of the negative effects of such forces for the young and the older generation.

Notes

1. Pedro Beltrao Calderon, *Sociologia dello sviluppo* (Sociology of development) (Rome: Editrice Pontificia Università Gregoriana, 1988), p. 210.
2. Ibid., p. 211.
3. Alessandro Pizzorno, "Développement Economique et Urbanisation," *Actes du Ve Congrès Mondial de Sociologie*, International Sociological Association, 1962.
4. United Nations Secretariat, "Growth of the World Megalopolises" (Paper presented by the Population Division at the symposium, Mega-cities and the Future: Population Growth and Policy Responses, Tokyo, October 1990).
5. Calderon, *Sociologia dello sviluppo*, p. 215.
6. Gustave Massiah, "L'explosion urbain est prévu pour l'an 2000," *La Recherche* 220 (April 1990).
7. Sidney Goldstein, "Demographic Issues and Data Needs for Mega-city Research" (Paper presented at the symposium, Mega-cities and the Future: Population Growth and Policy Responses, Tokyo, October 1990).
8. Massiah, "L'explosion urbain," table on p. 518.

9. Division for the Advancement of Women, United Nations Office at Vienna, "Women and Households in a Changing World," in Eleonora Masini and Susan Stratigos, eds., *Women, Households and Change* (Tokyo: United Nations University Press, 1991), 30–52.
10. W.F. Ogburn and F. Ninkoff, *Technology and the Changing Family* (New York, 1953).
11. Elise Boulding, *The Underside of History* (Boulder, Colo.: Westview Press, 1976).
12. Elise Boulding, *One Small Plot of Heaven* (Wallingford, Penn.: Pendle Hill Publications, 1989).
13. Peru Mujer, *Women Organizing for Development*," Path Papers, no. 5 (1982).
14. Eleonora Masini, "The Family and its Changes in the Italian Community in Canada," in Raimondo Cagiano de Azevedo, ed., *Società in Transizione: Italiani e Italo-Canadesi negli anni 80* (Society in transition: Italians and Italo-Canadians in the 1980s) (Milan: Franco Angeli, 1991).
15. Eleonora Masini and Susan Stratigos, eds., *Women, Households and Change* (Tokyo: United Nations University Press, 1991). Carmen Elisa Florez et al., *The Demographic Transition and Women's Life-course in Colombia* (Tokyo: United Nations University Press, 1990); Liliana Acero, *Textile Workers in Brazil and Argentina* (Tokyo: United Nations University Press, 1991).
16. Alice Goldstein and Sidney Goldstein, "China's Labor Force: The Role of Gender and Residence," *Journal of Women and Gender Studies* (Taipei), Jan. 1990, no. 1: 87–117.
17. S.N. Agarwala, "The Age of Marriage in India," *Population Index* (April 1957) (Washington, D.C.: Population Reference Bureau), p. 97.
18. Nancy Foner, "Age and Social Change," in David Kertzer and Jenny Keith, eds., *Age and Anthropological Theory* (Ithaca: Cornell University Press, 1984).

Part 3
Mega-city management policies

10

Mega-city management and innovation strategies: Regional views

Ellen Brennan

Chief, Population Policy Section, Population Division, United Nations, New York

Introduction

This paper draws upon material developed in the project, "Population Growth and Policies in Mega-cities," currently under way in the Population Policy Section of the Population Division of the United Nations. Studies are being prepared on some 20 developing country mega-cities. To date, 13 reports have been published (Bangkok, Bombay, Cairo, Calcutta, Dacca, Delhi, Jakarta, Karachi, Madras, Metro Manila, Mexico City, São Paulo, and Seoul). The discussion in this paper, which is limited to these 13 cities, focuses on a few selected topics: current spatial strategies, urban land policy, urban services, and institutional development.

Current spatial strategies

A large number of developing country mega-cities have adopted spatial strategies designed to promote a polycentric structure as a means of slowing the growth of the metropolitan region. In Bombay, for example, planners have attempted to promote an ambitious second metropolitan region across Thane Creek, in New Bombay. In two other mega-cities in India, Calcutta and Madras, ambitious decentralization strategies have failed to take into account the very slow growth of these metropolitan areas and the fact that economic stagnation does not create the right climate for effective and efficient decentralization. Delhi has a more propitious growth environment, but even Delhi has experienced difficulties in implementing its decentralization programme of 18 growth centres, including six ring towns [14].

Other cities, such as Cairo and Jakarta, have attempted to alter the axis of growth, changing it from the past north-south axis to an east-west one, but so far success has been limited [8, 19]. Dacca adopted a northern development corridor strategy after 1981, but its growth pattern is deviating widely from the proposed strategy. Seoul has been more successful in promoting a directional strategy by adopting a series of measures, such as new towns and satellite cities, industrial estates and complementary industrial location measures, public transport investments, land use controls, restrictions on the expansion of educational facilities, and residential taxes to promote development south of the Han River [11]. However, even the Seoul experience has been criticized. The large green belt zone has resulted in dramatic increases in land and housing prices; moreover, a World Bank study suggested that industrial decentralization occurred because of market forces and not as a result of government policies [29].

It is generally agreed that spatial restructuring is a necessary condition for successful adjustment to mega-city size. Many of the negative externalities of big city size, such as traffic congestion and pollution, can be reduced by decentralization and suburbanization. However, mega-city policy makers have frequently not promoted polycentric development very effectively. In part, this failure was the result of limited capital resources and a chronic inability to control land uses, but these constraints are not a total explanation. In some cities, results would have been better if policy makers had tried to follow and support locational adjustments by the market rather than attempting and failing to counteract market forces. Resources were often wasted by investing in infrastructure in the wrong places, or too soon (in advance of prospective demand). In other cities, planners proposed spatial strategies that were too ambitious relative to the current rate of mega-city growth. Clearly, the central issue is to learn how, when, and where to intervene to promote an efficient polycentric structure rather than to impede it.

Urban land policy

Whereas key questions in developing country mega-cities are how to increase the total supply of land accessible to low income households and how to make better use of the substantial underutilized land areas, most governments have not adopted effective policies. Certainly, a study of land policies in the 13 mega-cities under review in this paper underlines this point. The land supply problem is generally independent of the type of ownership. It is as severe in cities where much of the land is publicly owned, such as Karachi and Delhi, as in cities where most of the land is privately owned, such as Bangkok, Metro Manila, or Seoul [3]. In all cases, the price of land has increased much faster than the consumer price index, exacerbating the difficulty of acquiring land for low income housing. In some cities, this price increase is partially explained by special circumstances, such as the absolute scarcity of land not subject to flooding (Dacca), purchases by nationals returning from working in the Middle East (Karachi and Dacca), or the existence of a large green belt (Seoul).

A more general consideration, however, has been the appeal of land as an investment for storing capital and generating future capital gains. This speculation has occurred despite legislation and other measures to curb it. Because of the lack of enforceable measures for controlling land usage, the spatial structure of many cities has been determined primarily by private development, which is obviously governed by on-site profitability rather than long-term general welfare [1].

As a result of strong future demand for land in most developing countries and the lack of alternative investment channels, land is often seen as the only reliable avenue for investment. In countries where remittances from overseas earnings have been used for land purchases, this tendency is even more pronounced. In Dacca, for example, the world's poorest mega-city, there has been intensive speculation in the urban land market in recent years. It is estimated that one-third of the remittances of expatriate workers have been used to purchase land. Land prices have risen about 40–60 per cent faster than the prices of other goods and services and are now completely out of line with income levels [15]. Likewise, in Cairo, remittances from abroad have been involved in a majority of all residential land transactions in recent years and have been a major factor in fueling the rise in land prices [20].

In addition to creating an artificial scarcity and raising prices, speculation has had other undesirable effects. In many mega-cities, large betterment values – which are often due to improvements in accessibility resulting from public sector investments – have accrued to private developers, whereas the social costs of speculation (e.g., leapfrog development, longer commuting distances, higher commuting costs) have been passed on to the public. In other cities (e.g., Karachi), speculation has not only distorted the residential land market but also resulted in a highly dispersed, discontinuous pattern of urban development, with large vacant areas lying next to densely populated built-up areas. Servicing those areas has been highly uneconomical. Water and sewerage pipes, power lines, and other service lines have to be installed with a capacity sufficient for the eventual total development of a given area; they have remained underused for such a long period of time, however, that cost recovery from user charges has been nearly impossible.

Since land is an essential ingredient in all urban growth, devising equitable and efficient land development policies is one of the major challenges facing planners and policy makers in developing country mega-cities. Because land is not homogeneous – indeed, each parcel of land is unique – basic assumptions of perfectly competitive markets routinely fail to apply to land markets [7]. Since market mechanisms alone are unlikely to produce an efficient allocation of land uses in cities, interventions in some form (e.g., physical, financial, legislative, administrative) are required to increase efficiency, distribute benefits more equitably across income groups, and reduce the negative effects of inappropriate land development such as congestion and pollution [26]. Thus even the most capitalistic, free enterprise-oriented societies have increasingly imposed some measure of public control over the use of urban land.

The degree of intervention has varied widely among countries. In a number of mega-cities (e.g., Bangkok, Cairo, Metro Manila), there have been virtually no effective measures to influence or control land development. Seoul, which is one of the few cities in the world that have experimented as much with a broad range of metropolitan development strategies, probably represents the opposite extreme. Independent of the degree of intervention, there are a number of similarities. Many mega-cities have formulated master plans that have included some prescriptions about the future directions of urban growth. These master plans rarely, if ever, have been realized and have languished in metropolitan planning offices as irrelevant documents [3]. The reasons are simple. The population projections underpinning the master plans were widely off the mark, hence on-the-ground uses soon differed widely from land use patterns in the master plan. Moreover, most master plans were formulated in too rigid and inflexible a manner and did not allow for readjustments in the light of changing conditions.

Land use controls, which generally were included as part of these master plans, have been largely ineffective. Controls often reflected a mainly engineering/architectural concern with order and the clear delimitation of land uses inherent in developed country town planning ideals [26]. Desirable standards of plot size, infrastructure, and so forth were typically set at levels higher than could be afforded by the majority of low income residents. Moreover, there was little or no recognition of the limited powers of enforcement available to planning departments in most developing country mega-cities, where most land development has taken place outside the formal, regulated sector [2].

Briefly summarizing a number of other direct public actions that governments have employed in an attempt to increase land supply: Measures designed to reduce the attractiveness of urban land as a vehicle for the storage of capital generally have been unsuccessful, mainly because so many members of the middle and upper classes in almost all non-socialist countries have invested directly or indirectly in land [5]. In India and Pakistan, for example, where the authorities have long attempted to control speculation, restrictions on multiple holdings, the size of land holdings, and the warehousing of vacant land have been circumvented by a variety of tactics from legal appeals to the use of family proxies [2].

Governments have also attempted to increase land supply through the legalization of land tenure. Experience from many developing countries has shown that tenure security can have powerful effects on urban residents' incentive to invest in housing and associated infrastructure. Also, it is a precondition in many developing countries for access to formal mortgage financing.

In a number of developing country mega-cities, problems have been encountered in legalizing tenure, particularly in regard to cost recovery. In Karachi, for example, despite vigorous follow-up and motivational campaigns, less than 10 per cent of residents came forward to obtain title. In other instances, granting security of tenure has produced "upward filtration," that is, the buying out of lower income residents by middle income households [5]. Mexico City is a case in point. Ironically, in spite of official pronouncements seeking to control Mexico City's urban sprawl, the regularization programme has actually fostered the spread of unplanned urbanization. Indeed, once land on the urban fringes has been regularized and infrastructure introduced, land and housing prices have risen rapidly, forcing lower income residents to sell out and move to cheaper, unserviced areas further out on the periphery, where the process is once again repeated [21].

Modernization of cadastral and land registration systems represents a further attempt to increase land supply. There is growing recognition that a major reason why local administrations in most developing country cities have not coped successfully with urban population growth is because they are "flying blind," that is, they simply do not know what is going on in their local land markets [25]. The information base in many developing country mega-cities is improving, particularly with the aid of aerial photography, which eliminates much labour-intensive data gathering. By and large, however, most mega-cities lack sufficient accurate and current data on patterns of land conversion, the number of housing units (formal and informal) built during the past year, infrastructure deployment patterns, land subdivison patterns, and so forth. Frequently, urban maps are 20–30 years old and lack any description of entire sections of cities, and particularly of the burgeoning peri-urban areas. Without information, many planners and policy makers have been operating on the basis of assumptions or using standards (most often inappropriate ones) from other countries to develop land policies. Unless these assumptions or standards are on the mark, plans and policies are ineffectual at best and destructive at worst [25].

Land registration has traditionally been a serious problem in most developing country mega-cities. Information about who owns what is typically poor; squatter settlements increase uncertainty about property rights; moreover, the legal and administrative systems for establishing, recording, and transferring title are typically inadequate [7]. If land markets are to work properly, transactions need to be registered. Once facts are recorded, land can be bought and sold with fewer obstacles, which helps the pace of development [32]. Improved land registers, besides being associated with improved property tax systems, can also bring in substantial transaction fees, since approximately 10 per cent of property in urban areas worldwide changes ownership each year. Bangkok provides an example of a successful land titling project. The $76 million titling project, which was conducted with the financial assistance of the World Bank, aimed at producing up-to-date maps on a scale of 1 : 1,000 (the Bangkok Metropolitan Administration had been using cadastral maps that were 40–60 years old), and eliminating leakages in the current valuation system [16]. The photo maps were sufficiently detailed so that few parcels of land escaped identification for taxation purposes (before the titling project, it was estimated that one-third to one-half of the 1 million land parcels in Bangkok were not linked to a property tax record). In 1988 alone, Bangkok's land titling project brought in $200 million in fees [32].

There are also a number of examples of joint public-private actions to increase land supply. Land readjustment has worked very well in the handful of countries where it has been practiced. For example, Seoul's land readjustment programme is widely considered to be an example of successful intervention in the urban land market, as it involved only short-term holding of land by the public sector and resulted in significant improvements. The programme is not necessarily transferable to other developing countries, however, since it requires a considerable administrative infrastructure, a well-designed legal framework, an effective political consensus, and speed in its implementation [11]. Another example of public-private cooperation, although broader in scope than land readjustment, is the Guided Land Development (GLD) programme adopted in Jakarta. GLD, which is essentially a simplified form of land readjustment, attempts to guide development to the fringe areas on the east and west of the city by providing serviced urban land on a large scale affordable by low and middle income households.

To sum up, mechanisms to influence public control of the land market have not been in short supply. The major problem has been implementation. It is politically difficult to introduce effective policies because powerful vested interests aim to maintain the status quo. Despite the fact, for example, that new computer technology provides an excellent means of modernizing cadastral and land registration systems, the real reason why so many cities have such antiquated systems and why land and housing values have not been updated is that owners do not wish to pay taxes, and governments are highly sensitive to the complaints of landowners [6]. Similarly, the whole issue of land speculation comes down to a matter of political will and of competent management, both of which are frequently lacking in developing country mega-cities.

Urban services

Housing

Urbanization pressures throughout the world have created enormous pressures on urban housing markets. Indeed, during the early 1980s, nine new households were formed for each permanent dwelling built in low income developing countries [32]. The gap between supply and demand in most developing countries is widening. In Thailand, for example, against estimated demand for 300,000 urban housing units, the National Housing Authority (NAA) was able to build only around 6,000 units annually [16]. In 1983, the most recent year for which data are available, the Philippines's National Housing Authority produced less than 800 completed housing units [12]. In Madras, some 6,000 legal housing units have been produced annually by governmental housing agencies and the private sector – against an estimated annual demand for 30,000–40,000 new units [17].

There are a number of similarities in the housing policies that have been adopted in all world regions. Until the early 1970s, housing policies in most developing country mega-cities typically followed the model of many industrial nations, relying on heavily subsidized blocks of public housing that were often targeted to special groups, e.g., to civil servants, the military. The number of units constructed was constrained by their high standards and resultant high costs. In many instances, standards were adopted as derivatives from the colonial authorities or from developed countries with totally different land and construction circumstances. In other cases, high standards were demanded as evidence of modernization and economic progress [26]. Since most of the intended residents could not afford the units, rents were usually subsidized. Despite large subsidies, however, public housing often went unoccupied for long periods of time as a result of poor location, inadequate infrastructure, rents that were higher than residents could afford, or cultural unacceptability [7].

To cite a few examples, in Jakarta, public housing units were generally constructed in peripheral areas and were reserved mainly for public servants and the military. Although some of the units were offered for sale to the general public, they were costly and had limited appeal. For one thing, living in high-rise buildings was an alien way of life for most Jakarta residents. For another, not only were there limited opportunities for employment in the area, but also self-employed households were prohibited from selling food or operating cottage industries in the new high-rise units [19]. In Bangkok, the large multi-storey apartment blocks constructed by the NHA during the late 1970s were neither culturally acceptable nor financially within reach of the target groups. In fact, the illegal transfer of apartments for "key money" became a common practice. Because of the poor quality of construction and lack of maintenance, many of the public housing complexes constructed under the auspices of the NHA are now classified by the NHA itself as "potential slum areas" [16].

Regarding government policy towards slum and squatter settlements, governments have sometimes ignored the existence of slum and squatter settlements or have excluded them from public utilities and health and social services. Bulldozing squatter settlements was a common occurrence during the 1960s and early 1970s. Indeed, land policy often had a simplicity that was generally misguided: if squatter settlements were growing, simply evict the squatters [7]. Moreover, it failed to consider that squatter housing represented a large part of the poor's capital stock.

Outright destruction of squatter areas is now relatively uncommon, except in cases where the squatters are living in areas unsuitable for upgrading. The early "sites-and-services" projects consisted essentially of a "basic needs" approach, emphasizing lowering standards to the bare minimum by providing shelter that could be upgraded progressively over time. Typical projects included provision of land tenure; selected trunk infrastructure to connect the areas with existing utility and road networks; on-site infrastructure (water, sanitation, roads, drainage, and electricity), often based on communal solutions; core houses, ranging from a simple wall with utility hook-ups to completed buildings; social facilities such as schools, health clinics, community centres; and financing for the plots, core houses, and building materials [33].

Although sites-and-services represented a considerable improvement over previous shelter strategies adopted by developing country mega-cities, they were based on new construction, and even under the most optimistic scenario, the majority of low income residents of developing country mega-cities could never hope to be reached. Area upgrading projects, on the other hand, have built on the existing informal housing stock where the poor already live and thus are in a better position to target shelter production directly to them. Typically, area upgrading projects aim at improving infrastructure in a comprehensive package that includes water, sanitation, drainage, solid waste removal, and roads and footpaths. Also, some form of tenure security usually has been part of slum improvement projects.

Although Calcutta is one of the poorest cities in the world, it has mounted a very large area upgrading programme and made considerable progress during the 1980s in addressing some of the city's most serious infrastructure deficits. Under the aegis of the Calcutta Metropolitan Development Authority, major area upgrading efforts involving the construction of paved internal roads, electrification, and the provision of standpipes and sanitary latrines have improved living conditions for nearly 2 million persons [10].

Jakarta's Kampung Improvement Programme (KIP) is widely acknowledged to be one of the world's most successful area upgrading programmes, having improved more than 500 *kampungs* and provided basic services for an estimated 3.8 million residents [19]. The basic principles of KIP are simple – to make improvements, even if marginal, in the living standards of as many residents as possible. Because of KIP's longevity, it has been possible to conduct a number of longitudinal impact studies. In general, such studies found that KIP triggered substantial private investment in home improvement and led to significant property value increases [19].

Very little attention has been given to the possible renovation of slum housing in the deteriorating central areas of developing country mega-cities. In São Paulo, for example, where more than 3 million residents live in dilapidated tenements, until recently there have been no upgrading programmes. Several pilot projects have been conducted under the auspices of the Catholic Church, one in a tenement in the central city housing 60 families [22]. The central location of these slum areas poses a number of problems, particularly in market economies, where the price of land increases towards the centre of cities, making these sites potentially valuable for redevelopment. Increasing commercialization and gradual gentrification have been among the major threats to the inner-city poor, often resulting in their expulsion into peri-urban squatter settlements. Governments have rarely intervened to counteract these trends.

Redevelopment activities undertaken in inner-city areas, either through public or private sector intervention, have not been successful in providing alternative improved housing for the poor. The interesting lesson is that this phenomenon turns out to be pervasive in almost all redevelopment initiatives, whether from the private sector for clearly speculative reasons, from the public sector with a genuine concern for the housing stock and living conditions of the poor, or, at times, even when tenant households have organized themselves and promoted redevelopment [23].

Sites-and-services and area upgrading programmes have been an unquestionable improvement over the public shelter programmes that preceded them. They generally succeeded in changing the outlook of policy makers and public agencies, convincing them that heavily subsidized, high standard, high cost units could only be good-looking social failures [9]. Moreover, the new types of projects played a key role in exposing important constraints on the performance of housing markets, such as prohibitively costly building regulations, overlapping layers of traditional and modern property rights, further complicated by imported land use laws or other regulatory constraints. In evaluating these projects, an important fact to consider is that they were typically financed by bilateral or international agencies, hence access to foreign capital facilitated the emphasis on the affordability, design, and construction of housing units for low income families. However, the total numbers reached worldwide were small compared to demand (indeed, total capital funds available from all international lenders would not even be enough to finance urban investment needs in a single large country such as Brazil or India) [9].

The latest strategy – commonly referred to as an "enabling strategy" – is centred around the idea that governments should serve as "enablers" in the housing sector, drawing back from their role as providers of housing and playing a more forceful role in facilitating new construction by the private sector (both formal and informal), mainly by creating an appropriate regulatory environment and ensuring the availability of housing finance [31]. Indeed, it is now generally accepted wisdom that governments do not, in general, respond to demand faster or more efficiently than private markets (but they can do much to mitigate or remove market imperfections [7]). In order to facilitate incremental building by the poor, the idea is that local governments will have to alter local building codes and regulations. Another important governmental role will be the stimulation of appropriate building technologies by providing incentives (e.g., credit, technical support) to small-scale producers of local construction materials.

Water supply

Water supply problems are among the most serious problems facing developing country mega-cities. The deficits are severe in many places. Whereas a relatively large proportion of the population receives piped inside water in Mexico City, São Paulo, and Seoul (82, 95, and 94 per cent, respectively), the other cities are not so fortunate. Around 66 per cent of Bangkok's population has piped inside water. In Calcutta and Manila, coverage is around 50 per cent. Only 40 per cent of Karachi's population receives piped inside water, usually for only a few hours daily. In Bombay, the level of supply is so much below demand that it is restricted to between two and eight hours per day, depending on location. In Cairo, about 20 per cent of the population, mainly on the periphery, has no access to piped water and uses substitute sources such as canals, wells, and public water fountains. In Jakarta, around half of the population obtains water from vendors – at about 13 times the cost of piped water (see United Nations mega-cities studies, United Nations, 1986–1990).

Unlike housing, transport, and so forth, problems in the water supply sector reflect the unique geographical, topographical, meteorological, and geological conditions of each mega-city. Karachi, for example, is located some 160 kilometres from the Indus River, which is its major source of groundwater [18]. In Bombay, the water supply situation reaches emergency proportions when the monsoon fails, as occurred in 1966 and 1972 [13]. Madras faces a perennial scarcity of water. In 1981, following a two year drought, the water supply situation was so severe that the government discussed transferring the city to the banks of the Cauvery River some 125 kilometres to the south [17].

Mexico City provides an illustration of the severity of the water supply problem. Situated in a closed mountain valley, with relatively scarce precipitation, Mexico City has had to ensure an adequate supply of water by pumping an ever larger volume, at escalating costs, from remote supply sources at lower altitudes. Costly projects such as the Cutzamala River project have enabled the government to increase the supply of water steadily – from 20 metres per second in 1960 to 42 per second in 1976 and to 60 per second in 1983, even though rising demand has reduced per capita consumption [21]. Currently, the authorities are pumping 55 per cent more water from the aquifers each year than is replenished by rainfall. As the aquifers dry up, the ground above sinks, in some parts of the city by 12 inches a year. The remaining water is becoming more saline, requiring expensive treatment.

Whereas supplies have increased, Mexico City lacks an efficient distribution system. Systems losses are estimated at over 30 per cent. Leakages and unaccounted for water may explain the relatively generous provision of more than 300 litres per capita per day, which approaches United States design standards. Factories and businesses use 28 per cent of the capital's water, paying 620 pesos (21 cents per cubic metre); domestic users, who consume 57 per cent of the total, pay one-tenth as much; only 40 per cent of domestic users are metered, and the authorities collect only 30 per cent of the fees they should charge (*The Economist*, 29 September 1990). Without money for maintenance, damaged pipes do not get mended.

When the supply of water is a major problem, it absorbs a huge share of financial resources. In Cairo, for example, a 20 year programme to expand production capacity and extend Cairo's distribution system is under way at an estimated cost of US$2.9 billion [20]. In São Paulo, it is estimated that investments of US$100 million per year will be needed to eliminate deficits and provide for growing demand [22].

In most developing country mega-cities, financial resources are scarce because of the failure to introduce comprehensive cost recovery schemes, often reflecting the principle that basic services such as water supply are social services for which users should not have to pay. Clearly, the gap cannot be bridged by fiscal resources. External aid from higher levels of government or from abroad (bilateral/multilateral agencies) is not likely to increase. Cost recovery is a viable option because surveys suggest that even low income households will pay for basic services such as piped water if the alternative is doing without or paying more for an inferior substitute (e.g., water purchased from carriers). The managerial problems are to convince consumers that user fees will mean better services and to devise instalment financing schemes to make the capital costs of services (e.g., a house connection for water) affordable for low income households.

Another key managerial problem is to give greater attention to operations and maintenance (e.g., repairing leaking standpipes, replacing damaged water meters) and to maximize the use of existing facilities (a "systems management" approach) to relieve the burden on new capital investments. Examples of the latter include measures to address the water supply leakage problem (e.g., Cairo, Karachi, Jakarta, Metro Manila). Whereas these actions are very simple, they may be crucial to whether the expected benefits from the original capital investment are realized or not. Although the problems are easy to handle technologically, they are more difficult from an organizational perspective, at least in mega-cities and other large metropolitan areas, because effective maintenance requires a spatial network of field engineers for monitoring, assessment, and upkeep.

Transport

Urban transport conditions vary widely among mega-cities, both in terms of the severity of the problem and the degree of the response, but there is usually some correlation between the two. For example, considerable efforts have been made to improve the very severe congestion in Bangkok and Calcutta, although the results have not been overly impressive. The exceptions are Seoul, which has a moderate problem by developing country mega-city standards but a very ambitious and broad set of policy interventions, ranging from restrictions on automobile ownership to massive public transit investments, and Metro Manila, which has severe congestion and slow speeds, but a very limited policy response.

Congestion is severe in many mega-cities. In Mexico City, congestion slows down the movement on the roads to 16 kilometres per hour at peak times [21]. In Metro Manila, travel along one quarter of the primary road network is now less than 15 kilometres per hour, while speeds in the CBD during peak hours are down to 10 kilometres or less, or about twice the speed or walking [12]. In Bangkok, where traffic moves at an average of only 13 kilometres per hour, congestion is as high as anywhere in the world, reaching levels at which many people modify their behaviour by changing trip destinations and time of travel, relocating, or not making the trip at all [16].

Most mega-cities have experienced extraordinarily rapid growth in the number of private vehicles. In Cairo, for example, the number of private vehicles has been growing by 17 per cent per annum [20]. The reasons for this rapid growth in Cairo are fairly clear and are typical of a number of other mega-cities. Despite repeated recommendations of the numerous transport studies conducted in Cairo during the 1970s and 1980s to assign highest priority to public transport, most investment went into the construction of bridges and flyovers, which served private automobile users. Another factor was the heavily subsidized cost of fuel (the pump price of gasoline at 15 piastres per litre was only about half of the economic cost; whereas gasoline prices were increased in two stages to 30 piastres, that is still below the market price) [20]. With the exceptions of Hong Kong and Singapore, there have been relatively few examples of governments seriously trying to limit the use of private cars. In the mid-1980s, Bangkok considered setting up toll gates in central areas of the city, but the proposal was quickly dropped [16]. In 1990, Mexico City issued a ban on each car during one working day a week – clearly a case of too little too late.

A major response to transport problems in developing country mega-cities has been high cost projects, such as the construction of metros. Of the 13 cities in question, four – Metro Manila, Mexico City, São Paulo, and Seoul – have established metros. Cairo and Calcutta have recently opened systems. After years of delay, construction of Bangkok's sky train is finally about to get under way, whereas Bombay, Delhi, Jakarta, and Karachi all have been developing plans. A recent World Bank-funded study found that, whereas rapid transit systems did improve public transport in the cities in the study, they did little to relieve congestion. Moreover, they were phenomenally expensive, ranging on average from US$50 million to US$165 million per kilometre of track [34].

Much less attention has been paid in developing country mega-cities to improving public buses, which are almost universally overcrowded and poorly maintained. In Cairo, for example, passenger loadings per bus are up to 2,100 passengers daily [20]. Moreover, up to a third of Cairo's fleet is out of service on any given day; in Jakarta, the figure is around 40 per cent. In many developing country mega-cities, minibuses, microbuses, collective taxis, and other forms of para-transit have filled the gap caused by the shortage of standard size buses. In Metro Manila, for example, privately operated jeepneys are the dominant transport mode. Mexico City has experienced spectacular growth in the number of collective taxis, mainly in response to transport demand on the periphery. In Cairo, whereas the share of the formal public transport sector dropped from 73 to 40 per cent during 1972–1983, the share of informal public transport, e.g., microbuses, private buses, and taxis, nearly doubled, from 14 to 27 per cent [20]. Although attempts have been made to control the growth of para-transit through various licensing schemes, this has often proved to be elusive. In Bangkok, for example, whereas the city has some 4,500 licensed minibuses, there are at least 5,000–10,000 unlicensed ones.

Transport is an area where relatively low cost engineering and management measures can have a significant impact on relieving congestion. These include construction of key bus routes and reserved bus lanes, expansion of automatic traffic signals, improved signs and road markings, improvements to the circulation plan within the CBD, construction of pedestrian only rights-of-way, and so forth. Moreover, before mega-cities embark on metro projects, they should be encouraged to study and price the cheaper alternatives, such as light rail systems and extensions to suburban rail lines. In addition to developing sound public transport alternatives, governments should also be encouraged to attack congestion through a combination of measures that include the proper pricing of automobiles in the city centre – e.g., levying substantial charges on those who choose to drive into the CBD [34].

Environmental protection

A majority of the world's mega-cities suffer from severe negative externalities in the form of inadequate sewerage facilities, insufficient solid waste disposal, and poor air and water (river and ocean) quality. Unfortunately, because of inadequate records (e.g., stations for measuring air pollution), the lack of monitoring, and the sparsity of research, evidence on their magnitude is largely anecdotal and impressionistic. There are a few numbers available, invariably ad hoc and unsystematic. For example, the proportion of metropolitan population served by piped sewerage is 11 per cent in Metro Manila (optimistically, rising to 20 per cent after implementation of the proposed Sewerage Master Plan), 18 per cent in Dacca, less than 20 per cent in Karachi, 30 per cent in Delhi, 33 per cent in Madras, 40 per cent in Jakarta, 45 per cent in Calcutta, 80 per cent in Mexico City, and 86 per cent in Seoul [10–21]. The proportion of solid waste collected is 25 per cent in Jakarta, 33 per cent in Karachi, 55 per cent in Calcutta, 70–80 per cent in Madras, Metro Manila, Mexico City, and Bangkok, a high proportion in Dacca (because almost nothing is wasted in such a poor city), and almost 100 per cent in Seoul [10–21].

Quantification of the extent of air and water pollution is much worse, because monitoring stations are rare or non-existent. It is widely recognized (e.g., by the World Health Organization) that some mega-cities have serious pollution problems: air pollution in Mexico City, São Paulo, Bombay, Metro Manila, Bangkok, Calcutta, and Seoul; and water pollution in Dacca, Delhi, Seoul, Karachi, Bangkok, Metro Manila, and Cairo. The sources of pollution vary from case to case: in some cities air pollution is the result of automobile emissions, in others it arises because of polluting industries; similarly, water pollution is the result of industrial contamination in some cities and of leaking sewerage in others.

Some developing country mega-cities are more polluted because of different technologies (e.g., burning fuels generating heavy particulates, no automobile emission controls, leaded gasoline) and because of the absence or lax enforcement of environmental controls. Mexico City, which is usually regarded among the outliers in terms of air pollution, has all of the characteristics conducive to high air pollution: high altitude conditions tend to significantly increase the emissions of fine particles, HC and CO pollution from vehicles, and to make people more susceptible to certain of its effects; as a result of the city's elevation and the mountains that surround it, winds rarely blow with enough force to clear the air; the basin also has abundant sunlight, one of the key elements of photochemical smog.

Developing country mega-cities have been less successful in avoiding negative externalities such as pollution than the developed country mega-cities. In some cases (e.g., in regard to pollution control) this reflects too little intervention, in part because of insufficient pressure from those affected. Where measures have been adopted, there generally has been haphazard enforcement. For example, although the law prohibits discharge of waste water into the Nile, bacteriological and virological data indicate considerable pollution from sewerage. In Mexico City, the principal ordinance in the solid waste field dates back to 1941; whereas some modifications were introduced in the 1970s, the fines that can be legally imposed bear no relation to current monetary values [4].

Mexico's strategy to alleviate environmental pollution gained momentum during the 1980s. In 1987 the government adopted a number of strict policies in regard to automobile emissions (e.g., it was announced that automobiles manufactured between 1977 and 1982 would be required to be inspected periodically with pollution monitoring equipment; automobiles manufactured after 1988 would be required to have emission control systems, etc.). Compliance, however, was very slow, and the situation reached near crisis proportions in January 1989 when levels of harmful ozone led the authorities to announce an eight point programme, including extension of the school holidays for a one month period, pulling visibly polluting vehicles off the roads, mandatory emission checks for cargo vehicles, and so forth. In 1990 the government issued a car ban one working day a week according to the displayed colour of each car's license plate. Recently, an increasingly intensive effort has been under way to develop a comprehensive package of motor vehicle controls, including more stringent new car standards and inspection and retrofit of some older vehicles. To date, no country in the world has attempted, much less successfully carried out, the type of used vehicle retrofit programme contemplated in Mexico City. Such a programme probably should be attempted because of the large proportion of older vehicles in the fleet, which will dominate the inventory throughout the remainder of this century and into the next [27].

In São Paulo, on the other hand, emission checks are still voluntary, and the major emphasis of the government's campaign for air quality improvement is to raise the level of environmental awareness.

Institutional development

Mega-cities typically experience rapid population growth and an expansion of economic activities, both of which have strong locational impacts that spill over the boundaries of the core city into an ever expanding metropolitan region. Mexico City is a case in point. Within a few years, more than half of the population of the Mexico City Metropolitan Zone will be located in the State of Mexico. There is no single metropolitan region authority with responsibility for implementing a comprehensive and integrated strategy of metropolitan development. Events are occurring outside the Federal District that affect both it and the metropolitan area at large, yet the Federal District is currently powerless to respond [28].

A problem in managing the growth of mega-cities is developing the appropriate institutional framework. Municipal administrations cannot perform this task well because their jurisdictions are "underbounded," and they are usually fully occupied with the day-to-day problems of routine administration, service provision, and finance. In many mega-cities, metropolitan development and planning authorities have been established, but they tend to languish as weak institutions with nothing to do and little to say (e.g., the Dacca Improvement Trust, Bombay Metropolitan Development Authority, Karachi Development Authority, Metro Manila Commission, Bangkok Metropolitan Administration) or have evolved into public works agencies (e.g., Calcutta Metropolitan Development Authority, Delhi Development Authority). Other mega-cities, such as Cairo, Mexico City, Jakarta, and Seoul, do not have a metropolitan development authority. In some cases, there are conflicts between a metropolitan planning authority and the municipality, with the latter often turning out to be the stronger (e.g., as is the case in Bombay and Karachi). In other cases, key urban services/major metropolitan investments are the responsibility of the central or provincial governments instead of a metropolitan authority (e.g., in Seoul, Metro Manila, Bangkok, and Jakarta).

A metropolitan development authority may be an effective mechanism for managing mega-cities provided that its role is clearly defined. The limited territorial control of existing municipalities and the extensive jurisdictional fragmentation usually mean that metropolitan problems cannot be handled at the sub-metropolitan level. However, it is very important that the metropolitan development authorities do not usurp the functions of other agencies. Instead, they should perform functions that other bodies cannot do, such as identifying and promoting an appropriate spatial strategy (but not via heavy-handed government intervention), coordinating a capital investment budget for the metropolitan region, promoting economic development (e.g., giving strong political support for major economic infrastructure programmes that could increase metropolitan economic efficiency), seeking consensus among existing bodies and agencies for regional approaches to problem solving, and finding mechanisms to increase public participation and access.

Conclusion

A reasonable test of the effectiveness of management in developing country mega-cities is the ability to deliver basic urban services to a rapidly growing metropolitan population. Most mega-cities suffer from severe service deficits (often more than 50 per cent of the population lacks many basic services). The inability of mega-cities to solve all of the problems associated with providing urban services to their growing populations is only to be expected. For one thing, many of them are continuing to grow rapidly. It is very difficult from both a resource and a management point of view to expand urban service levels at a pace equal to the rate of metropolitan population growth. As a result, deficits tend to become larger. For another, all the countries, even those with an impressive growth record such as the Republic of Korea, have capital resource constraints and competing claims on public investment, so that the resources available for urban services are inevitably limited. Also, metropolitan efforts to improve revenue generation have been very mixed, with little across-the-board implementation of cost recovery mechanisms, except within the narrow context of internationally supervised (e.g., World Bank) projects.

Of course, urban service supply problems are not limited to mega-cities in developing countries. Mega-cities in developed countries have also faced difficulties, especially with respect to the maintenance and renovation of urban infrastructure. Given the scale of the problem and the constraints, many developing country mega-cities have made considerable progress in improving their capacity to deliver urban services to their rapidly growing populations.

If policy makers in developing country mega-cities could be implementing more effective urban land policies, housing policies, transport policies, and so forth, that would better manage the growth of mega-cities, why aren't they doing so? The explanation is due to a mix of complex factors. First, policies are often in harmony with the vested interests of the metropolitan élite. Urban policies are intended to be regressive in their impact and are not intended to change the distribution of interpersonal welfare. There is also the factor of pride and prestige. For example, there may be a reluctance to lower public service standards on the grounds that supplying a site with services rather than a modern apartment, a standpipe rather than in-house taps, open latrines rather than a modern toilet, is a sign of failure [1]. (Clearly, however, low service standards reaching a majority of a mega-city's population should be a greater reason for pride than ideal services for the few.) Another reason is the fact that, too frequently, inappropriate approaches have been adopted or transplanted from other cities [1]. Most policy makers and planners in developing countries have been trained in the United States or in Europe and find it difficult to adapt their skills and approaches to the reality of developing country city problems. Finally, there are often major institutional constraints. Effective action may be impeded by legislative obstacles, constraints imposed by the central government, poor municipal organization (e.g., divided responsibility among agencies for specific functions), and so forth.

There are some grounds for optimism that sound policy interventions may be able to ameliorate many mega-city problems. Direct attacks on negative externalities via anti-pollution strategies and policies to relieve congestion have hardly been tried, and could have a high pay-off. Capital cost constraints can be relieved by standards reductions and by cost recovery schemes. Mega-city economic efficiency can be improved by relaxing onerous regulations, selective improvements in public services, and congestion relief.

The absolute size of mega-cities necessitates spatial reorganization if they are to remain efficient. Most mega-cities are pursuing polycentric spatial strategies, but the question remains whether the transition to polycentricity can be facilitated by public policy intervention. Polycentric spatial structures may evolve more efficiently if policy makers respond to market signals and support spontaneous locational adjustments rather than attempt to promote new preselected sub-centres at a high investment cost.

Finally, establishing a metropolitan-level authority can enable the authorities to cope with metropolitan problems that spill over jurisdictional boundaries. Geographically large metropolitan regions are necessary to ensure over-bounding to encapsulate future population growth. Whereas a metropolitan development authority may be the most effective institutional tool to deal with the problems of megacity growth, experience suggests that there are severe obstacles in the way of efficient and cooperative coordination with pre-existing levels of government, both central and local.

References

1 Brennan, Ellen M. "Comparing Mega-cities." Paper prepared for the 1990 annual meeting of the Population Association of America, Toronto, 3–5 May, 1990.

2 ———. "Land and Housing Issues in Developing Countries." Paper prepared for the Population Committee Workshop on Urbanization, Migration, and Economic Development, National Research Council, National Academy of Sciences, Washington, D.C., 1990.

3 Brennan, Ellen M., and Harry W. Richardson. "Asian Mega-city Characteristics, Problems, and Policies." *International Regional Science Review* 12 (1989), no. 2: 117–129.

4 Dagh Watson SpA. *Waste Management and Resource Recovery in Mexico City*. UNDP Project GLO/8C/004. Milan, 1985.

5 Doebele, W.S. "Selected Issues in Urban Land Tenure." In H.B. Dunkerley, ed., *Urban Land Policy Issues and Opportunities*. World Bank Staff Working Paper, no. 283. Washington, D.C., 1978.

6 Gilbert, Alan. "Land and Shelter in Mega-cities: Some Critical Issues." Paper prepared for the Symposium on the Mega-city and the Future: Population Growth and Policy Responses. Tokyo, 22–25 October, 1990.

7 Mayo, S., S. Malpezzi, and D.J. Gross. "Shelter Strategies for the Urban Poor in Developing Countries." Paper prepared for the annual meeting of the American Real Estate and Urban Economics Association, New York, 1986.

8 PADCO, Inc., in association with Engineering Consultants Group and Sherif El-Hakim and Associates. *Final Report: The National Urban Policy Study*. Cairo, 1982.

9 Renaud, B. "Another Look at Housing Finance in Developing Countries." *Cities* (February 1987).

10 United Nations. *Population Growth and Policies in Mega-Cities: Calcutta*. Population Policy Paper, no. 1. New York: Department of International Economic and Social Affairs, 1986.

11 ———. *Population Growth and Policies in Mega-Cities: Seoul*. Population Policy Paper, no. 4. New York: Department of International Economic and Social Affairs, 1986.

12 ———. *Population Growth and Policies in Mega-Cities: Metro Manila*. Population Policy Paper, no. 5. New York: Department of International Economic and Social Affairs, 1986.

13 ———. *Population Growth and Policies in Mega-Cities: Bombay*. Population Policy Paper, no. 6. New York: Department of International Economic and Social Affairs, 1986.

14 ———. *Population Growth and Policies in Mega-Cities: Delhi*. Population Policy Paper, no. 7. New York: Department of International Economic and Social Affairs, 1986.

15 ———. *Population Growth and Policies in Mega-Cities: Dhaka*. Population Policy Paper, no. 8. New York: Department of International Economic and Social Affairs, 1987.

16 ———. *Population Growth and Policies in Mega-Cities: Bangkok*. Population Policy Paper, no. 10. New York: Department of International Economic and Social Affairs, 1987.

17 ———. *Population Growth and Policies in Mega-Cities: Madras*. Population Policy Paper, no. 12. New York: Department of International Economic and Social Affairs, 1987.

18 ———. *Population Growth and Policies in Mega-Cities: Karachi*. Population Policy Paper, no. 13. New York: Department of International Economic and Social Affairs, 1988.

19 ———. *Population Growth and Policies in Mega-Cities: Jakarta*. Population Policy Paper, no. 18. New York: Department of International Economic and Social Affairs, 1989.

20 ———. *Population Growth and Policies in Mega-Cities: Cairo*. Population Policy Paper, no. 33. New York: Department of International Economic and Social Affairs, 1990.

21 ———. *Population Growth and Policies in Mega-Cities: Mexico City*. Population Policy Paper, no. 32. New York: Department of International Economic and Social Affairs, 1991.

22 ———. *Population Growth and Policies in Mega-Cities: São Paulo*. New York: Department for Economic and Social Information and Policy Analysis, 1993.

23 United Nations Centre for Human Settlements. *Upgrading of Inner City Slums*. Nairobi, 1984.
24 ———. *Rehabilitation of Inner City Areas: Feasible Strategies*. Nairobi, 1986.
25 ———. "Analysis of Land Markets: Analysis and Synthesis Report." Draft synopsis, 1989.
26 ———. "Analysis and Synthesis Report." Revised draft, 1989.
27 Walsh, Michael P. "Motor Vehicle Emissions in Mexico: A Strategy for Progress." Paper prepared for the World Bank, 1989.
28 Ward, Peter M. "Mexico City." Paper prepared for the Mega-cities of the Americas Conference, State University of New York at Albany, 5–7 April, 1990.
29 World Bank. "Seoul: The Impact of Government Policies." *The Urban Edge* 8 (1984), no. 9.
30 ———. *The Mexico City Region: Issues and Perspectives*. Special Sector Report. Washington, D.C., 1984.
31 ———. "Enabling Shelter Strategy Urged by U.N. Body." *The Urban Edge* 12 (1988), no. 8.
32 ———. "Debate over Land Registration Persists." *The Urban Edge* 13 (1989), no. 7.
33 ———. "FY89 Sector Review of Urban Development Operations: Reaching the Poor through Urban Operations." Washington, D.C., 1989.
34 ———. "Metros in Developing Cities – Are They Viable?" *The Urban Edge* 14 (1990), no. 1.

11

Financing infrastructure in developing country mega-cities

Johannes F. Linn and Deborah L. Wetzel

The authors are respectively Director and Consultant, Country Economics Department, The World Bank, Washington, D.C.

Introduction

The number of cities with a population of 5 million or more continues to grow. In 1970 there were 20 urban agglomerations (a central city or cities surrounded by an urbanized area) with 5 million or more persons, accounting for 4.5 per cent of the total world population. By 1985, there were 30 such agglomerations containing 5.8 per cent of the total world population. By the year 2000, it is expected that there will be 45 such agglomerations encompassing 7.6 per cent of the world's population.[1] As seen in table 1, the majority of these "mega-cities" will be in developing countries. Seventeen of the 43 cities listed in the table are in Asia, seven are in Latin America, seven are in the Middle East/North Africa region, and one is in sub-Saharan Africa. Eleven of the cities are in developed countries. If these projections are accurate, by the year 2000, India will have six cities with a population greater than 5 million; China will have four such cities, and Brazil will have three.

Many of the findings reported here are based on research carried out by Roy W. Bahl and Johannes F. Linn under the auspices of a World Bank financed research project on urban finance in developing countries. The views expressed in this paper are those of the authors and do not necessarily reflect those of the World Bank or its member countries.

Table 1 **Urban agglomerations with projected population of 5 million or more in the year 2000**

Agglomeration	Population (in millions)		Average annual rate of growth	
	1985	2000	1970–1985	1985–2000
Tokyo-Yokohama (Japan)	19.04	21.32	1.65	0.75
Mexico City (Mexico)	16.65	24.44	4.30	2.56
New York (USA)	15.62	16.10	−0.24	0.20
São Paulo (Brazil)	15.54	23.60	4.38	2.79
Shanghai (China)	12.06	14.69	0.37	1.32
Buenos Aires (Argentina)	10.76	13.05	1.72	1.29
London (UK)	10.49	10.79	−0.04	0.19
Calcutta (India)	10.29	15.94	2.65	2.92
Rio de Janeiro (Brazil)	10.14	13.00	2.43	1.66
Seoul (Korea, Rep. of)	10.07	12.97	4.27	1.69
Los Angeles (USA)	10.04	10.91	1.20	0.55
Osaka-Kobe (Japan)	9.56	11.18	1.53	1.04
Greater Bombay (India)	9.47	15.43	3.26	3.25
Beijing (China)	9.33	11.47	0.79	1.38
Moscow (Russia)	8.91	10.11	1.50	0.84
Paris (France)	8.75	8.76	0.33	0.01
Tianjin (China)	7.96	9.96	0.98	1.49
Cairo-Giza (Egypt)	7.92	11.77	2.64	2.64
Jakarta (Indonesia)	7.79	13.23	3.93	3.53
Milan (Italy)	7.50	8.74	2.03	1.02
Teheran (Iran, Islam. Rep.)	7.21	13.73	5.23	4.29
Metro Manila–Quezon (Phil.)	7.09	11.48	4.65	3.21
Delhi (India)	6.95	12.77	4.52	4.06
Chicago (USA)	6.84	6.98	0.12	0.14
Karachi (Pakistan)	6.16	11.57	4.51	4.20
Bangkok (Thailand)	5.86	10.26	4.22	3.73
Lagos (Nigeria)	5.84	12.45	7.08	5.05
Lima-Callao (Peru)	5.44	8.78	4.33	3.19
Hong Kong (Hong Kong)	5.16	6.09	2.78	1.10
St. Pertersburg (Russia)	5.11	5.84	1.67	0.89
Madras (India)	4.87	7.85	3.16	3.18
Madrid (Spain)	4.83	5.42	2.40	0.77
Dacca (Bangladesh)	4.76	11.26	7.70	5.74
Bogotá (Colombia)	4.74	6.94	4.62	2.54
Baghdad (Iraq)	4.39	7.66	4.88	3.71
Shenyang (China)	4.11	5.50	1.79	1.94
Pusan (Korea, Rep. of)	4.02	5.82	5.32	2.47
Bangalore (India)	3.73	7.67	5.56	4.81
Lahore (Pakistan)	3.40	5.93	3.64	3.71
Belo Horizonte (Brazil)	3.17	5.01	4.60	3.05
Ahmedabad (India)	2.95	5.09	3.71	3.64
Ankara (Turkey)	2.91	5.19	5.53	3.86
Algiers (Algeria)	2.70	5.16	5.41	4.32

Source: Ref. 29, table 6.

The forces that lead to urbanization are obviously strong. Declining mortality rates in many developing countries are often not accompanied by reductions in fertility rates. The resulting increase in the population cannot be sustained by the rural economy. Urban areas are viewed as places of economic growth and opportunity, where the probability of finding employment and consumer goods is higher and where schools, public facilities, and cultural attractions are more likely to be found. Though the living conditions of the migrants in many of these large cities may be atrocious, for many the economic and social benefits of moving to the city outweigh the costs.[2]

There is no question, however, that the rapid rate of urbanization, particularly in large cities, poses a multitude of problems that in many cases seem unsurmountable. The massive inflow of people often leads to high levels of unemployment and underemployment because the market for labour may be unable to absorb the expanding number of job seekers. Housing and shelter are inevitably insufficient. As cities grow larger, the problems of inadequate sanitation and water supplies grow worse, as do those of overloaded and congested transportation systems. Air, water, and noise pollution grow worse, and in general the quality of life deteriorates. Rapid urbanization is frequently accompanied by municipal budget crises. Most cities are caught between ever increasing demands for both social and physical infrastructure and a lack of funds to provide these services.

In the early 1980s, the difficulties faced by the municipal governments were compounded by general economic crisis in many developing countries. Foreign finance, much of which was devoted to building large infrastructure projects such as powerplants, telecommunication systems, and roads, dried up. Higher rates of interest increased the part of national budgets that was devoted to servicing foreign and domestic debt, thus reducing the funds available for other purposes. The adoption of adjustment programmes emphasized reduction of public expenditure. Many of the cut-backs made were in capital spending. For a sample of 15 (mainly highly indebted) countries in which total real expenditure fell by 18.3 per cent, capital expenditure suffered a 35.3 per cent decline, whereas current spending fell only 7.8 per cent.[3] Such sharp cut-backs may reflect the greater flexibility of capital spending; it is easier to cancel or postpone a few large projects than to lay off government workers, reduce civil service pensions, or delay or renegotiate interest payments. Analysis by sector showed that infrastructure spending suffered the deepest cuts.[4]

While the general economic crisis affected countries as a whole, there is little doubt that it particularly affected large cities. Migration into major cities increased as activity in rural markets declined, thus increasing the demand for provision of services. Slow growth reduced the tax revenue received by both the national and municipal governments. As seen above, national governments cut back their spending on infrastructure, a good deal of which was targeted at major cities. Many national governments also reduced expenditure on the operation and maintenance of infrastructure already in existence (some of which is located in cities). Likewise, transfers to lower levels of governments were another area of expenditure susceptible to cuts given their discretionary nature in many countries. Municipalities in many countries receive a significant portion of their revenue in the form of transfers from the central government and thus also experienced a reduction in revenues from this source.

At present the cities contending with large populations and rapid urbanization find themselves in an extremely difficult situation. The demand for services and infrastructure such as water, sanitation, health facilities, housing, power, and transport is immense and growing. At the same time, many of these cities are ill-equipped to provide these services; many lack the administrative and technical ability; some cities are hampered by higher levels of government. Most important, however, is the fact that in many cities the poor provision of social and physical infrastructure is due to the difficulty of financing the expenditure necessary to provide these services. This applies not only to cities with populations over 5 million but to cities throughout the developing world. In order for countries to come to terms with rapid urbanization and to ensure that cities act as a vehicle for economic growth rather than as a bottleneck, they must find ways to finance the development of infrastructure.

Is it possible for cities to find ways to finance the ever increasing demands that are made upon them? We believe that the answer is yes, but that in order to do so, cities will not only have to take a fresh look at their traditional means of revenue mobilization; they will have to develop new and innovative ways of meeting their financial needs. Past studies have shown that the ability of developing countries to maintain and expand their stock of urban infrastructure in response to rapid population growth depends upon astute administrative and management skill with financial resources on the part of those in charge of financing urban services.[5] Given the immense need for infrastructure development, cities will have to make an effort to engage the private sector in the development of the city. The potential exists for the private sector to play a much greater role than it currently does in providing infrastructure in developing countries. We also believe that it is possible for cities, particularly the largest ones, to dramatically (if not completely) reduce their dependence on transfers from the central government.

The second section of the paper focuses on the question of responsibility for provision of social and physical infrastructure and its finance.[6] The third section of the paper provides an overview of the traditional approaches to raising revenue in large cities (such as the property tax, automotive taxation, user charges, etc.) and discusses efforts that have been made to improve these methods and whether they have been successful. The fourth section considers more recent and innovative approaches to financing urban infrastructure, relying on private sector involvement, including "build, own, operate, and transfer" (BOOT) projects and housing finance. A final section summarizes the major implications of our findings.

Who bears the responsibility for financing mega-city infrastructure?

In most large cities the institutional framework for the provision of public services is fragmented and unclear. Such fragmentation makes policy formulation and provision of services cumbersome and difficult. The fact that in most large cities rapid urbanization has outstripped the government's ability to provide basic urban services calls for a reassessment of the role of central and local governments in the urbanization process. Numerous studies have argued that in order for the provision of social and physical infrastructure to be improved, more responsibilities have to be delegated to municipalities and a better correspondence between local expenditure and revenue authority needs to be established.[7]

In most developing countries, there tends to be an overwhelming reliance on the central government to deal with local matters. In many cases local government does not have the authority to respond to pressing problems at the local level. In the area of social and physical infrastructure, the failure to address such problems results in large social and economic costs. In large cities, particularly capital cities (about half of the cities in table 1), the municipal government is likely to be more autonomous, but this does not necessarily mean that it has authority when it comes to decision-making concerning revenue intake. There are arguments both for and against the decentralization of the provision of urban infrastructure. In mega-cities, a strong case can be made that decentralization of revenue and spending authority will allow for better provision of infrastructure.

There are three general arguments in support of fiscal decentralization. The first is that if expenditure and tax rates are determined by those who run the city rather than those who run the country, local preferences will be better addressed, local services will improve, and local residents will be more satisfied with government services. The second argument made in support of fiscal decentralization is that stronger local governments will contribute to the development of democratic institutions because people can identify more closely with local rather than central government. The third argument is that local revenue mobilization will be increased, because local governments are more aware of and can tax more easily than the central government the parts of the local economic base that are growing quickly.

The arguments against decentralization of municipal finance are first that local governments often lack the administrative capacity to collect revenue and prepare budgets and investment plans. Second, improving local government's administrative capacity can unnecessarily duplicate the number and skills of staff at the central and local levels. Decentralization might thus lead to inefficient and expanding public employment. Third, public services provided by one jurisdiction often have spillover effects on other jurisdictions and the provision of such services calls for higher levels of government.[8]

Considering the case of mega-cities, it seems that all of the arguments in favour of decentralization would be applicable, while some of the arguments against decentralization are unlikely to hold in large cities. Large cities more than smaller ones are likely to attract individuals with the skills and administrative capability necessary to prepare budgets and make investment decisions. If such capability does not exist, there is much to be gained by training and technical assistance geared toward developing these skills. Decentralization, if effectively administered, should reduce the need for central government staff working on local issues, so that they can use their time more efficiently.

Finally, there is some credibility in the argument that services provided by one jurisdiction may spill over into another jurisdiction. Indeed, there are large externalities that exist in major cities, including air, water, and noise pollution. While some of these externalities may need to be addressed by higher levels of government, there is also the possibility that they are legitimately addressed by urban governments and could be appropriately financed by transfers from the central government.

Of particular interest is how, for a given set of expenditure functions, urban government expenditures should be financed. Based on a series of empirical case-studies, Bahl and Linn have set out a framework for pinpointing the sources of revenue that are appropriate to finance particular types of assigned urban expenditures. First, for publicly provided goods and services that are of measurable benefit to readily identifiable users within a jurisdiction, user charges are the most efficient means of financing the service. Such services include water supply, sewerage, power, telephones, public transit, and housing. Second, local services such as administration, traffic control, street lighting, and security, which are public goods of benefit to the general public within the urban area, are most appropriately financed by taxes on local governments. Third, the costs of services for which significant spillovers to neighbouring jurisdictions occur, such as health, education, and welfare, should be met by means of substantial state or national intergovernmental transfers. Finally, borrowing is an appropriate source of financing capital outlays on infrastructural services, particularly public utilities and roads.[9]

Of course, revenue authority has many dimensions. Even where local governments have the authority to levy a tax, central government may retain a major say over rates, base valuation, exemptions, enforcement, and so forth. For example, in countries such as Brazil and Colombia, where responsibility for raising and collecting revenue in urban areas is decentralized and formally rests with the local government, final authority over such items as the tax base and the rates that can be charged rests with the central government. Central governments commonly control property valuation and exemptions and influence the appointment of local government officers. In many countries the central government must approve local budgets. In such situations the local government may be hamstrung by the responsibility of providing services without the means to adjust revenue, and inadequate provision of essential services may be the result.

Capital cities, however, are often accorded special status with regard to revenue and expenditure authority because of the special burdens that they face. These cities with special status are often the most effective in providing social and physical infrastructure. The most extreme – and most successful – examples are city-states like Hong Kong and Singapore, where the city has full control over revenue and expenditure decisions (including determination of the tax base and rates charged) and thus is better able to deal with the problems of rapid urbanization. It is likely that other large cities would benefit from special status, which would provide them with greater autonomy and hence a greater capacity to meet the increasing demand for urban infrastructure. In order for urban governments to bear effectively the responsibility of providing social and physical infrastructure, they must have a reasonable amount of authority over revenue mobilization and expenditure decisions.

In practice, political considerations may limit the extent of decentralization that the central authorities are willing to permit. Strong city governments may provide a power base for the political opposition to the party or government in power at the centre. On the other hand, the strengthening of pluralistic checks and balances may be – as seen from a broader vantage point of long-term democratization – one of the desirable aspects of decentralizing decision-making to secondary centres, represented by the mayors or governors of mega-cities.

Control of revenues is at the core of the debate over decentralization. Without a strong revenue authority, urban governments have neither the scope to provide effective infrastructure services nor the potential to build up a lasting independent political base.

The remainder of this paper will concentrate on the financing of urban infrastructure in the mega-cities of the developing world. We consider first the traditional means of revenue mobilization that urban authorities have used.

Traditional means of raising revenue

Table 2 sets out the financing of local public expenditures by type of revenue for a group of cities, all of which have achieved or are expected to achieve mega-city status by the year 2000.[10] From the table we see that, typically, large cities in developing countries rely on locally raised revenue for a majority of their financing. The median share of revenue coming from locally raised revenue is 79.4 per cent for those years before 1980 and it is 72.3 per cent for the year 1980 and after. In most countries the largest portion of locally raised revenue comes from local taxes, and the next largest share from self-financing sources, such as user charges. Revenue from sources external to the urban area (e.g. grants, tax sharing, and net borrowing

Table 2 **Percentage distribution of financing of local expenditures in selected cities by type of revenue**

City	Year	Locally raised revenue				Revenue from external sources		
		Total	Local taxes	Self-financing services	Other	Total	Grants and shared taxes	Net[a] borrowing
Ahmedabad (India)	1971	86.3	28.6	41.8	5.9	13.7	4.2	9.5
	1981	65.9	60.1	4.5	1.3	34.2	8.6	25.6
Bombay (India)	1971	89.6	37.9	38.7	8.0	15.4	1.0	14.4
	1982	81.8	35.8	42.3	3.7	18.2	0.7	17.5
Calcutta Corp. (India)	1975	73.8	64.4	—	9.4	26.2	19.4	6.8
	1982	61.3	49.0	—	12.3	38.7	54.9	−16.2
Dacca (Bangladesh)	1983	113.4	48.9	30.5	34.0	−13.4	34.6	−48.0
Jakarta (Indonesia)	1973	78.8	40.6	15.2	23.0	21.1	21.1	—
	1981	65.7	38.8	17.6	9.3	34.3	39.1	−4.8
Karachi (Pakistan)	1975	84.1	67.6	2.2	14.3	13.9	2.8	13.1
	1982	101.5	93.3	0.9	7.2	−1.5	3.0	−4.5
Lagos (Nigeria)	1980	51.2	42.8	0.2	8.2	48.8	48.8	—
Lima (Peru)	1982	73.4	27.8	36.1	9.5	26.6	19.0	7.7
Madras (India)	1976	69.2	54.5	3.7	11.0	30.8	25.1	5.7
	1979	72.9	58.0	0.6	14.4	27.1	13.7	13.4
Manila (Philippines)	1970	70.0	55.0	10.0	5.0	30.0	30.0	—
	1985	71.6	58.3	6.0	7.4	28.4	24.1	4.3
Rio de Janeiro (Brazil)[b]	1967	88.4	74.5	7.2	6.7	11.6	1.7	9.9
	1984	92.2	72.3	12.0	7.9	7.8	0.4	7.4
São Paulo (Brazil)[b]	1984	72.9	62.0	4.2	6.7	27.0	0.4	26.6
Seoul (Rep. of Korea)	1971	80.0	30.3	36.3	13.4	19.9	15.8	4.1
	1983	70.1	38.7	26.8	5.5	29.1	22.0	7.0

Median							
For years prior to 1980	79.4	54.8	10.0	10.2	20.5	14.8	9.7
For 1980 and after	72.3	53.7	12.0	7.7	27.7	20.5	7.0

Source: Ref. 4, table 2.8.

a. Net borrowing consists of loan financing minus net changes in financial assets or reserves. Because net borrowing can be negative, totally locally raised revenue reported in column (1) can exceed 100 per cent of total financing.

b. Because of the exclusion of autonomous agencies, the contribution of self-financing revenues are probably understated.

from higher levels of government) ordinarily provides somewhere between one-fifth and one-third of financing for local public expenditures.

This section will provide an overview of the principal sources of urban revenue, both those raised locally and those from external sources, and the efforts that have been made to improve them. We first consider some of the more important local taxes, including the property tax, automotive taxes, and other, somewhat less productive, taxes and their potential as sources of revenue. We then move on to means of self-financing and user charges in particular. Table 2 indicates that in some countries self-financing is an important source of revenue. This suggests that self-financing via user charges may be an effective way of increasing local government revenues in order to finance the development of infrastructure. Finally, we consider transfers from, and tax sharing arrangements with, higher levels of government.

Property taxes

The property tax is the most common and, in many developing countries, the most important source of local government revenue. Table 3 shows that for our sample of countries in the 1980s, the property tax raised anywhere from 9.5 per cent (Jakarta) to 99.7 per cent (Lagos) of total local government tax revenue. The median of the sample for the years prior to 1980 is 50.8 per cent; from 1980 onward the median is 40.4 per cent. In the period from 1980 onward the property tax provided over 50 per cent of local revenue in Bombay, Calcutta, Dacca, Lagos, Lima, Madras, and Manila. In those countries where the share of property tax revenue is smaller, local governments are often assigned an additional tax instrument, such as the tax on municipal services in Brazil, the municipal tax on industry and commerce in Colombia, or the octroi in Pakistan. Still other cities, such as Jakarta, receive a good part of their income in the form of intergovernmental transfers and thus rely less on the property tax than do other cities.

Because the property tax is difficult to administer efficiently, is often overloaded with policy objectives, and is politically unpopular, it is not necessarily the most effective revenue raising instrument. Indeed, poor policy and weak administration often constrain the yield of the property tax. However, in many cities, the property tax is one of a very few instruments that urban governments have at their dis-

Table 3 **Percentage distribution of local tax revenues by source for selected cities**

City	Year	Local taxes as percentage of local expenditure	Property	Property transfer	Income	General sales	Octroi	Gasoline	Entertainment	Industry and commerce	Motor vehicle	Gambling
Ahmedabad (India)	1972	38.6	43.0	—	—	—	52.0	—	—	—	2.0	—
	1981	60.1	29.7	—	—	—	68.7	—	0.2	—	1.4	—
Bombay (India)	1972	37.9	55.6	—	—	—	37.7	—	0.3	—	3.7	—
	1982	37.4	51.9	—	—	—	46.8	—	0.2	—	1.1	—
Calcutta Corp.	1975	64.4	64.8	—	—	—	27.1	—	—	—	—	—
(India)	1982	73.1	58.5	—	—	—	32.9	—	—	6.4	—	—
Dacca (Bangladesh)	1983	48.9	51.1	8.5	—	—	31.9	—	4.3	3.5	0.6	—
Jakarta (Indonesia)	1973	43.7	—	—	—	—	—	—	16.9	—	50.2	26.9
	1982	42.7	9.5	—	—	—	—	—	12.2	—	64.5	—
Karachi (Pakistan)	1975	67.6	46.0	—	—	—	49.9	—	—	—	3.0	—
	1982	—	27.3	—	—	—	71.8	—	0.1	—	—	—
Lagos (Nigeria)	1980	42.8	99.7	—	—	—	—	—	—	—	—	—
Lima (Peru)	1982	27.8	57.5	—	—	—	—	—	20.4	—	—	—
Madras (India)	1976	54.5	68.9	5.1	—	—	—	—	16.0	—	—	—
Manila (Philippines)	1970	55.0	61.9	—	—	—	—	2.2	—	32.1	—	—
	1985	58.3	59.2	1.0	—	—	—	—	7.3	30.7	—	—
Rio de Janeiro	1967	84.4	3.9	1.0	—	89.2	—	—	—	—	—	—
(Brazil)	1984	72.3	15.7	—	—	50.1	—	—	—	—	—	—
São Paulo (Brazil)	1984	62.0	18.7	—	—	50.5	—	—	—	—	—	—
Seoul (Rep. of	1971	30.3	20.6	34.8	—	—	—	—	16.4	—	22.2	—
Korea)	1983	38.7	21.1	51.3	—	—	—	—	3.5	0.5	7.6	—
Median												
For years prior to 1980		54.5	50.8	5.1	—	89.2	43.8	—	16.2	32.1	3.7	—
For 1980 and after		53.6	40.4	8.5	—	50.3	46.8	—	3.9	6.7	1.4	—

Source: Ref. 4, table 2.9.

posal. As a result, substantial efforts have gone into improving the fairness and revenue productivity of the property tax.[11] Yet policy makers rarely consider reform of the entire property tax system, including the rate and base structure, valuation principles, and administration. As a result, reform measures sometimes have offsetting effects and often do not lead to the expected increase in revenue.

City governments have adopted a wide array of property tax practices, and there is no general pattern that gives any indication of the determinants of this variation, except for the colonial heritage of the countries concerned. In general, there are three basic forms of property taxation: that based on an annual or rental value system, a system based on the capital value of land and improvements, and that based on the site value of the land. In practice, no one system is uniformly superior to the others, although the capital value system has emerged as the one most frequently applied in urban areas, perhaps because it has the broadest base and lends itself most readily to mass appraisal. In all three systems, however, the objective assessment of the rental or capital value of land/building poses difficulties.

First, assessment practices and exemptions are often unsystematic and based on ad hoc decisions by administrators and politicians. In most cities exemptions to the property tax are given for a host of reasons. Governments are often exempt as are owner-occupants and low income families in many cities. Exemptions are also used as incentives to stimulate construction or increase investment. Any changes in assessment or exemption practices inevitably raise political opposition.

Second, a major difficulty with assessment in all three systems is keeping up with changes in the property ownership, occupancy, and value. Very often ownership is difficult to determine, because of poor records and often questionable reinforcement of property rights. When property does change hands, it may happen outside of the institutional framework of city government and therefore be difficult to determine. Assessing the value of land is also difficult, particularly in countries with high inflation or countries with rent control. Most reforms of property tax systems have focused on identifying ownership, developing a fiscal cadastre, and establishing assessment techniques. Affective assessment may also be hampered by other administrative problems, such as a shortage of skilled staff and poor coordination among urban institutions.

Another difficulty with property tax systems is that often the base and rate structure of the property tax are determined by the central government. Central government control of the base and rates often places a considerable constraint on the revenue raising ability of city governments, even in the cases where assessment practices are well developed. Central control over local property tax administration is particularly troublesome where it results in inflexible tax rates. This makes it impossible for urban governments to stem the erosion of effective tax rates and of tax revenues by raising nominal tax rates between (generally infrequent) across-the-board reappraisals of property values. When such a reappraisal takes place, the resulting dramatic increases in property tax bills cannot be offset by temporarily lowering rates. This tends to undermine the political acceptability of market value-based reappraisal and thus undermines the long-term viability of the property tax as an elastic revenue source.

Finally, property tax systems often have weak political support because the property tax is not identified with the provision of any particular service and therefore taxpayers are more reluctant to pay. In many cities this reluctance is compounded by the lack of enforcement and the absence of adequate incentives for prompt and full payment.

These difficulties with the property tax imply that collection costs are high and collection efficiency is low in many cities. Bahl and Linn find that the evidence indicates also that the property tax is income inelastic and that growth in the property tax base has lagged behind growth in income and in some cases behind the general price level (that is, the real property tax yield has fallen).[12]

All of these factors have made the property tax a target of reform in a number of developing countries.[13] Generally, there have been two areas of intervention: policy and administration. Policy reforms have focused on tax rates, exemptions, and inefficient adjustments for inflation. Administrative reforms have focused on incomplete tax rolls, haphazard valuations, and low collection efficiency.

Many reforms have focused on valuation and development of the cadastral system. In the Philippines, the Real Property Tax Administration project (RPTA project) aimed to address property tax evasion that was possible because the system was based upon owner declarations: owners could understate the characteristics of their properties or neglect to declare their properties altogether. The reform implemented field-verified inventories of properties. The objective of the reform was to complete the tax mapping process (identifying property, assessing its value, determining tax liability) in 800 local jurisdictions in a five year period. While the reform achieved 75 per cent of that target, the impact on actual tax revenues was negligible and actual collections increased by only 1.1 per cent.[14]

Dillinger presents a number of reasons as to why the RPTA did not lead to a greater increase in property tax revenues: Partly it was because the reform was too narrow; it did not address such items as the widespread underestimation of unit costs, which determine the capital value assessment. It also failed to address central government policies that constrain property tax yield. Dillinger cites an estimate that, "centrally decreed postponements, of the most general revaluation, combined with limits on tax rates and assessment ratios, reduce the effective rate of property taxation in the Philippines to less than 0.2 percent."[15] Finally, revenue mobilization did not improve much because the reform did not address the problems concerning collection and enforcement.

In Brazil's property tax reform, the Convénio de Incentivo ao Aperfeiçoamento Técnico-Administrativo das Municipalidades (CIATA), the objective was to use a short-term injection of manpower, supplies, and equipment to produce a complete and up-to-date set of documents in order to administer the property tax. The reform included updating the tax code and the tax map, developing a new set of property records, determining new unit cost tables, creating a new assessment role and a new set of tax bills incorporating the new assessments, and developing a ledger for recording payments against outstanding liabilities.[16]

CIATA's impact on tax revenues was immediate. In percentage terms, property tax revenues increased by 95 per cent in real terms in the first year following project implementation.[17] However, the early CIATA projects seem to indicate that this impact on revenues was short-lived. In general, moreover, the absolute levels of tax liability remained low as municipal officials used their autonomy over property tax policy to reduce nominal tax rates. And while collection efficiency was improved, it seems to have suffered from a lack of permanent procedural change.

In some cities property tax revenue improvements have been achieved with relatively simple measures. Delhi improved its collection by 96 per cent in one year, 1986/1987, mainly by requiring taxpayers to pay their assessed tax before appeals against assessments could be heard, and by freezing bank accounts of defaulters, awarding discounts for early payments, and decentralizing collection points. Sri Lankan urban authorities improved tax collection by instituting a system of reminders and warning notices.[18]

The least successful reforms have been those that have tried to increase the real revenue take of property taxation merely by higher tariffs and improved assessment. In Malaysia and Thailand, the introduction of new property tax systems have experienced long delays and have had disappointing results in terms of revenue collection.[19]

Experience shows that reforms of the property tax system do have some potential for increasing the resources of urban governments, but that some general lessons should be borne in mind. First, as emphasized by Dillinger, one should reform the property tax system by "working backwards." Extensive property tax reforms have often been ineffectual because they neglect collection issues. There is a strong argument for focusing on collection administration before adjusting rates or developing an extensive cadastral register. The latter steps may be useless if the capacity to collect, and the incentives for compliance, do not exist.

Second, and following from above, is that reforms should be based on a comprehensive diagnosis of the weaknesses in the property tax system, including the assessment of skill levels on the local level, and the capacity for permanent procedural change. While reforms that imply "quick fixes" are helpful, the ultimate objective is to make the property tax a buoyant source of revenue on a long-term basis.

Finally, one must keep in mind the constraints that are imposed by the central government. If the central government is hesitant to give up control of local tax bases and rates, it might be advisable to focus on relatively minor reforms of the property tax system and to place greater emphasis on developing other sources of revenue.

For mega-cities, property tax reform deserves special consideration: First, the property tax base in mega-cities tends to be a relatively large percentage of the total urban property tax base in a country, and so the payoff from any improvements in property tax design and tax administration tends to be particularly significant. Second, starting country-wide urban property tax reform in the mega-cities may be most appropriate, since the administrative capacity in these cities tends to be greatest and consequently implementation can proceed while efforts are made to strengthen the administrative infrastucture in the smaller urban centres. Third, in view of the large range of the types of properties likely to be found in large cities, it is appropriate to differentiate the approach taken to property tax reform in the mega-city. In particular, it will generally be appropriate to proceed with individual appraisal of large, high value commercial properties, complemented by mass appraisal of smaller, medium value commercial and residential properties, while allowing across-the-board exemption for the large number of small, low value residential properties found in the poor neighbourhoods of the cities.

Motor vehicle taxation

Motor vehicle taxation is an excellent, but often neglected, base for urban government taxation, particularly in large cities. In most large cities, the number of motor vehicles generally grows faster than the population, motor vehicle ownership and use are easily taxable, and the burden is likely to fall on individuals with higher income. Nevertheless, we see in table 3 that, in the years from 1980 onward, only one city in our sample of mega-cities collected more than 10 per cent of its total tax revenue from motor vehicle taxation. Jakarta received 64.5 per cent of its total tax revenues from taxes on motor vehicles. The example of Jakarta emphasizes the fact that motor vehicle taxation, if turned over to local authorities and if given sufficient attention, can make a major contribution to local urban revenues. Indeed, table 4 shows that revenue from motor vehicle taxation in Jakarta was more than twice local expenditure on urban roadways. The ratios for other cities for which data are available range between 4 and 19 per cent.

There are three arguments behind increasing the use of motor vehicle taxation. The first is that such taxes take advantage of a steadily increasing tax base, particularly in big cities. The second is that motor vehicle taxes are an effective means of recapturing the fiscal costs of motor vehicle use. The third argument for motor vehicle taxation is that it provides a means for controlling the social cost of motor vehicle use by reducing the differential between the marginal private cost of motor vehicle use and the marginal social cost of its use.

A strong case can be made that urban governments should be allowed to tax motor vehicles because it is the urban or local level of government that is often required to deal with the costs that result from rapid growth of urban vehicles and urban residents that suffer

Table 4 **Revenues from local motor vehicle taxation as a percentage of total local expenditure on urban roadways, selected cities**

City (Year)	Percentage
Ahmedabad (1981)	19.4
Bombay (1982)	4.1
Jakarta (1982)	286.9
Seoul (1983)	18.3

Source: World Bank data.

most from pollution and congestion due to heavy traffic. Local authorities are often responsible for the construction and maintenance of urban road infrastructure as well as for regulating city traffic and providing public transport. As seen above, revenue from motor vehicle taxation has the potential to cover a substantial part of these costs.

Usually local motor vehicle taxation consists of a very heterogeneous set of levies.[20] Most cities impose some form of annual licence taxes on all motor vehicles whose owners reside in the particular taxing jurisdiction. These taxes may take the form of a flat annual rate that differentiates only between the type of vehicle. In some cities, such as Bombay, Jakarta, and Seoul, the tax varies not only by type of vehicle but according to weight, cylinder size, and/or age. Some systems also have special features like lower tax rates for business vehicles, or taxation by number of seats.

Another form of motor vehicle taxation is a one time tax on the registration of motor vehicles or a tax on transfers of vehicle ownership. In some countries registration fees are only nominal. In Jakarta, the registration fee has played the role of a tax (levied at 10 per cent of the value of the vehicle for the initial transfer and 5 per cent for all subsequent transfers).

A third form of vehicle taxation is a tax on fuel. Fuel taxes are most commonly applied to gasoline. Local surcharges on national fuel taxes have been levied in a number of cities. One argument commonly made against spatially differentiated gasoline taxation is that it may encourage gasoline smuggling and unnecessary driving to refuel. However, in practice, fuel prices already differ substantially across regions due to differences in tax rates, differential transport costs, or local retail monopolies. In fact, fuel prices in rural areas are commonly significantly higher than those in urban areas. As long as urban fuel tax surcharges are kept within reasonable bounds (e.g., so as to offset or reverse the market determined rural-urban differentials), their negative side-effects will be negligible.

As mentioned above, motor vehicle taxation may provide a way to reduce congestion and traffic by making private users bear the cost to the public. Only in Singapore (as far as we know) has an effort been made to restrain central city congestion by the application of area- and time-specific licence fees and parking charges. A scheme was initiated in 1975 by which a restricted zone in the city was defined to include the most congested portion of the central business district, covering 22 hectares with 22 entry points. Between 7:30 a.m. and

10:15 a.m. an entry into this restricted zone by private vehicle was permitted only if the vehicle exhibited a licence costing US$26 a month, or US$1.30 a day (in 1976 prices). Buses, commercial vehicles, motor cycles, or car pools were exempt. The scheme was supplemented by a drastic increase in public and commercial parking fees.

Watson and Holland [30] provide an excellent evaluation of the Singapore scheme from which one can conclude that the scheme has proven to be technically, administratively, and politically feasible. Although Singapore's special circumstances certainly favoured a successful outcome, its experience should serve as an example for other cities. However, any attempts to follow Singapore's example should take note of the various practical aspects that helped the system work: adequate study and preparation; simplicity of regulation and flexibility of implementation; and unfettered authority by the metropolitan government to impose whatever scheme was regarded as most appropriate. The fact that such schemes have not been implemented elsewhere, even where explicitly considered and ostensibly adopted (as in Bangkok), reflects the powerful political opposition to any serious efforts to limit the use of private automobiles in large cities.

Given the evidence available, it does appear that motor vehicle taxation is an untapped source of revenue in most large cities. The optimal choice of action in motor vehicle taxation in large cities of developing countries is likely to include some combination of the instruments reviewed here. Unrestricted licences and fuel taxes can make major contributions to local revenue generation without causing major efficiency losses. Restricted licence taxes and parking fees and taxes could then be imposed mainly to control urban congestion and thus reduce the cost of maintaining urban roads.

Other taxes and their potential

Apart from property taxes and motor vehicle taxation, cities can and do make use of a large number of other taxes and licences. Local governments in developing countries usually have access to one major non-property tax. Table 3 shows that for a number of countries in South-East Asia, the octroi provides a significant source of revenue. Cities in Brazil have access to sales taxes. A good number of cities receive at least some revenue from taxes on entertainment. A host of smaller "nuisance taxes," such as stamp taxes and the like, are also available and appear in the "all other" category, which for some countries is significant. These other taxes tend in general not to be as productive as sources of revenue as property taxes or motor vehicle taxation, but they do have the advantage of being available. Many of these taxes give city governments the opportunity to tap the growing taxable capacity of urban areas.

Many of these smaller taxes are hold-overs from the colonial or precolonial practices applied to small and medium-size towns 50 or 100 years ago and have been adjusted on an ad hoc basis in order to deal with the rapidly rising revenue needs of urban areas. In most cases they have evolved with little regard to the overall objectives of the tax system as a whole, but rather with emphasis placed on immediate revenue needs. Cities have often been obliged to use such taxes for want of any alternative. This is particularly true in cities where the most broad-based and productive revenue bases are jealously guarded by the central government. In many cities this has led to a tax system that is burdened with a large number of taxes that are costly to collect but not productive or buoyant in terms of revenue.

There are four main issues to consider with regard to the revenue productivity of these types of taxes. The first involves defining a non-property tax system that is capable of raising adequate revenue for local government. Taxes with a small revenue yield imply that a proliferation of such taxes will be necessary to meet revenue needs. Second, the income elasticity of these taxes is important. This represents the degree to which the revenues of a tax grow more or less in proportion with the level of general economic activity in the area. Because expenditure needs are likely to grow at least in proportion to personal income and prices, one might argue that the revenue from these taxes should be equally buoyant in order to make their collection worthwhile. Third, one must consider the sensitivity of these taxes and the degree to which they are stable over time. Taxes whose income are unpredictable and unstable over time make planning difficult. Finally, one must consider the criterion of administrative ease. If the tax cannot be effectively collected at reasonable cost it may be more trouble than it is worth for the city government. Let us consider briefly each of these other taxes.[21]

Local income taxes

While local income taxes are an important source of local tax revenue in a number of industrial countries, they play little or no role in the tax systems of the cities covered in table 3. In those cities where local income taxes do exist, they have relatively limited coverage. This is at least partly due to the fact that local income taxes are often constrained by a central government fearful of tax base competition. It may also be the result of administrative weaknesses on the local level. The potential yield of a local income tax depends very much on the coverage of the tax and rate structure, and the actual yield depends on the effectiveness of assessment and collection. If a local income tax is placed piggyback onto the central income tax, it becomes a more viable revenue raising proposition; but in this case, local discretion is limited and the tax more often than not takes on the form of a transfer. The potential of a local income tax for raising revenue and helping in the financing of city infrastructure is thus conditioned on two factors: the administrative capacity of the city government and the discretion of the city authorities over the local income tax base, rates, and structure. The greater these two factors, the greater is the potential of the local income tax as a source of revenue for cities.

General sales taxes

Brazil is the only country in our sample where local governments are given access to sales taxes. The contribution of these taxes to total tax revenue in Brazil is significant, at 50 per cent of total tax revenue in both Rio de Janeiro and São Paulo in 1984. The success of the general sales tax in Brazil attests to its considerable revenue potential; however, in most developing countries, sales taxes are reserved for use by higher levels of government.

There are five basic types of sales taxes: the turnover tax is levied on every sale; the manufacturer's sales tax is levied at the stage of production; the wholesale sales tax is imposed upon the transactions between wholesaler and retailer; the retail sales tax is imposed on the sales to the final consumer; and the value added tax is levied on each transaction but is based only on the additional value generated by the establishment selling the good or service. In their discussion of general sales taxes, Bahl and Linn point out that only the turnover and the retail sales taxes are likely candidates for a local tax from the point of view of administration.[22]

The potential revenue performance of the local sales tax is its principal attraction and justifies its often high collection costs. The revenue elasticity of the tax is likely to be good because the tax is levied *ad valorem* and revenues thus increase with general economic activity and inflation. By the same token, the stability of local sales taxes may be found wanting because collections expand and contract in proportion to the level of economic activity – though the base of a sales tax is not likely to be as unstable as the base of the income tax.

Despite its substantial revenue potential there are two major difficulties with a local sales tax. The first concerns administrative difficulties, which stem from the small formal sector and from the preponderance of small retail establishments in most developing countries. An attempt to levy a retail sales tax on these enterprises poses tremendous administrative costs. Small retail establishments would almost certainly have to be exempt. In some countries the base would become so narrow, however, that statutory rates would have to be quite high. There is also the scope for considerable evasion with this type of tax. The second difficulty with the local sales tax is that, like sales taxes on a larger scale, it tends to be a regressive tax. This may be alleviated by exempting basic necessities and foodstuffs.

As development proceeds and the modern sector develops in the major cities, the potential for the use of local sales taxes will grow and it may become an important source of revenue in those cities where it is administratively feasible (as in Rio de Janeiro and São Paulo).

Local taxes on industry, commerce, and professions

While these taxes are a common source of local revenue in Latin America, the data in table 3 indicate that few mega-cities rely on such taxes as a major source of revenue. In Calcutta, local taxes on industry and commerce provided 6.4 per cent of total local tax revenue in 1982. In Dacca, 3.5 per cent of local tax revenue comes from these taxes. In contrast, Manila relied on industry and commerce taxes for 30.7 per cent of its total local tax revenue. In some smaller cities the reliance on such taxes as a source of revenue is much greater: in San Salvador they accounted for 84 per cent of local tax revenue and for 73 per cent in La Paz. This indicates that, for many cities, taxes on industry, commerce, and the professions may be an untapped resource. The nature of this tax varies widely among countries and even among cities within a country. The tax could take the form of a sales tax in some cities, a tax on business capital in others, an annual value tax on business real estate in yet others, and in many municipalities, a flat charge for a business licence.

The potential revenue yield for business taxes is quite substantial, particularly in large cities where the number and sizes of businesses are growing. Even though the base may be inadequately assessed, the tax yield can grow rapidly. An analysis of the business licence tax in the Philippines shows that even with quite poor assessment and collection practices, the income elasticity of the tax yield can be greater than one.[23]

Despite their revenue potential, taxes on industry and commerce are difficult to administer. It is very difficult to assess small firms that do not keep proper accounts. Moreover, it is difficult to get a complete enumeration of taxable firms within an urban area, and as a result there is a high degree of evasion. The business tax is also plagued by serious collection problems; delinquency rates are often high. In order to make such taxes work as a source of revenue for local governments, they must be differentiated from central government sales taxes. For example, the business licence tax in the Philippines is really a gross receipts tax on all businesses, but its administration and design are kept quite separate from central government sales taxes.

An argument can be made that there is the potential for developing the business tax in large cities on the grounds that it can raise substantial revenues; rate and base adjustments are often unfettered by higher level government restrictions; it is relatively costless politically; and it often has no suitable alternative. Focus must be placed, however, on alleviating its administrative shortcomings.

The octroi

In many of the South-East Asian countries, the octroi is a significant source of revenue. In Ahmedabad, it provided 68.7 per cent of total local tax revenue in 1981. In Karachi, it provided 71.8 per cent of total local tax revenue. While the octroi is a significant source of revenue for these cities, it is unlikely that its use is viable in other large cities.

The octroi is a tax levied on goods entering a city for the purpose of local processing or final consumption.[24] The base of the octroi is the value, weight, or number of items entering a local jurisdiction by road, rail, air or sea. Rates vary according to complicated schedules, and the taxes are collected at octroi stations: checkpoints on roads at the jurisdictional borders and at railway stations, airports, and docks. Ahmedabad assessors are equipped with a manual of market values that they use to double-check the invoice amount. The taxes are collected directly from the driver by the attending clerks.

Complications of the octroi are that it increases transport time and cost. Bribery of octroi staff is frequently reported. Like all tariffs, the octroi also gives locally produced commodities a pricing advantage over commodities imported from outside the metropolitan area and thus distorts production and consumption decisions; tariffs have been shown to be more inefficient than many other forms of modern taxation [33, ch. 4]. The tax can also provide a disincentive for metropolitan integration under area-wide authority, because consolidation of the fragmented local authorities would automatically reduce the octroi tax base by detaxing intra-metropolitan commodity flows. From the standpoint of efficiency, the octroi is therefore an unmitigated disaster.

Despite these problems, the octroi continues to be a major and buoyant revenue source in the cities where it is established. In other cities, the complications and inefficiencies of imposing the octroi, or a tax like it, make it unlikely that such a tax could be implemented in a way that makes the administrative burden and harmful efficiency effects worth the revenue collected.

Entertainment taxes

As seen from table 3, many urban governments levy taxes on various forms of entertainment, and while the percentage of such taxes in total local tax revenue is not enormous, in some countries they contribute over 10 per cent of total local tax income. Entertainment taxes are commonly levied on restaurants and hotels, theatres, movies, and on betting and gambling. Lotteries operated by local governments might also be thought of as an entertainment tax. Local taxes on betting and gambling may be a particularly important source of revenue, where racecourses or casinos provide readily identifiable tax opportunities. Assessment and collection, however, may be difficult; arrangements typically involve a considerable amount of bargaining and might lend themselves to under-the-table payments. In Jakarta during the 1970s, a substantial part of the revenues from gambling was channelled into a separate fund under the exclusive control of the Governor of Jakarta and was used without formal accountability for various local projects.[25] Although entertainment taxes represent a relatively accessible and desirable form of local taxation, they cannot be relied upon as a major and stable source of financing for urban governments.

Our brief review of taxes other than the property tax and motor vehicle taxation in large urban areas indicates that development of general sales taxes and taxes on commerce and industry have the greatest potential for increasing the revenue raising capacity of urban governments. Their effectiveness as a revenue source, however, is contingent upon the administrative capacity of the city and willingness of the central government to relinquish exclusive controls over sales taxes. Over time, as the major urban areas become more and more developed, such taxes are likely to become an important revenue source.

User charges

In the preceding section we argued that user charges (fees charged for the provision of a service) are the most efficient means of financing public goods and services that are of measurable benefit to readily identifiable users. Many such services are provided by local authorities in urban areas, including water, power, telephones, solid waste disposal, and mass transport. However, these forms of infrastructure are generally inadequately provided in rapidly urbanizing cities.

Inadequate services often result from poor pricing policies on the part of the local government. Indiscriminately subsidized services often lead to a level of demand that is higher than can be supplied, leading to congestion and interruption of services. Under such circumstances, individuals or companies are sometimes forced to provide their own costly substitutes for publicly provided services, and they have been found to be willing to pay more for an improved level of public service provision.[26] Poor pricing policies also place a heavy weight on the fiscal authorities of a given locality. If utilities and services cannot cover their own operating costs, their loss must be covered from other parts of the budget. Table 2 shows that, more often than not, the proportion of locally raised revenue from self-financing services is low, with a median of 12 per cent in the years from 1980 onward. More effective use of user charges has great potential as a source of finance for developing infrastructure in large cities. Indeed, given the appropriate pricing policies, there is no reason that the provision of such services should not be self-financing, especially in mega-cities.[27]

User charges are particularly well suited to local government finance, where there is a direct link between user and beneficiary. Given an appropriate pricing structure, user charges can increase efficiency, even while making allowance for the poorest members of society. Generally, when providers of public services are not operating at full capacity, they should price services at their marginal cost. In other words, the price should be set equal to society's cost of providing the last, or marginal, unit. Since the price the consumer is willing to pay measures the benefit of consumption, when price equals marginal cost, the cost of providing this last unit will just equal the benefit that it provides. If the price exceeds the marginal cost of service provision, then the benefit of its provision at the margin exceeds its cost, and therefore a higher provision at lower prices would be more beneficial for society. By the same argument, when the price is lower than marginal cost, society gains from a higher price and lower consumption.

There are a number of qualifications, however, that may alter the marginal pricing rule. First, when one individual's consumption of a publicly provided good affects other (when there are externalities), the individual should be induced to consider the social rather than the private costs of his or her behaviour. This can be undertaken by charging below or above marginal cost in order to align private costs with social costs. For example, if individuals are primarily concerned with their own well-being, they may not be willing to be immunized against a contagious disease as would be socially desirable; they must be charged a cost lower than marginal cost or in some cases no charge at all. In other cases, as in road use, individuals may cause costs that are borne by others (e.g., pollution and congestion costs). The "external" costs could be "internalized" by charging an emission fee, or a toll during peak periods.

Second, the development of many of the services provided by local authorities, such as power, telecommunications, transport, and water systems, requires a few large ("lumpy") investments rather than continuous small ones. In these cases, setting prices to short-run marginal costs will result in price instability; prices will rise as the provider of the services reaches full capacity and then will drop dramatically after capacity has been expanded. A way to avoid this problem is to use average incremental costs as the basis for pricing as opposed to marginal cost. Average incremental cost is a formula that provides an inexact but stable approximation of marginal cost.

A third difficulty arises in pricing the services of firms that experience economies of scale, i.e., the unit cost drops as the scale of operation increases. In these cases, it is often advisable to use a two part pricing scheme, because pricing based on marginal cost will not cover operating costs. One example of a two part pricing scheme is where there is a basic fee for connection and a fee equal to the marginal cost of consumption.[28]

One common argument against user charges, however, is that they hurt the poor, because, by placing user charges on public services, the poor will no longer have access to them. In practice, however, the poor often fail to get these services anyway. Because of fiscal constraints in most urban areas, only a limited amount of public services can be provided free of charge. When this happens, poor people are likely to be at a disadvantage. Subsidized water and electricity benefit heavy users, such as the more wealthy and industrial users.

In practice user charges can be structured to help the poor: first, by targeting subsidies in a way that limits them to services primarily consumed by the poor, such as health posts and primary schools in rural areas and poor urban settlements; second, user charges are also often structured to help the poor directly by "lifeline tariffs," where an initial portion of a service (usually that amount deemed necessary for basic human needs) is provided either free or below marginal cost. Consumption beyond first level is charged at or above marginal cost.[29] Third, access fees or one-time installation charges for infrastructure services, such as water and power, can be waived in poor neighbourhoods, while the actual use of the publicly provided service is charged for. The poor frequently cannot afford the high one-time capital charges but are able to pay the recurrent costs of use, especially as the publicly provided service tends to substitute for higher cost services offered by private vendors (e.g., water carriers, etc.).

The proper design of charges can help public authorities to meet the goals of efficiency, equity, and financial viability. This holds for the provision of water services, power, telecommunications, solid waste management, and a host of other services. While the individual circumstances of pricing may vary in each industry, it seems that better use of user charges can certainly help large cities finance more adequate and efficient infrastructure.

Two other methods of developing infrastructure in built up areas that are akin to user charges and that have demonstrated some success are land readjustment and valorization charges.[30] Land readjustment schemes usually involve the consolidation of numerous parcels of raw land at the urban periphery. The land is serviced and subdivided for urban use and then returned to the original owners. However, some of the land is retained by the public authority, in part to meet the needs of urban infrastructure (especially roads and green spaces) and in part to provide a source of finance to defray the cost of development. The land retained for this latter purpose is sold at market prices in commercial transactions or auctions.

The Republic of Korea has made extensive use of land readjustment programmes. By 1985, some 35 per cent of Seoul's total built up area was covered by completed or ongoing schemes. The system has opened up new land for urban use and thus has helped to increase the supply of housing and raise public funds. Such programmes, however, require fairly sophisticated methods of public land management, including effective land registration, cadastral records, and land redistribution formulas.

Valorization systems, which are often applied in Latin America, have been used to finance improvements in infrastructure in built up areas. According to this system of taxation, the cost of public works is allocated to affected properties in proportion to the benefits conferred, and it has been used to finance street improvements, water supply, and other services. Valorization charges are designed to recover project costs, not to recapture all the benefits the project is expected to confer. The system is intended to make urban services largely self-financing and thus to help reduce municipal tax burdens.

The valorization system in Bogotá has been carefully studied. At the height of its use in 1968 it contributed 16 per cent to the financing of all local public expenditures (including spending by state-owned enterprises). Its significance has decreased since then, but it has retained an important role in financing infrastructure development.

In practice, valorization schemes have not always recovered the cost of projects and have tended to rely on large financial transfers from the city's general revenue. An important reason for this is that some projects have been designed to improve living conditions in low income areas, and the beneficiaries have not been expected to pay valorization charges. Another reason that some valorization schemes have failed to cover costs has been the incomplete collection of charges. In Bogotá, for projects in the period 1968–1986, arrears amounted to 16 per cent of costs. The collection problem has arisen mainly from lack of payment by public agencies and by a few large properties. Projects for which the benefits were uncertain or not clearly concentrated in the areas bearing the valorization charge often created the greatest collection problems. The experience in Bogotá has demonstrated that the success of the valorization system depends heavily on the quality of investment planning and project preparation.

Under the appropriate circumstances and where the benefits of land and infrastructure development can be clearly discerned, land readjustment and valorization schemes clearly can help to recover the costs involved in the development of urban infrastructure. They are, accordingly, an additional type of user charge that large cities should consider when trying to expand their resources.

Grants, transfers, and tax sharing arrangements

From the information in table 2, we see that the importance of intergovernmental grants and shared taxes varies considerably in large urban areas. In Calcutta, revenue from grants and shared taxes in 1982 was 54.9 per cent of total local revenue. In Lagos, it was 48.8 per cent (for 1980) and in Jakarta, 39.1 per cent (for 1981). By contrast, grants and shared taxes provided only 0.4 per cent of total local revenue in São Paulo (1984) and 0.7 per cent in Bombay (1982). Bahl and Linn [4] find that in the cities for which data are available, there is no general trend toward an increasing reliance on grants and transfers. They also find that the degree to which expenditure is decentralized does not predict whether large cities will depend on grants. While the size and nature of grants are among the major components of the debate over centralization versus decentralization that was discussed in the preceding section, an argument can be made that large cities should depend less on grants and transfers than smaller cities. This argument goes hand in hand with the argument made above, that large urban areas are likely to benefit from increased autonomy.

Intergovernmental grants and transfers usually have three different functions.[31] The first is the provision of access to central government tax instruments. These grants compensate local governments for the fact that the central government often restricts the use of the most productive sources of revenue – they virtually always claim the highest yielding taxes. The second function of grants and transfers is equalization. Transfers are often used to shift resources from the more prosperous parts of the country to the less prosperous ones. The third function of grants and transfers from the central government is to encourage local governments to increase expenditure on functions that are either of national significance or that have spillover effects into other communities.

In the case of large cities, it is this last function that is the most relevant. As seen above, unless cities are prohibited from using certain tax bases by the central government, they will usually have a number of mechanisms for raising revenue. It is also likely that mega-cities will have higher levels of economic activity and therefore will not be the recipients of grants for equalization purposes. It is very likely,

Table 5 **Alternative forms of intergovernmental grant programmes**

Method of allocating the divisible pool among eligible units	Method of determining the total divisible pool		
	Specified share of national or state government tax	Ad hoc decision	Reimbursement approved expenditures
Origin of collection of the tax	A	—	—
Formula	B	F	—
Total or partial reimbursement of costs	C	G	K
Ad hoc	D	H	—

however, that large cities will provide services with benefits that will spill over into neighbouring communities and will be spending on services that might be considered to be of national significance. This is particularly the case in capital cities.

If cities receive grants for this purpose (or for other purposes), the most crucial factor is that they be predictable; erratic grants and transfers undermine local budgeting. In order to achieve this predictability, grant and transfer administration should be based on a system of rules. Generally grant distribution systems have two dimensions: the method of determining the size of the distributable pool and the method of determining the distribution among state and local units. Bahl and Linn [4] set out a taxonomy of such rules (table 5).

Current practice in determining the pool of resources suggests three principal approaches: a specified share of national or state taxes; an ad hoc decision that is usually made on the basis of an annual appropriation and voted upon; and third, the reimbursement of costs. Allocations among state and local governments are usually made in one of four ways: by returning shares to the communities from which they were collected (tax sharing); by formula; on an ad hoc basis; or by reimbursing costs.

As discussed above, in principle, large cities should expect to receive grants and transfers for their expenditure on services of national benefit (unless they have entered into a tax sharing arrangement). This suggests that for most large cities, grants and transfers will be based on reimbursement costs. As seen from table 5, the total pool available to reimburse costs may be determined as an earmarked tax or share of national revenue, on an ad hoc basis, or as a proportion of costs to be reimbursed. The amount of reimbursement (i.e., full vs. partial reimbursement) is likely to have implications for the fiscal authority of the city. Full reimbursement is likely to be accompanied by a rigid central government process; local fiscal choices will be minimized. Partial reimbursement leaves local governments with more authority and often provides an incentive for increasing the tax effort within cities. However, certain methods of partial reimbursement, such as matching grants, may also have unfavourable allocative effects if grants distort budgets in favour of the aided service and against other services desired by the community.

Thus, in determining to what extent they should rely on grants and transfers, large cities should consider the trade-offs involved. By a heavy reliance on grants, the city is virtually guaranteed to have reduced authority over its revenue mobilization and frequently over its expenditure allocation. In small cities where administrative skills are scarce, this may not be an issue, since there may not be any substantial alternative revenue source to central transfers. In mega-cities, it seems almost certain that local authorities can do better than relying on central funds, which tend to come with strings attached. If transfers are received at the price of reduced local autonomy, they may not be worth it, at least in mega-cities. If, however, transfers are provided within a framework allowing local authorities some significant degree of control, they are a useful means of financing (or helping to finance) services that may be necessary to both the city and the country. In general, however, large cities should not count on grants and transfers from higher levels of government as a major source of revenue for financing the development of urban infrastructure.

This conclusion is strengthened when considering the arguments for and against transfers to cities from the perspective of the central authorities. Low transfers force cities to self-finance expenditures that tend to have largely local benefits. This enhances the efficiency of urban areas. At the same time, since rural areas, small towns, and remote areas tend to be poorer and less able to raise revenues for public service provision, central governments frequently want to redistribute fiscal resources away from the large cities to the remainder of the country in the interest of equalizing revenues, and thus public spending, on a per capita basis.

Borrowing

Taxes, user charges, and transfers are primarily assigned to meeting the recurrent cost of services. Borrowing from other levels of government (and where possible from private institutions) is often regarded as the most reasonable source of funding for capital expenditure. In developed countries, and particularly in the US, the majority of cities raise funds through the use of municipal bonds and direct access to capital markets. In developing countries, financial markets are not usually sufficiently developed to support such a market, and municipalities rely on borrowing from the central government and from specialized credit agencies such as development banks. In table 2, we see that Ahmedabad and São Paulo have relied on external borrowing for about a quarter of their local revenue. Other cities have relied much less on such borrowing.

The principal argument for resorting to borrowing is that borrowing distributes the costs of projects over the life of the loan and therefore over successive beneficiaries.[32] Funding from recurrent surplus would unduly burden current users and restrict current demand, and would inhibit investment in worthwhile large projects.

The ability of large cities to effectively use borrowing as a means of financing urban infrastructure largely depends on two factors: the availability and channels of credit and the city's ability to service its debt, i.e., its creditworthiness. In developing countries, the potential for going directly to credit markets by issuing municipal bonds will depend on the level of financial sophistication in the country. Very often the financial networks and pool of investors are insufficient to support municipal bonds. In the few cases where municipal bonds have been issued, as in Lagos, the majority of the bonds have usually been purchased by state-owned entities such as the National Insurance Fund.

A more common channel of credit is a public credit intermediary, or a municipal credit institution. These institutions are thought to provide some advantages over borrowing directly from the government. They can foster greater financial accountability. If such institutions bear the risk of local government default, they are likely to be more rigorous in their assessment procedures. This will lead to better project selection. Specialized credit agencies also can protect borrowers from political interference.

The second issue concerning borrowing is the ability of the city to service its debt. This is of particular concern when the borrowing finances the development of infrastructure that does not have any specific revenue return, such as roads or drainage. The increased reliance on loans to finance such projects presupposes an effort and capacity to increase future tax revenues. Where this is not likely to materialize, debt finance should be considered with considerable caution. In principle, of course, mega-cities should be better able to raise additional revenues to finance their debt service than small towns and rural jurisdictions.

In practice, the use of municipal credit institutions has not lived up to expectations. In many countries, normal banking discipline has not applied, and these specialized agencies have not attained any degree of financial separation from the central government. In the Latin American countries, where these institutions are fairly common, they typically depend on support from the central government and are not removed from political infighting. Support from the central government often comes in the form of subsidies, which may lead to fiscal difficulties at a higher level of government. These agencies also may suffer from poor repayment. In general, the assumption that such specialized institutions will encourage both the lender and the municipality to ensure sound financial practices has not been borne out in practice.[33]

As large urban areas and financial markets become more developed, large cities in developing countries may be able to rely to a greater extent on borrowing, particularly in the private sector, to finance the development of physical and social infrastructure. While for many cities this may not immediately be an option, it is a potential source of finance that policy makers should keep in mind. The massive needs to be met also provide an incentive to national policy makers to implement programmes that will foster the development of deeper capital markets in developing countries.[34]

New means of financing infrastructure in big cities: Focus on the participation of the private sector

Our review of the traditional methods of raising revenue indicates that there is a good deal of potential for mega-cities to raise public revenue using traditional means. However, given the overwhelming demand for services and the renewed emphasis on cutting public expenditure in developing countries, they may not be sufficient nor represent the most efficient way to proceed. This points increasingly in the direction of developing the role of the private sector in providing urban infrastructure. There are a number of means through which the private sector may come to play a greater role in the provision of public services, including management contracts, deregulation and demonopolization, self-help and community-based contracts, and contracting out. Such practices have been important in some developed countries, but until recently, they have played a relatively minor role in the provision of public services in the cities of developing countries. Here we discuss very briefly the arguments for privately providing public services. We then focus on two areas where private participation may be particularly promising and important in the large cities of developing countries: build, own, operate, and transfer (BOOT) schemes and housing finance.

The private provision of public services

There is a large and growing literature on the private provision of public services, and there is in fact quite a rich history of the provision of social and physical infrastructure services by the private sector.[35] The principal argument that is usually put forth in favour of private sector involvement is that the private provision of goods and services is more efficient. There are two aspects to this argument. The first emphasizes property rights: private ownership and the claim on assets it involves push owners to monitor carefully the behaviour of private enterprise managers and employees. Public enterprises, in contrast, are not "owned" by anyone in particular, so the incentives to monitor managers and employees are not strong. The second aspect relates to the exposure to greater competition and "market discipline" of private compared to public firms, which makes the former more efficient. The empirical evidence on this issue is not conclusive, but the weight of the evidence seems to be on the side of competitive private enterprises.[36]

The important issue at stake is whether competition is in fact feasible, and therefore whether private markets can work efficiently. As pointed out by the World Bank [35], for many urban infrastructure services, such as housing, urban transit, curative medical care, and job training, there are no technological barriers to entry, and externalities are relatively minor or can be dealt with by government regulation. A classic example is public versus private buses. Table 6 shows a comparison of private versus public bus operations in a number of developing country cities. It shows that while public bus services are rarely able to cover their costs, in most cases private bus companies do. Public companies have higher fleet utilization rates, lower staffing ratios, and less fare evasion than do their public competitors. Private provision of urban bus transport (and other urban services) does not rule out targeted subsidies in support of poverty re-

Table 6 **Comparative operating conditions and costs of private and public bus services in selected cities in developing countries, 1985**

City	Ownership	Fleet utilization (%)	Staff-operating bus ratio	Cost per passenger (km/US cents)	Revenue-cost ratio
Ankara, Turkey	Public	65	6.0	2.5	0.67
	Private	95	2.6	1.2	1.70
Bangkok, Thailand	Public	80	6.2	1.9	0.74
	Private	80	—	1.2	1.10
Calcutta, India	Public	64	20.7	1.9	0.46
	Private	86	4.0	0.7	1.10
Istanbul, Turkey	Public	60	7.5	2.0	0.88
	Private	—	—	1.7	1.10
Jakarta, Indonesia	Public	59	14.5	1.8	0.50
	Private	76	7.3	0.9	1.20
Karachi, Pakistan	Public	40	12.4	2.8	0.49
	Private	72	6.4	1.0	1.15

Source: Ref. 1, table 1.
Note: Only data for comparable large bus types are included.

duction. For example, in Bogotá, bus operators whose vehicles are used predominantly by poorer commuters have been subsidized by public subsidies. It is critical, however, that competition not be inhibited by public intervention. For example, subsidies only for publicly owned and run firms, or restrictions on entry by private competitors to public service providers, will limit the scope and potential of competitive markets and thus the scope for efficiency gains.

For services where competition is not assured, such as for large-scale public utility networks or selected social services, private providers do not necessarily provide superior service as compared with public providers. However, in many developing countries (and cities), the organizational effectiveness and financial capacities of public authorities are generally weak. With governments frequently unable to provide timely and adequate resources – on both a national and municipal level – the effectiveness of public sector service provision is likely to remain low. Thus private provision of at least some public services may not even be a matter of choice. In some countries, in fact, the poor provision of public services has prompted private agents to fill the gaps left by the public sector. For example, in some cities of Nigeria, households pay a large premium to private water vendors in the dry season because water provision is poor and the quality of public water is low.[37] Nigerian manufacturers have also made considerable investments in generators in order to avoid frequent power outages and fluctuations in voltage that cause damage to machinery.[38] Obviously, one remedy is to improve the effectiveness of the public sector entities; however, another, and at times preferable, alternative is to support private provision of these services by reducing barriers to entry (e.g., permit private generation of power and sale to public grids) or by auctioning off, leasing, or subcontracting public service franchises to private providers. This is possible for a wide range of physical infrastructure, including power, water, road construction, port facilities and stevedoring, solid waste disposal, etc. For social services, such as education and health, private provision of services has a long and respectable history in many countries before public provision became the rule. Recently, there has been a trend in some developing countries to encourage, rather than hinder, private provision of these services, too, in some cases, with financial support from the government (as in the case of pilot education schemes in Chile and the Philippines [35, p. 22]).

Thus, in many instances services can be provided efficiently and effectively by private agents, and the case for increased reliance on private provision is particularly strong in large cities where the scope for competition is high and where regulation of private providers – to the extent necessary and appropriate – can be implemented relatively effectively. This allows limited fiscal resources to be released and used in the areas where market failure requires that the public sector provide the service. Let us now consider two cases of private sector involvement that may be of particular use in financing infrastructure in large cities.

Build, own, operate, and transfer (BOOT) schemes

Large cities require large infrastructure supply systems in the areas of transport, telecommunications, water, and power. For these systems, which have traditionally been provided and financed by the public sector, private involvement through BOOT schemes may be particularly attractive. BOOT schemes are projects in which the private sector takes over the development of infrastructure for a given period of time (usually between 15 and 30 years) and after this period passes control of the infrastructure back to the government. Private sector involvement in the provision of public infrastructure is not a new phenomenon. During the nineteenth and early twentieth centuries, the private sector frequently took on infrastructure projects. The Suez Canal and the Trans-Siberian Railway are two well-known examples. More recently, under the name of "limited recourse" projects, the private sector has financed the development of rigs in the North Sea. Recent use of BOOT schemes in Malaysia, the Philippines, and Thailand indicate that, under the right conditions, they may be an effective way to develop infrastructure in mega-cities.

A number of factors converged in the late 1970s that made schemes involving the private provision of infrastructure in developing countries more desirable. The debt crisis meant that governments had lower borrowing capacities and fewer budgetary resources available for the development of infrastructure. At around the same time, the major international contracting firms were facing a significant downturn and were looking for ways to promote additional business. With the onset of structural adjustment programmes, many countries became increasingly interested in promoting the development of the private sector and in "privatizing" traditionally public sector activities and enterprises. The BOOT approach to financing appeared as a way to help developing countries obtain needed infrastructure, while at the same time promoting private sector activity in the economy.

Under BOOT schemes, projects that are normally considered as public sector activities are temporarily placed in the hands of the private sector.[39] The process of planning, financing, designing, constructing, and operating is conducted under the auspices of a private sector organization – the project company. This company is typically composed of a consortium of firms that includes a major international engineering and construction firm and one or more equipment suppliers. The host government gives the project company a concession to build the infrastructure and to operate and collect the revenues that the project generates for a designated period of time. The project company raises the bulk of the financing required for the project from commercial lenders, usually supported by export guarantee agencies and sometimes with support from bi- and multilateral institutions. The project company owns and operates the facility for a period of time that is sufficient to pay off the debt incurred in financing the project and to provide a reasonable return on the equity of investors. At the end of the period, operation of the infrastructure is passed back to the government. In theory, this approach provides a means for an infrastructure project to be completely financed by the private sector. In practice, particularly in developing countries, extensive host government support is a prerequisite for a successful BOOT project.

A number of countries have employed BOOT schemes in the development of infrastructure. Malaysia has completed construction of three BOOT projects and has three under way.[40] It has completed two toll-road projects and a project involving a water treatment plant and a submarine pipeline to the island of Labuan. Projects under construction include the Labuan-Beaufort Interconnection, which involves laying a submarine cable for electricity, and two more toll-roads. Two factors have contributed to the success of the Malaysian projects. The first is that the government and the local financing community have taken an active role in financing the projects. For example, in the North-South Highway project, with total financing requirements of M$2.535 billion (US$921 million in 1989 dollars), at least M$1.6 billion (US$581 million) will be raised from banks and insurance companies within Malaysia. The balance is to be raised offshore in a syndicated Eurocurrency credit and/or syndicated letter of credit facilities at a maturity of 15 years.

The second factor that has contributed to the success of the Malaysian projects is the government's commitment to BOOT as a model. The government is providing supporting finance of M$165 million (US$60 million). It has also undertaken to reimburse the project company (United Engineers Malaysia) if for any reason, traffic flows, and therefore toll income, should fall below a mutually agreed upon level. It has also provided exchange rate guarantees and various guarantees against *force majeure* or government action.

Pakistan signed the basic contracts for its first major BOOT project, the Hab River project, in December 1989, and is seeking to develop others as part of its policy to encourage private sector involvement in the power sector. The Hab River project consists of a 1.300 MW oil fired power plant to be sited near the mouth of the Hab River, about 40 kilometres from Karachi. The sponsoring consortium is led by Hawker Siddeley Power Engineering of Great Britain and Xenel Industries of Saudi Arabia. The total cost of the project is estimated at just over US$1.1 billion.[41]

Multi- and bilateral official agencies have played an important role in the Hab River project. With the help of the World Bank, the Japanese Export-Import Bank, the UK Overseas Development Agency, the Government of Italy, and USAID, a Private Sector Energy Development Fund (the "PSEDF") has been set up under the control of Pakistan's National Development Finance Corporation. This fund is used to finance up to 30 per cent of the costs of BOOT projects. All loans to the PSEDF are guaranteed by the Government of Pakistan. These resources are on-lent at prevailing market interest rates. With 30 per cent of the project financed through the PSEDF and 25 per cent financed by equity, the remaining balance of 45 per cent is left to be financed by commercial lenders. The World Bank has also helped the Government of Pakistan in soliciting proposals for BOOT projects and in streamlining the procedures for the review and approval of investments. In addition to the Hab River project, the Pakistani government has three other BOOT projects in the works and is considering a number of smaller projects.[42]

The Philippines is also turning to BOOT projects to help meet increased demands for energy. A number of projects have been proposed; the first one to be implemented involves the development of a 200 MW gas turbine plant in Metro Manila. The facility is expected to be used primarily as a stand-by facility for "peak load" purposes. The project sponsor is Hopewell Holdings Limited of Hong Kong. Equity and debt are to be provided by the Asian Development Bank. Equity is also being provided by Hopewell and Citicorp. All of the electricity produced by the plant is to be purchased by the National Power Corporation (NPC); the NPC pays both a fixed monthly capacity fee and an additional energy fee based on the actual amount of energy generated. Total fee revenues are used to pay operating expenses, taxes, debt service, and dividends. The NPC also provides free fuel and free use of the project site for the entire contract period.

The Philippine government has provided a set of foreign investment incentives and guarantees to potential sponsors. These include the right to remit earnings, the proceeds from liquidation, and the sums required for payment of interest and dividends in the currency in which the investments were made; a guarantee that the property of the BOOT firm will not be expropriated by the government except for public use or in the interest of national welfare and upon payment of just compensation; a full exemption from income taxes by the Philippine government for four to six years; certain tax and duty exemptions; simplification of customs procedures; and exemptions of certain taxes on contractors.

Thailand is close to completing a BOOT project involving a 30 kilometre toll-road in the Bangkok metropolitan area, known as the Second Stage Expressway. The US$1 billion project is based on a toll concession that began on 1 March 1990 and runs for 30 years. The project is under the direction of the Expressway Rapid Transit Authority of Thailand (ETA), but the financing, building, and operation of the project have been given to the Bangkok Expressway Company, Ltd. (BECL), a company incorporated in Thailand and majority owned (about two-thirds) by Kumagai Gumi Company, Ltd., a major Japanese engineering and contracting firm. The remaining equity ownership is spread among Thai institutional investors and some international financial institutions. In order to finance the project, BECL was attempting to raise 5 billion baht (US$200 million at 1988 exchange rates) of equity subscriptions and 20 billion baht (US$800 million at 1988 rates) of debt with recourse only to BECL and its assets. The loans come mainly from commercial banks in Thailand and from multilateral and bilateral government lending institutions.[43]

The Thai government has helped to implement the project in a number of ways. It agreed to share with BECL, according to a revenue sharing formula, revenues from the *existing* government toll-road system. The government issued a decree enabling ETA to acquire the land necessary in order to build the new expressway and placed the expressway concession on the list of projects receiving investment privileges, which include income tax relief for eight years and tax exemptions on dividends. The government made provisions in the case of exceptional circumstances, allowing for some delays in the implementation schedule, adjustments in revenue sharing proportions, an increase in tolls, and an extension of the overall concession period. "Exceptional circumstances" include material increases in interest rates, material economic dislocation in Thailand, material delays in the relocation or diversion of utilities, unanticipated adverse ground conditions, significant disruptions in the local construction and building materials industry, and non-insurable events of *force majeure*.[44]

Thailand has also been negotiating a BOOT project with a Canadian firm for the construction of "Stage One, Phase One" of the Bangkok metro. Negotiations are well under way and it is hoped that the metro will be in operation by 1994.[45]

The experience with BOOT projects to date indicates that they involve a delicate and complicated balancing of public and private interests and involvement; however, they can be a successful method of financing infrastructure if certain essential ingredients exist. First, BOOT projects are unlikely to be successful in developing countries unless they have strong host government support. The government must be able to provide powerful bureaucratic support and a legal environment in which the various regulatory and other issues that arise may be addressed. The government must be able to negotiate the terms of the concession agreement and to provide logistical support. Often the government will be the sole purchaser of the output of a BOOT project (as in the case of power plants), in which case it must be able to assure a revenue stream that is essential in persuading investors and lenders to commit their funds on a long-term basis. Often also the host government is required to provide guarantees concerning inflation, foreign exchange, project risk, and *force majeure*. In general, while BOOT projects may reduce or eliminate the financing that the government must contribute to these projects, they require a substantial actual or contingent financial commitment on the part of the government.

The second important ingredient for a successful BOOT project is a financially strong and experienced sponsor or group of sponsors who will form the project company. The process of developing such a project is immensely time consuming and expensive. For example, Bechtel spent US$7 million over five years on unsuccessful power plant attempts and Kumagai Gumi spent US$5 million in pre-signing costs on the road project in Thailand.[46] Because of these high costs, the project company needs to work out cost sharing arrangements early in the process among members of the project.

The third ingredient is a clear demonstration to potential investors and lenders of the financial viability of the project. This implies that there is a clear and certain source of revenue that will be sufficient to pay interest and principal payments on debt and provide a return on equity that is commensurate with development and long-term project risk. As far as project costs are concerned, they must be reasonably predictable, and it must be clear that the project can be built and operated as planned.

The fourth ingredient that usually exists in successful BOOT projects is local participation. Foreign investors are unlikely to be willing to put their money into projects that local investors are unwilling to take part in. Countries with more developed financial markets, such as Malaysia and Thailand, also tend to have greater success with BOOT projects. In addition, it is also advisable to include among the sponsors some well-connected and well-respected private participants from the host country. This assists not only as far as the logistics of the project are concerned, but helps to assure that the local environment is well understood.

Where these conditions exist or can be brought about, it does seem possible that BOOT projects may be a means of financing the development of infrastructure in mega-cities. Indeed, projects that can be limited to one geographical area seem to be better suited to privatized development than do projects that are large networks.[47] The large scale of mega-city projects, the scope for cost recovery from users with relatively high incomes, the need for advanced technology and efficient management – all these are factors applicable to major infrastructure projects in mega-cities and to potentially facilitating and strengthening the case for BOOT projects.

Housing finance

One of the greatest challenges of rapid urbanization in mega-cities is keeping up with housing needs. Almost inevitably, large cities are surrounded by expanding squatters' settlements and shanty towns for lack of adequate housing. These areas usually lack the most basic services, including water and sanitation. Traditional public housing programmes have tried to improve these areas by relying heavily on subsidies from the government; the high level of subsidies required severely limited the ability to replicate such projects on the scale needed to meet ever increasing housing demands. Recent research in housing finance has emphasized the need to develop institutions able to provide long-term mortgage finance systems as a means of meeting housing needs.[48] The evidence available indicates that the development of a well-functioning system of market rate mortgage finance can contribute not only to meeting housing needs in mega-cities but to more dynamic urban investment. The development of such a system leads to more equitable resource mobilization than in housing systems that rely entirely on subsidies. Cities have an important role to play in the development of effective mortgage finance systems by providing an environment that enables such mortgage finance to operate. After briefly considering alternative traditional approaches of public housing provision and their difficulties in meeting housing needs in large cities, we discuss mortgage finance systems and how they may provide a means of meeting future housing finance needs.

During the 1950s and 1960s, many developing countries pursued public programmes of construction of high-cost housing units. Experience demonstrated, however, that most of these units benefited relatively high-income occupants and could not possibly be constructed in the numbers required to improve the abysmal housing conditions of the majority of urban dwellers.[49] In the 1970s, this approach was increasingly replaced by "sites and services" projects. Such projects provide government-sponsored packages of shelter-related services that range from a minimal level of a plot of land to an upper level of "core housing," complete with utilities and access to community services.[50] The level of services provided in the project typically depends on the ability and willingness of the beneficiary populations to afford them. Emphasis in these projects has typically been placed on both meeting basic housing needs of the poor and cost recovery (i.e. low or no subsidies). While many of these projects have been successful in meeting some housing needs, in practice, they required large subsidies and were often biased towards standards that were beyond the reach of the poorest members of society and that prevented large-scale replication of sites and service projects. In the economic environment of the 1980s, where subsidies were being cut back and fiscal concerns became of great importance, the ability of the sites and services approach to meet the large and growing housing needs of mega-cities turned out to be limited.

One alternative to sites and service projects, which was increasingly stressed in the 1980s, involved slum improvement programmes. These consisted of the upgrading of basic infrastructure services in poor neighbourhoods at low unit costs and with a degree of cost recovery that permitted the replication on a large scale. Another approach to increasing the availability of housing to a large number of urban households involves the development of mortgage finance institutions. Giving access to mortgage finance to those income groups that can pay for it reduces pressure for increased government subsidy programmes and prevents their recapture by social groups with higher incomes than originally targeted for.

Renaud [25] argues that housing finance systems can have large positive effects on urban development, financial development, and fiscal stability. Moreover, the lack of readily available mortgage lending explains the dominance of incremental housing construction in most developing countries. Financing housing through informal markets or through family and friends (two common sources of housing finance in developing countries) is usually more costly because of the inability to diversify risks and the lack of standardization. The availability of informal finance may also be limited.

Because of the major role that housing plays in domestic savings, an effective mortgage finance scheme can have an important impact on financial resource mobilization. The development of autonomous mortgage institutions can remove three bottlenecks in housing markets by developing deposit and savings services accessible to households, by orienting supplies of housing toward units that are affordable, and by diffusing better financial practices. Institutions that are financially autonomous have a vested interest in high quality loan origination and in timely portfolio servicing as loan losses would rapidly threaten their viability.

The experience with the development of mortgage financing systems in developing countries has shown not only that it can be an effective means of meeting housing needs but that it has positive side-effects as well, such as encouraging positive short-term interest rates. In Thailand, for example, the turn-around of the Government Housing Bank (GHB) has been at the centre of the present housing boom.[51] From a former position of having to source funds from overseas, the GHB in 1984 began successfully to tap the savings market directly with a number of attractive deposit instruments. Because of low overheads, fewer branches, and advanced operational techniques, it could offer higher deposit rates than those of commercial banks.

With adequate funding assured, the GHB embarked on an aggressive strategy of expanding and improving the terms of its mortgage lending activities so that it could consistently offer the lowest interest rate loans in the market (while offering higher deposit rates) and maintaining a healthy profit margin. From 1987, after the GHB had been demonstrating that the home loan business is attractive, coupled with a period of high liquidity, the commercial banks and finance companies went into mortgage lending seriously. All types of financial institutions competed for business, providing fuel for the current housing boom. During 1987 and 1988, mortgage interest rates offered by commercial banks were lower than the prime rate. The outstanding mortgage loan portfolios of all institutions grew at a compounded rate of 16.4 per cent per year from 1982 to 1986, and for 1987 and 1988 the growth exploded to 33.1 per cent and 42.9 per cent respectively.[52]

The development of the housing finance industry is the key to the present housing boom in Thailand and to the inroads that down-market housing have made in the housing market. Tanphiphat and Simapichaicheth [28] draw some lessons from the Thai experience.

The first lesson relates to the fact that the government recognized the importance of housing finance and has used the GHB as a key housing policy instrument to foster the "enabling environment" for the housing industry. This enabling environment is crucial to the successful development of a housing market and is the area in which large cities can play the greatest role in supporting the development of a mortgage finance system. Three major improvements are commonly needed in this domain: The legal procedures for determining ownership and facilitating property transfers need to be well established. Second, revisions are needed in ineffective foreclosure laws, which often provide a serious impediment to successful mortgage lending. Finally, the development of professional services for reliable appraisal of residential properties and the continuous monitoring of market conditions are needed. These improvements are effectively those that are necessary for better administration of the property tax (as discussed above); emphasis on them thus effectively kills two birds with one stone.

The second lesson from the Thai experience is that part of its success is due to the fact that the government has allowed market forces to determine the mortgage loan conditions. There are no interest rate directives (normally set to assist low income borrowers) that in the end impede the functioning of the financial system, and private firms were quick to pick up on the example of the GHB.

Finally, the Thai experience highlights the fact that the housing finance system is an integral part of the whole financial system. Not only does it contribute to improved housing but it helps to mobilize the substantial savings that are set aside for housing so that they can be used for the development of other types of urban infrastructure.

In Colombia, the unanticipated benefit of the housing finance system (the CAV – the Corporación de Ahorro y Vivienda) has been positive interest rates on short-term deposits; it was the first segment of the banking system to ensure positive returns on short-term deposits. By putting pressure on other banks to also provide positive real returns, the housing finance system has played a critical role in the urban economies.

In Ecuador, the provision of new mortgage instruments has allowed household credit to replace large implicit subsidies. The system also provides for the indexation of mortgage repayments to wages and recognizes that in an economy such as Ecuador's, real wage decreases may well imply temporary repayment problems for borrowers but not necessarily a long-term inability to pay. If real wages behave in such a way that repayments are not sufficient to amortize the loan, the shortfall is capitalized into the outstanding loan balance.

Addressing the substantial requirements for housing that will arise in the major cities of the world is an important concern in developed and developing countries alike. While subsidies will be needed to assist the very poorest in meeting minimal shelter and residential service needs, it is clear that it will not be possible for cities to subsidize housing on the scale that is required to meet all housing needs. The experience of Thailand, Colombia, and other countries indicates that establishing a mortgage finance system and providing an environment in which it can function effectively is perhaps the most efficient and equitable way to meet housing needs. This approach has the additional benefit of encouraging the role of the private sector in providing housing by providing reasonable rates of return, contributing to the development of the financial system, and mobilizing resources that may be used to meet urban development needs.

Financing infrastucture in the mega-city: A summary

The infrastructure needs of the mega-cities in developing countries are severe and apparently beyond the scope of traditional solutions. One of the most important constraints has been the lack of adequate financial means to support the needed investments as well as operation and maintenance of the required facilities. This paper has explored a large range of alternative measures that would permit redressing the obvious problems of infrastructure provision and financing in the mega-cities of developing countries. It has focused on three broad areas of possible reform of existing practices:

- decentralization of expenditure responsibility and revenue authority to urban governments from higher level authorities,
- improvement of traditional sources of urban public finance, and
- greater reliance on private sector involvement and financing of urban infrastructure.

While much of the discussion applies to urban finance in general, the points raised and the recommendations made in this paper have particular relevance to the financing of the mega-city in developing countries. The main conclusions are briefly summarized below.

1. Decentralization. Decentralizing more, rather than less, expenditure responsibility and revenue authority to urban governments in

the mega-cities is likely to result in more efficient infrastructure service provision, greater self-reliance by cities on their own resources, and the strengthening of a country's pluralistic political structure. Traditional arguments for central government involvement in infrastructure service provision (limited administrative capacity of local authorities, spillovers, etc.) apply less to mega-cities than to smaller cities and towns.

2. Improving urban public finances. Greater reliance on their own resources means that urban governments in mega-cities need to look principally towards a reform of the property tax, motor vehicle taxation, sales taxes, and user charges for efficient, equitable, stable, and growing sources of public revenue. Loans should be contracted to finance the capital costs of major public infrastructure investments, but their debt service should be met by local revenue sources. Transfers from higher level governments to fund mega-city infrastructure should be limited strictly to cases where sizeable nationwide spillovers clearly exist.

3. Increasing private sector involvement. Infrastructure in mega-cities offers scope for increased involvement by the private sector in the provision and financing of social and physical infrastructure services. By opening services traditionally restricted to public providers to entry by private enterprises competing with public entities on a level playing field (i.e., no differential subsidies or regulatory advantages accorded to public entities), the availability of such services can be significantly increased, while costs to users are lowered and the burden on public finances reduced. Build, own, operate, and transfer (BOOT) projects provide one way of involving private investors in large-scale infrastructure projects; the development of housing finance systems is a way to mobilize private resources for the private construction of urgently needed urban housing.

None of the above approaches will work in isolation. They represent a mutually reinforcing package of measures that need to be pursued across the board. Only then can serious progress be made in dealing with the mega-problems of mega-cities without endangering the macroeconomic stability of the country as a whole, and without imposing an undue burden on the economies of the cities themselves or on the economy of the rest of the country.

Notes

1. See United Nations, *Prospects of World Urbanization, 1988* (New York: United Nations, 1989).
2. See Mattei Dogan and John D. Kasarda, eds., *The Metropolis Era*, vols. 1 and 2 (Newbury Park, Calif.: Sage Publications, 1988) for several interesting discussions on the forces behind urbanization in general and in individual cities.
3. See World Bank, *World Development Report, 1988* (New York: Oxford University Press, 1988) p. 109.
4. Ibid., p. 110.
5. See R. Bahl and J. Linn, *Urban Finance in Developing Countries* (New York: Oxford University Press, 1992).
6. By "social and physical infrastructure" we mean the provision of goods and services that have the nature of a public good such as roads, street lamps, enforcement of law and order, etc. We also include the provision of certain services that are fundamental to human and economic activity and that may or may not be provided publicly. These include water, sanitation, shelter, health and education facilities, and power.
7. See Bahl and Linn [3], Bahl and Nath [5], Ljung and Farvacque [21], World Bank [33], Davey [9], Bartone and Mayo [7], and Bahl and Linn [4].
8. For a detailed discussion of the arguments for and against fiscal decentralization, see Bahl and Nath [5] and Bahl and Linn [4, chap. 12].
9. See Bahl and Linn [3] and Bahl and Linn [4].
10. In table 2, the data for two years are provided when available. This allows one to make a comparison of how financing methods in a particular country have changed over time.
11. This discussion treats only the revenue raising properties of urban property taxation. For an in-depth discussion of the incidence of the property tax and its allocative effects, see Bahl and Linn [4, chaps. 5 and 6].
12. Bahl and Linn [4, chap. 4, p. 45].
13. See Dillinger [10] for an in-depth discussion of the objectives and experience of urban property tax reform in developing countries.
14. See Dillinger [10, p. 45]. In his paper, Dillinger provides a detailed account of the measures taken in the Philippines.
15. Dillinger [10, p. 46].
16. See Dillinger [10, 13].
17. See Dillinger [13, p. 49].
18. See Davey [9, p. 43].
19. Ibid.
20. Linn [19] provides an in-depth discussion of motor vehicle taxation, including the incidence and allocative effects of different types of such taxation.
21. For an extensive review of these "other taxes," see chap. 8 of Bahl and Linn [4].
22. Bahl and Linn [4, chap. 8, p. 18].
23. See Bahl and Schroeder [6].
24. The name "octroi" is derived from the French word, which could best be translated as "impost." The octroi was levied extensively in pre-revolutionary France – Paris was surrounded by customs walls in 1789 – and was one of the sources of popular discontent that sparked the French Revolution (Schama [27, p. 73]).
25. See Bahl and Linn [4, chap. 8, p. 44].
26. See Whittington, Lauria, and Mu [32] and Lee and Anas [18] for discussion of the willingness to pay for water and other public services in Nigeria.
27. Provision is used here to cover operating costs and debt service expenses. It is unlikely that such firms will be able to finance major capital expenditures out of recurrent revenues. Therefore borrowing will also be necessary; but the costs of such recourse to loans should

be borne by the beneficiaries that live in the larger cities. The same may not be true for rural systems and their users.

28. For an in-depth discussion of the principals of pricing public services, and for a case-study of charging for urban water services, see Bahl and Linn [4, chaps. 9, 10, and 11].
29. Whittington [31] argues that in the case of water, such lifeline rates may not be advantageous to the poor if individual family water connections do not exist. Poor families often share one connection. The volume through that connection will be higher, and therefore the price charged will be higher. His argument highlights the need for careful consideration of individual city circumstances in developing a pricing structure.
30. See World Bank [33, p. 160].
31. See Dillinger [12].
32. See Davey [9].
33. See Davey [9] and Dillinger [12].
34. On this subject, see World Bank [34].
35. See Elliot Berg Associates [15], Roth [26], and World Bank [35] for a review of the literature in this field.
36. Elliot Berg Associates [15].
37. See Whittington, Lauria, and Mu [32].
38. See World Bank [33, p. 144] and Lee and Anas [18].
39. See Augenblick and Custer [2] and Joosten and Kranendonk [17] for detailed discussions of BOOT projects.
40. See Augenblick and Custer [2] and Carnevale [8].
41. See Augenblick and Custer [2, Appendix, p. 10].
42. See Augenblick and Custer [2].
43. See Augenblick and Custer [2, Appendix, p. 7].
44. Ibid., p. 8.
45. Note that Turkey, one of the first countries to promote BOOT projects (and to coin the phrase), has attempted to negotiate a number of BOOT projects for both power plants and bridges, but, as yet (as far as the authors are aware), has been unable to implement any of them. This is largely attributed to negotiating difficulties between the government, the various consortiums, and the financing agencies. Many of the companies involved have complained about the lack of coordination and communication among the various Turkish ministries involved. In some cases the government's unwillingness to provide guarantees has led to break downs in negotiation.
46. See Augenblick and Custer [2, p. 7].
47. See Joosten and Kranendonk [17, p. 56].
48. See Renaud [23–25].
49. See Linn [20, chap. 5], for a review of this experience.
50. For a review of the sites and services programmes, see Mayo and Gross [22].
51. See Tanphiphat and Simapichaicheth [28].
52. Ibid., p. 15.

References

1 Armstrong-Wright, Alan, and Sebastien Thiriez. *Bus Services: Reducing Costs, Raising Standards*. World Bank Technical Paper, 68. Washington, D.C., 1987.

2 Augenblick, Mark, and B. Scott Custer, Jr. "The Build, Operate, and Transfer ("BOT") Approach to Infrastructure Projects in Developing Countries." A report prepared for the World Bank, 1990. Mimeo.

3 Bahl, Roy W., and Johannes F. Linn. "The Assignment of Local Government

Revenues in Developing Countries." In: Charles E. McLure, Jr., ed. *Tax Assignment in Federal Countries.* Canberra: Australian National Press, 1983.

4 ———. *Urban Finance in Developing Countries.* New York: Oxford University Press, 1992.

5 Bahl, Roy W., and S. Nath. "Public Expenditure Decentralization in Developing Countries." *Government and Policy* 4 (1986): 405–418.

6 Bahl, Roy W., and Larry Schroeder. "The Business License Tax." In: Bahl and Miller, eds. *Local Government Finance in the Third World: A Case Study of the Philippines.* New York: Praeger Publishers, 1983.

7 Bartone, Carl R., and Stephen Mayo. "Economic Trends and Macroeconomic Policies Affecting Urban Development in the Third World." Background paper for the World Health Organization Expert Committee on Environmental Health in Urban Development. RUD/WP/90.15. Geneva: World Health Organization, 1990. Mimeo.

8 Carnevale, Francesca. "Putting BOT on the Road." *Trade Finance* (UK) 72 (April 1989): 65.

9 Davey, Kenneth. "Strengthening Municipal Government." Infrastructure and Urban Development Department Discussion Paper. Report INU 47. Washington, D.C.: The World Bank, 1989. Mimeo.

10 Dillinger, William. "Urban Property Taxation in Developing Countries." PPR Working Paper Series, no. 41. Washington, D.C.: The World Bank, 1988. Mimeo.

11 ———. "Property Tax Administration in Brazil and Nigeria." Paper presented at the International Symposium on the Property Tax, 21–30 November 1988.

12 ———. "External Sources of Local Government Finance: Intergovernmental Grants and Borrowing." Paper presented at the Workshop for Strengthening Local Government in Africa, Bologna, Italy, 1989.

13 ———. "Urban Property Taxation: Lessons from Brazil." Infrastructure and Urban Development Department Case-study. Washington, D.C.: The World Bank, 1989. Mimeo.

14 Dogan, Mattei, and John D. Kasarda. *The Metropolis Era.* 2 vols. Newbury Park, Calif.: Sage Publications, 1988.

15 Elliot Berg Associates. "Private Provision of Public Services: A Literature Review." Paper prepared for the Public Sector Management and Private Sector Development Division, Country Economics Department, the World Bank, Washington, D.C., 1989. Mimeo.

16 Hamer, Andrew M., and Johannes F. Linn. "Urbanization in the Developing World: Patterns, Issues and Policies." In: E.S. Mills, ed. *Handbook of Regional and Urban Economics*, vol. 2. New York: North Holland, 1987.

17 Joosten, Rik, and Sascha Kranendonk. *Infrastructure Build, Own, Operate and Transfer Projects.* Paris: Ecole Européenne des Affaires, 1988.

18 Lee, Kyu Suk, and Alex Anas. "Impact of Infrastructure Deficiencies on Nigerian Manufacturing." Washington, D.C.: The World Bank, 1990. Mimeo.

19 Linn, Johannes F. "Automotive Taxation in the Cities of Developing Countries." *Nagarlok* 11 (Jan.–Mar. 1979), no. 1: 1–23.

20 ———. *Cities in the Developing World: Policies for Their Equitable and Efficient Growth.* New York: Oxford University Press, 1983.

21 Ljung, Per, and Catherine Farvacque. *Addressing the Urban Challenge*. Infrastructure and Urban Development Department, General Operational Review. Report INU 13. Washington, D.C.: The World Bank, 1988.

22 Mayo, Stephen, and David Gross. "Sites and Services – and Subsidies: The Economics of Low Cost Housing in Developing Countries." *The World Bank Economic Review* 1 (Jan. 1987), no. 2: 301–335.

23 Renaud, Bertrand. "Financing Shelter." Water Supply and Urban Development Department Discussion Paper. Washington, D.C.: The World Bank, 1985. Mimeo.

24 ———. "Adjusting to the New Economic Environment: The Changing Perspective on Housing Finance." Paper presented at the Asia Pacific Housing Finance Conference, Hong Kong, 14–17 October 1987.

25 ———. "The Role of Housing Finance in Development: Issues and Policies." Infrastructure and Urban Development Department, Washington, D.C.: The World Bank, 1989. Mimeo.

26 Roth, Gabriel. *The Private Provision of Public Services in Developing Countries*. EDI Series in Economic Development. New York: Oxford University Press, 1987.

27 Schama, Simon. *Citizens: A Chronicle of the French Revolution*. New York: Knopf, 1989.

28 Tanphiphat, Sidhijai, and Pratak Simapichaicheth. "Private Sector Housing in Thailand." *Housing Finance International* (May 1990): 11–19.

29 United Nations. *Prospects of World Urbanization*. New York: United Nations, 1989.

30 Watson, Peter L., and Edward P. Holland. *Relieving Traffic Congestion: The Singapore Area License Scheme*. World Bank Staff Working Paper, no. 281. Washington, D.C., 1978.

31 Whittington, Dale. "Problems with the Use of Increasing Block Water Tariff Structures in Developing Countries." Infrastructure and Urban Development Department. Washington, D.C.: The World Bank, 1990. Mimeo.

32 Whittington, Dale, Donald T. Lauria, and Xinming Mu. "Paying for Urban Services: A Study of Water in Onitsha, Nigeria." Infrastructure and Urban Development Department Case-study. Washington, D.C.: The World Bank, 1989. Mimeo.

33 World Bank. *World Development Report 1988*. New York: Oxford University Press, 1988.

34 ———. *World Development Report 1989*. New York: Oxford University Press, 1989.

35 ———. *Developing the Private Sector*. Washington, D.C.: The World Bank, 1989.

12

Land and shelter in mega-cities: Some critical issues

Alan Gilbert

Professor, Department of Geography, University College London

Introduction

This paper is concerned with land and shelter in mega-cities located in the so-called third world. Its emphasis is on the housing of the poorer half of their populations, in some African and Asian contexts, the poorer three-quarters. The main focus is on the role of the state in helping poor people to marshall the main inputs necessary for the construction of self-help housing.[1] The paper argues that access to the necessary inputs for self-help home ownership is becoming more difficult in many mega-cities as a result of economic recession, the rate of urban expansion, and shortages of necessary inputs. The state cannot resolve this problem in most mega-cities, therefore it should consider carefully the situation of tenants and sharers and ways of increasing the supply of rental housing. It is possible to devise ways to improve shelter conditions but not necessarily in the form of owner-occupation.

From renting to ownership: An inevitable transition?

In general, cities in Africa, the Middle East, and the Indian subcontinent contain higher proportions of tenants than do most Latin American cities. In part, this is a function of the level of economic development and the pace of urban growth, in part a function of different urban traditions. In most cases, however, the past 30 or 40 years have seen a general tendency towards higher levels of home ownership. In Mexico City, only 27 per cent of households were owner-occupiers in 1950 compared to 54 per cent in 1980 [8]. In Bombay, only 10 per cent of households were owner-occupiers in 1961 compared to 39 per cent in 1981 [29].

The shift towards owner-occupation has occurred because of rapid urban growth, which was difficult to absorb in the existing rental housing stock, and through the proliferation of self-help housing. The latter was encouraged by improved forms of transportation, particularly the development of the motorized bus, and the availability of better infrastructure, notably water and electricity. In addition, the extensive connivance of the authorities was necessary, since land could normally be acquired only through illicit, or at least irregular, methods.

As self-help housing gradually became more acceptable in planning and architectural circles, governments realized that this form of accommodation represented the only real alternative for third world cities. Indeed, some politicians began to use irregular settlements as an ideological weapon, using the promise of owner-occupation as a means of placating the urban poor. In many third world cities, self-help home ownership is now seen to be the inevitable path along which most poor households will eventually be accommodated.

In practice, the continued transition to owner-occupation is by no means inevitable. Whether it continues depends upon the ability of the poor to acquire the resources necessary to engage in self-help housing. Without cheap access to land, building materials, infrastructure, and transportation, owner-occupation is likely to remain inaccessible to many families. Indeed, in Latin America, where economic recession bit deeply during the 1980s and the costs of access to land and building materials have risen, there are major reasons to question whether the transition to ownership has been continuing.

This is particularly the case in most mega-cities, where land has become extremely scarce. Bombay, Calcutta, Caracas, Mexico City, and Rio de Janeiro, for example, are all situated in terrain that makes continued expansion close to the city centre difficult. New peripheral settlements now have to be located a long way from the city. As a result, it is probably no coincidence that these cities have much higher levels of non-ownership than most smaller cities in their respective countries.

Certainly the assumption in much of the third world housing literature is that current trends, particularly in the cost of land, are leading inevitably to fewer home-owners and more tenants. Doebele [16, p. 16], for example, writes that "the realities of the future will more probably be a housing market in which a much larger proportion of the poor dwell in rental units, and for whom the hope of ownership of land and house will become increasingly remote." Similarly, Van der Linden [66, p. 7] speaks of the "stagnating bridgeheaders," those people who, 10 or 20 years ago, would have become owners in an autonomous settlement but can no longer afford to do so. Amis [2], too, has observed in Nairobi that "today's squatter is tomorrow's tenant."

In practice, the structure of tenure in any city does not depend only on the availability and cost of land. While land is vitally important, tenure is the outcome of a much more complex process. First, land prices are not the only ingredient determining the cost of self-help housing. The cost also depends on the price of building materials and services. In so far as evidence from many Latin American cities suggests that building costs have generally risen in real terms as a result of monopoly control over the supply of basic commodities such as bricks, glass, and cement, this rise is likely to have slowed the growth of owner-occupation. On the other hand, this is not inevitably the result. After all, owner-occupation expanded rapidly during the 1960s and 1970s, at a time when the prices of building materials were already rising rapidly. It is by no means certain, therefore, how rising costs of land and materials affect tenure choice among the poor. Rising land prices in irregular settlements, for example, may not deter home ownership so much as change the quality of housing. Thus, faced by higher prices, settlers may simply buy smaller plots, a tendency clearly evident in Bogotá and Mexico City in the 1970s [27]. Another likely response is for settlers to buy plots in less accessible or in worse serviced settlements. A further possibility is that they will pay more for the same plot and take longer to build and consolidate their home.

It is likely also that the tenure balance depends not on the absolute cost of ownership but on the relative costs of renting versus ownership. If there is a plentiful supply of cheap rental units, many families may choose to remain as tenants rather than suffering the responsibilities and difficulties of self-help construction. Where land is very cheap relative to rents, owner-occupation may become a much more attractive proposition. An influential factor in this relative cost equation is state policy. Where governments have introduced rent controls, tenants with secure tenure and cheap rents may be reluctant to move. Where governments encourage their supporters to occupy public land, the cost of ownership relative to renting may fall dramatically. The relative costs of ownership versus renting, therefore, vary dramatically from society to society as a result of very different kinds of state policy [65]. Different states have different attitudes towards home ownership; they have different approaches to increasing the supply of rental housing. Above all else, this variation in state policy explains the differences in tenure balance between countries and cities [28]. For this reason alone, there is no clear relationship between per capita income and housing tenure; as the table shows, national affluence certainly does not lead inevitably to widespread home ownership.

The cost and availability of transportation are also critical elements influencing tenure. Even today, unless good transportation is available, it is uncertain whether every family will choose owner-

Housing tenure in some third world mega-cities

<table>
<tr><th></th><th>Owners</th><th>Tenants</th><th>Others</th><th>Year</th></tr>
<tr><td>Cairo</td><td>31</td><td colspan="2">69</td><td>1981</td></tr>
<tr><td>Dacca</td><td>22</td><td>55</td><td>23</td><td>1973</td></tr>
<tr><td>Bombay</td><td>38</td><td colspan="2">62</td><td>1981</td></tr>
<tr><td>Calcutta</td><td>24</td><td colspan="2">76</td><td>1981</td></tr>
<tr><td>Delhi</td><td>53</td><td colspan="2">47</td><td>1981</td></tr>
<tr><td>Madras</td><td>32</td><td colspan="2">68</td><td>1981</td></tr>
<tr><td>Bangkok</td><td>55</td><td>31</td><td>14</td><td>1980</td></tr>
<tr><td>Istanbul</td><td>56</td><td colspan="2">44</td><td>1975</td></tr>
<tr><td>Jakarta</td><td>64</td><td>23</td><td>13</td><td>1985</td></tr>
<tr><td>Seoul</td><td>41</td><td>59</td><td>0</td><td>1987</td></tr>
<tr><td>Bogotá</td><td>57</td><td>40</td><td>3</td><td>1985</td></tr>
<tr><td>Caracas</td><td>63</td><td>31</td><td>6</td><td>1981</td></tr>
<tr><td>Lima</td><td>49</td><td>28</td><td>23</td><td>1980</td></tr>
<tr><td>Mexico City</td><td>53</td><td colspan="2">47</td><td>1980</td></tr>
<tr><td>Santiago (Chile)</td><td>64</td><td>20</td><td>16</td><td>1982</td></tr>
</table>

Sources: Refs. 60, 30, supplemented by the housing censuses of Colombia, Mexico, Peru, and Venezuela and by refs. 15, 33, 1, 70.

Note: Some census authorities classify data into only owners and tenants and exclude a category for other kinds of non-owners.

occupation even when they can afford it. Given increasing distances and the deteriorating transport situation in many cities, many may decide that the balance of advantage between renting a home near the city centre and ownership on the periphery favours the tenant option.

Finally, even if households are forced to forsake ownership in the immediate future, it is not certain that they will become tenants. There are alternative forms of tenure available. Some, for example, will share with friends or kin, a phenomenon that became increasingly apparent in Santiago during the Pinochet regime [4, 38] and that has long been common in Mexico City [52, 27, 67]. Rather than moving into rental accommodation or home ownership, young adults will postpone their departure from the parental home. Newly married couples will live with kin. The only obvious outcome of rising housing costs is greater overcrowding and deteriorating conditions [24].

Should the state seek to increase the supply of rental housing?

If many households are likely to find owner-occupation more difficult in the future, it would seem advisable to encourage the provision of rental housing. Such a policy may actually improve housing conditions in the short term, because, as research has shown, tenants often have superior access to services than do owners, especially owners in peripheral settlements [34]. Such a policy would also be beneficial in so far as it would enhance consumer choice. At present, it is arguable that many families own homes only because the balance of advantage is so often blatantly slanted in favour of ownership. If land and housing were not such a good hedge against inflation, if tax relief were available to landlords rather than home-owners, if tenants were protected from the abuse of landlords, and if some measure of tenure security were provided (without damaging the interests of the landlord), then many current owner-occupiers would switch to renting. As Lemer [34] has argued, in many countries there is no real choice between ownership and renting. It does not seem unreasonable to argue that a well-functioning housing market should provide a great deal of choice, not only of size and quality of units but also of tenure. Surely a fundamental task of government is to make more of a choice available.

To my mind, the only issue is how to do this. Certainly, few governments currently wish to build housing for rent, even fewer wish to continue as social landlords [65]. They have adopted this attitude partly because of their previous experience as landlords and partly because of the lack of financial resources available to them. There seem to be few good reasons why governments should act as social landlords if such housing is destined only for higher income groups or is going to be badly run. Similarly, given their lack of resources, governments are probably best advised not to build housing for rent. They would usually be better advised to concentrate on cheaper, and therefore more replicable, projects such as slum upgrading. In so far as governments continue to build public housing, it should normally not be subsidized. Subsidies are only defensible if allocation systems can guarantee that it is the very poor who occupy the housing. Even then it is difficult for governments to prevent poor people from subletting; indeed, prohibitions are almost certainly counter-productive.

If the state is not to provide rental housing, then perhaps private landlords should be encouraged. Of course, whether we wish to do so depends in large part on the nature, and the image, of private landlords. If they are rich, nasty, and exploitative, then the answer is presumably no. Unfortunately, it is difficult to make any categorical statement on this issue, because we know remarkably little about landlords in most third world cities [65, 26].

In Latin America, the affluent no longer invest in rental housing in the way they did in the past. They have been replaced by landlords living in the consolidated self-help settlements [11, 12, 26, 20, 23, 31]. As a result, the majority of owners seem increasingly to be drawn from the same strata of society as the tenants. Few landlords seem to own more than a couple of properties. A similar pattern seems to be characteristic of many parts of Asia and North Africa [39, 71, 56, 21]. Only in the cities of sub-Saharan Africa is there more evidence of a powerful landlord class [2, 62], even if most landlords "own only one or two buildings" [41, p. 191].

The profitability of renting naturally varies from city to city. It is influenced by public policy, notably rent control, and by the possibility that the poor can gain access to cheap land on which they can become owner-occupiers [12]. Most Latin American writers accept that public policy, together with a growing range of investment opportunities, has reduced the attractiveness of rental housing. In Africa, reports seem to differ on the profitability of rental housing [62, 5, 54]. In Asia, there is little information, although in Indonesia, Nelson [39, p. 24] argues that "rental units seem to be a good investment." Even so, it is "very uncommon for individuals to go out and purchase land or units explicitly to get involved in the rental market" (page 27).

Under such circumstances, there are few commercial investors willing to invest in rental housing. Admittedly, evidence from Korea and Saudi Arabia shows that investors can be tempted by financial incentives, but the cost of such incentives is high. As such, most governments are probably advised to spend their monies in other ways.

In any case, looking at renting as a business is following a form of logic that may not be shared by every landlord. In sites-and-services schemes, many poor families rent as a method of repaying the cost of purchase [32, p. ix; 62]. Similarly, in Mexico, Coulomb [11] argues that there is a stratum of landlords who are engaged in "domestic renting." Their rationale is not to make profits *per se* but to supplement their income, however minimally. This group of the population knows little about banks and interest rates. They do not calculate their profits in the same way as businessmen. For many, it is the only "investment" that they know anything about: for older people, often migrants from the countryside, putting their money into "bricks and mortar" to create extra housing space is a logical process.

Since small-scale landlords are continuing to build, either because this is the only business they know or because they eventually want the extra space to accommodate kin, then direct assistance to this group probably represents the best method of increasing the supply of private rental housing. In so far as many such landlords are relatively poor, this strategy offers a way of distributing government resources to lower income groups, combining goals of growth with distribution. And in so far as it is increasing the supply of housing and tenants do not inevitably live in worse housing conditions, it seems a worthwhile policy. The only issue is how to encourage the small landlord.

The offer of credit is one possibility. However, few banks are prepared to give loans without the security of a land title, something that many informal landlords cannot provide. Similarly, some governments are reluctant to offer loans without collateral in case this sets a precedent that will encourage further the informal alienation of land [26]. Nevertheless, small-scale informal credit schemes remain a real possibility under some circumstances.

Probably the most workable form of incentive, however, is simply the regularization of existing self-help settlements. In itself, this will encourage further investment by small-scale landlords. If roads are improved, bus services provided, water and electricity supplied to the settlements, new tenants will want to move into the area, and there is plenty of evidence that landlords are prepared to create many more rooms. The evidence suggests that there is little need for settlements to be fully legalized; landlords invest without title deeds. The only significant problem with a regularization strategy is that, in so far as owners are required to pay for the improved infrastructure and services, housing costs and therefore rents are likely to rise. While better services mean that living conditions are likely to improve, in some cases, poorer tenants may be gradually displaced by more affluent newcomers. Given that increasing the supply of housing is the highest priority, displacement of some households should be viewed as a necessary, albeit unfortunate, side-effect. In any case, there is some evidence that many poor tenants retain their accommodation in upgraded settlements.

Is land becoming scarcer in the mega-cities?

The concensus in the third world housing literature is that the cost of land is rising, thereby slowing the growth of owner-occupation and the prospects for self-help housing consolidation. This argument differs from earlier thinking. For many years, it was assumed that self-help housing flourished in most third world cities because land was easy to obtain. In Africa and parts of Asia, customary forms of land-holding allowed newcomers to obtain free plots on the fringe of the city [41, 43, 51]. In Latin America and the Middle East, land was often obtained through the medium of the land invasion, a process frequently encouraged by government and opposition parties alike [17, 21, 14, 73]. Indeed, it was in a city dominated by land invasions that the doyen of the self-help housing literature formed most of his ideas. The very fact that John Turner worked in Lima was vital in convincing him that low-income households could successfully build and consolidate their own homes [57, 58]. A series of governments in that city had encouraged the invasion of public land as a way of accommodating a burgeoning population and indeed garnering their political support [10]. Had Turner worked elsewhere, it would have been obvious that access to land was much more of a problem in most other large Latin American cities [22].

Today, many writers on third world housing contend that the period of free access to urban land is over. As Baross [6, p. 205] argues:

> The majority of people who came to the large cities in developing countries in the last two or three decades found or developed housing in popular settlements. It was an historical epoch of non-commercialized or cheap commercial land supply. . . . People did not have to pay or paid very little. . . . This era in many developing countries is drawing to an end.

Similarly, UNCHS [61, p. 25] have pointed out that "land, particularly in the cities, is being quickly transformed from a resource with a use-value to a commodity with a market value."

Access to free land has become much rarer for a variety of reasons. First, the combined forces of demographic growth and suburbanization have simply used up most of the accessible land [16, p. 14]. This is especially true in the mega-cities. Second, a fully commercialized land market has been established in most cities. Low-density suburban development has led to increasing numbers of middle class owners occupying peripheral land. This has meant that most owners, including the public sector, have become well aware of the market value of their land [25]. Growing commercialization has become a dominant characteristic of the land market and has encouraged the process of land speculation. Many owners of peripheral land have kept their property out of the market until the price of land has risen [55]. According to the literature, this has led to a rapid rise in land prices [61, 55, 69, 7].

Third, commercialization has been further encouraged by the action of the State. In particular, governments have been much more prepared in recent years to upgrade irregular settlement and even to grant full legal title. As McAuslan [36, p. 32] notes: "Country after country has abandoned its neutral role in private market transactions and adopted regulations." Clearly, this has brought benefits to many occupiers, particularly when it has given security of tenure to those living in fear of eviction. It has also led to major service and infrastructural improvements. But, legalization usually brings additional costs. As Payne [42, p. 47] argues,

> Regularisation or legalisation can be a double-edged sword. For owners, it represents their formal incorporation into the official city, and the chance to realise what may be a dramatically increased asset. For tenants, or those unable to pay the additional taxes that usually follow, it may push them off the housing ladder altogether.

Fourth, official intervention has sometimes brought additional problems for the poor. In particular, efforts to control urban sprawl have reduced the supply of land and particularly that available to low-income groups. As UNCHS [61, p. 25] note,

> Public authorities have taken strong measures to limit urban expansion into fertile agricultural areas, in efforts to preserve them for food production, for open space and for the control of pollution. Where such actions have been successful . . . [it has become] more difficult for low-income and disadvan-

taged groups to compete for sites . . . sometimes pushing them to distant fringe villages.

Finally, access to land has been hindered by the sheer physical growth of the city and worsened, in places, by the inadequate development of transport services. In most mega-cities, peripheral land is now very far from the city centre. While jobs in factories or urban sub-centres may still be accessible, work in the central city is only available to those prepared to spend several hours each day commuting.

Despite this general consensus, a few words of warning are in order. First, it is by no means certain that land prices are bound to rise perpetually. After all, circumstances have recently changed. While the 1960s and 1970s were a period of rapid demographic and economic growth throughout urban Latin America, the 1980s have seen both a slowing in population expansion and a dramatic decline in economic prosperity in a majority of cities [24]. The economic recession is bound to slow increases in urban land values in most parts of Africa and Latin America. Second, if peripheral land is rising rapidly in price as a result of the rural-urban conversion process, it is by no means certain that land within the already developed area will increase so dramatically. Certainly, land values in central Bogotá fell between 1955 and 1977 [69], and in low-income settlements, real prices began to fall after a couple of years [27, p. 113]. Third, generalizing about land is fraught with difficulty because the situations in different cities are so variable. Not only does the state of the local economy differ but also the rate and form of urban growth. Many cities, such as Managua, Valencia, and Monterrey, still have plenty of land. Elsewhere, however, the topography of cities such as Caracas and Rio de Janeiro makes land very much scarcer. Size of city, the degree of land concentration, and most important of all, the attitude of the State vary considerably.

In practice, therefore, land market behaviour is likely to vary considerably between cities. And, while it is likely that real land prices will rise during periods of economic and demographic growth, it is not inevitable that the poor will be excluded from peripheral land in every city. Indeed, that issue will not be determined wholly by economics. Equally important is the attitude of the State to the poor. Latin American governments intervene heavily in the land market; many States use land not only to reward construction and real estate companies but also as a means of seeking votes and political support.

For this reason, governments as diverse as Odría's populist military regime in Lima and Venezuela's democratic regimes since 1958 have encouraged land invasion [10, 25, 45]. Since governments change, there seems to be little consistency in the land allocation process. For example, in São Paulo, where land invasions were a rare occurrence before 1985, a change of national government in 1985 suddenly led to a major increase in this form of land alienation [53]. In Managua, the dreadful earthquake of 1972 cleared a large area of land in the centre of the city, which was later made available to low-income settlers. Elsewhere, the flow of free land may suddenly dry up. In Santiago, Chile, the wave of invasions that characterized the period from 1969 to 1973 was instantly reversed by the Pinochet regime [9, 38]. The result of this variation is that the precise nature of land allocation methods can only be determined at the local level.

As such, the cost of land access will vary considerably between cities. Gilbert and Ward [27, p. 110] found in their study of Bogotá, Mexico City, and Valencia, that there were considerable variations in the cost of land relative to incomes between low-income settlements in the three cities. Different methods of acquisition, forms of tenure, levels of incomes, and expectation of servicing were all ingredients in these differential prices. As a result, it is unwise to make too general a statement about land price trends and the cost of access by the poor to land. Reality has a strange habit of confounding all reasonable forecasts.

How the State might intervene in the land market

There is clearly little black and white advice that can be given to individual governments beyond that they should above all remain flexible in their policy response and sensitive to the needs of the poor. Since local circumstances vary so greatly and since the competence of government is so variable, there is little point in providing clear guidelines for policy. However, the following issues would seem worthy of consideration.

Controlling the urban perimeter

There is a clear need both to slow and to direct the pattern of urban growth. Informal suburban development can get out of hand. It can spread too quickly, creating very low-density suburbs that are very difficult to service. In addition, it often occupies land that should not be urbanized – because it is too high to be supplied cheaply with water or too low to be drained, because it is environmentally attractive or because it is too close to polluting or dangerous neighbours. The prohibition of informal urban development, however, appears to work only where there are authoritarian military regimes in charge. Where civilian or military governments are open to popular pressures, ways are usually found to ignore the urban regulations. Under such regimes, regularization or legalization of informal settlements regularly occurs. An armistice is called, all settlements are deemed to be safe from demolition, and a decree is promulgated that no future illegal development be permitted. The decree is ignored and a new round of informal settlement begins [27, 74].

While this situation is clearly unacceptable, so too is a total ban on informal sector expansion. This is demonstrated by experience in Santiago, where the Pinochet government has acted firmly against both land invasions and illegal subdivisions. For 17 years there has been virtually no informal settlement in Santiago. The result has been to increase urban densities and to force many families into overcrowded housing conditions. Eventually this became a significant political issue increasing the unpopularity of the Pinochet regime.

If both free licence and total prohibition are clearly wrong, what approaches can governments follow? There is no single panacea, but the following suggestions may be helpful.

First, sites-and-service schemes still offer some promise for future development. However, it has to be remembered that many previous schemes have not provided an answer for the very poor. World Bank research shows that few beneficiaries are drawn from the lowest income deciles [32]. While this does not render such schemes redundant, it does suggest that many schemes have been too expensive. In part, this is because there are few mega-cities that have introduced such schemes on a large scale. Indeed the number of sites-and-services plots created in most large cities is very small. In part, this is because, although the international conventional wisdom strongly supports sites-and-services programmes, few third world urban governments have been totally enamoured of the idea. The idea that governments should create what may be regarded as official slums has discouraged many from initiating such projects. But more critical has been the cost of land acquisition. In many mega-cities, land prices have reached levels that make sites-and-services projects unviable.

Indeed, the lesson in many mega-cities is that sites-and-services schemes have come too late. There is too little land close to the city centre that can be utilized. Obviously, such projects can be used in deconcentration programmes or in the distant periphery, but it is too late in cities such as Caracas or Mexico City; there is simply too little land left. Indeed, in some countries, national agencies are pursuing sites-and-services schemes mainly in smaller cities, where prices are more reasonable. This has been the approach of FONHAPO in Mexico, where between 1983 and 1988, only 15 per cent of plots were created in the three largest cities [18].

Second, the introduction of sites-and-services projects, where feasible, must clearly be linked to lower building and servicing standards. The higher the standard, the less accessible the plots. This was made clear in Bogotá during the 1970s when an attempt to produce legal settlement failed to discourage illegal developers. The official settlements were attractive, but mainly to the middle class. The illegal developers continued to sell plots to poorer families. Of course, standards should not be lowered so far that it makes servicing expensive in the future. Roads should be a certain width, open spaces must be left for communal facilities, some form of water supply must be available. In addition, low-income settlement should be directed into particular areas that will be relatively cheap to service. In effect, this is a policy of guided squatting as followed in Hyderabad (Pakistan) and Madras [42].

Third, land invaders and illegal subdividers will still operate where the costs of land acquisition are too great for most of the poor. Frequently, the new colonists are not aware of the full costs of land acquisition. Subdividers wishing to encourage sales pretend that they will instal full services. Professional invaders do not point out that future legalization procedures are likely to cost the settlers quite large sums of money. One approach is for the authorities to publish guidelines to informal settlers pointing out the dangers of participating in such schemes. If the public utilities make rough estimates of the likely cost of service installation and publicize those costs at the time of sales, this would alert many settlers to the real cost of a serviced plot of land. Leaflets could be circulated in the settlement at the time of sale. Such a programme would be cheap and would force the settlers to demand a better deal from the subdivider. It would spare the government some major problems in the future.

Fourth, landholders should be discouraged from selling their land without planning permission. In theory, this could be achieved through fines that would effectively form a betterment levy. The government takes, say, 50 per cent of the imputed sales value; while this would raise the cost of land, it would also provide a fund with which to subsidize service installation. There should also be a levy on sales with planning permission, although this would be lower than that on unplanned settlements.

Fifth, another method of discouraging excessive suburban development may be land banking. This is currently being employed in Mexico, and it has been used in the past in Delhi. It is not, however, something that has so far worked terribly well. All too frequently government bureaucracies have been too inflexible to manage the land they hold properly. In Delhi, the slow development of State land seems to have raised the price of vacant land in the city rather than reducing it [49, 50]. It seems to have excluded the poor and allowed developers to make even larger profits. To be successful, land banking requires skills that may be beyond the ability of many third world urban governments. "There are also the uncertainties of advance planning, land management and price setting, not to mention the increased risk of squatter invasion which can be resisted only at some political cost" [47, p. 21]. Land banking is not currently recommended by many authorities [42].

Treatment of existing informal settlements

Programmes of settlement upgrading are clearly critical for the future. They should aim to improve the quality of infrastructure and services. They should seek to improve the security of tenure for the occupants. They should try to involve the community in deciding the kinds of improvement to be made.

At the same time, it is important to recognize certain implicit dangers in upgrading programmes. First, some government upgrading programmes are wolves in sheep's clothing. They consist mainly of legalization programmes that bring little in the way of benefits to the community but do involve considerable costs. In Mexico, legal title rarely brings greater security for occupiers but does involve paying land taxes as well as costs of legalisation [67]. Second, upgrading can lead to the displacement of settlers [44, 37, 40]. Often these are tenants displaced by higher rents or sometimes owners who cannot afford to pay installation charges for services. In particularly well located areas, upgrading can lead to middle class families replacing the poor.

There is a major reason, in fact, for asking whether full legalization is necessary. Owners appear to make improvements without formal title. What is essential is that they be assured that they will be allowed to remain; normally, the introduction of services is adequate proof of that fact. Certainly the assumption of writers such as de Soto [15] that full legal title is essential has to be questioned. While he is right that credit is easier to arrange when the collateral of a property can be set against the loan, it is doubtful whether the lack of credit is the major constraint on housing improvement. In a city such as Lima, the main current constraint is falling real incomes; credit will hardly help under such circumstances.

A question should also be raised against the idea of issuing title deeds to individual households. There is perhaps a case for issuing some kind of collective title, a deed that can only be dispensed with after permission has been gained from the neighbourhood association. Alternatively, future planning might be assisted by the issue of leasehold titles rather than freehold, the lease on the land eventually reverting to the community. Both methods might slow the commercialization of land, helping to keep more poor families in the community. On the other hand, it would prevent those families that wished to speculate in land using perhaps their own way of accumulating capital.

Discouraging land speculation

There are a number of well-known methods of discouraging land speculation. Within the urban perimeter, higher taxation on empty lots is an obvious method. The disadvantage is that this method, like most other forms of control, requires an effective cadastral system. There is no technical reason why most governments in mega-cities cannot establish such a system. With powerful microcomputers, a database would be easy to establish and, given cheap labour, easy to maintain. The real reason why so many cities have such disastrously antiquated systems and why land and house values have not been updated is that owners do not wish to pay taxes. Governments are highly sensitive to the complaints of landowners. Clearly, without the political will, cadastral systems will not be improved.

On the edge of the city, perhaps the best method of controlling land speculation is to maintain an adequate rate of growth in serviced and unserviced but authorized land. The provision of more serviced land obviously requires effective forward planning by the service authorities, something that cannot be relied upon in every mega-city.

Similarly, the provision of authorized unserviced land requires competent management.

Ultimately, the whole issue of land speculation is a matter of political will and of competent State management. Both are in question in most mega-cities throughout the world. There is also the issue of densification, which was discussed above. If the authorities wish to encourage densification so as to reduce service costs, the implication is that this will raise land prices and fuel land speculation. Governments cannot have their cake and eat it.

Infrastructure, building materials, and regulations

It is now accepted that government has a key role to play in guaranteeing the provision of services. There is, of course, a major debate about whether government should itself provide the services, but there is no doubt that it should monitor, regulate, and plan for the gradual expansion of infrastructure. Indeed, this is a key implication of the recent acceptance of self-help housing as an architecture that works; if individual households with the necessary resources are capable of planning and constructing their own homes, they are generally not capable of providing their own electricity, roads, transportation, water, and drainage. Perhaps the key shelter role of government, therefore, is to make infrastructure and service available to the urban population.

If it is accepted that governments should organize the provision of these services, the issue then becomes their capacity for doing so. Currently, there is a debate about the virtues of privatization in both developed and less-developed countries, even if that debate is dominated by rhetoric and motivated by ideology [48]. There is no space here to discuss this important issue beyond noting that, despite the current conventional wisdom, it is easy to identify numerous examples of efficient public enterprise in third world countries, as well as examples of inefficient private utilities. In practice, it does not matter greatly whether infrastructure is supplied by private, public, or mixed enterprises; the important issues are that there is sufficient capacity, that sensible pricing policies are employed, and that some kind of welfare criterion informs distribution policy.

The issue of pricing and subsidies can also be touched on only briefly here. Clearly, the idea that all services can be provided at a huge subsidy is erroneous. Few third world governments have sufficient resources to heavily subsidize water, electricity, and other key services. The result of attempting to do so is, as Linn [35] convincingly argues, likely to prove inequitable. Excessive subsidies undermine the budgets of the service agencies, which prevents them from investing for the future. If service capacity does not expand, then the people who suffer tend to be the poor, particularly those living in new urban settlements. These people are forced to pay more for water and electricity but, in addition, tend to pay, through regressive taxation systems, for the service subsidies. In places, the poor pay the taxes to support the subsidies that go to higher income groups.

The general argument that public utilities should set their prices on a marginal cost basis seems to be convincing. Households should be charged for their use of services, and overall the agencies should broadly break even. However, a strong measure of cross-subsidization should be introduced into the pricing structure. This has benefits in terms of efficiency as well as equity. If consumers of large quantities of water are charged more per unit than small consumers, the more affluent are dissuaded from using so much. If they persist, then at least they are contributing to the cost of servicing the poor. Sensible pricing conserves scarce resources while at the same time making key services available to the poor. However, the argument that is now appearing in the literature that service and infrastructure provision should be taxed in order to create funds for development appears highly dangerous [3].

The rising price of services is posing a major problem in a number of third world cities. This is a consequence of the debt crisis and the financial situation in which many governments have recently found themselves. Excessive price rises are due in part to the very success of public utilities in the past. Until recently, many agencies in Asia and Latin America have been quite successful in increasing supply, mainly on the basis of large loans from commercial banks and multinational agencies. With the rise of international interest rates, however, many of these institutions have been placed in financial jeopardy. Essentially efficient agencies are now being placed in impossible positions. Their external debts are so great that they are being forced to raise charges excessively. The danger is that public institutions, such as those in Bogotá and Mexico City, which have worked well in the past, will be subjected to excessive political pressures to modify their methods of operation. It will be a tragedy if the debt crisis, rather than improving third world government behaviour, undermines already effective public utilities. If charges and tariffs rise too rapidly, public agencies will come under tremendous local criticism. Their management will be forced to respond to populist demands, undermining the capacity of those agencies for longer term planning.

In planning for services and infrastructure, it is also necessary to consider carefully the standards and minimum specifications employed. It is my impression that all too many mega-cities are struggling to provide services at excessively high standards. The result may be pleasing to the engineers but the additional costs involved are beyond the ability of the consumer to pay. We are seeing the unfortunate results of what I shall perhaps unfairly call the "engineering ethos" in far too many countries at the present time: too many huge dams, too many underground railways, too many urban motorways. If it has belatedly been accepted that minimum standards can be applied in shanty towns, perhaps it can be accepted that lower standards be applied throughout the world's expanding cities. Let us plan for more bicyles and buses and fewer cars.

A similar argument is applicable to building materials. All too often the use of traditional materials is being phased out of local construction. Sometimes this is good sense; where insects eat wood perhaps cement is a more sensible building material; nylon pipes are certainly an improvement on previous materials. But often perfectly good materials are forsaken for the less adequate. Sometimes this is because companies have decided that the new is more profitable; sometimes builders and consumers are seduced by the fashionable. Whatever the reason, the State should act to discourage the introduction of inappropriate technologies. They should encourage local producers to make local materials available. Not only will this keep production out of the hands of monopolies but in many countries it will keep down the cost of foreign exchange.

A research agenda

Rental housing

Despite a recent upsurge in research on rental housing, we still know remarkably little about the mechanics of housing supply, the rationale behind housing choice, landlord-tenant relations, the effects of government policy, and the operation of the law. And, while we know something about a handful of cities, we are still profoundly ignorant of how rental housing markets operate in most mega-cities. Given this situation, several issues would repay further attention.

First, we should certainly seek to understand more about the nature of the small-scale landlord and the reasons why he or she invests. We should also explore ways of encouraging more investment of this kind. This is a high priority if any effort is to be made to stimulate rental housing production by this group.

Second, we need to know more about the tenure preferences of low-income populations. Most important is to establish the reasons why so many prefer to be home-owners. Understanding the basis of tenure preferences will open up new opportunities for governments to modify current behaviour.

Third, we need to understand more clearly the causes of good and bad landlord-tenant relations and the role that the law plays in improving or worsening those relations. Indeed, the role of the law in establishing the nature of rental arrangements should have high priority.

Finally, the role of cooperative organizations in rental accommodation should be considered carefully. Why are there so few rental cooperatives and to what extent is this a feasible way of improving housing conditions particularly in inner-city areas?

Land

First, although we know a great deal about how poor people acquire plots of land in self-help settlements, we know much less about how they buy and sell plots within established settlements. That there is an active land and housing market is well established. However, we know little about how transactions are conducted given the lack of title deeds and how the money is found to purchase a house when there is no formal system of credit. We also know very little about what determines the frequency of sales and whether the difficulty of selling a plot or house impedes household mobility. Are people unable to sell their homes and, therefore, find themselves unable to change their jobs or, if they do change jobs, to avoid long journeys to work?

Second, the legalization movement is proceeding powerfully in third world cities. In so far as this recognizes the viability of self-help housing, it is a good thing, but, as I have argued above, it can have negative effects on the poor. What needs to be established, within a given society, is the minimum necessary to guarantee *de facto* tenure. What do poor households require in the way of official sanction before they will begin the consolidation process? In so far as full legalization is required, how can this process be simplified so that it is both quicker and cheaper to implement?

Third, much is written about the displacement that occurs after upgrading and legalization. This has become a highly polemical issue but one where serious research is still lacking. We need to know the circumstances under which poor people are forced out of self-help settlements. Is it the tenants who move or do owners move too? Are owners forced to move because of higher costs or do they choose to move so as to capitalize the rising value of their homes?

Infrastructure, servicing, and technology

First, it is clear that effective infrastructure provision is a key to successful housing programmes. It is less obvious how effective provision can be achieved. Again, this is an area that is becoming polemicized with extravagant claims being made for private versus public enterprise. We need to examine carefully the effectiveness and consequences of service privatization. We also need to establish more scientifically why some public enterprises in third world cities work effectively and well. The World Bank has gathered a great deal of information on public utility performance; this data bank should be interrogated by the Bank's own staff and by independent researchers.

Second, in some countries, traditional building materials and methods are being displaced by imported systems. Sometimes this represents a form of improvement, sometimes a deterioration. At present we know too little about why such changes in technology and materials are occurring. Is it due to commercialization and advertising? to the exhaustion of traditional supplies? to new sophisticated building regulations? These are important questions, with respect to both improving the housing of the urban poor and helping rectify national balance-of-payments deficits.

Conclusions

The problems of land and shelter in mega-cities in third world countries are similar to those in most poor urban areas. In mega-cities, such problems are eased by the fact that real incomes are generally higher than in other urban areas. Similarly, treatment is eased by the generally higher capacity of service agencies in the major metropolitan cities. On the other hand, mega-cities face additional problems with respect to the availability of land; in some, there is simply no land for expansion close to the city. They also face more severe problems with respect to transportation. If this paper has not emphasized the differences between mega-cities and smaller urban centres, it is because the essential causes of poor housing – low incomes, inequality, lack of well-remunerated jobs, shortage of services and adequate transportation – are very similar throughout the urban realm. In practice, the differences between mega-cities across continents are greater than the differences between cities of different sizes within continents.

Clearly, the problems of land and shelter are so severe in many mega-cities that it is futile to pretend that they can be solved. They can only be reduced, and this paper has attempted to suggest ways in which that can be done. Few of these suggestions are very original, for the simple fact that the literature of self-help housing, in which the majority of the poor live, is now very sophisticated. We already know a great deal about how to treat the problems of land and shelter. The problem, as always, is one of mobilizing sufficient political will to make any real difference to the existing situation.

However, there is one area where I have laid particular emphasis. Rental and shared housing has been neglected by both governments and the research literature for a number of years. Although there are signs that this is now being redressed, I believe that there is much to do. If my argument that self-help housing is becoming less accessible to the poor is broadly correct, more attention to rental housing is essential. The danger is that if governments continue to neglect rental housing, living conditions in third world mega-cities will start to deteriorate seriously.

Note

1 By self-help housing I mean housing that is normally constructed in neighbourhoods that lack legal title and that often offend the planning regulations because they lack services and infrastructure and occupy land that is often unsuitable for urban development. Most self-help dwellings are built mainly, although not entirely, by the family with the help of friends and relations. It should be underlined that most self-help housing, particularly that which is more than 10 years old, is a much more solid structure than the stereotypical third world slum or shanty town.

References

1 Abt Associates, Inc. "Informal Housing in Egypt." Washington, D.C., 1982. Mimeo.

2 Amis, P. "Squatters or Tenants? The Commercialization of Unauthorised Housing in Nairobi." *World Development* 12 (1984): 87–96.

3 Anderson, D. "Infrastructure Pricing Policies and the Public Revenue in African Countries." *World Development* 17 (1989): 525–542.

4 Bahr, J., and G. Mertins. "Desarrollo poblacional en el Gran Santiago entre 1970 y 1982: análisis de los resultados censales en base a distritos." *Revista de Geografía Norte Grande* 12 (1985): 11–26.

5 Barnes, S.T. *Patrons and Power: Creating a Political Community in Metropolitan Lagos*. Manchester University Press, 1987.

6 Baross, P. "The Articulation of Land Supply for Popular Settlements in Third World Cities." In: S. Angel et al., eds. *Land for Housing the Poor*. Singapore: Select Books, 1983, pp. 180–209.

7 Carroll, A. *Pirate Subdivisions and the Market for Residential Lots in Bogotá*. World Bank Staff Working Paper, no. 435. Washington, D.C.: The World Bank, 1980.

8 CENVI (Centro de la vivienda y estudios urbanos). "Vivienda y propiedad en cinco colonias populares de la Ciudad de México, Primer documento de interpretación." Mexico City, 1990. Mimeo.

9 Cleaves, P. *Bureaucratic Politics and Administration in Chile*. Berkeley: University of California Press, 1974.

10 Collier, D. *Squatters and Oligarchs*. Baltimore: Johns Hopkins University Press, 1976.

11 Coulomb, R. "La vivienda de alquiler en las áreas de reciente urbanización." *Revista de Ciencias Sociales y Humanidades* 6 (1985): 43–70.

12 ———. "Rental Housing and the Dynamics of Urban Growth in Mexico City." In: A.G. Gilbert, ed. *Housing and Land in Urban Mexico*. San Diego: Center for U.S.-Mexican Studies, University of California, 1989, pp. 39–50.

13 Cuenya, B. "El submercado de alquiler de piezas en Buenos Aires." *Boletín de Medio Ambiente y Urbanización* 17 (Suplemento especial 1986): 3–8.

14 Danielson, M.N., and R. Keles. *The Politics of Rapid Urbanization in Turkey*. New York: Holmes and Meier, 1984.

15 De Soto, H. *El otro sendero*. Mexico City: Editorial Diana, 1987.

16 Doebele, W.A. "The Evolution of Concepts of Urban Land Tenure in Developing Countries." *Habitat International* 11 (1987): 7–22.

17 Drakakis-Smith, D.W. "Slums and Squatters in Ankara: Case Studies in Four Areas of the City." *Town Planning Review* 47 (1976): 225–240.

18 Duhau, E. "Política habitacional para los sectores populares en México. La experiencia de FONHAPO." *Medio Ambiente y Urbanización* 7 (1988): 34–45.

19 Durand-Lasserve, A. *L'exclusion des pauvres dans les villes du tiers-monde*. Paris: L'Harmattan, 1986.

20 Edwards, M. "Cities of Tenants: Renting among the Urban Poor in Latin America." In: A.G. Gilbert, J.E. Hardoy, and R. Ramirez, eds. *Urbanization in Contemporary Latin America*. New York: John Wiley & Sons, 1982, pp. 129–158.

21 El Kadi, G. "Market Mechanisms and Spontaneous Urbanization in Egypt: The Cairo Case." *International Journal of Urban and Regional Research* 12 (1988): 22–37.

22 Gilbert, A.G. "Pirates and Invaders: Land Acquisition in Urban Colombia and Venezuela." *World Development* 9 (1981): 657–678.

23 ———. "The Tenants of Self-help Housing: Choice and Constraint in the Housing Markets of Less Developed Countries." *Development and Change* 14 (1983): 449–477.

24 ———. "Housing during Recession: Illustrations from Latin America." *Housing Studies* 4 (1989): 155–166.

25 Gilbert, A.G., and P. Healey. *The Political Economy of Land*. Aldershot: Gower, 1985.

26 Gilbert, A.G., and A. Varley. *Landlord and Tenant: Housing the Poor in Urban Mexico*. London: Routledge, 1991.

27 Gilbert, A.G., and P.M. Ward. *Housing, the State and the Poor: Policy and Practice in Three Latin American Cities*. Cambridge: Cambridge University Press, 1985.

28 Harloe, M. *Private Rented Housing in the U.S. and Europe*. London: Croom Helm, 1985.

29 India, NIUA. *Rental Housing in India: An Overview*. Delhi: National Institute of Urban Affairs, 1989.

30 ISHOC (International Symposium on Housing Organizing Committee). *Country Profiles: Housing and Human Settlement Conditions*. Yokohama: City of Yokohama, 1987.

31 Jaramillo, S. "Entre el UPAC y la autoconstrucción: comentarios y sugerencias a la política de vivienda." *Controversia* 123–124 (CINEP, Bogotá) (1985).

32 Keare, D.A., and S. Parris. *Evaluation of Shelter Programs for the Urban Poor: Principal Findings*. World Bank Staff Working Papers, no. 547. Washington, D.C., 1982.

33 Keles, R., and H. Kano. *Housing and the Urban Poor in the Middle East – Turkey, Egypt, Morocco and Jordan*. M.E.S. Series, no. 20. Tokyo: Institute of Developing Economies, 1987.

34 Lemer, A.C. *The Role of Rental Housing in Developing Countries: A Need for Balance*. World Bank, Water Supply and Urban Development Department, Discussion Paper, no. UDD-104. Washington, D.C., 1987.

35 Linn, J.F. *Cities in the Developing World: Policies for Their Equitable and Efficient Growth*. New York: Oxford University Press, 1983.

36 McAuslan, P. *Urban Land and Shelter for the Poor*. London: Earthscan, 1985.

37 Moitra, M.K., and S. Samajdar. "Evaluation of the Slum Improvement Program of Calcutta Bustees." In: R. Skinner et al., eds. *Shelter Upgrading for the Urban Poor: Evaluation of Third World Experience*. Manila: Island Publishing House, 1987, pp. 69–86.

38 Necochea, A. "El allegamiento de los sin tierra, estrategia de supervivencia en vivienda." *Revista Latinoamericana de Estudios Urbano Regionales (EURE)* 13–14 (1987): 85–100.

39 Nelson, K.W. *Choices and Opportunities: Low-Income Rental Housing in Indonesia*. Urban Institute Working Paper, no. 3780–12. Washington, D.C., 1988.

40 Nientied, P., and J.J. van der Linden. "Evaluation of Squatter Settlement Up-

grading in Baldia, Karachi." In: R. Skinner et al., eds. *Shelter Upgrading for the Urban Poor: Evaluation of Third World Experience*. Manila: Island Publishing House, 1987, pp. 107–126.

41 O'Connor, A.M. *The African City*. London: Hutchinson, 1983.

42 Payne, G. "Informal Housing and Land Subdivisions in Third World Cities: A Review of the Literature." Report prepared for the Overseas Development Administration, Oxford Polytechnic. Oxford, 1989.

43 Peil, M., and P.O. Sada. *African Urban Society*. New York: John Wiley & Sons, 1984.

44 Rakodi, C. "Upgrading in Chawama, Lusaka: Displacement or Differentiation?" *Urban Studies* 25 (1988): 297–318.

45 Ray, T. *The Politics of the Barrios of Venezuela*. Berkeley: University of California Press, 1969.

46 Robben, P.J.M. "Measurement of Population Dynamics Following Squatter Settlement Improvement in Ashok Nagar, Madras." In: R. Skinner et al., eds. *Shelter Upgrading for the Urban Poor: Evaluation of Third World Experience*. Manila: Island Publishing House, 1987, pp. 87–106.

47 Rodwin, L., and B. Sanyal. "Shelter, Settlement, and Development: An Overview." In: L. Rodwin, ed. *Shelter, Settlement, and Development*. London: Allen and Unwin, 1987, pp. 3–33.

48 Roth, G. *The Private Provision of Public Services in Developing Countries*. New York: Oxford University Press, 1987.

49 Sarin, M. *Urban Planning in the Third World: The Chandigarh Experience*. London: Mansell, 1982.

50 Soussan, J. "Urban Planning and the Community: An Example from the Third World." *Environment and Planning* A14 (1982): 901–916.

51 Stren, R.E. *Housing the Urban Poor in Africa: Policy, Politics, and Bureaucracy in Mombasa*. Berkeley: Institute of International Studies, University of California, 1978.

52 Sudra, T. "Low-Income Housing System in Mexico City." Ph.D. diss., MIT, 1976.

53 Taschner, S.P. "Diagnosis and Challenges on Housing in Brazil." Paper presented at the Conference on Housing, Policy, and Urban Innovation, Amsterdam, 27 June–1 July 1988.

54 Tipple, A.G. *The Development of Housing Policy in Kumasi, Ghana, 1901 to 1981*. Centre for Architectural Research and Development Overseas, University of Newcastle Upon Tyne, 1988.

55 Trivelli, P. "Access to Land by the Urban Poor: An Overview of the Latin American Experience." *Land Use Policy* 3 (1986): 101–121.

56 Turan, M. "Poverty, Prudence, and Place-making: Strolling through Gecekondus." *Habitat International* 11 (1987): 77–102.

57 Turner, J.F.C. "Barriers and Channels for Housing Development in Modernizing Countries." *Journal of the American Institute of Planners* 33 (1967): 167–181.

58 ———. "Housing Priorities, Settlement Patterns, and Urban Development in Modernizing Countries." *Journal of the American Institute of Planners* 34 (1968): 354–363.

59 United Nations. *United Nations Compendium of Housing Statistics 1975–77.* New York, 1980.
60 ———. *Compendium of Human Settlement Statistics, 1982–84.* New York, 1985.
61 United Nations Centre for Human Settlements (HABITAT). *Upgrading of Inner-City Slums.* Nairobi, 1984.
62 ———. *Case Study of Sites and Services Schemes in Kenya: Lessons from Dandora and Thika.* Nairobi, 1987.
63 ———. *Shelter, Infrastructure and Services for the Poor in Developing Countries: Some Policy Options.* Nairobi, 1987.
64 ———. *Renovación Habitacional Popular en el D.F. La reconstrucción de vivienda en el centro histórico de la Ciudad de México después de los sismos de setiembre de 1985.* Nairobi, 1987.
65 ———. *Strategies for Low-Income Shelter and Services Development: The Rental-Housing Option.* Nairobi, 1989.
66 Van der Linden, J. *The Sites and Services Approach Reviewed.* Aldershot: Gower, 1987.
67 Varley, A. "Urbanisation and Agrarian Law: The Case of Mexico City." *Bulletin of Latin American Research* 4 (1985): 1–16.
68 ———. "The Relationship between Tenure Legalization and Housing Improvement: Evidence from Mexico City." *Development and Change* 18 (1987): 463–481.
69 Villamizar, R. *Land Prices in Bogota between 1955 and 1978: A Descriptive Analysis.* World Bank City Project Paper, no. 10. Washington, D.C., 1980.
70 Wadhva, K. "Rental Housing in India: Compulsion or Choice." Paper presented at the Expert Group meeting on Rental Housing in Developing Countries organised by UNCHS (HABITAT) at the Institute of Housing Studies in Rotterdam, 9–13 October 1989.
71 Wahab, E.A. *The Tenant Market of Baldia Township: Towards a More General Understanding of Tenancy in Squatter Settlements.* Free University Urban Research Working Paper, no. 3. Amsterdam, 1984.
72 Ward, P.M. "Land Values and Valorisation Processes in Latin American Cities: A Research Agenda." *Bulletin of Latin American Research* 8 (1989): 47–66.
73 ———, ed. *Self-help Housing: A Critique.* London: Mansell, 1982.
74 Zorro, C., and A. Gilbert. "Tolerancia o rechazo de los asentamientos urbanos irregulares: el caso de Bogotá." *Revista Interamericana de Planificación* 16 (1982): 138–170.

13

Six strategic decisions for transportation in mega-cities

Ralph Gakenheimer

Professor of Urban Planning and Civil Engineering, Massachusetts Institute of Technology, Cambridge

At the current four per cent urban population growth rates, there will be 17 cities of over 10 million by the end of the 1990s. Mexico City and São Paulo will have 25 million people. Some of these cities will house over a fifth of their national populations (Cairo, Buenos Aires, Bangkok); others will comprise a small portion (Shanghai, at 1.5 per cent). They will be found in the higher income developing countries (São Paulo) and in the lower income countries (Dhaka). All will play important national roles in producing wealth, information, intelligence, and leadership – and also in consuming revenue. Their problems are already awesome in magnitude, endangering a positive difference between their productivity and the resources they consume. Transportation has a great deal to do with this difference. My aim here is to discuss how transportation can be used as a tool to improve their viability and their contribution to development and welfare.

I will work toward six crucial decisions in transportation for mega-cities, first by introducing their strategic context. I begin with three basic objectives of urban development planning at large, and con-

An earlier version of this paper was presented at the Megacities Transport Seminar at the World Bank, Washington, D.C., May 1991.

tinue with a set of general strategic objectives, from which I will derive strategic decisions for urban transportation.

Basic objectives

The World Bank has just provided the development community with what I believe will be a stable set of basic objectives [3]; I paraphrase:

1. Since cities account now for a large portion of national economic productivity, and potentially for much more of it, planning should emphasize the productivity of the urban economy and the need to alleviate the constraints on productivity.
2. Since increasing urban poverty is sapping away the productivity and welfare of the urban poor, their condition should be enhanced by increasing the demand for labour and improving their access to infrastructure and social services.
3. The deteriorating urban environment threatens the livability and productivity of cities, so policy should be addressed to reversing this trend, improving the urban environment.

Part of the quest for improved productivity, then, is at the same time one to alleviate poverty and reverse the environmental deterioration that make urban development unsustainable and jeopardize productivity itself.

General strategic objectives

Now consider general strategic objectives for all sectors of urban policy and planning.

1. The guidance of physical development

Should we encourage megalopolitan growth? Probably not, particularly if there are other large cities in the country, since they can probably accommodate new economic activities at similar levels of high productivity and with fewer diseconomies of urbanization. Should we attempt to suppress or cap growth? Probably not, since suppressing urban growth has never worked, even in command economies with great presumed authority to make it work. Growth will surely continue and there are several reasons to marshal our strength to guide it. One is to decentralize development, minimizing the problems of overconcentration. Mega-cities have severe problems of high central density. Seoul houses more than 300 persons per hectare. In many cities, downtown rebuilding is raising densities higher than can be sustained by water, sewerage, and transportation systems. Many businesses are caught in city centres because of the need for business services and allied economic activities that could be decentralized altogether. The objective is to decentralize so as to retain the effectiveness of agglomeration economies.

While decentralizing from congested centres, a second objective of guidance is to raise the concentration of peripheral development, avoiding the non-sustainable consumption of peripheral agricultural land. Many cities are located in areas of scarce agricultural land. Cairo alone consumes an additional one per cent of Egypt's agricultural land each year.

A third reason for managing growth is to make more land available for housing within reach of work places, especially for the poor. One of the disadvantages mega-cities impose on the poor is to force them to live long distances from work, which raises unemployment and jeopardizes health. Though the poor are especially disadvantaged by urban locational systems, the journey to work problem afflicts many groups. Studies in Santiago showed that a substantial part of the population undertook journeys to work of considerably longer distances than if workers were allocated at random to the job locations of the city. The megalopolis represents a specially exacerbated form of this problem because urban trips on average are significantly longer than in smaller cities, and pockets of land currently available for housing the poor are apt to be the most removed from work centres.

Thus, all three of the basic objectives – productivity, poverty alleviation, and environmental sustainability – are importantly served by gaining leverage on the location of urban growth.

2. Enhancing productive relationships among economic activities

Productive relationships usually require deliveries or other forms of face-to-face contact to achieve agglomeration economies. Related industries benefit, and government can help by clustering them in districts providing good infrastructure endowments, granting them tax holidays, and making special loan possibilities and business services available. Inter-industry relationships are enhanced by special facilities such as freight airports, union freight terminals, superior mode change facilities for goods and passengers, and adequate solid waste service. Highways and transit are very important elements of these services to enhance productivity.

3. Improving the programming and pricing of infrastructure

The World Bank's urban policy paper [3] says the greatest impediment to urban productivity is the weakness of the public sector. This is most evident in the infrastructure shortfall. The services are typically far underpriced and insufficient. Sixty per cent of Cairo's area has no surfaced street network. Forty per cent of São Paulo's population lacks household water and sewerage services. Revenues from infrastructure systems do not serve to expand or even maintain those systems, even though the individual substitutes used by urban dwellers often cost many times the full cost of public service.

Correction of this problem is urgent for many reasons. Inadequate infrastructure deters economic development, since many firms would have to supply their own, as shown by Kyu Sik Lee's studies in Nigeria [1]. The serviced parts of the city attract excessive densities of activity, causing overconcentration and deterring decentralization. The environment is damaged by inadequate storm drainage and the entry of waste water into the water-table.

Inadequate infrastructure leaves the poor with a deteriorated environment, much higher prices to pay for substitutes, and/or also a shortage of housing, since only serviced land is developable. And in the serviced areas, the infrastructure itself deteriorates from lack of maintenance and repair. Transportation is only a single case of this problem, but one of the most serious.

4. Structuring governance

Mega-cities present greater problems than other cities in development management because they attract attention by government agencies at all levels and their physical size means they are comprised of more local governments. The need is to create a single voice to preside over the development management of the city and to coordinate the attention of national and regional government agencies. Whether the area is made up of 39 local governments as São Paulo is or only 3 as is Cairo, the problem of organizing spatial patterns of development and providing network infrastructure requires a comprehensive view. Otherwise the city may have little voice at all in national agency initiatives and may fail to achieve efficiencies in the distribution and servicing of activities. There is a need for at least some key elements of metropolitan government to be put in place, or metropolitan authorities with responsibility for the key services. Transportation is one of the sectors that suffers the most from lack of adequate metropolitan institutions.

Each of these general strategic objectives – physical planning, enhancing agglomeration economies, programming and pricing infrastructure, and structuring governance – includes transportation facilities and services as one of its key elements. Within their context, the far-reaching consequences of strategic decisions for transportation itself are more apparent.

Strategic decisions for transportation

Stated otherwise, the transportation decisions are, for the most part, elements of a more general strategic approach that are specialized to the transportation sector. This paper is organized to highlight that fact because there are few problems that can be solved within a single sector. Most of the following policy and action decisions would be very weak unless they were complemented by supporting decisions for other infrastructures, poverty alleviation, housing, and land development. This is not to say the transportation sector is weak. In many cases it is indispensable to a sufficient strategy.

I lay out the whole pattern in the table. My original intent was to draw arrows between the higher ones and related lower ones. In fact, however, each one above is related to all below, so that arrows would not be an accurate representation.

The strategic pattern for urban policy and planning

Basic objectives			
Productivity	Poverty alleviation	Environment	
General strategic objectives			
Guide physical development	Enhance productive economic relationships	Programme and price infrastructure	Structure metropolitan governance
Transportation strategies			
How to price and finance transportation		How to control automobile usage	
How to choose modes		How to protect the environment	
How to improve the mobility of the poor		How to create sustainable institutions	

1. How to improve the pricing and financing of urban transportation

Transit, like the other public services, is underpriced in most cities, either as a matter of political expediency or because of a belief that commuters cannot afford a higher fare. The result is that the city is damagingly underserved, and the poor are apt to suffer the most from the service shortfall because of their peripheral housing locations. In fact, the entire working and school population – or at least the more than 80 per cent of it that uses the transportation system – suffers reduction of its productivity.

Option one is to raise the fare toward the marginal cost of service. It should be done in small increments that follow inflation in accordance with a formula, rather than by large increments that stimulate public reaction as sudden large burdens. Fares should be raised in parallel with rates for other public services so it is clear that public service rates are responding to conditions of the economy. In addition, cities should look for ways to require all beneficiaries to share the burden of expense.

In general, the rule should be that the city should not operate a service that it cannot self-finance. At the same time, it is reasonable to reach out as broadly as possible among beneficiaries in order to finance the service. A new transit line benefits its own passengers, to be sure. It also benefits passengers in parallel transit lines by alleviating congestion on them. It benefits employers, motor vehicle users, and nearby landowners, whose property value is enhanced. Indeed, I hope I have by now clarified by the form of this argument that eventually everyone profits from improved access, back up to our three "basic objectives" of productivity, poverty alleviation, and environment.

Such widespread benefits might seem to justify a high subsidy. Maybe they would if the taxing system were reliably equitable and the corresponding cut-backs could be wisely distributed among all alternative uses of revenue. Under real circumstances, however, the subsidy comes from the non-remunerative public services such as health, education, and the other infrastructures. That should not be permitted. Further, a heavily subsidized service is not utilized prudently. In any case, adequate subsidies are not forthcoming.

The question, then, is how to levy charges on secondary beneficiaries. There is little precedent for subsidizing one form of public transportation from the fare box of another, since they all are likely to be in serious need. In France there is a tax on employers to finance urban transportation, based on the size of the company payroll. In Brazil companies pay part of the commuting costs for employees. It could be done in other countries. There is a widespread precedent for charges on land that appreciates in value as a result of public expenditure in the form of benefit levies (valorization), used to the greatest extent in Colombia but in minor ways in several other Latin American countries and throughout the world (e.g. until recently in Indonesia). Simplified forms of betterment charges in the form of special assessment districts (charged by their level of service in the transit network) would also be a possibility.

Privatization is an alternative possibility. On a world-wide basis, there are hundreds of cities with privatized bus transport, most of them dividing the service into individual route concessions that are unsubsidized. They survive in both higher and lower income cities. Some concessionaires form cooperatives or syndicates; some even rotate routes so that each gets a chance at the more profitable ones (Buenos Aires). Transit service provided by pubic agencies tends to become inefficient, to decline in quality, and to absorb increasing government subsidies.

Hundreds of cities have informal sector transport using a variety of motorized and non-motorized vehicles under minimal public control that also survive. These services are often suppressed by governments because they are difficult to regulate and they are sometimes politically aggressive. Leadership needs to require them to form syndicates or other organizations that would constitute units with which public authority can bargain and that require these small firms or individual drivers to share responsibility for enforcement of regulations.

The important decision in privatization is whether the system is a unitary company serving under a public service agreement, as in Great Britain, or a number of contractors each serving only a part of the network. We have little evidence on the performance of unitary companies in the developing world, but there is reason to be wary. They could turn out to have the same deficiencies as a public agency without the advantage of direct government control. They might work better as simply operations contractors, while a metropolitan authority retains ownership of the equipment. This is a practice familiar in France. The best solution may be the use of several contractors serving part of the system, with careful attention in advance to the way they are contracted and recontracted. The traditional concession system is not well adapted to this service. Authorities cannot choose concessionaires equitably because the rigid constraints of service leave little basis to compete for the contract – the routing, scheduling, and pricing are fixed. Also, they are likely to disinvest their equipment toward the end of a concession, fearing they will not be continued. That results in substandard equipment in service. We need to create new modes of contracting and public service regulation.

Now that there is attention to "build, operate, and transfer" (BOT), it may be appropriate to recall the use of that system in Europe during the late nineteenth century as a means of introducing trolley-cars. The private system builders were given 30 or 40 years to amortize their original investment, after which they transferred all assets to the municipality at no charge. BOT for very large scale projects, as currently discussed, may have a doubtful future because of the complicated assurances required by multi-party investment groups. For modest priced transit systems there is more hope.

Transit ownership is a complicated issue subject to different pressures in every city. It is important to have in mind, none the less, that privatization is a financially viable idea for all but the most capital intensive technologies.

We should remember that the most underpriced urban transportation mode is the automobile. The result is that in nearly all countries, the greatest part of the public works backlog is the need for the repair and rebuilding of streets and highways. There are new possibilities emerging. There is a resurgence of toll-roads in several countries (as with the Jasa Marga of Indonesia). In Mexico roads are concessioned to private operators responsible for maintaining them in exchange for user payments. There is a great deal of current research on automatic tolling through the use of electronic devices that may soon make tolling practical for urban highways, since the vehicles will not have to stop.

Urban congestion pricing is arriving – that is, motorists using roads pay a user fee that increases with the level of congestion at the time of use. The idea is that peak hour users are responsible for the costly need to expand the facility and therefore should pay more. After experiments in Hong Kong, a full test of this idea will be undertaken in Cambridge, England. Urban congestion pricing is a practice that has been advocated by economists for several decades but only recently made possible by the appearance of affordable electronic devices that can identify the vehicles passing a point without stopping them. This approach is only the beginning of a list that includes schemes that require special paid licences for automobiles to enter downtown areas, as in Singapore, local gas taxes as proposed in Indonesia, the targeting of automobile import duties to areas of the vehicles' use, and so on.

The important conclusion is that urban commuters are getting a highly subsidized ride, but they are suffering acutely from it through lack of adequate service and terrible congestion in mega-cities. They would do themselves a favour by paying more and getting better service. The strategic problem is to choose combinations of charges that alleviate these problems.

2. How to choose public transit modes

For the vast majority of megalopolitan commuters, the bus is the basic form of urban transit and will remain so for the foreseeable future. But mega-cities make crushing demands on access through certain radial corridors where the maximum capacity of buses (about 30,000 passengers/hour in one direction) is exceeded.

The need to serve such corridors brings the possibility of rail rapid transit into focus with its capacity of up to 75,000 or 80,000 passengers/hour/direction. But such a transit system is very expensive. The capital cost for elevated sections is US$22 million to US$60 million per kilometre. Underground sections cost US$50 million to US$165 million. The rolling-stock and other costs are very high too. Studies of metro systems in the developing world by TRRL/Halcrow Fox [2] show that no metro, however successful in moving quantities of people, has been able to pay its way, except for those in very high income cities (Hong Kong and Singapore) whose fares would be unsustainable in low income countries. Even those that carry very high passenger volumes (e.g., Mexico City) with apparently very good urban structure impacts still impose burdensome, unsustainable subsidy payments on government.

This presents a difficult dilemma. We should honour the assertion of my last section, that we should not build what we cannot make financially self-supporting. But what can we do if the urgent needs of major corridor access are high and the continued vitality of the city centre requires more passenger arrivals? The possibility of sharing the burden among more of the beneficiaries should be further examined. Only one metro (Hong Kong) has succeeded in taking advantage of value rises in surrounding land parcels, and only two have succeeded in redesigning the routes of surrounding bus systems to feed the metro. None have obligated automobile users to sustain part of the cost.

Bus ways (isolated right of ways at grade or elevated to be used only by buses) are a currently hopeful option. The ongoing TRRL/ Cornwell and Cracknell study has revealed tentatively that capital costs for bus ways are only a fraction of those for metros, about US$1 million at grade and US$10 million elevated. Their capacity is at least 39,000 passengers/hour/direction, and possibly greater. Evidence is limited because there are no long stretches of bus way yet in existence. Bus ways have certain advantages compared with metros. A bus way can be built for just parts of routes where transit would run into congestion, otherwise leaving the buses on ordinary streets and highways. It can accommodate buses on the long stretches after they have collected passengers in neighbourhoods. It can be built incrementally, rather than having to be built all at once. Cities could build several bus ways in parallel corridors for the price of one metro. At the same time, bus ways have some disadvantages. They are institutionally more complicated because they engage existing agencies responsible for bus operations, traffic control, and highways. They would often remove existing street lanes from general use, and their land development impacts (and consequently possible benefit assessments) are weak.

Final opinions are not yet available. When they are, this strategic decision will still be a difficult one. If we accept that new transit should not impoverish the government budget, the urgent question that needs to be answered – differently for each city – is how much penetration into the indirect beneficiaries of transit service can we gain to pay its costs.

While considering special systems technologies for urban transportation, we should not forget the simplest. There is good evidence that bicycles could take a much more important part in urban transportation than they have up to now. They account for enormous volumes of passenger flow in such diverse countries as China and the Netherlands, yet they are little used in much of the developing world. The problem appears to be that cycling is dangerous as long as bicycles are only a small part of the traffic. When they are a substantial part of the traffic, they take their own place in the system and can be operated more safely. A good many mega-city trips are too long for regular bicycle use, but a large number are not. There are good indications that a city that would promote bicycle use through an educational programme, combined with the availability of modest priced bicycles and the judicious provision of cycling lanes, could push the volume of bicycle use over the minimum threshold that would make the mode the standard for a significant part of the population. It would not be expensive to try. The pay-off could be large in congestion relief and reduction of air pollution.

3. How to control the use of automobiles

The automobile is the mode of transport of an affluent, low-density, and land-consuming society with plenty of public capital to supply facilities for travel. Even the northern countries are not in this category.

In the developing world the automobile serves as personal transport for 20 per cent of the population at most and still jams the roadways with congestion that delays everyone. The justifications for controlling the use of private vehicles are responsive to all the basic objectives of development planning: productivity, poverty alleviation, and sustainability. Automobiles cause low density use of peripheral land, at the same time causing congestion that exacerbates the problems of overconcentration at the centre. They exclude the poor from participation in urban life since transit cannot follow the low density urban patterns that the automobile encourages. They cause more than half of the air pollution in many cities and deteriorate the viability of public transportation by competing with it.

The northern countries have largely foregone the possibility of successfully restraining automobile use because they have generated land use patterns that cannot be adequately served by alternative modes. In the developing world the majority of the population still uses other modes, so there remains a chance.

We have learned that gentle actions do not work. No significant number of automobile users are attracted to any new transit system in the short run, no matter how well it performs. The options, none the less, are numerous and combinable. City centres can be protected by regular driving bans, parking enforcement, parking space reduction, pedestrianization of central streets, and special licensing schemes that require payment to enter with an automobile. More generally, there are congestion fees, tolls, gas taxes, and other user charges that can be used to curb automobile use as well as to finance facilities. The best time to put restraining actions in place is when a new transit route opens. This is the time to increase parking enforcement and to pedestrianize selected routes. These actions may not result in significant reductions of automobile use immediately, but they create a balance of access at the destinations, include an available alternative to automobile travel, provide needed additional space for pedestrian traffic, and encourage a long-term shift toward public transit. It is no coincidence that New York City has the most complete transit system and the lowest car ownership in the US. In the long term people adapt to the realities of congestion. On these grounds we might question the wisdom in Cairo of opening massive parking garages around the city centre just as the new metro was beginning operations.

For all mega-cities the question is not whether to control automobile use, but how. We should review the performance of existing measures and consider the institutional and technical feasibility of new ones. This is an essential part of transportation policy.

4. How to improve the mobility of the poor

One of the major challenges of the mega-city is incorporating the immigrant poor into the working economy. Most mega-cities have severe problems of unemployment. In Manila there is 16 per cent unemployment and 45 per cent underemployment. One of the major obstacles is access, how to circulate in search of work and to reach work daily.

During the period of strategically targeting the poor with special services in the 1970s and later, we learned an important lesson: it is often futile to create special services and heavy subsidies. They disappear when watchful eyes are withdrawn, evolve into expensive commitments, and deteriorate the system-wide service within which they are offered. The solution is not so much creating special services for the poor as incorporating the poor into broader sectoral transportation improvements.

It is probable that the best solution for mobility of the poor is to repair local roads adequately and provide good quality transit service at full cost. If one more family member gets an additional part-time job that way, it will far more than pay the cost. The poor suffer in many ways from poor location and poor access. They pay up to twice as large a proportion of their income for housing as the average (figures from Tunisia), partly because of the limited options of accessible location. It was discovered in early squatter studies that the families in the more comfortable peripheral settlements were those with regular employment. The occasionally employed had to live in expensive city centres where they could grasp ephemeral opportunities. The tenuous supply lines to low income settlements cause the poor to pay more for daily survival if they cannot get out to purchase essentials – up to 55 per cent more for food than in rural areas of Tunisia.

We need to know much more about the value of access. Our blunt tool of analysis that uses simply aggregate time saved in travel as a basis for justifying transportation investments is of very limited value. The effort here meshes our concern for productivity with the effort to alleviate poverty. Where does endowment of transportation service improve employment possibilities, improve education, or lower consumer prices? What current travel behaviours of the poor show they would benefit from better transit? The conclusions would be quite different for different cities. These are questions that should be asked and answered. Some of them can be answered by analysing the urban structure, others by conferring with individual commuters. Indications provided by brief studies would be adequate as a basis for experimental action.

The potential pay-off from incorporating the poor in the public transportation system is very high in social, political, and economic terms for everyone.

5. How to protect the environment through transportation policy

Two principal impacts of transportation on the environment are air pollution and land consumption.

Of all the problems of transportation, atmospheric pollution is the greatest focus of concern in many mega-cities. Cities in air shed basins with problems of inversion (e.g. Mexico City) have been the first to act. They have intervened deeply into private behaviour in the quest for relief. In Santiago it is forbidden to drive in the city centre three days a week, and on one day a week, to drive at all is forbidden (the restricted days are indicated by the license number). Other cities will follow. With the rapid annual increases of vehicle miles travelled in cities of the developing world, the problem is daunting. At current rates of increase, many cities – Mexico, Jakarta, Santiago – will have levels of pollution unsustainable to human health within a decade. To a greater extent than for any other problem, cities will simply *have to act* to preserve minimally livable environments. There is no other problem in which public action is so inevitable. There remains only what action to choose.

Given the high level of achievement in policy that is minimally required, the choices are not many. They are basically either to limit automobile use in dense areas or to require technology that reduces emissions. Land planning to reduce trip lengths may be advisable separately, but will not achieve enough results to overcome the general increase of vehicle miles travelled. Transit will be useful to restore mobility where controls on personal vehicles reduce it, but transit alone would be ineffective. To the small extent that it converts personal vehicle users, it merely makes room for new automobile users on the roads.

Engineers in the automobile industries of the northern countries are taking the lead in engine design, engine control, reformulated petroleum fuels, and alternative fuels. There has been progress in the use of alcohol as a fuel in Brazil. There has been a rapid increase in the stringency of emission standards. In the US emission standards have reduced emissions since 1969 for hydrocarbons by a factor of 14, for carbon monoxide by a factor of 16, and for nitrous oxides by a factor of 3 in grams per mile. It is important to stay abreast of these improvements in the automotive industry, particularly in the acquisition and maintenance of buses, which are responsible for a lot of pollution and are the easiest for local governments to control.

The strongest intervention a local government can make, however, is limiting automobile use, especially in downtown areas of high contamination. This should be done anyway for additional purposes mentioned in the section above and promises significant pay-offs. The stringent requirements in Santiago are tolerated by the public because people can see directly the difference in air quality through improved visibility in the city. They can smell the difference. Nothing supports enforcement as well, nor improves citizens' respect for responsible government so much.

In limiting the consumption of rural land by urbanization transportation plays a supporting rather than a proactive role. The principal tools of restraint are other infrastructures, especially water and sewerage, along with direct controls over building, which ensure that land development is contained within strong urban boundaries, limits that are expanded outward as the city grows. This policy of contained development facilitates efficient transportation and is facilitated by it.

6. How to create robust transportation institutions that ensure good service and the implementation of decisions

At a meeting of public transportation specialists in the summer of 1990 at UN HABITAT, Nairobi, there was disagreement on many matters, but very strong concurrence on one thing: urban transportation decisions are made at the wrong level. Important decisions are made at the national level, where the financing comes from, but purely national initiatives cannot be expected to deal successfully with details of the fit of a new system to its full local context. Service and locational decisions are often made at the municipal level. But the scope of the problems and the solutions is *metropolitan* or *megalopolitan*, not national or municipal. Whether the question is pricing, network planning, controlling the use of individual motor vehicles, integrating the poor, or protecting the environment, the scopes of concern of national and municipal governments are not the right scales. I will add that when the actions are metropolitan in scope they are apt to be in the hands of special purpose agencies with only the survival and health of a single mode in mind, and that does not work either. Some means has to be created to grasp the problems comprehensively at the metropolitan level. Transportation institutions need, then, to be both *metropolitan* and *comprehensive*.

They have to be metropolitan because municipal boundaries in an area-wide network are arbitrary. Local autonomy produces discontinuities, makes the impacts of one locality's actions on the others unmanageable, makes system integration impossible, makes cross subsidy very difficult. Histories of success in urban transportation confirm this. The source of the word "metro" is in the name of the "metropolitan" company that built the one in Paris. System integration has been most successful in cities such as Toronto, Hamburg, and Miami, where political integration preceded it.

The matter is in fact difficult to resolve. Metropolitan authority alone is ineffective because only a national government can contract and guarantee large loans. In many situations only national authority can set transit fares, successfully carry out land acquisition, or even reliably supervise the construction and afterwards assure responsible operation as the authority holding the debt.

We need strong metropolitan authority, well supported by national government. The nation must be willing to release some authority to the metropolitan level, subject to constraints that assure adequate financial performance. The latter, of course, is a difficult condition to meet, given the poor performance of public transit systems throughout the developing world.

Adequate mega-city institutions are very difficult to design because metropolitan areas do not correspond to any level of government. In Brazil, which exhibits one of the few useful models of national metropolitan policy, there was substantial resistance to the metropolitan acts of the 1970s by cities arguing that they suppressed home rule.

It is important that authority be comprehensive, linked to the planning of all modes, land, and the environment. The first five headings immediately above make that need evident. Single mode initiatives are necessarily isolated. They are likely to be built by single-minded effort, concerned only with efficient completion and unmindful of related urban systems. Their efforts are likely to be brusquely imposed on unfriendly vested interests. They encourage no collaboration; that would delay the project schedule. In the case of transit, they produce facilities forced to sustain themselves as isolated subsystems, taken at best to be a contribution of national largesse and expected to be accompanied by sufficient continuing subsidy to function with little local effort.

Comprehensive authority is difficult to achieve but essential to strategic transportation planning.

Are there problems and solutions unique to mega-cities?

I conclude there are none. Every transportation problem suffered by cities of over 10 million people is also suffered by cities considerably smaller. The magnitude of severity of mega-city problems may be proportionally larger than the cities' difference in size, but the problems are not qualitatively different. Some solution technologies may require a large scale of urbanization, but all the thresholds known to me are considerably lower than 10 million. Metros are needed by travel demand of over 40,000 passengers/hour/direction in smaller cities. The key variable is personal income levels. The currently most successful metros in the developing world are in non-mega-cities.

Is there a role for mega-city collaboration in transportation development? There certainly is. In fact, my conclusion implies there is a more crucially important role than if mega-cities were to collaborate only to solve their own problems. Mega-cities potentially have more capability to deal with problems that they share with smaller cities. They can be trial sites and showcases for solutions to be adopted by other cities.

Why? Mega-cities hold a large part of their countries' stake in development. As a result, they command more attention from national policy, from the national and international press, and from public investment. National leadership needs to and does invest more effort and funds in mega-cities. At the same time, mega-cities attract the best development professionals in their countries – in many countries practically the entirety of high quality local development professionals. Mega-cities are clearing-houses for international intelligence about problems and solutions. As a result they are the cities that have the skills and the budget to seek, design, and implement new, robust solutions. Just as small firms cannot afford research and development but need to depend on results achieved in large firms, so the secondary metropolises of the developing world must look to the mega-cities for guidance and for prototype solutions. Mega-cities must serve as the models of determined commitment to be followed by others in solving these problems. They must innovate, achieve, and diffuse the answers to these quandaries that suppress the effectiveness of urban areas in the development process.

References

1 Lee, Kyu Sik, and Alex Anas. *Manufacturers' Responses to Infrastructure Deficiencies in Nigeria: Private Alternatives and Policy Options*. World Bank Discussion Paper, INU 50. Washington, D.C., July 1989.

2 Transport and Road Research Laboratory of Great Britain, and Halcrow, Fox and Associates. *Rail Mass Transit in Developing Cities*. Crowthorn, UK: TRRL, 1989.

3 The World Bank. *Urban Policy and Economic Development: An Agenda for the 1990s*. World Bank Policy Paper. Washington, D.C., April 1991.

14

The dual challenge of poverty and mega-cities: An assessment of issues and strategies

Om Prakash Mathur

HDFC Professor of Housing and Urban Economics, National Institute of Public Finance and Policy, New Delhi

Introduction and scope

An extraordinarily large amount of work has been done in recent years on issues relating to poverty in the developing countries.[1] Studies have been undertaken in several countries to define the thresholds of poverty, to estimate the number of the poor, and to ascertain their demographic, economic, social, and other characteristics.[2] Attempts have been made to explore the causal relationship between poverty and selected macroeconomic parameters. Attempts have also been made on a limited scale to assess the reach and efficiency of the poverty alleviation strategies and interventions. The effects of structural adjustments on the poor have also been studied in the context of countries like Chile, the Philippines, Thailand, Kenya, and Ghana.[3]

What is somewhat puzzling is that despite the increasing global and country-wide attention, issues relating to poverty in the mega-cities, which account for a significant proportion of the urban poor, have not been separately or specifically examined. Public policy responses and poverty alleviation strategies, too, have not distinguished the

The views expressed in the paper are those of the author.

poverty-related problems of mega-cities from similar problems in other places. It is the thesis of this paper that the incidence of poverty in mega-cities is quantitatively very large, and qualitatively complex and different, and the two together, that is, the qualitative and quantitative dimensions of poverty in such cities today, present to the developing countries their biggest and most formidable urban agenda for the 1990s. Drawing attention to the susceptibility of the poor of mega-cities to deteriorating economic environment and outlook and structural adjustments, this paper, which has been euphemistically titled as "The Dual Challenge of Poverty and Mega-cities: An Assessment of Issues and Strategies," points out that this dual challenge cannot be addressed by conventional poverty alleviation strategies and service delivery systems. These are costly, unaffordable, and unsustainable. This paper argues that while community based approaches have proved to be more effective in reaching the poor and creating among them an awareness of more efficient utilization of infrastructure and service networks, it is far from clear whether these can be multiplied and scaled up to levels where they can replace the existing public policy and programme interventions. This paper stresses the need to mount a more organized research effort to better understand the syndrome of poverty in mega-cities.

The paper is in three parts. In the first part, I present evidence on the levels of poverty and service deprivations in the mega-cities, pointing to the fact that in terms of magnitude, these deprivations have no precedent in human history. The second part deals with the nature of public policy responses to poverty problems. The thrust of this part is that such responses have at most had a marginal impact on the living conditions of the poor. Further, these responses have not been specific to the poverty problems of mega-cities. I also provide in this part a few examples of community initiatives in dealing with poverty, and state that given the lessons that these initiatives have provided, it would seem that more in-depth work is needed in order to determine their sustainability on a larger scale. The final part of the paper points out that the world will witness in the 1990s the emergence of many more mega-cities that will wield enormous economic power within and across the developing countries. In many cases, the future economic growth in many of the countries will heavily depend on the productivity of mega-cities. Maintaining the productivity of these cities will, therefore, mean greater attention to overcoming the deficiencies in their infrastructure and services.

The basic material for this paper has been drawn from the *World*

Development Report (WDR) (The World Bank, 1990), the *Human Development Report* (HDR) (UNDP, 1990), the United Nations, DIESA Monographs on *Population Growth and Policies in Mega-Cities*, the three regional papers on the *Access by the Urban Poor to Basic Infrastructure Services* (Economic Development Institute of the World Bank, 1989), and the *Global Report on Human Settlements* (UNCHS, 1986). I have made no reference in this paper to issues relating to the problems of the definition and measurement of poverty or of intercountry comparisons of poverty data. Such issues have been extensively discussed and debated in a number of studies, including the *World Development Report* (1990).

Poverty, service deprivations, and mega-cities

Urban poverty in the developing countries

I will begin this paper by pointing out that the existence of large-scale poverty in the urban areas of developing countries is now established and recognized. According to a recent estimate (1988), approximately 330 million persons, or 27.7 per cent of the total urban population of developing countries, live below the poverty line.[4] In Africa, which is urbanizing at an extremely rapid rate of about 7 per cent per annum, nearly 42 per cent of the urban population do not have

Table 1 **Incidence of urban poverty in developing countries, 1988**

Region	Urban population (in millions)	Percentage share in each region	Population below poverty level (in millions)	Percentage share in each region	Ratio of population below poverty line to total urban population (%)
Africa	133.24	11.2	55.46	17.0	41.6
Asia	591.91	49.7	136.53	42.0	23.0
EMENA	174.14	14.7	59.53	18.0	34.2
Latin America	291.66	24.5	77.27	24.0	26.5
Total	1,191.95	100.0	328.79	100.0	27.7

Source: The World Bank, Infrastructure and Urban Development Department, *Reaching the Poor Through Urban Operations* (Washington, D.C., November 1989).

Table 2 **Incidence of urban poverty in developing countries, 1988**

Region	Urban population (in millions)	Percentage share in each region	Population below poverty level (in millions)	Percentage share in each region	Ratio of population below poverty line to total urban population (%)
Low-income	654.08	54.9	176.66	53.7	27.0
Lower-middle	320.18	26.8	99.16	30.2	31.0
Upper-middle	217.69	18.3	52.97	16.1	7.4
Total	1,191.95	100.0	328.79	100.0	27.7

Source: The World Bank, Infrastructure and Urban Development Department, *Reaching the Poor Through Urban Operations* (Washington, D.C., November 1989).

adequate incomes to purchase a minimum basket of goods and services considered essential to stay above the poverty line. A little over one-third of the urban population of EMENA (East and Middle Europe and Africa), which includes several low-middle and upper-middle income countries like Algeria, Egypt, Jordan, Turkey, Pakistan, and Hungary, is poor. Although in terms of the proportion, the incidence of urban poverty in Asia may appear to be low – being only 23 pr cent, the absolute numbers of the urban poor are staggering.

The incidence of urban poverty appears to be generally high in low-income and low-growth economies (see tables 1 and 2 in Appendix for details). Though the correlations between poverty levels, GNP per capita, and GNP growth rates are not significant in a statistical sense, the levels of poverty in countries like Bangladesh (GNP per capita of US$160 and GNP annual average growth rate of 0.4 per cent), Ethiopia (GNP per capita of US$130 and a negative GNP growth rate of −0.1 per cent), Nepal (GNP per capita of US$160), Burundi, Madagascar, Togo, Somalia, and Chad are noticeably high, putting these countries in an extremely difficult situation of, on the one hand, channelling investments in sectors that would raise the GNP per capita and, on the other, finding resources to bring about basic improvements in the conditions of the poor.

There are several other developing countries where despite the high GNP per capita and high GNP growth rate, the incidence of urban poverty is extremely high, notable among them being Brazil (GNP per capita of US$2,020 and GNP annual average growth rate of 3.6 per cent), Colombia (GNP per capita of US$1,240), Equador, Peru, and Botswana. Evidently, the high GNP and the GNP annual average growth rates have not made much of an impact on the pattern of income distribution and poverty levels in these countries.

Further examination of the poverty and income data shows that the poverty incidence can be low, in fact significantly low, even in countries that have low GNP per capita, China being one of the most exceptional in this group. Sri Lanka has also been mentioned in this category, though the *World Development Report* (1990) provides no urban poverty data for this country. Evidently, there are diverse groups of countries with no clear patterns or relationships between the incidence of poverty, GNP per capita, or the GNP growth rates.

Interestingly, the urban poverty levels seem to be appreciably high in countries that have a high incidence of rural poverty. In countries like Bangladesh, Guatemala, Haiti, Ethiopia, Nepal, Burundi, Lesotho, the Philippines, and Madagascar, both the urban and rural poverty rates are extremely high, exceeding 50 per cent of the population. This fact too places several of the developing countries in situations where they have to make difficult investment choices between urban and rural poverty.

Poverty as measured in terms of incomes or expenditures necessary to purchase a minimum basket of goods and services represents only one of its facets. There are other manifestations of poverty such as the absence or inadequacy of shelter and basic services that are no less disconcerting. According to the UNCHS report on shelter and urbanization,[5] 100 million people worldwide are estimated to have no form of shelter at all. Such homeless people combined with those who live in shanty towns are now found in most of the cities of the developing world. The United Nations report on the achievements of the International Drinking Water Supply and Sanitation Decade 1981–1990 estimates that 18.3 per cent of the urban population of developing countries have no access to water supply, and another 28.3 per cent remain unserved by sanitation (Appendix tables 3 and 4). In Asia and the Pacific region, urban population unserved by water supply is 23 per cent of the total; this proportion is as high as 35 per cent in the case of sanitation. The important point to note is that although the proportions of unserved population registered a decline during the period 1981–1990, the absolute numbers increased from

212.70 million to 243.70 million in the case of water supply, and 292.08 million to 377.0 million in the case of sanitation.

Poverty and deprivations in the mega-cities

There is virtually nothing in the literature that sheds light on the nature and dimensions of poverty in different cities or the different population classes of cities, suggesting that the city size effects on the nature of poverty have not been separately examined by urban scientists and scholars. Thus, while the broad approximations on the number of the poor and those deprived of shelter and basic services as given above are able to provide us with some sense of the overall urban poverty dimensions, the understanding of the phenomenon of poverty in mega-cities has remained essentially obscure and remote. There are no comparable estimates of the number of the poor, that is, those who are below the poverty line, in mega-cities. Also, it is arguable whether such conventionally used income-expenditure measure or the criterion of the basket of goods and services are at all relevant for assessing the incidence of poverty in the mega-cities since they have incomes and consequently expenditures that are substantially higher than the national and urban income averages. It can also be argued that the basket of goods and services necessary for people to stay above the poverty threshold in mega-cities may itself vary from that of cities in other population classes.

This controversy apart, there is no denying the fact that the mega-cities of developing countries today present the worst forms, on the one hand, of visible poverty, for example, slums and squatter settlements and unsanitary living conditions, and, on the other, less easily discerned poverty such as the high rates of infant mortality and high degree of drop-outs from the primary stage of schooling. According to the UNCHS report cited above, in Cairo, "the tombs in the city cemeteries are home to hundreds of thousands people who have nowhere else to go apart from their City of the Dead," and in India, the same report cites, "half a million people will be forced to sleep on the streets of Calcutta and a further 100,000 men, women and children will spend the night on the pavements of Bombay." The UNCHS *Global Report on Human Settlements* (1986) has pointed out that in Mexico, 40 per cent of the total population live in what are called "informal settlements"; in São Paulo, this proportion is 32 per cent; in Manila, 37 per cent; and in Ankara, 51 per cent.

When translated into updated population figures (see data sources

Table 3 **Estimates of the percentage of city population in informal settlements, 1980**

City	Total population (000s)	In informal settlements	
		Number (000s)	Percentage
Mexico City	15,032	6,013	40
São Paulo	13,541	4,333	32
Manila	5,664	2,666	47
Bogotá	5,493	3,241	59
Karachi	5,005	1,852	37
Ankara	2,164	1,104	51

Source: United Nations Centre for Human Settlements, *Global Report on Human Settlements* (UNCHS, 1986).

for Appendix table 3), it may mean 7 million persons living in some form of uncontrolled or unauthorized settlements in Mexico City; up to 2 million people living in very substandard accommodation in São Paulo; 3 million people living in bustees and refugee settlements in Calcutta, and another 2.5 million people in similarly blighted and unserviced areas; and some 3.5 million slum dwellers living on about 8,000 acres of Bombay's land.

In Cairo, more than 1 million people are estimated to live in cemeteries of the city, with many more sleeping in mosques. Close to 2 million inhabitants squat on 415 sites dotted through the Manila urban region – this number does not include families living in legal but otherwise substandard housing. Nearly 2.6 million persons, or 40 per cent of Karachi's population, live in squatter settlements, or "katchi abadis," as these are called in Pakistan. Approximately one-half of Lima's city population lives in inner city settlements (*tugurios*), and another 25 per cent live in squatter settlements (*pueblos javaneses*).

Evidence of other forms of deprivation is invariably ad hoc and unsystematic. I have, nevertheless, drawn from various sources some information on the levels of deprivation for some of the mega-cities and present the same in table 3 of the Appendix to obtain a general understanding of the existing situation.

Of all the basic needs, water is undeniably the most essential to survival and to individual health and family welfare. Yet it is one commodity that people are least able to provide for themselves. Urban poor also lack the information to minimize the effects of their unsanitary conditions.

Generally speaking, the water supply and sanitation situation is extremely serious in the low income settlement areas of mega-cities, where few dwellers have access to water supply and sewage systems. In Mexico City, tap water reaches 80 per cent of the population, but in most squatter settlements, it reaches less than 50 per cent of the population. More than three-quarters of Jakarta's population have no direct connection to piped water. Some 10 per cent depend solely on water vendors, with water costing five times that of the piped water. Thirty-five per cent of the population of Metro Manila who live outside the water distribution system either purchase water from private vendors or are served by groundwater. Lower income groups in Lima spend three times more per month on water from vendors but consume less than a sixth as those with running water.

The position of mega-cities with respect to other essential services is even more appalling. For instance, of the more than 13 million people living in the São Paulo metropolitan region, 64 per cent live in houses not served by the sewage system. Cairo has no publicly organized domestic solid waste disposal system. Jakarta, too, has no water-borne sewage system. Septic tanks serve only about 25 per cent of the city's population; others use pit latrines, cesspools, and ditches along the roadside. Only about 11 per cent of the population of Metro Manila is served by piped sewerage. In the large number of unserved areas, sewage is conveyed via gutters, open ditches, and canals into water courses. In Delhi, 70 per cent of the total population do not have access to water-borne sewerage. The proportion is nearly 100 per cent in the unauthorized colonies. Only 20 per cent of Karachi's households have sewerage connections.

An estimated 100,000 persons in Bangkok obtain water directly from canals and waterways that are grossly polluted by human waste and industrial effluents. The water-borne sewage system serves only about 18–20 per cent of the population of Dacca. About 30 per cent of this city's population use a total of 50,000 septic tanks, which typically overflow into the streets and drains.

The spread of health and educational services is limited to only a few sections of the mega-cities, the effects of which are visible in high infant mortality rates, chronic malnutrition, recurrent gastroenteritis, and non-utilization of governmental hospitals and dispensaries. Almost invariably, the share of poor households in publicly subsidized health and educational services is low compared to the better-off and high-income households.

Studies have shown that in Mexico City, the infant mortality rate in the poor areas is up to three times higher than in the rest of the city. Protein-energy malnutrition is an important contributory cause of death among children between the ages of one and four years in Mexico City. Infant mortality rates in São Paulo vary from 42 per thousand in the core areas to 175 per thousand in one of the peri-urban municipalities. In some of the *favelas*, it is over 100 per thousand live births. Infectious diseases account for one-third of all infant deaths in the core areas and almost one-half in the periphery.

Many of the women living in Bombay slums complain of generalized weakness and anaemia (70–75 per cent), and 50–60 per cent suffer from chronic malnutrition, avitaminosis, recurrent gastro-enteritis, and helminthic infections. Malnutrition, blindness, and paralysis are common causes of morbidity. There are also other equally important social conditions that affect the population, such as sexually transmitted diseases, early teenage pregnancy, smoking, and drug addiction among school children of Bombay slums.

With the prevalence of environmental deficiencies, Cairo is plagued by countless illnesses. In addition to bacterial infections, viruses, and parasitic infections, there are serious problems associated with malnutrition. In the Manila slums, infant mortality is three times as high, rates for tuberculosis nine times as high, and diarrhoea twice as common as in the rest of the city. The city has a high incidence of morbidity caused by poor sanitation and environmental pollution.

A significant proportion of Karachi's population is served by private practitioners who are frequently untrained. Community surveys found that even in the presence of several governmental hospitals and dispensaries, only 10 per cent of residents of squatter settlements surveyed who were sick utilized these facilities, relying instead on private practitioners.

The people of Dacca have a high incidence of bronchitis and other respiratory diseases. People often bypass lower order health care facilities such as the dispensaries because of what is perceived to be inadequate care, and go directly to one of the city's large and overburdened general hospitals. Many of the urban poor receive no medical attention or go to indigeneous doctors, whereas pregnant women normally go to untrained midwives.

In Jakarta, the household groups that receive more than their due of publicly subsidized health services are the better-off households.

The present distribution of government subsidies in health (and education) is highly skewed towards the upper middle and upper income groups, and this inequitable transfer of public resources to various income classes tends to accentuate the existing socio-economic inequalities.

School enumeration rates in Jakarta vary by income class and geographical location. Although primary school subsidies are more or less equitably distributed at the higher levels of schooling, subsidies become increasingly skewed towards better-off households in the levels beyond primary school. Children in the upper income classes account for 28 per cent and 33 per cent of the junior and secondary school age groups, but receive 33 per cent and 55 per cent of the subsidies at these levels.

This description of deprivation levels in mega-cities is illustrative, and it may be possible to add a few more statistics, but it is adequate to make at least two observations. Firstly, the mega-cities have a major problem of, on the one hand, extreme polarization in respect of the availability of basic social services and, on the other, of environmental degradation. Indeed, if there is one feature that distinguishes mega-cities from other urban areas, it is the non-accessibility of the poor to such basic services. Secondly, such deprivations are unprecedented in terms of scale and character, the likely effects of which are still to be fully assessed.

Public policies and interventions for poverty alleviation

Evolution of public policy responses

Reviews of the literature show that concern for urban poverty in the developing countries is of a comparatively recent origin, with claims being made that the turning point was Robert McNamara's annual address of 1975, wherein he drew attention to the fact that in the developing world, "the urban poor exist in thoroughly squalid conditions, afflicted by malnutrition, devoid of rudimentary sanitary facilities, lacking employment, possessing minimum shelter if at all." Until this address and perhaps more appropriately the beginning of the 1970s, public policy responses to poverty issues were far from developed, did not distinguish between rural and urban poverty, and paid little attention to urban poverty issues. Most developing countries worked under the assumption that urbanization was necessary, that it was central to any economic transformation, and postulated that economic transformation will itself trickle down and gradually spread out to the different population and income groups. The countries overlooked the likely adverse consequences of urbanization. Programme interventions too were aimed essentially at removal and clearance of slums, considered until then the main manifestation of poverty in the urban areas.

The decade of the 1970s, however, opened under totally different sets of conditions and circumstances, with countries painfully recognizing that urbanization and the manner in which it had come about was not an unmixed blessing, and, while, on the one hand, the urban areas, particularly the large and mega-cities, brought about massive economic gains and productivity, they were equally the centres of large-scale poverty and deprivation.

More concretely, if we look at it in a historical perspective, it would seem that the development of public policy responses grew out of at least three simultaneously operating forces:

- the failure on the part of the developing countries to anticipate the scale and pace of urbanization, and their relative unpreparedness to address urbanization issues;
- the inability of the formal sector to expand and correspondingly absorb the increasing urban labour force; and
- the incapacity of the formal institutional systems to expand the infrastructure and basic urban services for meeting the needs of the fast growing urban population.

There were two principal schools of thought about the problem of burgeoning urbanization and urban poverty in the developing countries. One stressed policies designed to lower out-migration from rural areas. This was one of the main justifications for the rural development policies of the 1970s. A second policy response was urban decentralization and development of small and intermediate-sized cities. The most common instruments were fiscal incentives designed to alter the location of investment and the subsidization of urban infrastructure in smaller cities.

Sectoral strategies for alleviating urban poverty

Neither of the two policies seemed to have any impact on the problems arising out of urbanization. Such efforts were frequently undertaken with little systematic rationale. The doubts that rural development or industrial decentralization policies could solve the fundamental urbanization problems led many developing countries to conclude that large urban agglomerations were a fact of life. They were unlikely to disappear. The realistic question thus was what to do about the poor population in such cities. Should there be policy interventions analogous to those designed to deal with rural poverty? Or should there be different policy packages? Facing up to the fact of the growing number of the poor meant, among other things, improving urban housing, generating employment, and expanding urban water supply, sewage disposal, and other health and educational services. The public policy responses as they grew in many countries thus involved

- expansion of employment and income earning opportunities, particularly in the informal sector, which employed most of the poor;
- establishment of realistic shelter policies and norms;
- provision of basic services such as water supply, sanitation, education, and health services; and
- improvement in the mechanisms of delivering services to the poor.

The principal emphasis in the anti-poverty strategies in most developing countries was on shelter for the low-income groups. Most typical were sites and services projects, by which land parcels fitted with rudimentary urban services were provided to poor people who then constructed their own dwellings or contributed to their construction. Another emphasis was on upgrading existing slum settlements, employing largely self-help methods. Compared to sites and services and slum upgrading, the employment generation components of anti-poverty strategies were small. Following the basic needs strategy, several developing countries emphasized the linkages between services such as water supply, sanitation, primary health, education, and nutrition with poverty alleviation, and established separate programmes for the provision of services. These programmes were directed mainly at women and children, considered by many to be the poorest of the poor.

Lessons and experiences

Experience gained and registered in several countries shows that public policies and programme interventions have made at best a marginal impact on the urban poverty problems in the developing countries. Several studies of anti-poverty policies and programmes have led to the following conclusions:

- Sites and services projects have reached few poor people over the years, and the justification for such projects is questionable.
- Whether sites and services plots are affordable to the poor remains controversial. However, there is considerable evidence to point out that within the present system of shelter and services provision, market forces tend to operate against the poor. Many shelter projects developed for the low-income groups become private housing after allocation and thereafter operate on the ruling market prices. Consequently, the houses become occupied by higher income groups while the poor remain in squalid conditions.
- In slum upgrading projects, the income range of beneficiaries is even broader, supporting evidence that a significant share of families living in unserviced areas are not as poor as their housing conditions might lead us to believe.
- The shelter projects remain unaffordable to low-income groups without subsidies.
- In many such projects, while the component of direct subsidies is low, there are substantial indirect subsidies. Thus, in many cases the interest rates on loans are not only below the market but also below the prevailing rate of inflation. In several projects, interest rates are negative in real terms.
- Inability on the part of governments to cover the cost of shelter and services is also seen as subsidization.
- Access to shelter and urban services is hampered by public regulatory policies, including planning laws and regulations, building standards, and rent controls.

Community-centred approaches

The last few years have witnessed in several developing countries increasing reliance on community-based approaches to urban poverty. These constitute, in a sense, a reaction to the poverty alleviation approaches of the 1960s and early 1970s, when it became clear that cities on their own could not solve the problem of services or shelter effectively by slum clearance, relocation, and public shelter policies. Most governments turned to policies involving, as stated above, development of sites and services, upgrading of slums, and more critically, the promotion of self-help and community participation in several poverty alleviation programmes. Yue-man Yeung, who carried out extensive studies of the community-based and participatory approaches to urban poverty alleviation, points out in his study that "the gradual realisation of the ineffectiveness of a service delivery model, i.e. government-provided services, has promoted experimental and innovative efforts to mobilise people's resources towards improving the urban living environment."[6] According to Yeung, the main rationale of the experimental community-centred approaches is to make use of community resources for the delivery of basic physical and social services. These attempts evidently require "new organisations and mobilisation, usually taking the form of participatory, self-help, cooperative, self-sustaining, and community-based styles of management characterised by popular participation." Because urban service provision in most situations, and more so in the mega-cities, is more often unevenly distributed and skewed in favour of high-income communities, it is a pragmatic strategy for the urban poor to organize themselves and arrange to provide and manage the needed services to themselves, preserving indirectly scarce capital for the government to pursue other developmental purposes that might also benefit them.

From the position of the developing countries, participatory approaches to poverty alleviation seem beneficial in many ways, including:

- reduction in the cost of social services, thereby enhancing the public sector's ability to pursue development options;
- generation of information on the socio-economic characteristics of the poor;
- assisting the government to identify community leaders who can help both the community and the government in realizing their respective goals;
- strengthening of the socio-economic structures of poor communities, giving rise to a sense of community that is often weakly developed in urban areas; and, finally,
- creation with very small subsidization by the government to carry out participatory urban services of income earning opportunities for low-income communities.

Several lessons have emerged from the evaluation of poverty alleviation programmes currently operating on a community participation basis in several countries.[7] Firstly, it is evident that the nature and extent of participation by the people in their desire to improve urban services varies between what may be described as a partnership with the government (i.e., the government has a definite say as to the content of and manner in which urban services are to be improved) and the case where the slum settlements organize themselves to make available those services the government fails to provide and deliver to improve their well-being. Secondly, most people-oriented programmes require strong leadership, which may be formal or informal. Almost all studies have pointed to the need for improvement of leadership qualities if participatory urban services are to improve.

Thirdly, one of the main responsibilities of community leaders in slum settlements is to help the poor to articulate their needs for services in a more effective and organized manner. In several urban poverty alleviation programmes, the package of services does not reach the lowest socio-economic groups. The real needs and problems of poor communities are quite different from those assumed under the programmes. Finally, the activities provided under the various programmes are generally not diversified enough to cater to a broad spectrum of needs. As the studies point out, this is a consequence of the bias that tends to favour physical and visible services at the expense of social services specific to individual communities.

The dual challenge of poverty and mega-cities: Issues and perspectives

Almost all projections indicate that the urban population of the developing countries will increase from approximately 1.38 billion in 1990 to about 1.97 billion by the turn of the century and cross the 4 billion mark by the year 2025. In terms of percentages, it will mean a phenomenal increase from an estimated 34 per cent to nearly 40 per cent in 2000, and over 55 per cent by 2025. One of the distinguishing features of this pattern of growth will be the rise of mega-cities. In 1985, there were 20 cities (excluding Hong Kong) with more than 5 million people, accounting for 15.4 per cent of the total urban population of the developing countries. By the turn of the century, the number of such cities will rise to 33 and their share of urban population will grow to more than 17 per cent.[8]

In several countries, the demographic weight of mega-cities is already large and overwhelming. As table 4 shows, Mexico City accounts for over 30 per cent of Mexico's total urban population; the population of Buenos Aires is nearly 42 per cent of the total urban population of Argentina; and Bangkok accounts for 57 per cent of Thailand's urban population. Seoul contains 37.5 per cent of South Korea's total urban population.

While there may be historical and other differences between Mexico

Table 4 **Population of mega-cities and their share in total urban population**

Mega-city	Population (in millions) 1970	1985	Average annual rate of growth 1970–1985 (%)	Percentage of country's total urban population, 1985
Mexico City	8.74	16.65	4.30	30.10
São Paulo	8.06	15.54	4.38	15.80
Shanghai	11.41	12.06	0.37	5.52
Buenos Aires	8.31	10.76	1.72	42.00
Calcutta	6.91	10.29	2.65	5.24
Rio de Janeiro	7.04	10.14	2.43	10.40
Seoul	5.31	10.07	4.27	37.50
Greater Bombay	5.81	9.47	3.26	4.83
Beijing	8.29	9.33	0.79	4.27
Tianjin	6.87	7.96	0.98	3.64
Cairo	5.33	7.92	2.64	35.80
Jakarta	4.32	7.79	3.93	18.50
Teheran	3.29	7.21	5.23	29.20
Metro Manila	3.53	7.09	4.65	32.50
Delhi	3.53	6.95	4.52	3.54
Karachi	3.13	6.16	4.51	20.00
Bangkok	3.11	5.86	4.22	57.40
Lima	2.84	5.44	4.33	19.80
Dacca	1.50	4.76	7.70	41.00

Source: United Nations, *Prospects of World Urbanization 1988* (New York, 1989).

Table 5 **Demographic and economic hold of mega-cities**

Mega-city	Percentage of total for country: Population	Output measure
Greater São Paulo (1970)	8.6	36.0 of NDP
Shanghai (1980)	1.2	48.0 of net industrial production
Mexico City (1970)	14.2	12.5 of gross industrial production
Karachi (1974–1975)	6.1	16.1 of GDP
Lima (1980)	28.0	43.0 of GDP
Metro Manila (1970)	12.0	25.0 of GNP
Metro Bangkok (1981)	47.0	70.0 of GNP

Source: Friedrich Kahnert, "Improving Urban Employment and Labour Productivity," World Bank Discussion Paper No. 10, May 1987, as quoted in "Structural Adjustment and Sustainable Growth: The Urban Agenda for the 1990s" (Unpublished paper, The World Bank, July 1990).

City, São Paulo, Cairo, Manila, Calcutta, Beijing, and Shanghai, what they share is that each performs major economic functions and consequently wields massive economic power that is clearly disproportionate to its share in population. Table 5 presents data for selected mega-cities on the share of GDP/GNP and industrial output in the respective countries and suggests that future economic growth in these countries will depend heavily on the productivity of such cities.

It also seems evident that the urban poverty situation will worsen over the years. Estimates indicate that while the proportion of the poor in developing countries may decline over time – from about 27.7 per cent in 1988 to 24 per cent in 2000 – the absolute numbers are projected to increase from about 330 million to 425 million persons.[9] Also, from all counts, it would seem that the share in poverty of mega-cities will also be large and they will encounter bigger pressures, particularly in respect of social services. A recent study on the proportion of population in the 0–19 age group in selected mega-cities (which bears critically on health and education services) shows that, compared with the relatively small proportion of people in this age group in the large cities of developed countries, the proportion is extremely large in the mega-cities of the developing countries. Forty-four per cent of Bangkok's population is in the 0–19 age group; in Cairo, it is 47.7 per cent. Almost invariably, the population in the 0–19 age group exceeds 40 per cent of the total (table 6), which means that the provision of educational and health services will become a major task in the developing countries.

How to respond to this scenario – growing poverty and an increasing number of mega-cities – is perhaps the biggest challenge for the developing countries in the 1990s and beyond. This challenge has to be seen in the light of other equally powerful trends overtaking many developing countries, of which the deteriorating economic environment is perhaps the most important. There is a serious resource problem facing developing countries, particularly in Africa, Latin America, and parts of Asia. Coincidentally, the urban poverty situation is worse in the countries in these regions on account of structural adjustments. Not to be belittled is the fact that the developing countries themselves place a low priority on health and education expenditures, ignoring the vital effects that these have on urban productivity. Table 1 in the Appendix shows that expenditure on health as a percentage of GNP varies between 0.2 per cent in the case of Pakistan to a little over 5 per cent in Panama. In as many as 18 out of 48

Table 6 **Proportions of population in 0–19 age group in selected cities (%)**

Budapest (1981)	23.2
Buenos Aires (1980)	25.4
Chicago (1980)	32.0
Frankfurt	24.8
London (1981)	27.6
Los Angeles (1980)	28.8
Madrid (1980)	33.5
Milan (1981)	27.7
New York (1980)	28.1
Osaka (1980)	31.0
Paris (1982)	18.7
Rome (1981)	29.6
Tokyo (1981)	28.2
Warsaw (1981)	23.0
Bangkok (1981)	44.1
Bogotá (1973)	51.5
Cairo (1976)	47.7
Delhi (1980)	48.9
Istanbul (1975)	43.5
Jakarta (1981)	52.9
Manila (1978)	51.4
Mexico City (1980)	48.5
São Paulo (1980)	40.0
Santiago (1982)	41.7
Seoul (1980)	42.5

Source: J.T. Martin, I. Ness, and S.T. Collins, *Book of World City Rankings* (New York: The Free Press, London: Collier Macmillan, 1986).

countries for which data are available, health expenditures are less than 1 per cent of GNP; and in 21 countries, it ranges between 1 and 2 per cent of the GNP. Expansion of these expenditures where they can effectively meet the shortage of health services will be formidable for developing countries in the coming years.

The World Bank's Task Force on Poverty Alleviation has drawn attention to significant limitations of the existing approaches to poverty alleviation.[10] According to the Task Force, efficiency investments towards poverty related sectors may not be able to bring relief to large numbers of the poor in the medium term. Orienting investments towards poverty related sectors is not necessarily poverty specific and benefits have only partly accrued to the poor. Narrowly targeted micro-programmes also have limitations. For these reasons, poverty policies and programmes need to redefine the respective roles of public institutions and the poor themselves, which would include the reallocation of public resources for social services to complement the more traditional investment-oriented interventions.

Amidst all this, the classic debate on the sufficiency of growth, distribution, and direct targeting of programmes to the poor continues both globally and in individual countries. Much research tends to suggest that growth may be a necessary though not a sufficient condition for alleviating poverty. Likewise, growth without distribution may not be able to affect any reduction in the number of the poor; direct targeting of programmes to the poor may be essential as growth does not trickle down, but it must be accompanied by growth.

It is worth ending this paper by quoting from Janice Perlman's paper, where she argues that,

> the sheer size of these mega-cities presents a situation of which we have no collective experience. No precedent exists for feeding, sheltering, or transporting so many people . . . , nor for removing their waste products or providing clean drinking water. . . . The question now is how to find creative ways to apply these advances to the building and maintenance of the urban infrastructure, urban management and service delivery, and the regeneration of the urban environment.[11]

Appendix

Table A–1.1 **Poverty in developing countries: A statistical profile**

Country	Total population (in millions) 1988	Population below absolute poverty level (in millions) 1977–1986	GNP per capita (US$) 1987	GNP per capita average annual growth rate (%) 1965–1988	Rate of inflation (%) 1980–1987	Debt service as a percentage of GNP 1988
Bangladesh	108.90	94.00	160	0.40	11.10	1.60
Guatemala	8.70	6.20	950	1.00	13.30	4.40
Haiti	6.30	4.70	360	0.40	7.90	0.90
Ethiopia	47.40	29.00	130	−0.10	2.10	4.30
Ghana	14.00	6.20	390	−1.60	46.10	3.80
Nepal	18.00	11.00	160	NA	8.70	1.20
Burundi	5.10	4.30	250	3.00	4.00	3.30
Lesotho	1.70	0.90	370	5.20	12.20	3.00
Philippines	59.90	35.00	590	1.60	15.60	7.00
Madagascar	10.90	5.60	210	−1.80	17.30	9.30
Peru	20.70	7.20	1,470	0.10	119.10	1.20
Dominican Rep.	6.90	3.00	730	2.70	16.80	5.50
Togo	3.40	0.30	290	0.00	6.10	7.00
India	815.60	394.00	300	1.80	7.40	1.50
Ecuador	10.10	5.20	1,040	3.10	31.20	5.60
Somalia	5.90	4.20	290	0.50	38.40	0.40
Botswana	1.20	0.60	1,050	8.60	10.00	5.70
Myanmar	40.00	16.00	200	NA	NA	NA
Brazil	144.00	NA	2,020	3.60	188.70	0.20
Colombia	31.70	13.00	1,240	2.40	24.10	7.50
Pakistan	106.30	34.00	350	2.50	6.50	3.40

Chad	5.40	2.60	150	−2.00	3.20	0.70
Côte d'Ivoire	11.20	3.20	740	0.90	3.80	5.10
Rwanda	6.70	5.80	300	1.50	4.10	0.70
Morocco	24.00	8.90	610	2.30	7.70	6.40
Mali	8.00	3.90	210	1.60	3.70	2.50
Indonesia	174.80	68.00	450	4.30	8.50	9.90
Malawi	8.00	6.10	160	1.10	12.60	4.10
Zambia	7.60	1.10	250	−2.10	33.50	4.90
Uruguay	3.10	0.60	2,190	1.30	57.00	6.70
Egypt	50.20	12.00	680	3.60	10.60	3.70
Panama	2.30	0.60	2,240	2.20	3.30	0.20
Nicaragua	3.60	0.70	830	−2.50	86.60	NA
Tunisia	7.80	1.40	1,180	3.40	7.70	10.90
Mexico	83.70	NA	1,830	2.30	73.80	5.70
El Salvador	5.00	1.40	860	−0.50	16.80	2.90
Algeria	23.80	2.10	2,680	2.70	4.40	12.70
Paraguay	4.00	1.40	990	3.10	22.10	4.90
Korea (Rep. of)	42.00	6.80	2,690	6.80	5.00	3.80
Thailand	54.50	16.00	850	4.00	3.10	4.30
Cameroon	11.20	3.00	970	3.70	7.00	2.00
Honduras	4.80	1.80	810	0.60	4.70	6.40
Jordan	3.90	0.60	1,560	NA	2.20	19.60
Malaysia	37.90	4.60	1,810	NA	30.50	13.00
Mauritius	1.10	0.10	1,490	2.90	7.80	7.40
China	1,088.40	87.00	290	5.40	4.90	1.00
Kenya	22.40	10.00	330	1.90	9.60	4.40
Papua New Guinea	3.70	2.50	700	0.50	4.70	8.40

Table A–1.2 **Poverty in developing countries: A statistical profile**

Country	Daily per capita calorie supply as percentage of requirements	Life expectancy at birth (years) 1988	Infant mortality rate (under 1) 1988	Percentage of population without access to health services 1985–1987	Percentage of population without access to safe water 1985–1987	Percentage of population without access to adequate sanitation 1985–1987	Health expenditure as percentage of GNP 1986
Bangladesh	83	51	118	55	54	94	1.60
Guatemala	105	62	57	66	62	76	0.70
Haiti	84	55	116	30	62	79	0.90
Ethiopia	71	47	135	54	84	NA	1.00
Ghana	76	54	88	40	44	70	0.30
Nepal	93	51	126	NA	71	98	0.90
Burundi	97	49	73	39	74	42	0.70
Lesotho	101	56	98	20	64	85	1.60
Philippines	104	64	44	NA	48	33	0.70
Madagascar	106	50	119	44	68	NA	1.80
Peru	93	62	86	25	45	50	1.00
Dominican Rep.	109	66	63	20	37	72	1.40
Togo	97	53	92	39	45	86	1.60
India	100	58	97	NA	43	90	0.90
Ecuador	89	66	62	38	42	33	1.10
Somalia	90	47	130	73	66	82	0.20
Botswana	96	67	41	11	46	58	2.90
Myanmar	119	60	68	67	73	76	1.00
Brazil	111	65	61	NA	22	36	1.30
Colombia	110	68	39	40	8	30	0.80
Pakistan	97	55	107	45	56	80	0.20

Chad	69	46	130	70	NA	NA	0.60
Côte d'Ivoire	110	53	95	70	81	NA	1.10
Rwanda	81	49	120	73	50	43	0.60
Morocco	118	61	71	30	40	NA	1.00
Mali	86	47	168	85	83	81	0.70
Indonesia	116	61	68	20	62	63	0.70
Malawi	102	47	149	20	44	NA	2.40
Zambia	92	53	78	25	41	44	2.10
Uruguay	100	72	23	18	15	41	2.70
Egypt	132	63	83	NA	27	NA	1.00
Panama	107	72	22	20	17	19	5.40
Nicaragua	110	64	60	17	51	73	0.50
Tunisia	123	66	48	10	32	48	2.70
Mexico	135	69	46	NA	23	42	1.70
El Salvador	94	63	57	44	48	40	1.10
Algeria	112	64	72	12	32	43	2.20
Paraguay	123	67	41	39	71	14	0.40
Korea (Rep. of)	122	70	24	7	23	0	0.30
Thailand	105	65	30	30	36	47	1.30
Cameroon	88	56	92	59	67	54	0.70
Honduras	92	64	68	27	50	70	2.60
Jordan	121	66	43	3	4	39	1.90
Malaysia	121	74	23	NA	16	24	1.80
Mauritius	121	67	22	0	0	8	1.80
China	111	70	31	NA	NA	NA	1.40
Kenya	92	59	70	NA	70	NA	1.10
Papua New Guinea	96	54	61	NA	73	55	3.30

Table A–1.3 **Poverty in developing countries: A statistical profile**

Country	Primary net enrolment (%) 1987	Education expenditure as a percentage of GNP 1986	Primary education expenditure as a percentage of total education expenditure	Female as a percentage of male literacy rate 1985	Percentage of population below absolute poverty level 1977–1987	
					Rural	Urban
Bangladesh	53	2.20	39.10	51	86	86
Guatemala	NA	1.80	38.20	75	74	66
Haiti	NA	1.20	56.80	88	80	65
Ethiopia	27	4.20	52.80	NA	65	60
Ghana	NA	3.50	29.30	67	37	59
Nepal	NA	2.80	35.70	31	61	55
Burundi	NA	2.80	45.00	60	85	55
Lesotho	NA	3.50	39.10	135	55	50
Philippines	NA	1.70	61.80	99	64	50
Madagascar	NA	3.50	42.30	84	50	50
Peru	NA	1.60	31.10	86	NA	49
Dominican Rep.	NA	1.60	44.40	99	43	45
Togo	73	5.50	34.00	53	NA	42
India	NA	3.40	43.30	51	51	40
Ecuador	NA	3.60	37.10	94	65	40
Somalia	NA	6.00	NA	33	70	40
Botswana	NA	9.10	36.80	95	55	40
Myanmar	NA	2.10	NA	NA	40	40
Brazil	84	3.40	52.30	96	73	35
Colombia	NA	2.80	39.90	100	NA	32
Pakistan	NA	2.20	40.20	48	29	32

Chad	38	2.00	82.90	28	56	30
Côte d'Ivoire	NA	5.00	46.80	58	26	30
Rwanda	64	3.20	68.00	54	90	30
Morocco	57	5.90	36.50	49	45	28
Mali	18	3.20	48.40	48	48	27
Indonesia	NA	3.50	NA	78	44	26
Malawi	49	3.70	47.00	60	85	25
Zambia	NA	4.40	44.20	80	NA	25
Uruguay	NA	6.60	36.10	NA	NA	22
Egypt	NA	4.80	67.30	51	25	21
Panama	NA	5.50	36.30	99	30	21
Nicaragua	76	6.10	36.70	NA	19	21
Tunisia	95	5.00	45.00	60	15	20
Mexico	100	2.80	26.50	96	49	20
El Salvador	71	2.30	60.30	92	32	20
Algeria	88	6.10	28.50	59	NA	20
Paraguay	NA	1.40	36.60	93	50	19
Korea (Rep. of)	99	4.90	NA	92	11	18
Thailand	NA	4.10	59.00	94	34	15
Cameroon	NA	2.80	77.70	66	40	15
Honduras	NA	5.00	46.60	95	55	14
Jordan	NA	5.10	89.90	72	17	14
Malaysia	NA	7.90	37.90	81	38	13
Mauritius	94	3.30	44.20	87	12	12
China	98	2.70	28.50	68	10	10
Kenya	NA	5.00	61.90	70	55	10
Papua New Guinea	NA	5.60	0.00	64	75	10

Table A–2.1 **Urban poverty in developing countries: A statistical profile**

Country	Total urban population (in millions) 1988	Urban population as a percentage of total population 1988	Urban population annual average growth rate (%) 1980–1988	Percentage of urban population in largest city 1980	Percentage of urban population in cities of over 500,000 persons 1980	Number of cities of over 500,000 persons 1980
Bangladesh	14.20	13	5.60	30	51	3
Guatemala	2.90	33	2.90	36	36	1
Haiti	1.80	29	4.00	56	56	1
Ethiopia	6.20	13	5.20	37	37	1
Ghana	4.60	33	4.20	35	48	2
Nepal	1.60	9	7.40	27	0	0
Burundi	0.40	7	9.50	NA	0	0
Lesotho	0.30	19	7.20	NA	0	0
Philippines	26.60	41	3.70	30	34	2
Madagascar	2.60	24	5.90	36	36	1
Peru	14.30	69	3.10	39	44	2
Dominican Rep.	4.10	59	4.30	54	54	1
Togo	0.90	25	7.00	60	0	0
India	220.20	27	4.00	6	39	36
Ecuador	5.60	55	4.70	29	51	2
Somalia	2.20	37	5.60	34	0	0
Botswana	0.30	22	8.40	NA	NA	NA
Myanmar	9.60	24	2.30	23	23	2
Brazil	108.30	75	3.60	15	54	14
Colombia	21.90	69	3.00	26	51	4
Pakistan	33.00	31	4.50	21	51	7

Chad	1.70	31	7.40	39	0	0
Côte d'Ivoire	5.00	45	6.60	34	34	1
Rwanda	0.50	7	8.20	NA	0	0
Morocco	11.30	47	4.40	26	50	4
Mali	1.50	19	3.50	24	0	0
Indonesia	47.20	27	4.80	23	50	9
Malawi	1.10	14	7.90	19	0	0
Zambia	4.10	54	6.70	35	35	1
Uruguay	2.60	85	0.80	52	52	1
Egypt	24.10	48	3.50	39	53	3
Panama	1.20	54	3.00	66	66	1
Nicaragua	2.10	59	4.60	47	47	1
Tunisia	4.20	54	2.90	30	30	1
Mexico	59.40	71	3.10	32	48	7
El Salvador	2.20	44	1.90	22	0	0
Algeria	10.50	44	3.90	12	12	1
Paraguay	1.80	46	4.50	44	44	1
Korea (Rep. of)	29.00	69	3.70	41	77	7
Thailand	11.50	21	4.70	69	69	1
Cameroon	5.30	47	7.20	21	21	1
Honduras	2.00	42	5.60	33	0	0
Jordan	2.60	67	5.10	37	37	1
Malaysia	15.50	41	4.90	27	27	1
Mauritius	0.50	42	0.80	NA	NA	NA
China	544.20	50	NA	6	45	78
Kenya	4.90	22	8.20	57	57	1
Papua New Guinea	0.60	15	4.50	25	0	0

Table A–2.2 **Urban poverty in developing countries: A statistical profile**

Country	Percentage of population below absolute poverty level 1977–1987 (urban)	Percentage of population without access to health services 1985–1987	Percentage of population without access to safe water 1985–1987	Percentage of population without access to adequate sanitation 1985–1987
Bangladesh	86	NA	76	76
Guatemala	66	53	28	59
Haiti	65	20	41	58
Ethiopia	60	NA	31	4
Ghana	59	8	7	39
Nepal	55	NA	30	83
Burundi	55	NA	2	16
Lesotho	50	NA	35	78
Philippines	50	NA	51	17
Madagascar	50	NA	19	NA
Peru	49	NA	83	88
Dominican Rep.	45	NA	15	59
Togo	42	NA	1	69
India	40	NA	24	69
Ecuador	40	70	69	71
Somalia	40	50	42	56
Botswana	40	0	16	7
Myanmar	40	0	64	67
Brazil	35	NA	44	99
Colombia	32	NA	24	87
Pakistan	32	1	17	49
Chad	30	NA	NA	NA
Côte d'Ivoire	30	39	70	NA
Rwanda	30	40	21	23
Morocco	28	0	0	NA
Mali	27	NA	54	10
Indonesia	26	NA	57	67
Malawi	25	NA	3	NA
Zambia	25	NA	24	24
Uruguay	22	NA	73	41
Egypt	21	NA	8	NA
Panama	21	36	36	39
Nicaragua	21	40	89	84
Tunisia	20	0	0	16
Mexico	20	NA	53	87
El Salvador	20	20	32	18
Algeria	20	0	15	20
Paraguay	19	62	92	17

Table A-2.2 (*cont'd*)

Country	Percentage of population below absolute poverty level 1977–1987 (urban)	Percentage of population without access to health services 1985–1987	Percentage of population without access to safe water 1985–1987	Percentage of population without access to adequate sanitation 1985–1987
Korea (Rep. of)	18	14	52	0
Thailand	15	NA	34	54
Cameroon	15	56	57	0
Honduras	14	15	44	76
Jordan	14	5	12	NA
Malaysia	13	NA	24	40
Mauritius	12	0	0	14
China	10	NA	NA	NA
Kenya	10	NA	39	NA
Papua New Guinea	10	NA	5	1

Data sources for appendix tables 1 and 2

Category	Source	Page no.
Total population (in millions) mid-1988	*World Develpment Report 1990*	178
Population below absolute poverty level (in millions) (1977–1986)	*Human Development Report 1990*	132
GNP per capita (US$) 1987	*Human Development Report 1990*	158
GNP per capita average annual growth rate (%) 1965–1988	*World Development Report 1990*	178
Rate of inflation (%) 1980–1987	*World Development Report 1990*	178
Debt service as a percentage of GNP 1988	*World Development Report 1990: Poverty*	224
Daily per capita calorie supply as percentage of requirements	*Human Development Report 1990*	134
Life expectancy at birth (years) 1988	*World Development Report 1990: Poverty*	178
Infant mortality rate (under 1) 1988	*World Development Report 1990: Poverty*	232
Percentage of population without access to health services 1985–1987	*Human Development Report 1990*	130
Percentage of population without access to safe water 1985–1987	*Human Development Report 1990*	130
Percentage of population without access to adequate sanitation 1985–1987	*Human Development Report 1990*	130
Health expenditure as percentage of GNP 1986	*Human Development Report 1990*	148
Primary net enrolment (%) 1987	*World Development Report 1990*	234
Education expenditure as a percentage of GNP 1986	*Human Development Report 1990*	154
Primary education expenditure as a percentage of total education expenditure 1985–1988	*Human Development Report 1990*	154
Female as a percentage of male literacy rate 1985	*Human Development Report 1990*	144
Percentage of population below absolute poverty level 1977–1987 rural, urban	*Human Development Report 1990*	158
Total urban population (in millions) mid-1988	*Human Development Report 1990*	160
Urban population as a percentage of total population 1988	*World Development Report 1990*	238
Urban population annual average growth rate (%) 1980–1988	*World Development Report 1990*	238
Percentage of urban population in largest city 1980	*World Development Report 1990*	238

Data sources for appendix tables 1 and 2 (*cont'd*)

Category	Source	Page no.
Percentage of urban population in cities of over 500,000 persons 1980	*World Development Report 1990*	238
Number of cities of over 500,000 persons 1980	*World Development Report 1990*	238
Percentage of population below absolute poverty level 1977–1987 (urban)	(a) *Human Development Report 1990;* (b) The World Bank, "Measuring Levels of Living in Latin America: An Overview of Main Problem," Living Standards Measurement Study Working Paper, no. 3, Washington, D.C., 1980	158; 42
Percentage of population without access to health services 1985–1987	*Human Development Report 1990*	142
Percentage of population without access to safe water 1985–1987	*Human Development Report 1990*	142
Percentage of population without access to adequate sanitation 1985–1987	*Human Development Report 1990*	142

Table A–3 **Mega-cities: The levels of deprivation**

Mega-city	Shelter	Water supply and sanitation	Health and education
Mexico City	At least 7 million people live in some form of uncontrolled or unauthorized settlement. Eighty per cent of all dwellings in the city display some form of physical irregularity.	In Mexico City, tap water reaches 80 per cent of the population, but in some squatter settlements, it reaches less than 50 per cent of the population.	The infant mortality rate in the poor areas is up to three times higher than in the rest of the city. Protein-energy malnutrition is an important contributory cause of death among children between the ages of one and four years.
São Paulo	Up to 2 million people are estimated to live in very substandard accommodation in inner-city slums and squatter settlements.	Of the more than 13 million people living in the metropolitan area, 64 per cent lived in houses not served by the sewage system in 1980, and very little sewage was treated.	Infant mortality rates vary from 42 per thousand in the core areas to 75 in one of the peri-urban municipalities. In some of the *favelas*, it is over 100 per thousand live births. Infectious diseases account for one-third of all infant deaths in the core areas and almost one-half in the periphery.
Calcutta	Some 3 million people live in "bustees" and refugee settlements. Another 2.5 million live in similarly blighted and unserviced areas.	People living in bustees and refugee settlements lack potable water, endure serious annual flooding, and have no systematic means to dispose of refuse or human waste. Piped water is available only in the central city and parts of some other municipalities. The sewage system is limited to only a third of the area in the urban core.	

Bombay	Some 3.5 million slum dwellers live on about 8,000 acres of Bombay's land – over 400 persons an acre. Of these, the Dharavi slum, with over half a million people, is considered to be the largest slum in Asia.		Many of the women living in slums complain of generalized weakness and anaemia (70–75 per cent), 50–60 per cent suffer from chronic malnutrition avitaminosis, recurrent gastro-enteritis, and helminthic infections. Malnutrition, blindness, and paralysis are common causes of morbidity. There are also other equally important social conditions that affect the population, such as sexually transmitted diseases, early teenage pregnancy, smoking and drug addition among school children.
Delhi	Nearly 45–50 per cent of Delhi's population live in slum settlements. Recent studies place the number of those living in substandard areas at 56 million persons.	Seventy per cent of Delhi's total population does not have access to water-borne sewerage. The proportion is nearly 100 per cent in the unauthorized colonies. Currently, of the 242 million litres of liquid waste that is generated daily, only 46 million litres receive full treatment and 72 million litres receive partial treatment.	The overall infant mortality rate for the slums of Delhi is 221 per thousand live births.

Table A–3 (*cont'd*)

Mega-city	Shelter	Water supply and sanitation	Health and education
Karachi	Nearly 2.6 million persons, or 40 per cent of Karchi's population, live in squatter settlements, or "Katchi Abadis," as these are called in Pakistan.	Only 20 per cent of Karachi's households have sewerage connections.	A significant proportion of Karachi's population is served by private practitioners who are frequently untrained. Community surveys found that even in the presence of several governmental hospitals and dispensaries, only 10 per cent of residents surveyed in "Katchi Abadis" who were sick utilised these facilities, relying instead on private practitioners.
Bangkok		At least 100,000 persons are estimated to obtain water directly from canals and waterways that are grossly polluted by human waste and industrial effluents. Bangkok has no water-borne sewerage system and relies mainly on pour-flush latrines and septic tank systems.	
Lima	Approximately one-half of the city's population lives in inner-city slums (*tugurios*) and another quarter in squatter settlements (*pueblos jóvenes*).	Lower income groups in Lima spend three times more per month on water from vendors but consume less than a sixth as those with running water at home.	

Cairo	More than 1 million people are estimated to live in the cemeteries of the city, while many others sleep in mosques.	Cairo has no publicly organized domestic solid waste disposal system. For sewage and waste water, Cairo is a municipal nightmare. Sewers are often misused. Solid wastes are shoved into manholes and plug up sewers.	With the prevalence of environmental deficiencies, Cairo is plagued by countless illnesses. In addition to bacterial infections, viruses, and parasitic infections, there are serious problems associated with malnutrition.
Jakarta		More than three-quarters of the city's population have no direct connection to a piped water system. Some 10 per cent depend solely on water vendors, with water costing five times that of piped water. The city has no water-borne sewage system. Septic tanks serve only about 25 per cent of the city's population; others use pit latrines, cesspools, and ditches along the roadside.	The household groups that receive more than their share of publicly subsidized health services are the better-off households. The present distribution of government subsidies in health (and education) is highly skewed towards the upper-middle and upper income groups, and such inequitable public transfer of resources to various income classes tends to accentuate the existing socio-economic inequalities. School environment conditions vary by income class and geographical location. Although primary school subsidies are more or less equitably distributed at the higher levels of schooling, the subsidies become increasingly skewed towards better-off households: children in the upper income classes account for 28 per cent and 33 per cent of the junior and secondary school age groups, but receive 33 per cent and 55 per cent of the subsidies at these levels.

Table A–3 *(cont'd)*

Mega-city	Shelter	Water supply and sanitation	Health and education
Metro Manila	Close to 2 million inhabitants squat on 415 sites dotted through the Manila urban region. This number does not include families living in legal but otherwise substandard housing. Manila's squatter settlements vary in size from the very large Tondo Foreshore area, with over 27,000 families, or Bagong Barrio to mini squatter settlements.	About 11 per cent of the population of Metro Manila is served by piped sewerage. In the large number of unserved areas, sewage is conveyed via gutters, open ditches, and canals to water courses. The 35 per cent of the population of Metro Manila who live outside the water distribution system either purchase water from private vendors or are served by groundwater. Overuse of groundwater has lowered the water-table by up to 200 meters below sea level in many areas of Metro Manila, resulting in growing pollution of the water supply from saline intrusion.	In the Manila slums, infant mortality is three times as high, rates for tuberculosis nine times as high, and diarrhoea twice as common as in the rest of the city. The city has a high incidence of morbidity caused by poor sanitation and environmental pollution.

Dacca		The water-borne sewage system serves only about 18–20 per cent of the population of Dacca City. Around 30 per cent of the population use a total of 50,000 septic tanks that typically overflow into the streets and drains.	Dacca has a high incidence of bronchitis and other respiratory diseases. Persons often bypass lower order health care facilities such as the dispensaries because of what is perceived to be inadequate care, and go directly to one of the city's large and overburdened general hospitals. Many of the urban poor receive no medical attention or go to indigeneous doctors, whereas pregnant women normally go to untrained midwives.

Data sources for appendix table 3

Title	Author/Publisher
Population Growth and Policies in Mega-cities, Calcutta	United Nations, DIESA, New York, 1986
Population Growth and Policies in Mega-cities, Seoul	United Nations, DIESA, New York, 1986
Population Growth and Policies in Mega-cities, Metro Manila	United Nations, DIESA, New York, 1986
Population Growth and Policies in Mega-cities, Bombay	United Nations, DIESA, New York, 1986
Population Growth and Policies in Mega-cities, Delhi	United Nations, DIESA, New York, 1986
Population Growth and Policies in Mega-cities, Dhaka	United Nations, DIESA, New York, 1987
Population Growth and Policies in Mega-cities, Bangkok	United Nations, DIESA, New York, 1987
Population Growth and Policies in Mega-cities, Karachi	United Nations, DIESA, New York, 1988
The State of World Population	United Nations Fund for Population Activities, New York, 1986
Environmental Issues in Urban Management, A Programme for Research Policy Formulation and Technical Cooperation to Address Urban Environmental Issues in Developing Countries	The World Bank, Infrastructure and Urban Development Department, Washington, D.C., 1989
The Metropolis Era	Mattei Dogan and John D. Kasarda, Sage Publications, 1988
In the Shadow of the City	Trudy Harpham, Tim Lusty, and Patrick Vaughan, Oxford University Press, 1989

Table A–4 **Urban water supply coverage by region, 1980–1990**

Region	1980			1990		
	Total urban population (in millions)	Urban population unserved by water supply (in millions)	Percentage unserved	Total urban population (in millions)	Urban population unserved by water supply (in millions)	Percentage unserved
Africa	119.77	20.36	17.0	202.54	26.33	13.0
Latin America and the Caribbean	236.72	42.61	18.0	324.08	42.13	13.0
Asia and the Pacific	549.44	148.35	27.0	761.18	175.07	23.0
Western Asia	27.54	1.38	5.0	44.42	0.17	3.85
Total	933.47	212.70	22.8	1,332.22	243.70	18.3

Source: United Nations, "Achievements of the International Drinking Water Supply and Sanitation Decade 1981–1990," Report of the Economic and Social Council (New York, July 1990).

Table A–5 **Urban sanitation coverage by region, 1980–1990**

Region	1980			1990		
	Total urban population (in millions)	Urban population unserved by sanitation (in millions)	Percentage unserved	Total urban population (in millions)	Urban population unserved by sanitation (in millions)	Percentage unserved
Africa	119.77	41.92	35.0	202.54	42.53	21.0
Latin America and the Caribbean	236.72	52.08	22.0	324.08	68.06	21.0
Asia and the Pacific	549.44	192.30	35.0	761.18	266.41	35.0
Western Asia	27.54	5.78	21.0	44.42	0.0	0.0
Total	933.47	292.08	31.3	1,332.22	377.00	28.3

Source: United Nations, *Prospects of World Urbanization, 1988* (New York, 1989).

Table A–6 **Number, aggregate population, and percentage of total urban population of cities of 2 million and more, 1985**

Class (in millions)	Number of cities: World	Number of cities: Less developed regions	Population in millions: World	Population in millions: Less developed regions	Percentage of total urban population: World	Percentage of total urban population: Less developed regions
10.0 and over	11	7	140.7	85.5	7.0	7.4
7.5–9.9	9	5	77.2	42.5	3.9	3.7
5.0–7.4	10	8	61.7	49.7	3.1	4.3
4.0–4.9	10	7	44.4	31.1	2.2	2.7
3.0–3.9	14	6	47.8	20.5	2.4	1.8
2.5–2.9	27	18	74.0	49.2	3.7	4.2
2.0–2.4	19	9	41.5	20.2	2.1	1.7
Total	100	60	487.3	298.7	24.4	25.8
Urban total			(1,997)	(1,185)		

Source: United Nations, *Prospects of World Urbanization, 1988* (New York, 1989).

Notes

1. World Bank, *World Development Report 1990* (New York: Oxford University Press, 1990).
2. World Bank, Policy Planning and Research Staff, FY 89 Sector Review Urban Development Operations, *Reaching the Poor Through Urban Operations* (Washington, D.C., Nov. 1989); John P. Lea and John M. Courtney, eds., *Cities in Conflict: Studies in the Planning and Management of Asian Cities* (Washington, D.C.: World Bank, 1985); and *Report of the Task Force on Poverty Alleviation* (Washington, D.C.: World Bank, April 1988).
3. International Monetary Fund, *The Implications of Fund-Supported Adjustment Programmes for Poverty: Experiences in Selected Countries* (Washington, D.C., 1988).
4. World Bank, *Reaching the Poor* (see note 2 above).
5. United Nations Centre for Human Settlements, *Shelter and Urbanization*, World Habitat Day Information Kit, Nairobi, October 1990.
6. Yue-man Yeung, "Provision of Urban Services in Asia: The Role of People-Based Mechanism," in Hidehiko Sazanami, ed., *Regional Development Dialogue*, vol. 6, no. 2, pp. 148–169 (Nagoya: United Nations Centre for Regional Development, 1985).
7. Yue-man Yeung and T.G. McGee, eds., *Community Participation in Delivering Urban Services in Asia* (Ottawa: IDRC, 1986).
8. United Nations, *Prospects of World Urbanization 1988* (New York, 1989).
9. World Bank, *Reaching the Poor* (see note 2 above).
10. World Bank, "Report of the Task Force on Poverty Alleviation" (Draft, 1988).
11. Janice Perlman, "Mega-Cities: Global Urbanization and Innovation" (Paper presented at the International Workshop on Improving Urban Management Policies, East West Center, Honolulu, January 1989).

15

Myths of environmental management and the urban poor

Yok-shiu F. Lee

Fellow, Program on Environment, East-West Center, Honolulu

Introduction

Deteriorating environmental conditions in cities throughout the developing world are threatening the positive role of cities as engines of economic growth, as well as the health of urban dwellers – the poor in particular – who are exposed to increasingly high levels of air and water pollution and a growing volume of solid waste that remains uncollected or untreated. Government policies and actions thus far have failed to ameliorate the harmful effects of growing environmental problems that result from the combined stress of an increasing rate of urban population growth, accelerating demands for energy and natural resources, intensified land development, and land-use conflicts that are typical of rapidly changing urban regions. Underlying many of the inappropriate and ineffective actions by governments and international agencies is a set of questionable judgements regarding the nature of the problem of urban environmental degradation and the urban poor.

An earlier version of this article was presented at an International Meeting and Workshop on Urban Community-Based Environmental Management in Asia at Mahidol University, Bangkok, October 1991.

There are at least six major policy areas in which the perceptions of public officials in developing countries and international agencies are at odds with the reality of environmental deterioration and the urban poor, who must daily cope with worsening living conditions. While this is understandable given the social distance between the public officials and the urban poor, the policies that flow from the misconceptions have had devastating consequences, not only for the low-income groups but for entire cities as well. Unfortunately, the attitudes and approaches of both governments and aid agencies have largely developed into myths that have proved hard to eradicate. It is therefore of value to illuminate these myths so that future policies can be well grounded in reality and better positioned to address the stated objectives. Before we examine in detail the six myths of environmental management and the urban poor, it is instrumental to review the scope and nature of urban environmental problems.

Urban environmental problems

"Urban environment" refers to the "physical, social, economic, political and institutional features of the ecosystems that surround and support human life and ultimately determine the quality of life" in cities [3, p. 1]. Defined as such, the notion of urban environment is human-centred, and it concerns both the built environment of the city and the natural environment that provides resources for the city and is in turn affected by urban growth.

Scale of urban environmental problems

The conventional approach to examining urban environmental management issues is to organize discussions in terms of sectoral categories such as air, water, sanitation, and solid waste [44]. Focusing on these sectoral issues is understandable, perhaps unavoidable, because they reflect the way by which data are classified and government agencies are organized. But exclusive use of these sectoral categories has the unfortunate tendency of often channelling discussion into technical areas in which critical social and institutional factors are ignored [25].

An alternative approach is to classify environmental impacts of urbanization on a spatial scale. In the figure, the urban environmental issues remain sectorally oriented but are spatially distinguished. At each spatial scale, the characteristic problems and the related infrastructure and services needed to address such problems are spe-

Spatial scale	Household workplace	Neighbourhood / community	Metropolitan area	Region	Continent / planet
Key infrastructure and services	Shelter Water storage On site sanitation Garbage storage Stove ventilation	Piped water Sewerage Garbage collection Drainage Streets/lanes	Industrial parks Roads Interceptors Treatment plants Outfalls Landfills	Highways Water sources Power plants	
Characteristic problems	Substandard housing Lack of water No sanitation Disease vectors Indoor air pollution	Excreta laden water/soils Trash dumping Flooding Noise/stress Natural disasters	Traffic congestion Accidents Ambient air pollution Toxic dumps	Water pollution Ecological areas lost	Acid rain Global warming Ozone layer

Spatial scale of urban environmental issues (Source: ref. 3)

cified. The consideration of the spatial scale of impacts reveals several important issues for developing countries:

– health impacts are greater and more immediate at the household or community level and tend to diminish in intensity as the spatial scale increases;
– equity issues arise in relation to (a) the provision of basic services at the household or community scale and (b) intertemporal externalities at the regional and global scale – particularly the intergenerational impacts implicit in non-sustainable resource use and global environmental issues; and
– levels of responsibility and decision making should correspond to the scale of impact, but existing jurisdictional arrangements often violate this principle. [4]

Urbanization, environmental degradation, and urban poverty

In examining environmental problems associated with rapid urbanization in developing countries, it is necessary to realize that urban growth has also been associated with positive impacts on the economy and the environment. From an economic standpoint, urbanization has been closely linked with economies of scale from the centralization of capital, technology, and skilled labour and improved standards of living from higher household incomes. From an environmental perspective, urbanization has historically been associated with declining birth rates, which reduce the pressure for the unsound use of agricultural land and natural resources. The higher population densities in cities also lead to lower per-capita cost of providing energy, transportation, water, sewerage, waste treatment, and other services [49].

However, population growth and economic activities in cities strain the natural resource base in and around cities and they generate ever increasing amounts of waste that is beyond the capacity of urban authorities to dispose of and beyond the capacity of nature to absorb [41]. The inability of many local and municipal governments in developing countries to provide adequate infrastructure and services has led to the degradation of the living and natural environment in and around cities. Less than 60 per cent of the urban population in developing countries have access to adequate sanitation, and only one-third are connected to sewer systems [55]. Moreover, the collection and disposal of household garbage is a persistent problem for local authorities. Uncollected waste ends up in neighbourhood dumps, where disease-carrying insects and rodents proliferate, or in street drains, where it causes flooding and traffic obstruction. Solid wastes collected and put in open dumps often lead to groundwater pollution.

Industrial wastes pose another pressing problem for city governments, which usually have inadequate waste management capacity. It is difficult to monitor discharges and ensure that hazardous wastes do not end up in city sewers. The disposal problem is compounded by the fact that almost all developing countries do not have facilities or sites to treat hazardous wastes [3].

Air pollution is another growing problem in large cities with poor natural ventilation and significant mobile or stationary emissions. Air quality in most large cities of developing countries is far below internationally accepted standards for good health [48]. Indoor air pollution is particularly serious in low-income urban communities where fuel wood is commonly used for cooking and heating purposes in poorly ventilated housing [53].

Rapid urbanization and the growth of population in cities of all sizes are also quickly encroaching on arable land in developing countrics. Between 1980 and 2000, the physical size of urban areas in the developing world is expected to double from about 8 million hectares to more than 17 million hectares [48]. Arable land will be removed from production to accommodate urban growth at the same time that demand for food and other agricultural products will increase.

These problems have different impacts on different income groups. For example, ambient air pollution is relatively "income-blind," while water-related diseases tend to affect the poor more severely. In developing countries, studies of urban health conditions reveal that significant intra-urban health differentials exist between the rich and the poor, and in many cases, children and women are most vulnerable to adverse environmental conditions [3, 19].

Pollution affects the poorest most severely because many of them live at the periphery, where manufacturing, processing, and distilling plants are built and where environmental protection is frequently the weakest. The urban poor also tend to settle on environmentally sensitive sites such as steep hillsides, flood plains, desert land or the most polluted sites near solid waste dumps and next to open drains and sewers. Such sites are often the only places where low-income groups can build or rent houses without fear of eviction. It is virtually always the poorest groups that suffer the most from floods, landslides, or other disasters that have become increasingly common occurrences in cities of developing countries.

While a lack of piped water, drains, and garbage removal service may be the main cause of deteriorating environmental conditions and of the high incidence of disease, inadequate incomes and poor diets can greatly exacerbate the health threat such conditions pose [22, 19]. Low incomes also underlie the inability to move away from dangerous and polluted residential areas. Thus, urban environmental issues in developing countries are much wider in scope than those conventionally considered by environmental groups in the West.

Myths of environmental management and the urban poor

Myth no. 1: Global environmental concern is a first world problem, not a third world issue

Most of the international attention in the 1980s has been focused on global environmental concerns, such as depletion of the ozone layer and the increasing concentration of carbon dioxide in the atmosphere. These issues of the "global commons" are increasingly well covered in the mass media. They have also come to the top of the agenda of Western governments and environmental groups.

Concern about long-term global environmental issues is no doubt overdue, but these global issues have come to dominate Western concerns as they consider environmental problems in the third world. Paradoxically, the immediate, household level environmental pollution problems associated with unprecedented urbanization in the developing countries are often ignored or given slight treatment by Western environmental groups and international agencies. This distortion is sometimes reproduced within third world nations where national environmental groups become active to save endangered species but give no consideration to the acute public health hazards and environmental pollution problems that so seriously affect the health and well-being of many of their nation's less fortunate citizens [19].

The adverse effects of indoor air pollution and water-borne diseases on child mortality and women's life expectancy among the urban poor are of a global significance as great as that of the destruction of tropical rain forests. In immediate human terms they may be the most urgent of all worldwide environmental problems. Even modern toxic pollution concerns may be of less immediate priority than traditional fecal contamination in many cities in the third world, because for those without basic sanitation services, human excreta is still at the top of the list of toxic wastes [3]. The immediate threats to the urban poor of hazardous household airborne pollutants and inadequate sanitation, therefore, exceed the adverse effects of global warming or even vehicular pollution [8].

At least 600 million people living in urban areas of the third world are estimated to be housed in what might be termed health and life threatening homes and neighbourhoods. Virtually all the homes and neighbourhoods of poorer groups share two characteristics that have serious health impacts: the presence in the environment of pathogenic micro-organisms, and overcrowded housing conditions. Poor people die young in the third world. Among poorer households, a child is 40–50 times more likely to die before the age of five than a child born in a Western nation [7]. These facts about the urban poor are hidden, however, because figures for their health status are often omitted from the official statistics or presented as aggregated data along with the well-off population that enjoys a relatively good standard of health.

In spite of the evidence, environmental problems faced by the urban poor in third world nations have received only slight attention from international agencies and environmental groups. The lack of interest of environmental groups in urban environmental issues in the third world may stem in part from the revival of the "anti-city syndrome," which identifies the city as the centre of all the ills of society and as opposed to the virtues of rural life. Environmentalists often see the large cities in developing countries as symptomatic of environmental decay: they are overcrowded, congested, polluted, and have grown out of proportion to their ecological settings. In the view of many environmental activists, the city became

> an alien or inimical concept: something "other" from the environment, an embarrassing and inexplicable blur on the ecological map, or something decisively hostile to the cause of environmental conservation and enhancement: a place of concentration and irradiation of some of the worst agents of ecological degradation – air and water pollution, blight, noise, and overconsumption of nonrenewable resources. [18]

The scope of global environmental policy and action over the past 15 years has been focused more on large-scale international issues of managing the global commons than on the environmental conditions facing the urban poor worldwide. It is time to recognize that the plight of the urban poor is a global environmental problem.

Myth no. 2: Environmental management can be ignored in the "early stages of development"

There are various factors that prevent third world governments from taking action on pollution control. The most important is their overriding concern to expand industrial production and the exploitation of natural resources to create jobs and for export earnings. Pressing problems with repayment of debts, in particular, have increased pressure on governments to encourage foreign investors, increase exports, and defer considerations about the environmental consequences of their actions [19].

The indifference of governments to environmental issues in many third world nations, an attitude that also prevails among many developed country governments, can also be traced to the belief that environment and development are opposed to each other: development can only be achieved at the price of an increased level of pollution and some environmental damage. Conversely, if pollution is to be controlled or reduced, development will inevitably diminsh or fail. Many developing countries believe that the path to development is to follow the "Japan model": "get dirty, get rich, and clean up later."

The idea that environmental quality and pollution control are expensive luxuries to be pursued when a country is rich enough is in part based on the perception that pollution is a reversible process that can be handled at reasonable cost once governments decide to allocate resources to this end. This view is not necessarily valid, however. Certain environmental impacts are not reversible, and some environmental pollution problems can only be reversed in the very long term and at high costs. For example, the depletion of groundwater can lead to permanent changes in the characteristics of the aquifer, such as salt water intrusion in coastal regions and land subsidence. Contamination of groundwater by chemicals can take years or decades to correct [10]. Moreover, health effects from environmental pollution can be both long-term and insidious. Toxic elements can build up slowly in humans and lead to irreversible adverse health impacts [39]. More importantly for developing countries, deferred pollution control expenditures, like deferred maintenance, can build up and reach unmanageable costs.

Gradually, in the past decade or so, some developing countries have established ministries or departments of environment, and a few countries have passed comprehensive legislation relating to the environment. The major problem typical of many of these countries is implementation [6]. Often the environmental laws and ordinances are not enforced in developing countries because the responsible agencies have very few trained staff, insufficient authority, and little or no equipment for measurement and analysis. Some countries have attempted to decentralize responsibility for environmental management to urban authorities of the largest cities and capitals of provinces. Such a decentralization of responsibilities, however, has usually not been accompanied by a real transfer of power. Neither are funds allocated to the lower levels of government nor are the lower levels granted the financial authority to raise funds for environmental management [19].

Myth no. 3: Environmental management is too expensive

Many third world governments say they cannot afford environmental management measures because they are too expensive. Experience in the past 15 years, however, informs us that for most industrial operations, a substantial reduction in pollution emissions is possible for a small fraction of production costs. Some industries could actually reduce cost or increase profits through recycling of materials and reclamation from waste [19]. Moreover, evidence accumulated over the past decade or so shows that appropriate urban infrastructure and services are not expensive and a high proportion of costs can be recovered by charges that even many of the poor can afford [7].

With few exceptions, the technologies currently adopted in urban infrastructure in developing countries are the same as those employed in the developed countries: piped water, full internal plumbing, and conventional water-borne sewerage [36]. However, such services tend to be provided only to those sectors of the urban population with developed country incomes. Conventional wisdom suggests that aid-giving and consultants from developed countries encourage the use of costly imported equipment and materials that are produced in their land of origin. Gakenheimer and Brando [17] argue, however, that there are strong influences within the developing countries themselves – an "unintentional conspiracy" – that insists on unnecessarily high standards. These include: engineers who are familiar with modern solutions, government agencies that pursue failure-proof and maintenance-free construction, and politicians who wish to avoid being accused of "demodernizing" services. Taken together, these actions and inactions result in an unfortunate tendency toward increasingly high and costly standards.

The solutions to many of the existing urban environmental pollution problems that affect the urban poor the most require no great technological breakthroughs and expensive imported equipment. Rather, the application of relatively well-known, low-cost technologies and alternative planning practices can lead to great improvements as long as the interests of the urban poor are taken into consideration.

For example, in many cities in the third world, around 50 per cent of the water that is treated and distributed at public expense is not accounted for by sales [26]. There is no record of it having been delivered to consumers and it does not earn revenue for the water supply authorities. World Bank research suggests that, as a rule, if more than 25 per cent of the treated water is not accounted for, a programme to control the losses may prove to be cost-effective [47]. Implementing a formal control policy to reduce both physical losses (through leakage detection and repair) and non-physical losses (through improved management practices) will typically cost US$5–10 per capita. Studies have shown that savings and increased revenue will repay this cost within one or two years [35]. Investment to improve the performance of existing assets is thus highly cost-effective.

Another low-cost and unorthodox approach to improving water supply services to the urban poor is to provide assistance to water vendors to make their service more efficient. In both Bangkok and Jakarta, about one-third of the city's population has to purchase water from vendors at a much more expensive price than tap water [26]. Compared with further investment in expanding the formal water supply system, a strategy to increase the number and efficiency of vendors might produce a more rapid and replicable improvement in the standard of service. Since most of the purchasers are the urban poor, the intervention could thus also be an effective form of aid to the poorest [7].

A full-scale attack on urban sanitation problems in developing countries would require huge increases in investment only if third world governments insist upon adopting conventional water-borne sewerage. Conventional sewerage is inappropriate for use in low-income communities because of its high costs, which are in turn the result of the use of inappropriate construction standards [34, 40]. World Bank research has demonstrated that a wide range of household and community systems could greatly improve the sanitation conditions at costs affordable to the urban poor [38]. The solutions involve low-cost, locally manufactured hardware (plumbing, sanitary sheds, concrete caps for pit latrines) that can be installed using labour-intensive techniques. The central technologies range from improved ventilated pit latrines to simple modifications of standard sewerage designs that reduce diameters, excavation, inspection chambers, and other standard specifications [8]. The total annual cost per household of several of these options was only one-tenth to one-twentieth that of the conventional sewerage systems. Most demand far less water to allow for their efficient operation, and it is possible to install one of the lowest cost systems initially and then upgrade it gradually [19].

Solid waste is an another persistent urban environmental pollution problem whose harmful effects would be mitigated without incurring expensive technologies. In many third world cities, a large number of families depend for their subsistence on urban waste [16]. In the course of their work in collecting and recycling waste, they are exposed to a wide variety of health threats. Such hazards include both traditional health risks of bacteria and disease, which can be tackled by basic public hygiene measures, and modern risks associated with the presence of hazardous and toxic substances in urban wastes, which pose a more serious problem [39]. We do not know the types and quantities of hazardous materials that are contaminating the poor who engage in picking and recycling wastes. The separation of household and industrial wastes at source through administrative and planning measures, which do not require huge sums of investment, could reduce the risks of low-income households from contamination by toxic materials.

Myth no. 4: Poverty "causes" environmental deterioration; the urban poor generate wastes that degrade their habitat

Low-income squatter settlements in the third world have often been viewed as visual symbols of "cancerous growth" on the healthy body politic, and their inhabitants are labelled with a wide variety of other stigmas [32]. A Unesco report published in 1976 depicted the urban poor as socially, economically, politically, and spatially marginal; it implied that they are incapable of improving the situation themselves. The report attributed the rapid urban growth in developing countries to

> the ever increasing migratory movement – in practice beyond control – of families from rural areas attracted by the glitter and the fallacious promises of consumer society. . . . These newcomers, potential parasites, consist in the main of large families – 8 to 10 persons – only two or three of whom are economically active; . . . squatters tend to settle on land that falls outside the scope of authorizations to build – areas regarded as unhealthy, subject to flooding, etc. [22]

Systematic research, conducted mostly in Latin American cities, reveals quite the opposite picture: that the urban poor are not marginal but socially, culturally, economically, and politically integrated into the "official" city. Socially, the squatters are quite well organized and cohesive and make wide use of the urban milieu and its institutions. Culturally, they are highly optimistic and aspire to better education for their children and to improving the condition of their living environment. Economically, they work hard and they build – not only their own dwellings but also much of the overall community and infrastructure facilities. Politically, they are neither apathetic nor radical. They are aware of and actively participate in those aspects of politics that directly affect their livelihood the most [32].

In essence, the urban poor are not separate from, or on the margin of, society, but are tightly integrated into the system, albeit in a severely asymmetrical manner detrimental to their own interests. "Rather than being passively marginal in terms of their own attitudes and behavior, they are being actively marginalized by the system and by public policy" [32].

Unfavourable stereotypes about the urban poor that tend to "blame the victim" are very difficult to eradicate, however. Despite the pressures created by rapid urban population growth, most third world governments have given relatively low priority during the last three decades to the provision of appropriate, affordable housing and infrastructure for their urban populations, particularly the poorer households [52]. The result is that the majority of urban residents have *no alternative* but to live in self-built settlements or in dilapidated tenements.

The environmental pollution problems evident within the homes and around the neighbourhoods of so many poor households in third world cities are a direct result of the refusal by government to provide basic services. In order to bring down housing costs, low-income households have to make sacrifices in the nature and structure of accommodation. And they usually decide to make sacrifices in environmental quality. Although this may result in higher health risks and considerable inconvenience, these are much less important for immediate economic survival than other items [19].

In the developing countries, the true city builders are the urban poor. Their largely self-built houses are the largest source of new accommodation, but they are systematically denied access to environmental amenities and services. As such, the problems of urban environmental degradation are not the results of the urban poor's attempt to make room in cities for their survival, but reflect the inability (or unwillingness) of a legal and institutional structure to cope with the needs of the population and the tasks of providing adequate basic services.

Myth no. 5: The urban poor should be more self-reliant in managing their living environment

There are by now numerous case-studies describing the development of the different illegal or informal settlements where the urban poor have built most of the new housing stock in the developing countries in the last three decades or so. These case-studies describe the ingenuity with which new housing has been built at low monetary cost and with scarce resources; they also reveal a sophisticated capacity among the urban poor to organize and plan [7]. But individual actions and collective organizations among low-income households cannot address environmental pollution problems resulting from the lack of piped water supply, sewers, drainage, and services to collect garbage without some form of outside support.

The idea of self-help in infrastructure and services is largely borrowed from the experience of self-help in housing construction without much critical thinking on the transferability of that experience. There are important differences between housing and infrastructure – for example, in terms of their relationships to individual households and their requirements for community coordination – that warrant a careful reconsideration of the question of the extent of self-help in the provision of infrastructure and services among the urban poor. Many low-income households are willing to invest in their own houses because they represent household assets that have resale and rental income value. On the other hand, infrastructure such as piped water supply systems, drains, and sanitation facilities are community assets and common property that cannot be easily translated into individual household possessions. That is, whereas putting money into housing could be a form of acquisition of capital by individual households, there is no strong economic incentive for individual households to invest in community-wide infrastructure.

Moreover, the construction of self-help housing allows much flexibility for the individual households. As income opportunities expand and diminish, housing work can stop and start and construction materials can be acquired piecemeal over a long period of time. However, the installation and operation of infrastructure through self-help schemes require, among other things, close coordination and cooperation among all the household members of the community, which are sometimes difficult to secure. Therefore, the most striking negative perception of self-help settlements is often not associated with the self-built houses, which are painted and decorated, but with the lack of infrastructure and public facilities, which are dependent upon public investment well beyond the capabilities of the self-helpers themselves [32].

Furthermore, there is a fundamental constraint – access to land by the urban poor – that greatly limits the extent of self-help schemes in both housing and infrastructure [12]. We do not yet have a complete picture of how public policies and regulations shape the system of housing provision, but we can be sure from the evidence we have so far that public interventions are critical: roads, land tenure regularization, and recognition of community organization all affect the value of real estate throughout the entire city, including marginal settlements. Use of land for upper-income developments will affect the price of accommodation in marginal settlements in the same city [31]. The root cause of informal or "illegal" settlements is an urban land market that, through prices or government decisions, does not allocate land to the poor for housing [28].

The lack of access to land or an adequate supply of land by the urban poor often limits the scale of provision of infrastructure. The components in a good physical environment require physical space for their installation: neither piped water systems nor latrines can be provided without land being made available. The cleaning of drains and the collection of garbage is greatly facilitated if some minimal planning of pathways has been undertaken [2].

In short, without the right kind of technical advice, access to cheap credit, land, and appropriate equipment and materials, a community's capacity to install or improve infrastructure and services is limited. Government action could be needed to greatly increase the supply and reduce the cost of all the components of the basic infrastructure, including land sites within easy reach of employment opportunities and construction materials.

Myth no. 6: The only choices in managing the urban environment are the market and the State

Privatization and the decentralization of government have recently been promoted in many developing countries and by international agencies as two mainstream approaches to managing in urban environment [24, 14, 5]. Participatory management by non-governmental organizations (NGOs) and community-based organizations (CBOs) has been given slight attention in official documents, and their potential contribution to reviving the environmental basis of urban life, for the poor particularly, is largely neglected by third world authorities [27].

Many governments and aid agencies have recently subscribed to a usually overstated idea that privatization can improve the provision of infrastructure and services to low-income groups in most cities of the third world. The justification for privatization given by its proponents is often that the government is short of capital. The private sector, they contend, will provide the capital required to expand and improve services. But in most third world cities, many of the poorer households already rely upon the private sector for accommodation and certain services. Privately and illegally developed rental housing is the main source of accommodation. The lack of infrastructure and services in these illegal subdivisions supplied by these private developers do not support the idea that privatization will necessarily improve the environmental conditions for the urban poor [20].

Moreover, private companies are selective in their provision of services. They are reluctant to improve and extend piped water supplies, sewers, drains, and roads as one package, especially to low-income communities, although the simultaneous installation of these infrastructures would result in substantial cost savings. Water supply is the most attractive because people pay as they consume and often the user also pays for the initial cost of connection. Payment for services can be easily enforced because supplies can be cut off. Garbage collection may also be attractive because the capital investment to set up the service is not high and the services can be stopped if households do not pay [37]. However, the use of drains and roads cannot be terminated if households stop payment.

Furthermore, privatization is favoured in part in the belief that the private sector can operate more efficiently than the public sector in providing basic services such as solid waste collection, provided that there are contestable markets and competition [5]. But the privatization of natural monopolies such as piped water, sewers, and drains presents special regulatory problems for governments because there are no competitive pressures to help keep down prices and improve quality of service. Once a piped water supply system or a sewer system is built, it is virtually impossible for another company to compete by building another water or sewer system [20].

Decentralization of government functions to the local and municipal authorities is nowadays frequently referred to as an important strategy for meeting the needs of the urban population. There is, however, a large gap between the rhetoric and actual policy actions regarding strengthening the role of local governments. Lower levels of government have been given greater legal and institutional responsibilities for the planning, provision, and maintenance of urban infrastructure and services. Almost all municipal authorities in the third world, however, lack the power to collect enough revenue or mobilize local resources to fulfil their responsibilities. Local governments are usually highly constrained by central governments in their power to increase revenue [51]. The result is often ironic: middle- and upper-income groups receive water supply, sewer, and garbage collection services at less than the full costs of their provision, whereas the urban poor receive no public service and no publicly funded infrastructure.

Experience in the past three decades indicates that neither government nor the conventional private sector has contributed much to the installation of basic residential infrastructure or to the provision of basic services to the poor in the third world [20, 22]. In most cases, the urban poor have been provided access to water, sanitation, and drainage through innovative projects that have been conceived and carried out by non-governmental or community organizations. They have shown how services and facilities that meet the needs of the poorer households can be provided at low per capita costs and with good cost recovery [20]. Such innovative projects have reached only a tiny proportion of those in need, however.

There is tremendous potential in mobilizing NGOs and CBOs to address the concerns of local level environmental pollution problems. Part of the reason for such an emphasis on local resources is based upon the understanding that most third world governments will remain financially strapped and the low-income groups will mostly remain poor. Another reason relates to the positive experience of the informal cooperative systems among the poor in the management and control of local urban environments. As demonstrated in the work of the International Drinking Water Decade, the success of projects is highly dependent upon the degree of community participation in the projects and on the acceptance by the users of responsibilities for operation and maintenance [29].

Community participation as an ideal has been accepted almost universally, yet there are huge gaps between the understanding and the actual practice of such a concept in project development. It is praised by the right as a way to promote entrepreneurship and self-reliance, and by the left as a process of consciousness-raising and mass mobilization [46]. Between these two positions is a pragmatic view that enhanced communication through a carefully structured participatory mechanism will result in better designed and more cost-effective projects. For the poor, it means more direct attention to local level problems and potentials. For the lender, it means direct access to local knowledge about specific conditions in the project area.

Unfortunately, among many government planners, "participation" becomes a euphemism for getting the people in the communities to accept what has already been decided by the authorities. Thus participation in such a circumstance becomes nominal and does not actively involve the community in the decision-making process whose outcome could affect them directly. Community participation is frequently seen as merely the provision of residents' labour. In its most complete form, however, it places planning and final decision-making power in the hands of the residents themselves, usually in the form of neighbourhood organizations [42].

Conclusion

If present trends of urbanization continue and the attitudes of third world governments and international agencies continue to be dominated by these myths of environmental management and the urban poor, the quality of many basic services such as water, sanitation, and garbage disposal will deteriorate further and the problem of contamination of urban living environments will be aggravated. Despite the lack of comprehensive scientific data on the impacts of urban environmental problems, there is a growing consensus that in the third world, "the largest and most pressing environmental issue is to improve the housing and living environment of the underprivileged majority of citizens by reducing or eliminating the most serious health hazards present within their homes, workplaces and neighborhoods" [19].

Environmental improvements in developing countries – especially those often preferred by higher income groups – could be costly, even though low-cost appropriate technologies are readily available. Efforts to address urban environmental pollution problems must make room for the rights of the poor to be informed about environmental threats, to define their own priorities, and to participate fully in the decision-making process on environmental matters. Partly because of the false myths that have negatively affected the perception of environmental management and the urban poor in the developing countries, however, we are still very much behind in the development of a body of knowledge necessary to inspire and substantiate alternative approaches to urban environmental management.

The alternative approaches – "community-based approaches," "popular approaches," or "bottom-up approaches" – recognize the limited role of government in managing the urban environment at the lower spectrum of society. They call for governments to begin to consolidate a process by which the initiatives of citizens and community organizations are encouraged, supported, and built upon [11, 19]. There is no lack of examples of innovative *joint* government-community programmes to improve infrastructure and service provisions [20]. The problem is that these examples are the exceptions and they are not currently the conventional approach.

The focus of attention on the neighbourhood and household levels is opening up new, largely unexplored fronts. One of the limiting factors that have prevented the further elaboration of alternative approaches to urban environmental management is that there are knowledge gaps in fundamental areas, such as the nature of "coping mechanisms," kinship networks, reciprocal exchange, and sharing and bartering, that reduce risk and make survival possible for low-income households and neighbourhoods. Although collective self-help could have resulted in positive changes in the living environments, we know very little about how user-developed systems evolve in low-income communities where real barriers to communal action are common [15, 36]. For example, unconventional sanitation systems have recently been installed with apparent success in low-income communities in parts of some developing countries; we still need to find out how well the users of such systems are coping with the maintenance tasks [50].

Despite a steadily growing body of literature on urban environmental problems in developing countries, information available to researchers thus far is still relatively scarce, with documentation often supplied by developing country non-governmental organizations and citizen's groups rather than by international and national agencies. Recent case-studies of urban environmental problems in developing countries provide us some useful data for future analysis [9, 23, 33]. However, all of these studies are good at depicting the symptoms but weak on analysing the societal processes that have led to the creation and persistence of urban environmental problems; they tend to focus primarily on describing regional and metropolitan impacts of urban and industrial growth on air and water quality without going much into an analysis of the social and institutional context within which many urban environmental issues arise.

The elaboration of alternative approaches will benefit from a discussion at a somewhat lower level of abstraction in which the intermingling of social and institutional considerations is frankly taken into account. One component of an information and research strategy should probably focus on developing a grounded understanding of urban environmental issues by working in close collaboration with the individuals and community organizations themselves. It needs their inputs to define the categories of analysis as well as to verify the findings. This means qualitative data, interviews, and a greater use of case-studies upon which to draw general lessons.

Acknowledgements

I would like to thank Professor Mike Douglass and Professor Kem Lowry of the Department of Urban and Regional Planning at the University of Hawaii for sharing with me their thoughts on this topic while we conducted a research project on community-based urban environmental management in 1991. This article has benefited enormously from their insights. Discussion with Dr. Jim Nickum and Dr. Kirk Smith, two of my colleagues at the Environment and Policy Institute, has contributed to my understanding of institutional issues and environmental processes, respectively. Regina Gregory provided useful editorial assistance. Angelina Lau helped prepare the manuscript in an efficient and pleasant manner.

References

1 Anonymous. "Summary of Discussions on Urban Growth and the Environment." 1990.

2 Bapat, Meera, and Nigel Crook. "Behind the Technical Approach to Slum Improvement." *Waterlines* 8 (1989), no.1: 24–26.

3 Bartone, Carl. "Sustainable Responses to Growing Urban Environmental Crises." Paper presented at the IULA World Development Forum, Brussels, 4–6 April 1990.

4 ———. "Annotated Outline of a Report on Strategic Options for Managing the Urban Environment." Washington, D.C.: World Bank, 1991. Draft.

5 Bartone, Carl, et al. "Private Sector Participation in Municipal Solid Waste Service: Experience in Latin America." Washington, D.C.: World Bank, 1990. Mimeo.

6 Bower, Blair, et al. "Urbanization and Environmental Quality." In: *Urbanization and the Environment in Developing Countries*. Compiled by the Office of Housing and Urban Programs, U.S. Agency for International Development, Washington, D.C., 1990, pp. 1–39.

7 Cairncross, Sandy, et al. 1990. "New Partnerships for Healthy Cities." In: Jorge Hardoy et al., eds. *The Poor Die Young*. London: Earthscan, 1990, pp. 245–265.

8 Campbell, Tim. "Environmental Dilemmas and the Urban Poor." In: Jeffery Leonard, ed. *Environment and the Poor: Development Strategies for a Common Approach*. New Brunswick: Transaction Books, 1989, pp. 165–187.

9 CSE (Center for Science and Environment). "The Environmental Problems Associated with India's Major Cities." *Environment and Development* 1 (1989), no. 1: 7–15.

10 Dixon, John. Personal communications, 1991.

11 Douglass, Mike. "Poverty and the Urban Environment in Asia: Circuits of Production, the State and the Household Economy." Paper prepared for a Meeting of the Working Groups on Analytical Approaches to Urban Environmental Issues, Environment and Policy Institute, East-West Center, Honolulu, September 1990.

12 ———. "Poverty and the Urban Environment in Asia: Access Empowerment and Community-Based Management." Paper prepared for an International Meeting and Workshop on Urban Community-Based Environmental Management in Asia, Mahidol University, Bangkok, October 1991.

13 ESCAP (Economic and Social Commission for Asia and the Pacific). *State of the Environment in Asia and the Pacific 1990*. Bangkok: ESCAP, 1990.

14 Foster, David. "Viewing Environmental Protection as Investment in Urban Infrastructure." In: *Urbanization and the Environment in Developing Countries*. Compiled by the Office of Housing and Urban Programs, U.S. Agency for International Development, Washington, D.C., 1990, pp. 65–86.

15 Friedlander, Paul. "Water for the Urban Poor." *Waterlines* 9 (1990), no. 1: 6–8.

16 Furedy, Christine. "Social Considerations in Solid Waste Management in Asian Cities." *Regional Development Dialogue* 10 (1989), no. 3: 13–35.

17 Gakenheimer, R., and C.H.J. Brando. "Infrastructure Standards." In: Lloyd

Rodwin, ed. *Shelter, Settlement, and Development*. Boston: Allen & Unwin, 1987, pp. 133–150.

18 Garau, Pietro. "Urbanization and Eco-development." Paper prepared for the International Meeting on Environment and Development, 24–26 March 1988. Milan.

19 Hardoy, Jorge, and David Satterthwaite. *Squatter Citizen*. London: Earthscan, 1989.

20 ———. "The Future City." In: Jorge Hardoy et al., eds. *The Poor Die Young*. London: Earthscan, 1990, pp. 228–244.

21 Hardoy, Jorge, Sandy Cairncross, and David Satterthwaite, eds. *The Poor Die Young; Housing and Health in Third World Cities*. London: Earthscan, 1990.

22 Harpham, Trudy, et al., eds. *In the Shadow of the City; Community Health and the Urban Poor*. Oxford: Oxford University Press, 1988.

23 Jimenez, Rosario, and Sister Aida Velasquez. "Metropolitan Manila: A Framework for Its Sustained Development." *Environment and Urbanization* 1 (1989), no. 1: 51–58.

24 LaNier, Royce, et al. "Urban Environmental Management in Developing Countries." In: USAID, ed. *Urbanization and the Environment in Developing Countries*. Washington, D.C.: Office of Housing and Urban Programs, U.S. Agency for International Development, 1990, pp. 41–59.

25 Lee, Yok-shiu F. "Major Social and Institutional Factors in Examining Urban Environmental Issues in Developing Countries." Paper prepared for a Meeting of the Working Group on Analytical Approaches to Urban Environmental Issues, Environment and Policy Institute, East-West Center, Honolulu, September 1990.

26 ———. "Water Supply and Sanitation in Cities in Developing Countries in Asia and the Pacific." In: Jim Nickum and William Easter, eds. *Water Use Conflicts in Asian Metropolises*. Boulder, Colo.: Westview Press, forthcoming.

27 Lowry, Kem. "Community-Level Urban Environmental Management: Towards a Research Agenda." Paper prepared for an International Meeting and Workshop on Urban Community-Based Environmental Management in Asia, Mahidol University, Bangkok, October 1991.

28 McAuslan, Patrick. *Urban Land and Shelter for the Poor*. London: Earthscan, 1985.

29 Najlis, Pierre, and Anthony Edwards. "The International Drinking Water Supply and Sanitation Decade in Retrospect and Implications for the Future." *Natural Resources Forum* 15 (1991), no. 2: 110–117.

30 Oberai, A.S. "Problems of Urbanization and Growth of Large Cities in Developing Countries: A Conceptual Framework for Policy Analysis." International Labour Office, Population and Labour Policies Programme Working Paper, no. 169. Geneva, 1989.

31 Peattie, Lisa. "Shelter, Development, and the Poor." In: Lloyd Rodwin, ed. *Shelter, Settlement, and Development*. Boston: Allen & Unwin, 1987, pp. 263–280.

32 Perlman, Janice. "Misconceptions about the Urban Poor and the Dynamics of Housing Policy Evolution." *Journal of Planning Education and Research* 6 (1987), no. 3: 187–196.

33 Phantumvanit, Dhira, and Winai Liengcharensit. "Coming to Terms with

Bangkok's Environmental Problems." *Environment and Urbanization* 1 (1989), no. 1: 31–39.
34 Pickford, John. "Urgent Urban Water and Waste Problems." *Waterlines* 9 (1990), no. 1: 2–5.
35 Richardson, Harry. "Urban Development Issues in the Pacific Rim." In: Chuan-Fang Wang et al., eds. *Proceedings of Conference on Urban Development in the Pacific Rim*. Los Angeles, 1989, pp. 1–25.
36 Ridgley, Mark. "Services in a Colombia Shantytown: Speculations on the Limits of Collective Self-help." *Conference of Latin Americanist Geographers* 15 (1989): 56–69.
37 Rondinelli, Dennis, and John D. Kasarda. "Privatizing Public Services in Developing Countries: What Do We Know?" *Business in the Contemporary World* 3 (1991), no. 2: 102–113.
38 Sinnatamby, Gehan. "Low Cost Sanitation." In: Jorge Hardoy et al., ed. *The Poor Die Young*. London: Earthscan, 1990, pp. 127–157.
39 Smith, Kirk, and Yok-shiu Lee. "Urbanization and the Environmental Risk Transition." In: John Kasarda and Allan Parnell, eds. *Urbanization, Migration, and Development*. Newbury Park, Calif.: Sage, 1993, pp. 161–179.
40 Taylor, Kevin. "Sewerage for Low-Income Communities in Pakistan." *Waterlines* 9 (1990), no. 1: 21–24.
41 TDRI (Thailand Development Research Institute). *Urbanization and Environment: Managing the Conflict*. TDRI Year-End Conference Research Report, no. 6. Bangkok: TDRI, 1990.
42 UNCHS (United Nations Center for Human Settlements). *Global Report on Human Settlements*. Oxford: Oxford University Press, 1987.
43 ———. *A Methodological Framework of Environmental Assessment for Urban Development*. Nairobi, 1988.
44 ———. *People, Settlements, Environment and Development*. Nairobi, 1991.
45 United Nations. "Growth of the World's Megapolises." Paper prepared for Symposium on the Mega-city and the Future: Population Growth and Policy Responses, 22–25 October 1990, Tokyo.
46 *Urban Edge*. "Participation in Urban Development." 8 (1984), no. 5.
47 ———. "Tackling the Problem of 'Lost' Water.' 10 (1986), no. 6.
48 USAID (United States Agency for International Development). "Urbanization in the Developing Countries." Interim Report to Congress, 1988.
49 ———. *Urbanization and the Environment in Developing Countries*. Washington, D.C.: Office of Housing and Urban Programs, U.S. Agency for International Development, 1990.
50 Vines, Marcus, and Bob Reed. "Low-cost Unconventional Sewerage." *Waterlines* 9 (1990), no. 1: 26–29.
51 WCED (World Commission on Environment and Development). *Our Common Future*. Oxford: Oxford University Press, 1987.
52 WHO (World Health Organization). *Improving Environmental Health Conditions in Low-Income Settlements*. Geneva, 1987.
53 ———. *Urbanization and Its Implications for Child Health*. Geneva, 1988.
54 World Bank. "Summary of Discussions on Urban Growth and the Environment." Washington, D.C.: World Bank, 1990. Mimeo.
55 ———. *Environmental Assessment Sourcebook* (*Volume II: Sectoral Guidelines*). World Bank Technical Paper, no. 140. Washington, D.C., 1991.

16

Priority urban management issues in developing countries: The research agenda for the 1990s

G. Shabbir Cheema

Principal Technical Adviser, Bureau for Programme Policy and Evaluation, United Nations Development Programme, New York

Urbanization trends in developing countries

Urbanization has been taking place rapidly over the past four decades in developing countries of Asia, Africa, and Latin America [23, 22]. In 1970, the world's urban population was 1.4 billion. It is expected to reach 2.9 billion by the year 2000 and 5.1 billion by the year 2025. The urban population of the developing countries is projected to increase from 675 million in 1970 to 1.9 billion in the year 2000 and 4 billion in the year 2025. Thus, the share of the world's urban population living in the developing countries will increase dramatically over the next decades. In 1970, this share was only 49 per cent. In 1985, it was already 58 per cent. This share is expected to increase to 67 per cent in the year 2000 and 79 per cent in the year 2025.

An important feature of urbanization in the developing countries is that the rate of growth of large cities has been greater than that of small cities [12]. In 1950 the population of cities of 100,000 or more was 49 per cent of the total urban population. By 1980, it had in-

The views expressed in the paper are those of the author and not necessarily those of the UNDP.

creased to 64 per cent. While in 1950 there were only four cities with a population of 5 million or more, it is projected that in the year 2000 there will be 32 such cities, and 11 of these cities will have a population of 10 million or more.

Most of the growth in large cities is projected to take place in developing countries. The number of cities of more than 4 million inhabitants is estimated to increase to 66 by the end of the 1990s, with 50 out of these in the developing world, and to 135 by the year 2025, with 114 out of these in developing countries.

There are, however, significant variations among developing countries in the rate of growth of urban population and urban agglomerations. Africa is the least urbanized but the most rapidly urbanizing region of the world, with average urban population growth rates of about 5 per cent in the 1970s and 1980s. Though the urban population growth rates are expected to decline during the first quarter of the next century, the average growth rate is still expected to be about 3 per cent. Latin America is already the most urbanized region of the world, with 69 per cent of its population living in urban areas in 1985. The average annual rate of growth of urban population in Asia during the past three decades has been more than 3 per cent. East Asia is the most urbanized part of Asia, followed by South-East and South Asia, respectively. Because this region has some of the world's most populous countries – such as China, India, and Indonesia – the region contains a sizable urban population.

The United Nations Population Division's projections indicate that from 1975 to the year 2000, the percentage of the population living in the urban areas of developing countries will increase from 28 per cent to 44 per cent. By the end of the 1990s, it is estimated that about 42 per cent of the population in Africa, 40 per cent in Asia, and 76 per cent in Latin America will be living in cities [21].

Rural to urban migration and natural population increase are the main causes of rapid growth of urban populations in developing countries. Many factors contribute to migration from rural to urban areas: Urban areas have better employment opportunities and provide higher wage levels. Furthermore, urban areas have better education, health, and social services. Political, financial, and administrative power is usually concentrated in large cities. Finally, improvements in transportation and communication facilities have made rural people more aware of the opportunities that are available in cities to improve their economic status and the futures of their children. The most common perception of the cities by the rural population is that cities provide better opportunities for raising household income levels.

In addition to the aforementioned "pull" factors, migration from rural to urban areas has also been accelerated by increasing population pressures on agricultural land, which create unemployment in rural areas; effects of distortionary fiscal policies, which reduce incentives to live in rural areas; inability of governments in developing countries to implement agrarian reforms, which leads to continued dependency relationships and low income levels for the landless and sharecroppers in the rural settings; and lack of complementarity in macro- and micro-level economic and urban planning policies, which negatively affects optimal utilization of resources.

The role of cities

Cities in developing countries are making vital contributions to economic growth by performing crucial service and production functions. In many countries, cities account for about two-thirds of the national output. For example, the Bangkok Metropolitan Area accounts for 74 per cent of manufacturing, although it has only 10 per cent of Thailand's population. Manila, with less than 15 per cent of the country's total population, produces one-third of the country's gross national product and contains about two-thirds of all manufacturing establishments. The modernization of the agricultural sector and increase in agricultural production depend largely on the emergence and efficient functioning of a network of smaller urban centres and market towns to provide financial, marketing, and processing and distribution functions. These towns also serve as places of commerce, where modern consumer goods can be purchased by the rural populace. The creation of such networks also leads to an increase in employment opportunities [17].

In addition to the achievement of the aforementioned economic benefits, cities also contribute to the achievement of social development objectives [1]. Urbanization is related to decline in birth rates over time, as indicated by the experience of the Latin American countries. Cities also facilitate the provision of diverse career and income generating opportunities that are not found in rural areas. Other advantages of cities are increases in the level of education and socio-political awareness, and the creation of a disciplined and skilled workforce, which is the necessary condition for future growth and development.

Negative consequences of urbanization

Rapid urbanization in developing countries over the past four decades has led to several negative consequences: increasing incidents of urban poverty, inadequate access to housing and such basic urban services as primary health care and water supply, proliferation of slums and squatter settlements, and urban environmental degradation.

The World Bank estimates show that in 1980 the number of urban poor households in developing countries was 41.1 million. According to these estimates, by the end of the 1990s, more than half of the absolute poor will be concentrated in urban areas [25]. About 90 per cent of the poor households in Latin America, 40 per cent in Africa, and 45 per cent in Asia will be living in the urban areas by the year 2000. A growing proportion of residents of large cities is poor. The incidence of urban poverty has been estimated to be 60 per cent in Calcutta, 35 per cent in Manila, 64 per cent in Guatemala City, and 45 per cent in Karachi.

The provision of basic urban services has not kept pace with the rapid increase in the urban population. A vast majority of the urban poor do not have adequate access to such urban services as low-income housing, urban transport, water supply, and public health services. In urban Asia, for example, it has been estimated that the average number of persons per room is 2.17, and about one-third of all dwellings have three or more persons per room. In Calcutta, about half of the residents live in one-room shelters. An estimated 77 per cent of the households in Greater Bombay have an average of 5.3 persons per room [26]. As regards the provision of piped water to individual households, there are wide variations among the developing countries. The percentage of urban population served by water supply in 1980 was 26 per cent in Bangladesh, 35 per cent in Indonesia, and 38 per cent in Myanmar. It was more than 70 per cent, however, in India, Malaysia, Pakistan, Republic of Korea, and Singapore. The sewerage system in Asia is serving primarily higher income areas.

In Africa, too, the basic urban services are inadequate and the existing services are not adequately maintained. As Obudho [13] notes, the inadequate access to housing, education, and health services has led to the deteriorating quality of life in the East African cities. Given the present economic situation in the African countries, the prospects of governments being able to make large-scale investments to improve the access of the urban poor to basic services are dim.

For the speed with which urbanization has been taking place in developing countries of Asia, Africa, and Latin America, most municipal governments have lacked financial and administrative resources to provide basic urban services. Government investments have largely been allocated to improve middle- to high-income settlements. Left to themselves, the urban poor, however, have found informal sector mechanisms to obtain basic services. They have, in most cases, occupied government or privately owned land and built shelters with their own resources without necessarily following the building codes and standards and other government regulations. This has led to the proliferation of slums and squatter settlements in developing countries. The availability of services tends to be the lowest in these settlements [4, 18, 19]. It has been estimated that 30–50 per cent of the residents of most large Asian cities are living in such settlements. The percentage of squatters and slum dwellers has been estimated to be 70 per cent in Addis Ababa, 40 per cent in Bogotá, 67 per cent in Calcutta, and 35 per cent in Manila.

Though cities are making contributions to output and income of developing countries, rapid population growth and uncontrolled industrial development are degrading the urban environment.

While the aforementioned consequences are discernible, the costs of urbanization are difficult to measure. The literature suggests, however, that these are substantial and differ from one country to another because of, among others, differences in standards of provision, technology, and cost of construction. Regarding the optimal city size, Richardson [16] argues that while smaller cities are able to absorb urban residents at a lower per capita cost than larger cities, this advantage is offset by higher absorption costs in peripheral regions and the cost of population distribution in favour of smaller urban areas.

The inevitability of urbanization

Over the past four decades, governments in developing countries have adopted many explicit population distribution policies and programmes to deconcentrate urbanization and facilitate a more balanced spatial development. The "closed city" programmes were aimed at reducing migration to metropolitan regions through such instruments as tax incentives, limitations on investments, and demolition of squatter settlements. Rustication policies and programmes were designed to resettle urban residents in rural areas. The "accommodationist" policies and programmes attempted to improve urban housing and services and deconcentrate growth of large cities by promoting dormitory towns and satellite cities.

The governments also promoted intermediate-sized cities and regional centres by extending support services to these, improving infrastructure, and strengthening linkages between intermediate-sized and large cities. Integrated rural development programmes were implemented to provide agricultural inputs and social services, increase infrastructure investments, and improve agricultural productivity and income. Finally, "land colonization" programmes were introduced by some of the governments to resettle residents from overpopulated rural areas to frontier regions or underutilized areas. The policy instruments commonly employed for this purpose have been transfer of land titles and provision of credit and other facilities to increase productivity and income of settlers.

Experience shows that the above policies and programmes did not have a significant impact on population redistribution and, indeed, cities have continued to grow rapidly. In most cases, population redistribution was not the primary objective of the above policies and programmes. The reasons for the insignificant impact of these policies and programmes vary depending upon the economic and political context of developing countries. Two reasons, however, seem to be the most common. First, the objectives of spatial strategies were not adequately reflected in the government's sectoral decisions that shaped public and private investments [9]. Consequently, most of the programmes could not be implemented. Second, these policies could not offset market forces that overwhelmingly favoured concentration of social and economic activities in large urban centres [19].

The challenge of urban management

Because policies and programmes to control rural to urban migration and diffusion of urban population have not been successful, there is an increasing recognition that the growth of cities is inevitable and that the solutions to the problems of cities depend heavily on their effective management. Urban management is a holistic concept. It is aimed at strengthening the capacity of governments and non-governmental organizations to identify policy and programme alternatives and to implement these with optimal results. The challenge of urban management therefore is to effectively respond to the problems and issues of individual cities to enable them to perform their functions. The most common issues faced by these cities are improving financial structure and management, providing shelter and basic urban services and infrastructure, improving urban information systems, strengthening the role of the urban informal sector, and strengthening urban institutional capacities, including the role of municipal governments.

The first issue: Improving financial structure and management

Several revenue raising instruments have been suggested to improve the resource base of municipal governments [6, 14, 18, 24]. First, user charges can be an important instrument for financing capital costs of urban facilities as well as maintenance and operating expenditures for urban infrastructure and services. The main reason in favour of user charges is that without some form of cost recovery, governments in developing countries do not have adequate resources to provide urban infrastructure and services. Yet, the role of user charges needs to be examined within the context of (a) investment requirements, levels of savings, and estimated operating and maintenance requirements and (b) affordability of different income groups and political and administrative capacity of urban local governments to ensure the collection of user charges.

Second, local taxes are a critical resource raising instrument. To varying degrees, the potential for local resource generation exists in cities in property taxes, income taxes, consumption-based taxes, and automobile taxes. This requires, however, that municipal governments be authorized to levy taxes presently reserved for central/provincial governments and that their tax administration capacity, including property assessment procedures, be strengthened.

Third, tax sharing is an important instrument for financial transfers from the central to municipal governments. Experience shows that among factors that need to be considered in delineating the tax sharing arrangements among the municipalities are the need to reduce interregional disparities, the need to provide incentives for local resource mobilization, and equalization of infrastructure and services among various urban regions.

Fourth, allocation from the centre may also be made in the form of grants, subsidies, loans, and investment of equity capital. Where grants are a major percentage of revenue, the municipal government's financial autonomy would be negatively affected.

Fifth, the private sector, including non-governmental organizations (NGOs) and the informal sector, provides an important source for mobilization of resources. In some areas, urban transport for example, the private sector might have an advantage. Experience shows that a major portion of low-income housing in urban areas is financed through private domestic savings. The urban poor do not have adequate access to financial institutions, largely due to their low income levels, and the collateral arrangements and collection techniques of these institutions.

Finally, administrative capacities and political support are crucial in implementing resource mobilization programmes. Resource mobilization policies and programmes are unlikely to succeed where there is a severe shortage of trained manpower, particularly trained accountants and financial managers; where the morale of the concerned staff is low because of personnel policies and practices such as low wages and limited career opportunities; and where monitoring and evaluation systems are not effective. The implementation of resource raising strategies also requires a decentralized local government system and political support at the central and local government levels for surmounting pressures from vested interests.

Past government approaches have paid inadequate attention to capital and maintenance and operating costs of urban development programmes and to the financing measures. As Prakash [14] points out, policy makers need to examine macro questions related to economic feasibility of urban development polices as well as micro questions concerning affordability, cost recovery, and subsidy requirements. He has identified a model for national urban development investment planning. The components of the model are estimating capital investment requirements, examining preliminary feasibility of the investment programmes, preparing a perspective plan and a short-term roll-over investment programme, and assessing the affordability and adequacy of cost recovery measures.

The relative significance of the aforementioned instruments in mobilizing resources varies from one metropolitan region to another. For example, in Karachi, the revenue from locally levied taxes in 1984–1985 was about 59 per cent, shared taxes 14 per cent, local non-tax 18 per cent, other non-tax 7 per cent, and central government grants and loans 2 per cent [3]. In Calcutta, the revenue from locally levied taxes has been declining while the revenue from shared taxes has been increasing. Central government grants and loans accounted for more than 20 per cent of the average yearly revenue between 1966 and 1985 [2]. In Bangkok, the revenue from locally levied taxes in 1985 was about 53 per cent, from shared taxes 17 per cent, and from central government grants and loans about 16 per cent [8].

Decentralizing power and resources from central government to municipalities and mobilizing municipal revenue through local sources with active participation of private sector and community organizations are two of the urban development challenges facing developing countries. The agenda for future research should, therefore, concentrate on the following priority issues:

- Central-local allocation of functions, financial flows, and access to credit;
- Assignment and administration of revenue sources including user charges;
- Participation of the private, including informal, sector and community-based organizations in local revenue generation and urban management.

The second issue: Providing urban shelter, services, and infrastructure

Policy and programme responses of the governments in developing countries to the deficiencies of urban shelter, services, and infrastructure have been disjointed and ad hoc. Initially, the focus was on public housing schemes and slum clearance. Soon it became clear, however, that the governments did not have the financial resources and administrative capacity to meet the increasing demand for shelter and basic urban services. The access of the urban poor to shelter, services, and infrastructure was constrained by many factors. These include:

(a) high price of land for housing;
(b) inadequate access of the urban poor to financial institutions;
(c) lack of participation by poor urban households in planning and implementing shelter projects;
(d) inadequate cost recovery of government investment programmes;
(e) too rigid building codes and standards; and
(f) the high cost of building materials.

However, as Hardoy and Satterthwaite [10] point out, new government attitudes and policies are emerging that are more appropriate to the situation in urban areas of developing countries. The right of those in squatter settlements to live there and obtain basic infrastructure and services is being recognized. Building codes and standards are being gradually reformulated. Many governments are supporting the production of cheap building materials utilizing local skills and resources and releasing unused land for low-income housing. The role of the private sector, including NGOs and community-based groups, in facilitating the provision of shelter and services is being recognized. New types of housing finance institutions are emerging that target low-income groups. Though replicating innovative project approaches and moving from publicly sponsored projects to "enabling" policies has been constrained by such problems as the high price of legal land sites, the new government attitudes and increasing interest of donors and international organizations provide new opportunities in the 1990s to facilitate participatory, self-help housing.

Staggering sums of investments would be required to provide adequate urban infrastructure and services. It has been estimated, for example, that annual investments during the 1990s will need to be tripled from US$10 billion to US$30 billion in order to ensure adequate access to drinking water and sanitation. Therefore, the governments in developing countries will have to find alternative mechanisms to increase the participation of the private sector in providing infrastructure. It would also require the application of innovative, low-cost, and simple to use and maintain technologies.

The research agenda dealing with urban shelter and services should concentrate on (a) the process through which informal settlements in developing countries are planned, managed, and constructed at the initiatives of individuals, community-based organizations, and NGOs and (b) the mechanisms through which the state can effectively perform its role as the facilitator of local initiatives. Some of the areas of priority research are as follows:

- What are the conditions that are conducive to local and community-based initiatives to meet shelter and basic urban service needs of the urban population? What are innovative partnerships between local governments and community organizations? What are the limits of self-help in the provision of urban infrastructure and services?
- What are the present and potential roles of NGOs in serving as intermediaries between local community and municipal and central governments?
- What are mechanisms through which innovative local initiatives can be replicated and incorporated in national programmes to maximize impact of government interventions?
- How can municipal governments be restructured to promote and support community-based initiatives?

- How can research findings be more effectively disseminated to community organizations and municipal and national governments so that these are incorporated in government decisions at the municipal and national levels?
- What are the administrative, financial, and technical means to improve infrastructure maintenance?
- What are the constraints on urban land and related markets? How can informal sector mechanisms be regularized?

The third issue: Improving urban information systems

The lack of adequate information has been one of the impediments to the formulation and implementation of urban management policies and programmes. As Masser points out [11], two types of barriers must be overcome before effective use can be made of computer-based information systems for urban management. The technical barriers relate to data availability rather than to computer technology. The existing data are often not compatible and thus are difficult to integrate. The data sets are not adequately updated. Finally, long lead times are needed for obtaining information for urban management.

The second type of barrier is organizational. As Masser [11] argues, the degree to which technological innovations are likely to be utilized fully after their initial adoption by an organization depends upon several factors: social context and national attitudes toward technological innovation, capabilities of technical staff, the extent to which innovations are associated with improvements in established administrative procedures, and degree of personal commitment among the non-technical staff.

The state of the art suggests that the challenge of information systems for urban management is to identify perceived needs of data use, to evaluate alternative approaches to information management in a multi-user environment, and to monitor actual use of information systems as a tool for management.

Some of the priority issues related to information systems for urban management are as follows:

- reasons for which central government agencies are sometimes unwilling to release small area statistics to urban management agencies; mechanisms through which disaggregated data could be made available to these agencies;
- use made of information within different types of urban management agencies and organizational cultures that have evolved to im-

plement urban management activities, including constraints on utilization of computer-based technology;
- assessment of the potential of the microcomputer for urban management in developing countries from the perspective of the requirements of the organizations concerned.

The fourth issue: Strengthening urban informal sector roles

The informal sector is significantly contributing to the urban economy and has strong backward linkages with commercial and government enterprises. About 50 per cent of the labour force in the third world cities has been estimated to be engaged in the formal sector. Mathur [12] points out that the informal sector produces a variety of goods and services, a greater part of which enter into the "consumption basket" of individual households.

The benefits of the urban informal sector are widely recognized by governments in developing countries. The International Labour Organisation (ILO) studies during the early 1970s led to an increasing interest at the national and international levels in the practices of the informal sector and its potential in absorbing surplus agricultural labour and providing urban services to the vast majority of the poor. The ILO estimates that the size of the economically active urban population will double from about 409 million in 1980 to more than 825 million at the end of the 1990s. New jobs will be needed to accommodate this rapid growth of urban population.

The main strength of the urban informal sector is its ability to generate employment opportunities. In Pakistan, for example, the creation of employment opportunities in the urban informal sector is not necessarily dependent upon direct public costs and commitment of public investments in advance. The other advantages of the informal sector in the country are that it uses simple technology appropriate to the resource base of the communities and that it produces jobs at lower cost. At present over 70 per cent of the urban labour force in the country is employed by the informal sector.

The informal sector has played an even more important role in the Latin American countries, where the employment opportunities in the formal sector have deteriorated, especially in the large urban areas. Schteingart [20] points out that in Mexico, the modern sector of the economy employs less than 25 per cent of the labour force. A survey in Mexico City showed that those employed in the informal sector in 1980 were over 36 per cent of the city's population. About

50 per cent of the urban housing is provided through the informal sector. In Lima, Peru, over 42 per cent of all housing is in informal sector settlements. Over 300,000 people are dependent on street vending for their livelihoods. Ninety-five per cent of total public transport is provided through the informal sector [7].

Governments in developing countries have adopted two types of policies. The "supply-oriented" policies are those that are geared towards increasing the productivity of supply of informal sector goods and services. This includes providing credit and technical assistance, creating production cooperatives, and broadening the access of those involved in the informal sector activities to the required inputs. The "demand-oriented policies" are aimed at increasing the demand of informal sector products by private consumers who purchase wage goods from the informal sector, by private firms in the formal sector that may subcontract part of their production activities to firms in the informal sector, and by the public sector, which can increase procurements from the informal sector. One of the future challenges is to provide a framework through the above and other types of policies and programmes to fully utilize the potential role of the informal sector in the process of urban development.

The urban informal sector provides a rich and rewarding agenda for policy and management related research. Among the areas of high priority are the following:

- assessment of the effects of direct policies and programmes on the informal sector, including credit and self-employment, spatial coverage, institutional mechanisms to implement policies, and impact of such policies on the productivity of the informal sector;
- analysis of the effects of indirect policies and programmes on the informal sector, including liberalization, pricing, tariffs, and recession;
- examination of the management structures and functioning of the informal sector organizations to determine the extent to which these organizations are able to utilize the developmental infrastructure such as loans, marketing, training, and skill development;
- productivity of different branches of the urban informal sector.

The fifth issue: Strengthening urban institutional capacities

The effectiveness of urban policies and programmes largely depends upon the quality of institutions responsible for planning and implementing them. The components of the urban institutional capacity in a country comprise the horizontal and vertical coordination among the concerned agencies, delineation of responsibilities and functions among the agencies, technical and human relation skills of the agencies to perform their assigned tasks, and decentralization of planning and management authority to urban local governments [4].

The proliferation of government and semi-government agencies has led to a lack of coordination and consistency by the concerned agencies. Sectoral authorities, for example, tend to provide physical infrastructure facilities without ensuring that local governments have the capacity to maintain them. It is partly due to the fragmentation of the institutional machinery that often capital works programmes have not been effectively linked with operational policies such as pricing and cost recovery.

Due to the speed with which urbanization has been taking place in developing countries, urban local governments have lacked financial and management capacity to provide adequate urban infrastructure and services. In most countries, semi-autonomous urban development authorities were established to undertake urban planning and coordination functions. Examples of such organizations are the Calcutta Metropolitan Development Authority, Karachi Development Authority, and the Metro-Manila Commission. Over the past three decades, most of the international assistance in the urban sector has been channelled through these development authorities. For all practical purposes, these authorities have functioned as an extension of government ministries and departments. In the meantime, the role of urban local governments has continued to decline, which is demonstrated by the inability of many local governments to adequately maintain urban infrastructure provided through the development authorities.

Lack of clarity in allocation of functions and responsibilities to agencies in urban areas has also impeded effective delivery of urban shelter and services. Often responsibilities are allocated to agencies without delineating mechanisms through which the assigned roles of these agencies are to be coordinated with those of the existing agencies. International agencies such as the World Bank and the Asian Development Bank have in the past encouraged the establishment of "project management units" and "project implementation units." While such units have facilitated the monitoring of project inputs, activities, and outputs, experience shows that these units lead to further fragmentation of the local institutional machinery.

A shortage of qualified staff is one of the main constraints on the effective provision of urban services. The personnel practices are usually characterized by unequal promotion opportunities to various civil service cadres, political intervention and favouritism in recruitment, red tape, and inadequate policies for staff development.

One of the most pressing issues in urban management is to strengthen the financial and management capacity of urban local government. Among the options are expansion of taxation and revenue-raising authority of local governments, provision of technical assistance and training to local officials, and the improvement of the system of intergovernmental transfers and allocation of funds from the central to municipal governments.

The future research agenda should include such issues as:

- effective combinations of centralization and decentralization to improve service delivery as well as community participation in urban management;
- mechanisms to strengthen planning and management capacities of small and intermediate-sized cities;
- delineation of functions and responsibilities of government and non-governmental agencies in the process of urban development in order to facilitate interagency coordination and strengthen capacities of the concerned agencies to perform their assigned tasks.

The sixth issue: Improving the urban environment

While cities are making contributions to output and income of developing countries, rapid urban population growth and uncontrolled industrial development are degrading the urban environment, placing strains on natural resources, and thus undermining sustainable and equitable development.

The growing amount of wastes generated by the urban communities outstrips the capacity of cities to collect and dispose of them safely and efficiently. Only between 25 and 55 per cent of all waste generated in large cities of the developing world is collected and disposed of safely by municipal authorities. Though significant progress has been made during the International Water Supply and Sanitation Decade, about 40 per cent of the urban residents are still not served by sanitation services, and 25 per cent do not have access to safe drinking water. Air pollution in most large cities is getting worse due to emissions from fossil fuels used for transport and industry. Inappropriate land development and inappropriately disposed toxic wastes generated by industry are causing damage to groundwater, wetlands, and other sensitive ecosystems. These environmental consequences have directly translated into negative impacts on human health and quality of life, especially for the urban poor, who live in the most polluted fringe areas of major cities.

Some of the areas of priority research dealing with the urban environment are as follows:

- legal and regulatory framework for environmental protection; assignment of jurisdiction for legislation, monitoring, and enforcement;
- environmental implications of land use control and property rights;
- effective mechanisms for solid waste collection coverage and solid waste treatment and disposal;
- impact of alternative technologies, transportation systems, and energy on the urban environment;
- mechanisms to incorporate environmental planning and management techniques into city wide strategy planning and implementation.

Conclusion

Rapid urbanization in developing countries is neither a crisis nor a tragedy; it is an opportunity to identify and implement innovative policies and programmes for socio-economic transformation. Because population distribution policies have largely failed, the solutions to urban problems should be found in the more effective management of cities. The urban research agenda for the 1990s, therefore, should focus on the identification of innovative approaches to deal with complex issues in urban management and on strengthening national capacities to plan and implement urban development programmes.

References

1 Angel, Shlomo. "Urbanization and Human Development." Paper prepared for the United Nations Development Programme, New York, 1989.

2 Banerjee, Tapan Kumar. "Issues in Financial Structure and Management: The Case of Calcutta Metropolitan Area." *Regional Development Dialogue* 10 (1989), no. 1.

3 Bengali, Kaiser, Aisha Ghaus, and Hafiz Pasha. "Issues in Financial Structure and Management: The Case of Karachi." *Regional Development Dialogue* 10 (1989), no. 1.

4 Cheema, G. Shabbir. *Urban Shelter and Services: Public Policies and Management Approaches*. New York: Praeger, 1987.

5 ———, ed. *Urban Management: Policies and Innovations in Developing Countries*. New York: Praeger, 1993.

6 Davey, Kenneth. *Financing Regional Government: International Practices and Their Relevance to the Third World*. Chichester: Wiley, 1983.

7 De Soto, Hernando. *The Other Path*.

8 Dhiratayakinant, Kraiyudht. "Issues in Financial Structure and Management: The Case of Bangkok Metropolis." *Regional Development Dialogue* 10 (1989), no. 1.

9 Fuchs, Roland. *Population Distribution Policies in Asia and the Pacific: Current Status and Future Prospects*. East-West Population Institute Papers. Honolulu: East-West Center, 1983.

10 Hardoy, Jorge E., and David Satterthwaite. "Housing Policy: A Review of Changing Government Attitudes and Responses to City Housing Problems in the Third World." In: Cheema, *Urban Management*. See ref. 5 above.

11 Masser, Ian. "Technological and Organizational Issues in the Design of Information Systems for Urban Management in Developing Countries." In: Cheema, *Urban Management*. See ref. 5 above.

12 Mathur, Om P. *Role of Small Cities in National Development*. Nagoya: United Nations Centre for Regional Development, 1984.

13 Obudho, R.A. "Urbanization and Urban Development Strategies in East Africa." In: Cheema, *Urban Management*. See ref. 5 above.

14 Prakash, Ved. "Financing Urban Services in Developing Countries." In: Rondinelli and Cheema, *Urban Services in Developing Countries*. See ref. 18 below.

15 ———. "The Urban Development Sector: A Case for a National Urban Development Programme." In: Cheema, *Urban Management*. See ref. 5 above.

16 Richardson, Harry W. "Problems of Metropolitan Management in Asia." In: Cheema, *Urban Management*. See ref. 5 above.

17 Rondinelli, Dennis A. *Secondary Cities in Developing Countries: Policies for Diffusing Urbanization*. Beverly Hills: Sage, 1983.

18 Rondinelli, Dennis A., and G. Shabbir Cheema. *Urban Services in Developing Countries: Public and Private Roles in Urban Development*. London: Macmillan, 1988.

19 Rodwin, Lloyd. *Shelter, Settlement and Development*. Boston: Allen & Unwin, 1987.

20 Schteingart, Martha. "Role of the Informal Sector in Providing Urban Employment and Housing in Mexico." In: Cheema, *Urban Management*. See ref. 5 above.

21 United Nations. *Patterns of Urban and Rural Population Growth*. New York: United Nations, 1980.

22 ———. *World Demographic Estimates and Projections, 1950–2025*. New York: United Nations, 1979.

23 ———. *World Population Trends and Policies: 1989 Monitoring Report*. United Nations, 1989.

24 United Nations Centre for Regional Development (UNCRD). *Regional Development Dialogue*. Nagoya: UNCRD, 1989.

25 World Bank. *Shelter*. Poverty and Basic Needs Series. Washington, D.C.: World Bank, 1980.

26 Yeung, Yue-man. "Access by the Urban Poor to Basic Infrastructure Services: Asia Region." Paper prepared for the Economic Development Institute of the World Bank, 1989.

Index